Between Slavery and Capitalism

Between Slavery and Capitalism

THE LEGACY OF EMANCIPATION IN THE AMERICAN SOUTH

Martin Ruef

PRINCETON UNIVERSITY PRESS

Princeton and Oxford

Contents

List of Illustrations

List of Tables

Preface

> On December 31, 1862, our Nation marked the end of another year of civil war. At Shiloh and Seven Pines, Harpers Ferry and Antietam, brother had fought against brother. Sister had fought against sister.... Slavery still suspended the possibility of an America where life and liberty were the birthright of all, not the province of some. Yet, even in those dark days, light persisted. Hope endured. As the weariness of an old year gave way to the promise of a new one, President Abraham Lincoln issued the Emancipation Proclamation ... today, it is a legacy we choose not only to remember, but also to make our own.
> —President Barack Obama, December 31, 2012, the 150th anniversary of the Emancipation Proclamation

Barack Obama, the first black president of the United States, observed the sesquicentennial of Lincoln's proclamation by issuing a release through the White House press secretary. In contrast to earlier events, such as a viewing of the Emancipation Proclamation in the Oval Office with African American seniors and their grandchildren on January 10, 2010, there was no public ceremony nor much effort to draw attention to the anniversary. The event received some coverage from the black press, but went largely unnoticed by the national media.[1] Despite popular fascination with the history of slavery and emancipation—as reflected in the box office sales of movies such as Steven Spielberg's *Lincoln*, Quentin Tarantino's *Django Unchained*, and the film adaptation of Solomon Northup's *Twelve Years a Slave*—the public's deeper engagement with the topic has been limited. Even in the White House, there seems to be little interest in stirring discourse around the legacy of slavery. In the absence of further commemorative events and dialogue, it is not clear how Americans will follow Obama's mandate to remember "the spirit that made emancipation possible," much less to come to grips with the economic and social implications that slavery and emancipation hold for current generations.[2]

Dedicated poll watchers are unlikely to be surprised by such political ambivalence. Over the past twenty years, surveys of representative swaths of the American population have revealed a considerable amount of quiet uncertainty and division about the role of the Civil War in ending slavery, the responsibility of the U.S. government to the descendants of slaves, and the ongoing need of American society to confront the symbols and inequality associated with slavery. In 2011, a CBS News poll prompted respondents to think about the reasons for the American Civil War on the occasion of the 150th anniversary of its initiation. Opinions were split. While nearly 37 percent of the surveyed individuals suggested that slavery was the root cause, another 53 percent believed the conflict revolved primarily around states' rights. The remaining 10 percent of respondents reported that they did not know or had no answer.[3]

In a poll conducted by the ABC News *Nightline* program fourteen years earlier, respondents were asked to reflect on the possibility that the federal government might offer a formal apology or reparations to black Americans with slave ancestors. Among American adults as a whole, nearly 38 percent thought that the government should apologize for slavery, while 54 percent believed that it should not. Considering the possibility of monetary compensation, 19 percent thought the government should pay reparations to slave descendants, while 75 percent believed it should not. Differences of opinion were especially pronounced across race and party lines. Among black respondents, 80 percent believed that an apology and/or reparations were needed. Among white Democrats, the percentage favoring an apology was 35 percent, while the percentage favoring reparations fell to 12 percent. Only meager numbers of white Republicans (24 percent and 7 percent, respectively) supported these federal actions to make amends to African Americans for the ills of slavery.[4]

Debates regarding the legacy of slavery continue in judicial battles over affirmative action, in claims regarding African American culture and family life, around monuments and flags dedicated to the Southern Confederacy, and in the way that black bondage and its effects are portrayed in popular culture. One more example serves to illustrate how divisive and persistent these issues can be. Until a vote by South Carolina's state legislature in May 2000, the Confederate battle flag flew above the state capitol in Columbia, along with the Palmetto state flag and the U.S. stars and stripes. In a national poll conducted in April of that year, respondents were asked whether the flag was a symbol of slavery that should be removed, or an aspect of Southern heritage that should remain. In all, 45 percent of those polled believed that the flag should be removed, while 42 percent thought that it should stay above the capitol dome. A small percentage of respondents (1 percent) volunteered that a compromise could be reached by moving the flag to a different location. The state legislature soon adopted the compromise solution, lowering the flag over the Capitol and raising a similar flag at the Confederate Soldier Monument on the grounds of the State House. Mirroring the schism in public opinion polls, the resolution seemed to satisfy no one, neither the NAACP, which had catalyzed the vote through boycotts and rallies, nor Southern heritage groups, which opposed the removal of the flag in the first place. Most politicians running major campaigns in South Carolina, from George W. Bush and Al Gore to Mitt Romney to Nikki Haley, have since been dogged by questions regarding their view on the flag.[5]

In academic circles, the usual bromide for such dissensus involves a call for greater historical literacy, supported by earnest efforts to make the fruits of scholarship accessible to a wider audience. The problem with this solution, in the case of slavery and emancipation, is that academic consensus itself is lacking. Discussion and surveys among historians and social scientists reveal fundamental disagreement on many of the effects of emancipation. In the mid-1990s, the historian Robert Whaples distributed a survey to 178 randomly selected members of the Economic History Association. Asked whether "American blacks [had] achieved substantial economic gains during the half-century after 1865," 37 percent of all respondents voiced agreement, 27 percent agreed only with provisos, and 36 percent voiced disagreement. On the question of whether "the system of sharecropping impeded economic growth in the postbellum South," 36 percent agreed, 21 percent agreed only with provisos, and 43 percent disagreed. A lack of consensus among scholars was also evident for numerous other factual questions regarding the period after slavery, ranging from the convergence of Southern economic development with that of the U.S. North to the efficiency of cotton monocropping to the impact of postbellum merchant monopolies on poor white and black farmers. Differences in opinion between scholars holding a Ph.D. in history (or currently teaching in a history department) and those holding a Ph.D. in economics (or currently teaching in an economics department) were especially stark.[6]

When considering legal prescriptions regarding issues such as reparations, the scholarly view seems equally muddled. In a review of work on the topic, John Torpey and Maxine Burkett acknowledge that there is "little consensus about the cause of action for which reparations are sought, whether for [antebellum] slavery or for [postbellum] segregation, or about the appropriate remedies." While demands for government intervention have existed since the end of the Civil War, reparation lawsuits have not fared well in court, owing to technical reasons ranging from the statute of limitations and sovereign immunity to a lack of plaintiff standing and difficulty in establishing causation.[7]

Why does there continue to be so much public and scholarly discord about the aftermath of the Civil War—perhaps more than any other event in American history? How we answer this question undoubtedly has something to do with our conceptions of race, something to do with our conceptions of economics, and something to do with our conceptions of sectional disparities between North and South. The point of departure for this text, however, is that uncertainty tends to be an inherent feature of profound institutional transformation, especially one as dramatic as that confronted by the United States between the bookends of the Civil War and Radical Reconstruction. The uncertainty is rooted in the construction of new social categories—of freedmen and women where there had been slaves, of sharecropping and tenancy where there had been plantations, of the progressive rhetoric of a New South where there had been a planter aristocracy. It is rooted in a change in economic institutions, in the difficulty of reconciling differences between slavery and capitalism. And it is rooted equally in the question of continuity, the tendency of mechanisms of identity and inequality to reproduce themselves across economic systems, despite superficial change. Before grappling with the political divisions and diversity of opinions that confront us today, it is necessary to examine the uncertainty of emancipation in its own time.

Acknowledgments

Appropriately, this book started in the South and ends in the South, though there have been many journeys in between. The beginning was marked by my move to the University of North Carolina as a newly minted faculty member. A budding interest in the sociological study of the American South was sparked by my introduction to the "UNC School" of Southern studies, which dates back to the arrival of Howard W. Odum in Chapel Hill in 1920. Odum founded UNC's Department of Sociology and wrote prodigiously on Southern regionalism over his three decades at the university. His "school" continued eighty years after its inception in various forms—in the scholarship of Peter Coclanis on the economic development of the South and in John Shelton Reed's astute observations of Southern culture; in Richard Cramer's sizable collection of texts on Southern economic history (many of which I inherited) and in the activities of the Center for the Study of the American South. Entranced by the region and its complex history of race relations, I started using the extensive archive of primary sources available at UNC to conduct research on the process of black emancipation.

From Chapel Hill, we moved cross-country to Stanford and, two years later, made another cross-country transition to Princeton. Both universities offered vibrant intellectual environments and the possibility to engage new topics. However, as the cliché goes, "you can leave the South, but the South will never leave you." Though my work took me in different directions in the fields of economic and organizational sociology, I remained convinced that the South had borne witness to one of the most fundamental organizational and economic transitions in American history. The crucible of race, as Joel Williamson has suggested, lay in the South and in the effort of Southerners to remember, transcend, or erase the region's history of slavery.

In 2012, fortuitous circumstances took us back to North Carolina, where I accepted a position at Duke University. Paralleling Howard Odum's influence at UNC, Duke's Department of Sociology bore the strong imprint of Edgar Tristram Thompson, another native Southerner turned social scientist. Thompson had been born on a plantation and devoted much of his thirty-three-year career at Duke, beginning in 1937, to making sense of his youthful exposure to plantation society, as well as the evolving race relations of the South. Inspired by Thompson's example, I decided it was finally time to bring together the essays I had written on the South's transition to capitalism and to articulate their common narrative in book form.

A journey is made all the better with fellow travelers, and I have had the benefit of having a number of wonderful students and collaborators help me along the way. Kelly Patterson did much of the leg work required to map businesses and credit ratings in the Southern economy between 1860 and 1900, drawing on the archive of Dun Reference Books at the Library of Congress and the credit ledgers at Harvard's Baker Library. Chapters 6 and 7 would not have been possible without his ingenuity and ceaseless energy. Alona Harness diligently helped me to synthesize and critically analyze over one hundred articles on plantation management published in the antebellum South between the 1820s and 1865. Ben Fletcher worked with me at UNC when the project was still in its earliest stages. The fruits of his labor are reflected in many of the life histories of former slaves coded from the interviews of the Works Progress Administration, as well as the analysis of postbellum status attainment in Chapter 3. As the manuscript was approaching its penultimate state, Jeff Rosenthal, another UNC alumnus, read a draft of the book from cover to cover, providing careful (and much-needed) fact-checking and reference updates. At different stages of the project, Bart Bonikowski and Dahlia Nahol also provided able research assistance. Special thanks goes to Paul Escott, professor of history at Wake Forest University, who provided the data set of WPA interviews that he and his graduate students first coded in the 1970s.

One benefit of inhabiting many places over the course of writing this book is that I have been rewarded by the input and company of gracious colleagues at a number of excellent institutions. At UNC, discussions with Judith Blau, Peter Coclanis, and Howard Aldrich helped propel the project in its formative stages. During my time at the Stanford GSB, the ecological lens developed by Michael Hannan and Glenn Carroll shaped my analysis of the decline of the Southern plantation. I gratefully acknowledge the suggestions and support from Princeton's Paul DiMaggio and Viviana Zelizer, as well as participants in the Economic Sociology and Theorodology workshops. New colleagues at Duke, including Eduardo Bonilla-Silva, Bai Gao, Kieran Healy, Lisa Keister, Nan Lin, Jim Moody, Lynn Smith-Lovin, Ken Spenner, Ed Tiryakian, and Steve Vaisey, served as a sounding board for some of my latest ideas on the emergence of free labor markets and a Southern middle class. Over the years, I have also received encouragement, advice, and friendly heckling from Jim Baron, David Brady, Matthew Brashears, Ron Burt, Sandy Darity, Jerry Davis, Avinash Dixit, Stanislav Dobrev, Roberto Fernandez, Neil Fligstein, Jennifer Green, Carol Heimer, Chris Marquis, Mark Mizruchi, Joeri Mol, François Nielsen, Damon Phillips, Mikolaj Piskorski, Woody Powell, Huggy Rao, Gabriel Rossman, Brian Rubineau, Rainer Schwabe, Art Stinchcombe, Toby Stuart, Jonathan Wells, Filippo Wezel, Valery Yakubovich, Tiantian Yang, and Ezra Zuckerman.

Versions of several ideas in this book appear in earlier articles and have been incorporated here in substantially modified or extended form (in some cases, with new data). Chapter 2 draws on a recent article in the *American Sociological Review*, titled "Constructing Labor Markets: The Valuation of Black Labor in the U.S. South, 1831 to 1867" (Ruef 2012). Chapter 3, as noted above, builds on an analysis with Ben Fletcher, published as "Legacies of American Slavery: Status Attainment among Southern Blacks after Emancipation" (Ruef and Fletcher 2003). Chapter 4 combines ideas from two chapters on Southern middle-class formation (Ruef 2011; Ruef and Reinecke 2011). The discussion of plantation decline in Chapter 5 originally appeared in the *American Journal of Sociology* as "The Demise of an Organizational Form: Emancipation and Plantation Agriculture in the American South, 1860–1880" (Ruef 2004). Two articles with Kelly Patterson contained the germs of the ideas for Chapters 6 and 7 (Ruef and Patterson 2009a; 2009b).

Although it would be tedious to enumerate the workshops, presentations, and conferences at which I have tested some of the ideas in the book, two events (both in August 2008) helped to transform the project from a series of loosely connected essays on the nineteenth-century South into a more integrated whole. One event was a conference jointly sponsored by the U.S. National Science Foundation (NSF) and the German Forschungsgemeinschaft (DFG) in New York City. Under the thematic umbrella of "Contextualizing Economic Behavior," the conference highlighted a need, in my mind, for an approach to economic history that would more fully combine the disciplinary agendas of economists and sociologists. The other event was a special session at the 2008 American Sociological Association conference, "Uncertainty and Social Order." Preparing for the conference, I thumbed through my papers on the postbellum South and found that the issue of uncertainty came up time and time again. Perhaps a bit exasperated by the number of articles that I sent to him before the conference, the discussant—the eminent sociologist Harrison White—concluded, "Mr. Ruef . . . it is time that you write the book!"

Professor White, I am pleased to report that the book has been written. It would not have been possible without the unfailing love and support of my wife Jennifer. Jen is a Southern girl and a committed social worker at UNC. Intriguingly, the School of Social Work was also founded by Howard Odum (as the School of Public Welfare) around the same time that he created the Department of Sociology. I would like to think that the bond between Jen and me was decided by fate when those events occurred nearly a century ago.

Finally, I would like to dedicate this book to my boys, Edison and Donovan. In his short life, Edison taught me the wisdom of quiet courage. We will forever miss his smile and approving "thumbs up." Donovan's courage is less quiet, but no less inspiring. His smile always contains the promise of a new day.

Martin Ruef
November 2013, Durham, North Carolina

CHAPTER 1

Institutional Transformation and Uncertainty

For many observers, the transformation of the South after the U.S. Civil War was one of the most dramatic institutional changes they had witnessed. As Mark Twain and Charles Warner wrote in *The Gilded Age* (1873), "The eight years in America from 1860 to 1868 uprooted institutions that were centuries old, changed the politics of a people, transformed the social life of half the country, and wrought so profoundly upon the entire national character that the influence cannot be measured short of two or three generations."[1] Although the emancipation of former slaves and political upheavals of Radical Reconstruction are perhaps the most evident features of this institutional metamorphosis, it touched upon almost every aspect of Southern society, ranging from urban life to class structure to the organizations that populated the region's agriculture and industry.

The Civil War itself left the country in a shambles, with a human and financial toll that has few parallels in American history. When the war ended, in April 1865, roughly 750,000 men in the North and South were dead, representing the greatest number of American casualties in any military conflict.[2] The direct economic cost of the war to the Union and Confederacy combined has been estimated conservatively at $6.6 billion, or one and a half times the gross domestic product of the United States in 1860.[3] The institutional interventions of the immediate postwar period seemed to bear the fruits of these costs and casualties of war. Slavery and indentured servitude were abolished by the Thirteenth Amendment in 1865. Emancipation was soon accompanied by an unprecedented federal effort to transition four million black men, women, and children into freedom and to incorporate the American South more fully into the economic and political life of a nation. In the twenty-first century, when sectarian struggles and civil wars again rage in many parts of the world, the experiences of the postbellum United States would appear to hold valuable lessons for those facing the challenge of intervention and institution building in developing countries.

Despite the sheer scale of federal intervention in the South, however, its necessity and effect continue to be widely debated. A majority of scholars now agree that the institution of chattel slavery was not economically moribund at the eve of the Civil War, though some informed voices contend that the American political system was equipped to eradicate it peaceably and that the war was avoidable.[4] Many others suggest that bondage persisted in the institutions of the postbellum era in subtle and not-so-subtle ways, including the convict leasing system, debt peonage, and the path dependence of black labor.[5] Yet others have argued that the economic institutions of the antebellum South were not as different or inefficient as one might suspect. Among economic historians, the late Robert Fogel has advanced perhaps the most cogent argument for continuity between the essentially capitalist character of American slavery and the market institutions that we recognize today. Even considering the property rights that it granted in human life and labor, Fogel and his collaborators have argued that the antebellum South possessed "a flexible, highly developed form of capitalism."[6]

Whether one emphasizes the advanced capitalism of the antebellum South or the rejection of free labor in the postbellum era, the conclusion with respect to institutional continuity remains the same: the effects of federal intervention in the South were superficial and, in many respects, temporary. With the departure of federal troops and the end of Reconstruction governments in the late 1870s, the region simply reverted to its old pattern of exploiting black labor and ensuring the dominance of the planter class. In lieu of transformation, this historical narrative thus highlights the *path dependence* of institutional arrangements in the late nineteenth-century South. Social scientists have often located the roots of such path dependence in the inertia afflicting organizations in preindustrial and industrial society, as well as in the durable inequality that results when old status distinctions—such as those between slaves and owners—are mapped to new ones—such as tenants and landlords.[7]

By contrast, this book begins with the premise that postbellum transformation of the South's organizations and economy was profound and that, by many measures, the New South that resulted after Radical Reconstruction evidenced a more capitalist and market-driven society than its antebellum counterpart. As I will argue later in this chapter, support for this premise could be found in the spatial dispersion of financial institutions and capital in the Cotton South, in the extensive rating of Southern businesses for credit markets, in the transition from subsistence to commodity agriculture among small farmers, in the rise of urban economies in the interior of the region, and in the availability of laborers who could be hired at will or on short-term contracts. These changes did not always portend unambiguous improvements in the lives of Southerners, black or white. And, in many cases, they existed alongside the vestiges of institutions imported from the era of slavery, leading to contention and confusion around the logics guiding the economy of the New South.

A key component of this premise is that the transformation involved a *transition and clash in economic institutions*, not simply political ones. Many of the influential treatments of the postbellum era have offered "top-down" political histories, in which the actions of great men, feeble carpetbagger governments, and fickle coalitions contributed to the reversal of Radical Reconstruction.[8] This reversal culminated in the alleged compromise between the presidential candidates Rutherford B. Hayes and Samuel Tilden in 1876, purportedly giving Hayes the presidency while relaxing the federal presence in the South.[9] The emphasis on politics has led scholars to contend that Reconstruction was a failure—indeed, judged on the criterion of political inclusion of Southern blacks, that it was a unique failure in Western history.[10] By contrast, the perspective offered here is one of "bottom-up" history, in which institutional transformation is reflected in thousands of economic transactions and trajectories among blacks and whites who were learning to navigate the shoals of a Southern economy that was transitioning between slavery and capitalism.

A second key premise of the book is that *enduring uncertainty* was a defining feature of this transition between precapitalist and capitalist institutions. As the historical sociologist Rebecca Emigh has pointed out, there has been an appropriate trend toward using "the plural forms 'transitions' and 'capitalisms' to emphasize their variability and complexity."[11] The idiosyncrasies of the New South economy reflect many of the virtues of this nomenclature. It is not surprising, therefore, that some historians speak of "Reconstructions," while others acknowledge that the postbellum era merely offered "one kind of [economic] freedom" to emancipated blacks. These labels are not mere scholarly hedges, but reflect the contention and heterogeneous views of institutional transformation among Union authorities and ex-Confederates, freedpeople and planters, Redeemers and Scalawags, townsfolk and rural farmers.[12]

Uncertainty goes beyond mere contention to reflect the difficulty that participants and observers have in making sense of a situation. It is understood, as Jens Beckert has pointed out, "as the character of situations in which agents cannot anticipate the outcome of a decision and cannot assign probabilities to the outcome."[13] Attention to uncertainty has been understated in previous treatments of economic transitions between precapitalist and capitalist institutions, owing partially to disciplinary orientations.[14] Among historians, there has been a tendency to document the factual features of Radical Reconstruction and the emergent New South using a retrospective lens. Among economists, the tendency has been to deploy precise models of individual or organizational productivity (or regional growth), eliding the tremendous ambiguity surrounding the folk models employed by historical participants. In a paper written half a century ago, the Canadian economist W. T. Easterbrook suggested that uncertainty could be "a possible key to the study of economic change," though the "categories of uncertainty" employed by economists and historians at the time were too restrictive to offer much leverage in the analysis of capitalist transitions. Easterbrook concluded, optimistically, that uncertainty might be "a unifying concept ... in working toward a systematic approach to long-run economic change" and he expected to "hear much more about [it] in the historical areas of economics and related disciplines."[15]

In this book, I reflect on the uncertainty affecting historical participants—including former slaves, Freedmen Bureau agents, planters, merchants, and politicians—during the period of Reconstruction and ask how it continues to influence our understanding of this era. Following the Civil War, uncertainty was one of the most pervasive features of everyday life, leading to fundamental questions about the valuation of labor (How should emancipated slaves be reimbursed in wage contracts?), social stratification (What occupations and class positions would be available to blacks and whites in the postbellum South?), organizational arrangements (What forms of agricultural tenure could persist? To what extent would the antebellum system of merchandising be replaced?), and regional development (What paths to economic or demographic growth would be viable for postbellum communities?). By interpreting the economic changes associated with emancipation through the lens of uncertainty, social scientists can come closer to the lived experience of institutional transformation than they would exclusively with the certitude of facts that have been collected (or models that have been deployed) with historical hindsight.[16]

To draw out the implications of these premises, the next two sections consider the concepts of uncertainty and economic transformation in more detail. I begin by formulating a general theory regarding the evolution of uncertainty over the course of institutional transformation, and then discuss the specific transitions toward capitalism that occurred in the economy of the U.S. South during the postbellum era. A concluding outline for the book connects those transitions back to the outcomes experienced by individuals, organizations, and communities in the aftermath of American slavery.

The Problem of Uncertainty

A distinctive feature of the sociological perspective on economic institutions and institutional change is its emphasis on uncertainty. While modern economics is well versed in analyzing situations of risk, where probabilities or payoffs can be assigned to outcomes even if those outcomes are indeterminate, the technical apparatus of economics is ill equipped to deal with contexts of uncertainty, where probabilities and payoffs cannot be assigned and actions can no longer be deduced from the preferences of agents.[17] The problem of uncertainty is magnified in circumstances where economic institutions—the understandings, norms, routines, and governance structures that constrain economic action—are themselves in flux. Sociologists and heterodox economists have traditionally looked to institutions as "devices" that help coordinate economic action when markets are imperfect or the knowledge of market participants is incomplete. In the absence of these devices (i.e., under conditions of institutional change), individuals must reassemble elements of older traditions and organizational forms in order to confront uncertainty and find a new basis for social order.[18]

The incorporation of uncertainty as a central element in explanations of institutional change carries several analytical advantages. One important insight comes from recent work on social fields, which may be conceptualized as institutionalized arenas in which individuals, organizations, social movements, and the state vie to influence one another and structure the rules and perceptions that govern behavior.[19] Uncertainty in social fields is typically seen to be a result of destabilizing changes that are introduced exogenously. In the field of Southern agriculture after the Civil War, uncertainty arose due to new rules (e.g., the Thirteenth Amendment's ban on slavery and involuntary servitude), new types of actors (the Freedmen's Bureau), new relations among actors (the transition from paternalistic to arm's-length employer-worker relationships), and new meanings (such as the unusual connotation of "freedom" under Black Codes and other restrictions on Southern blacks).[20] A simple view of uncertainty maintains that field participants experience it most intensively in the immediate aftermath of the introduction of such changes, which then gradually become taken-for-granted elements of daily life.

Recent perspectives on social fields offer a more nuanced view of uncertainty in the process of institutional change. In their *Theory of Fields*, Neil Fligstein and Doug McAdam argue that destabilizing changes, by themselves, do not automatically generate pervasive uncertainty. The critical question is what attributions are made to those changes by field participants (who may characterize them as threats or opportunities), how those attributions contribute to the mobilization of claims and resources, and whether that mobilization leads to forms of collective action that were previously prohibited or unthinkable. With these mechanisms, Fligstein and McAdam argue, we obtain the conditions for profound uncertainty following destabilizing institutional changes. Moreover, the "generalized sense of uncertainty and chaos" feeds back into contention among field participants, contributing to *escalating*—not decreasing—uncertainty as time following the initial destabilizing changes passes.[21]

Two historical examples of reactions to Abraham Lincoln's Emancipation Proclamation help to illustrate the conditions under which we might expect to observe (or not observe) escalating uncertainty. Given that Lincoln issued the proclamation under his war powers on September 22, 1862, uncertainty about its constitutional validity and effects prevailed from the beginning. This uncertainty was augmented because it applied to people of color, whose political and citizenship status in the United States—even considered outside the context of slavery—had been stripped by the Supreme Court's *Dred Scott* ruling six years earlier. Among white abolitionists, the vagaries surrounding the Emancipation Proclamation meant that it could be celebrated more for its symbolism than as an opportunity. Lincoln's efforts to mobilize support invoked two provisions that were widely criticized by the abolitionists. One, which became part of the proclamation, was the exclusion of Union-occupied territory and border states from the president's executive order.[22] The other provision, which did not make it into the proclamation, was Lincoln's advocacy for compensated emancipation, in which slaveholders would be remunerated for the loss of human property that they would incur. The result was a document that was treated as decidedly equivocal by abolitionists, both in its content and in Lincoln's intent. As the leading abolitionist William Lloyd Garrison quipped, the president could "do nothing for freedom in a direct manner, but only by circumlocution and delay." Given the initial uncertainty generated by the document, many abolitionists were disappointed and treated it as a preservation of the status quo.[23]

The reception of the Emancipation Proclamation among Union military officials and black "contrabands" fleeing enslavement was more spirited. Lincoln's executive order contained a key provision allowing for "such [slaves] of suitable condition [to be] received into the armed service of the United States."[24] Northern military authorities seized upon it as an opportunity for efforts, already under way, to mobilize former slaves for the Union army. Fugitive slaves, viewing it as a path toward freedom and a certain form of citizenship rights, initiated an exodus toward Union lines. In reaction, other actors highlighted the threats from Lincoln's executive order. This included not only Southern slaveholders, but also Northern politicians who emphasized the "Negro Influx Question" in the state and congressional elections held between the preliminary proclamation and the executive order issued on January 1, 1863.[25] As the Union military characterized Lincoln's declaration as an instrument of war, slaves near Union lines characterized it as an opportunity, Southerners underscored the legal threat to their property rights, and some elements of the Northern public raised the specter of black immigration, uncertainty around the effects of the proclamation grew. The more military authorities sought to enlist the assistance of fugitive slaves, the more they attracted dependent families and freedpeople who would not be able to offer military service or support; the more they sought to regulate the behavior of former slaves and relocate some blacks North from the battle lines, the more they undermined the political impetus behind the military effort.[26] As a result of this potentially vicious circle, the Emancipation Proclamation was no longer the tepid symbolic statement lamented by some abolitionists, but a contingency that could dictate the course and political support for the entire war.

This example echoes an important proposition derived from Fligstein and McAdam's framework: *the escalation of uncertainty following profound institutional change depends on the attributions and mobilization of participants within an institutional field*. Additional analytical insights into institutional change may come from unpacking the concept of uncertainty further. In his influential formulation, the economist Frank Knight distinguished three forms of the concept: risk, "classical" uncertainty, and "true" uncertainty. As noted previously, economic decision making under a condition of *risk* involves a known probability distribution across outcomes, where the outcome itself is unknown. *Classical uncertainty* involves decision making where the probability distribution across outcomes is unknown, but the possible outcomes themselves are classifiable. Both risk and classical uncertainty thus hinge on the assumption that there are a "finite, practically manageable number of *kinds* of [outcomes]," which may be ascertained and categorized by field participants. This assumption is violated under conditions of true uncertainty, where the possible outcomes of economic action can no longer be identified or classified and, consequently, the probability distribution across them is not just unknown, but unknowable.[27] Given that the root cause of this form of uncertainty is the inability to categorize possible outcomes, I refer to it as *categorical uncertainty*.

The idea of categorical uncertainty is alluded to in Frank Knight's work, but deserves a more central place in the analysis of institutional change. Knight repeatedly acknowledges that uncertain situations are encountered when there "is no valid basis for classifying instances [of outcomes]" or "it becomes impossible to classify instances objectively." Since, in his theory, such uncertainty is rooted in the mind-set of an economic actor engaged in rational planning, the method for dealing with uncertainty is simply "securing better knowledge of and control over the future."[28] What Knight omits is the source of categorical uncertainty. From an institutionalist perspective, this source lies in circumstances of institutional flux and contention, not only where extant rules and social norms fail to provide expectations as to what outcomes are more or less likely, but also where the categories of possible outcomes are themselves in the process of being redefined.[29]

Again a historical example from the postbellum South serves to illustrate distinctions among risk, classical uncertainty, and categorical uncertainty. Sharecropping emerged during Reconstruction as a contract between landlords and workers, in which landlords rented out parcels of farmland (and generally provided agricultural equipment, seed, and some level of managerial supervision), while agricultural laborers agreed to give up a share of their crop (most typically half, but often one-third or one-quarter). By 1920, the U.S. Census enumerated over half a million croppers in the American South.[30] In deciding whether to offer a sharecropping contract, Southern landowners faced several shortcomings in information. First, the income from agricultural production was indeterminate, owing to variability in weather conditions, catastrophes (such as pests), worker effort, and demand for commodity crops. Insofar as landowners were able to ascribe some rough probabilities to these sources of income variation based on a track record from previous years, they faced a situation of *risk*. Under this circumstance, sharecropping could be seen as an organizational form that allowed risk to be divided between croppers and landlords, roughly in proportion to their contractual shares. Despite its condemnation by classical thinkers such as Adam Smith and Karl Marx, a considerable body of economic theory has developed to account for the persistence of sharecropping as a function of its risk-sharing properties.[31]

A second source of uncertainty facing landowners was the changing political context of production. While the institution of slavery had ceded property rights and control to the planters, the period of Radical Reconstruction augured an era when emancipated blacks (and poor whites) might exercise leverage in negotiating the terms of work. Indeterminacy regarding the amount of leverage was magnified because of the changing role of the state in regulating land and labor, especially under Union occupation. Because there was no basis for ascribing probabilities to the consistency of labor supply under these novel political circumstances, landowners faced a situation of *classical uncertainty*. They could enumerate how many (and what categories of) laborers they needed to work their fields, but were uncertain about who they would recruit for this purpose and how they could control them. Within this context, as the anthropologist Miriam Wells has suggested, an alternative explanation for the emergence (or resurgence) of sharecropping is that it "counter[ed] the growing leverage and associated uncertainty of labor," by "undermining the solidarity of the work force," dispersing workers into separate contracts and plots, and improving the negotiating position of landowners.[32]

A third, and perhaps more fundamental, source of uncertainty for landowners was that they did not know what forms of agricultural tenure and contract might be possible in the aftermath of slavery. While sharecropping had existed in Western Europe since the late medieval period, it was relatively rare in the Old South.[33] The period after the Civil War gave rise to a bewildering array of options with respect to agricultural tenancy and labor, including not only sharecropping but also wage labor, share tenancy (in which farm laborers provided agricultural implements and work stock, in addition to their own labor), standing rent tenancy (in which farmers paid a fixed rent for land in agricultural commodities), and cash tenancy (in which farmers paid a fixed rent in cash). In the late 1860s, these possibilities—and the distinctions among them—were so ill defined that even expert observers spoke merely of the "small farm" system as an alternative to plantation agriculture.[34] Landowners thus faced a problem of *categorical uncertainty*, in which they not only found it difficult to say what forms of agricultural tenure were more likely to be viable, but also could not even categorize the possible forms of agricultural tenure. The process of defining, categorizing, and selecting forms of tenure was the result of contention between planters, who hoped to reinstate large-scale and centralized gang-system labor, and freedmen and poor whites, who valued economic autonomy. Through the "constriction of possibilities" in this conflict-driven process, Edward Royce has noted that sharecropping emerged over time as a dominant—but initially indeterminate—form of agricultural tenure.[35]

These examples suggest some additional propositions regarding the nature of uncertainty during periods of economic and institutional change. First, *profound instances of institutional transformation will generate problems of* **classical or categorical uncertainty** *for economic actors, not simply problems of* **risk**. On the one hand, if the political and organizational arrangements of the postbellum South had evidenced considerable continuity with those of the antebellum era, then indeterminacy in agricultural output could have been reduced to probabilistic calculations on the part of landowners. Sharecropping would have emerged as a substitute for wage labor primarily to manage risk, owing either to fluctuations in labor supply or to fluctuations in crop yield and crop value, such as those generated by the disastrous 1866–67 growing season.[36] On the other hand, if political and organizational indeterminacy made it impossible for landowners to anticipate how much labor they could recruit, or even what types of contracts might be possible, then the planters faced a problem of uncertainty. From this perspective, sharecropping thrived not as a mechanism for sharing risk, but as a tool for dividing workers (and thus managing political uncertainty) and as an outcome of contention between farm laborers and landlords.[37]

Another proposition builds on the idea of escalating uncertainty in fields, as discussed earlier. When participants in a field mobilize claims and resources following institutional change, they initially draw on established categories of economic action, even if the outcomes of such action are indeterminate. Thus, many former slaves hoped that emancipation would lead to land ownership, as proposed in General William T. Sherman's policy of promising "forty acres and a mule" to freedmen and women.[38] Meanwhile, many white landowners believed that gang-system labor would persist, albeit (nominally) under wage labor arrangements. With the escalation of contention and mobilization among groups of field participants, these established categories of economic action were pushed aside in favor of new possibilities, such as sharecropping, rental farming, share tenancy, and other contractual arrangements that began to emerge in the postbellum South. Consequently, we can propose that *profound instances of institutional transformation will tend to initially generate problems of* **classical uncertainty**, *as field participants struggle to understand new social circumstances with extant categories, followed by* *problems of **categorical uncertainty**, as contention among participants leads to the introduction of new categories of actors and activities.*

TRANSFORMATION OF ECONOMIC INSTITUTIONS IN THE SOUTH

By generating new markets, new organizations, and new rules in the postbellum South, capitalist transformation rendered it difficult for historical participants to predict the behavior of one another, much less the anticipated course of the economy in the aggregate. The uncertainty of the relationship among newly emancipated slaves, former slaveholders, and other whites was at the heart of the altered economic and social landscape. On a broader scale, capitalist development in the region touched on all major components of the economy, including banking and the credit market, the urban economy, investment in human capital, and the emergent market for free labor.

For each of these components, we can obtain a preliminary portrait of capitalist transformation over the latter half of the nineteenth century by considering indicators of economic change in the five states—Alabama, Georgia, Louisiana, Mississippi, and South Carolina—that derived much of their income from cotton cultivation.[39] With respect to financial infrastructure, these states were remarkably underdeveloped in the antebellum period. As documented in Homans's *Bankers' Magazine and Statistical Register*, Alabama had only a single chartered bank in 1849 and Mississippi had none.[40] The situation was only slightly improved in 1860, when the *Bankers' Magazine* identified four banks in Mississippi and nine banks in Alabama (see Table 1.1). On the eve of the Civil War, much of the Southern capital under bank management was concentrated in the city of New Orleans, where eleven banks held $24.5 million in assets, or 44 percent of all bank capital in the Cotton South.[41] By contrast, the rural South was particularly bereft of banking institutions. In the late antebellum period, only one out of every twelve farm proprietors lived in a county with a bank. The limited banking infrastructure of the region was largely oriented toward the needs of the planter elite and their cotton factors.[42]

Credit markets in the antebellum South were likewise available in only an opaque and highly personal form. While Southern merchants and farmers relied heavily on goods that were purchased on credit from Northeastern wholesalers (in 1859, an estimated $131 million was shipped to the South from New York City alone), most of these transactions occurred in the absence of formal credit ratings.[43] Credit reporting had been pioneered in the early 1800s by the British Merchant Banks and, in the United States, by John Bradstreet and Lewis Tappan's Mercantile Agencies, but it had made limited inroads in the South. During the antebellum period, the

Table 1.1. Statistics on Banking in the Cotton South, 1849–80

	1849		1860		1880	
	# of Banks[a]	Assets (millions of dollars)	# of Banks[a]	Assets (millions of dollars)	# of Banks	Assets (millions of dollars)[b]
Alabama	1	1.5	9	5.4	38	9.5
Georgia	20	4.9	34	10.4	81	19.6
Louisiana	6	17.7	14	24.5	19	21.0
Mississippi	0	0.0	4	0.8	33	3.9
South Carolina	14	11.4	20	14.9	35	10.3
Total	41	35.6	81	56.0	206	64.3

Sources: Homans (1849: 242; 1860: 974–1000); U.S. Comptroller (1880: lxxxv–lxxxvii); Ransom and Sutch (2001: 307).

[a] Including branches and banks that were closed over the course of the year.

[b] Lower bound based on capital, bonds, and deposits held by national, state, and other banks (missing some private banks that did not provide reports to the U.S. Comptroller).

abolitionist sensibilities of industry leaders constrained penetration in the region; in turn, Southern newspapers denounced credit reporters as agents of Yankee espionage.[44] As a consequence, formal credit assessments before the Civil War were often restricted to a few sizable enterprises located in the largest cities. Examining a basic measure of credit market integration, we find that the estimated percentage of capital in credit-rated businesses was a mere 3 percent in 1860 across all of the counties of the Cotton South, with negligible credit rating in rural counties and more (33 percent) for businesses in counties with urban centers (Figure 1.1).[45] As Christopher Kingston and Robert Wright have pointed out, the absence of formalized credit rating in the rural South led to a heavy reliance on personal credit markets and an emphasis on "honor" that would serve to maintain a debtor's reputation via word of mouth.[46]

While banks and credit markets were concentrated in the cities of the South, those urban centers were few and far between during the antebellum period. In 1860, the Cotton South had only three major cities—Charleston, Mobile, and New Orleans—with more than twenty-five thousand inhabitants; only two other urban centers—Savannah and Augusta—had more than ten thousand residents. Before the Civil War, the South was substantially less urbanized than any part of the country, including the Western frontier.[47] This demographic pattern was reflected in the economy, since much of the specialized productive activity of the South (including craft and small manufacturing) occurred on the plantation. On the eve of the Civil War, many planters and Southern nationalists viewed the region's largest cities with suspicion, mostly as a potent source of urban ills that were inimical to the preservation of slavery. As the historian Frank Towers has pointed out,

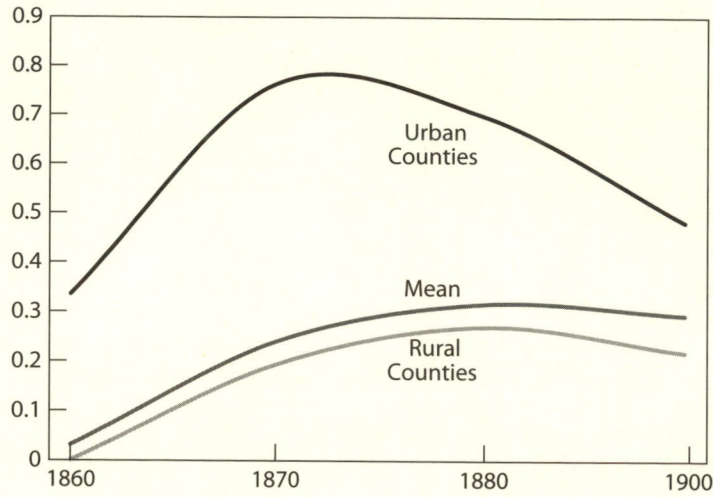

Figure 1.1. Formal Credit Market Integration in the Lower South, 1860–1900
Notes: The measure of market integration is the ratio of capital in credit-rated businesses to total capital investments in a county. Averages are reported across all counties for "mean," counties with at least one urban center (2,500+ inhabitants) for "urban counties," and counties without an urban center for "rural counties."

the economic vision of Southern traditionalists "promoted the building of Southern cities to expand market services for plantation agriculture" but excluded "the kind of industrial-based urban economy that had promoted excessive growth and class conflict in the North and in England."[48]

In institutional terms, of course, the most peculiar feature of the antebellum economy was its heavy reliance on chattel slavery. While much of the precapitalist-capitalist debate on slavery has focused on the mind-set of slaveholders, the relative productivity of the slave workforce, and the profitability of the slave trade, these discussions have tended to muddle rather than clarify the extent to which the structure of labor markets in the antebellum South deviated from the "free" labor markets observed in the nineteenth-century United States.[49] Three structural differences can be noted. First, despite an active domestic slave trade, turnover in slaves was low compared to the flow of wage labor from one employer to another. Michael Tadman, an economic historian, estimates that the typical slaveholder in the Upper South made a sale every ten to twelve *years*. In the period immediately after the Civil War, labor contracts signed by freedmen in the Upper South averaged less than twelve *months* in duration.[50] Second, in contrast to wage labor, the relatively high sunk costs in slaves were offset by very low maintenance costs, leading to strong incentives in favor of exploitation and against the turnover of slave labor. One cost calculation, advanced by Congressman George McDuffie (later governor) of South Carolina in 1832, suggested that the maintenance costs of field slaves were merely one-sixth those of the wages and board paid to free agricultural labor in the South Atlantic region.[51]

Third, while there was an ostensible shift toward allowing slaves to hire themselves out on short-term contracts in the late antebellum period, particularly in urban areas and in the Mountain South, the numbers of slaves who were granted this privilege was dwarfed by those who remained tethered to the plantation system. In Charleston, which had some of the most extensive regulations supporting slave hires, the number of hire badges issued every year rose from slightly over two thousand in 1800 to over five thousand in 1860 (Figure 1.2). While slave hires enjoyed some autonomy in selecting employers and trades, they remained a relatively small percentage of the local slave population. Hiring out in Charleston peaked at less than 14 percent of the county's slave population in 1860 and was consistently below 10 percent of the slave population before then.[52] In some Appalachian counties, slave hires approached one-fifth of the slave population in the late antebellum period. But the best available estimates for the South as a whole suggest that only 7.5 percent of slaves were hired out at any given time.[53]

These features suggest, prima facie, that the institution of slavery imposed "a limitation on the flow of labor between occupations and areas" and that the antebellum Southern labor market exhibited structural constraints that were consistent with precapitalist economies.[54] Flexibility in

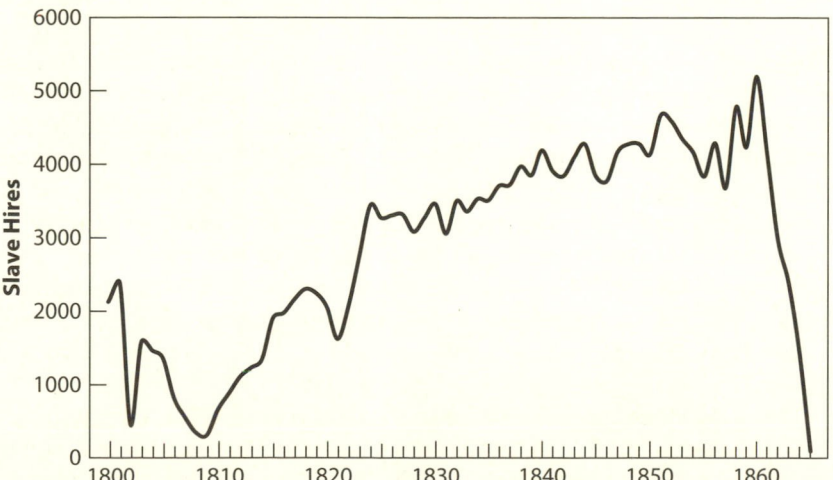

Figure 1.2. Estimated Number of Slaves Hired Out in Charleston (SC), 1800–65
Note: Estimates based on city income derived from sale of slave badges (Greene, Hutchins, and Hutchins 2004: Appendix 1).

hiring was often at the mercy of the relatively small size of the wage labor market in the South, particularly when it was limited to adults. In 1850, the U.S. census enumerated nearly 85,000 white adults (age fifteen and over) working as agricultural, manufacturing, construction, or service laborers in the five states of the Cotton South; the number of adult black slaves in Alabama, Georgia, Louisiana, Mississippi, and South Carolina was over 930,000, or more than ten times the number of whites.[55]

Viewed in these terms, the institutional interventions of the Union—both during and after the Civil War—would appear to have had a potential for dramatic effect on the Southern economy. In 1865, the passage of the Thirteenth Amendment and founding of the Freedmen's Bureau represented an unprecedented effort by federal authorities to construct and regulate a market for (nominally) "free" black labor. The passage of the National Banking Acts in the preceding two years created a system of national currency and removed banking from the control of the states. Formal supports for credit markets diffused rapidly as Northern credit rating agencies, such as Dun's, sent credit reporters to and established branch offices in the postbellum South. Some urban development was spurred during the Civil War by Union forces that built garrisoned towns and relied on the logistical infrastructure of Southern cities. More occurred in the aftershocks of the Civil War, as emancipated slaves and destitute whites migrated to urban centers in search of economic opportunity.

By some measures, these interventions, though short-lived, generated deep shifts in the Southern economy. Owing to the fairly restrictive conditions for obtaining a charter under the National Banking Acts, relatively few national banks were established in the South after the war—roughly forty existed in the five cotton states at the end of Radical Reconstruction. But the postwar boom in banking produced more state-chartered banks and nearly three times as many private banks, leading to a total of 206 banking institutions across the region in 1880 (Table 1.1). The average capitalization of the postwar banks, particularly the private banks, was modest compared to those that existed before the war, but the total assets of Southern banks were comparable to those observed in 1860. The result was a far greater geographic dispersion of banks and capital after the war. In the postbellum period, roughly one out of every three farm proprietors lived in a county with a bank, and the average Southern storekeeper or wholesaler lived in a county with nearly five banks.[56]

The mercantile agencies that had conducted formal credit ratings for decades in other parts of the United States penetrated the postbellum South at a brisk pace. At the time of the Civil War, R. G. Dun and Company only had two branch offices in the Lower South, located in New Orleans and Charleston. By 1890, the numbers of these offices had swelled to ten, with new locations in Atlanta, Birmingham, Columbus, Macon, Mobile, Montgomery,

Savannah, and Shreveport. Within five years after the war's end, the estimated proportion of capital in credit-rated businesses ballooned to 24 percent across all counties of the Cotton South and, by 1880, to 32 percent across all counties (Figure 1.1).[57] Although some scholars have suggested that the financial markets of the New South (and the United States, more generally) were less integrated than those of the antebellum period, a direct assessment of credit evaluations suggests that postbellum financiers and wholesalers in the Northeast had unprecedented access to information and ratings on Southern businesses.[58]

The urban economy of the Cotton South also flourished in the decades after the Civil War. By 1910, the five states in the region had nearly a dozen cities with more than 25,000 inhabitants. Atlanta was a prototype for the cities of the New South. Although it had been subjected to Sherman's "hard hand of war" like no other Southern locale, the city's population nearly quadrupled in the succeeding years, increasing to 37,409 by 1880. With its entrepreneurial spirit and diversified economy, Atlanta attracted frequent comparison with the thriving cities in the North and West.[59] More subtle, but equally impressive, was lower-order urbanization in the Cotton South. In Alabama, for instance, the number of incorporated towns with more than two hundred residents grew from 34 in 1870 to 91 in 1880 to 165 in 1890. The spatial pattern of economic activity in the antebellum period had emphasized two urban centers (Mobile and Montgomery) coupled with self-sufficient plantations and yeoman farmers in the hinterland; following the Civil War, the spread of railroad networks and commercial opportunities pushed merchants to the interior of the state. Credit markets served as a crucial institutional support to such urban development.[60]

The most pronounced institutional intervention into the postbellum Southern economy was also perhaps the one with the most ambiguous effect. As a matter of both regulation and norm, Northern authorities sought to import the free-labor ideology—with its attendant institutional devices of labor contracts and human capital investment—into a region that had resisted the idea of a wage labor market for two hundred years.[61] Central to this effort was the Bureau of Refugees, Freedmen, and Abandoned Lands. As a federal agency, the bureau was tasked with the massive responsibility of assisting four million former slaves in the transition from slavery to freedom. By some measures, the agency's organizing activities were unprecedented. The bureau reported the development of 740 black schools in the former slave states in 1866, with 90,589 students; by 1870, those numbers had grown to 4,239 schools under the supervision of the bureau, educating some 247,333 students.[62] Several hundred thousand labor contracts were signed under the auspices of the bureau and existing evidence suggests that they were enforced to a considerable degree.[63] Still, the bureau's efforts at education and labor reform reached only about one in ten freedmen, women, or children. Moreover, the widespread passage of Black Codes between 1865 and 1866—coupled with the ongoing use of coercion by many employers—threatened the very foundations of so-called free labor.

The limits of federal intervention and the contention in the transformation of the Southern labor market highlight a more general pattern. Economic transition in the postbellum South did not occur seamlessly, but rather in fits and starts. It is because of these institutional frictions that uncertainty was such a pronounced feature of capitalist transformation in the South. And it is because of the gradual diffusion of capitalist institutions that uncertainty escalated. Uncertainty was not merely in the heads of historical actors, hoping to come to an understanding of life in the New South, but in the progressive conflict between the logics of capitalist and precapitalist institutions.

OUTLINE OF THE BOOK

In this book, the implications of a theoretical emphasis on uncertainty are traced by considering the effects of change in economic institutions at different levels of analysis, with a particular emphasis on the transition between slavery and capitalism (see Table 1.2). At the individual level, this entails an examination of the wages and occupational status attainment of blacks and whites in the decades after the Civil War. Chapter 2 considers the extent to which the Freedmen Bureau's effort to reinstate plantation labor for former slaves in the mid-1860s was associated with changes in the valuation of black labor. Despite similarities in coercion and the organization of labor, I argue that the valuation of wage labor under the bureau was linked to human capital investments and statistical discrimination in ways that were fundamentally different from the valuations observed in appraisals, purchases, and hires within the antebellum slave market. This shift in the logic of valuation produced uncertainty among bureau agents, employers, and former bondsmen and women themselves as to how black workers would be compensated within the emerging free labor market of the American South.

Despite the uncertainty of wage rates within the labor market regulated by the bureau, employers and workers alike continued to operate with the occupational categories that had been established in the plantation system of the Old South. As this effort to regulate the labor market began to crumble, emancipated blacks faced a more fundamental form of uncertainty: what occupations (and class statuses) would be open to them with the demise of slavery? Chapter 3 explores this question by analyzing the legacy of slavery for status attainment among the first generation of blacks who were liberated from this peculiar institution. My quantitative findings suggest

Table 1.2. A Framework for the Analysis of Uncertainty and Change in Economic Institutions

Level of Analysis	Classical Uncertainty	Categorical Uncertainty
Individual	*Topics:* Worker Earnings and Income Inequality *E.g.,* How would wages for former slaves be set after the Civil War? (Chapter 2)	*Topics:* Jobs or Class Status *E.g.,* What social positions were possible for blacks and whites during Reconstruction? (Chapters 3 and 4)
Organization	*Topics:* Organizational Workforce and Performance *E.g.,* How many former slaves would remain as laborers in the plantation system? (Chapter 5)	*Topics:* Forms of Organization *E.g.,* What organizational alternatives to plantations were conceivable? (Chapters 5 and 6)
Community	*Topics:* Allocation of Regional Investments *E.g.,* How much would communities invest in agriculture versus industrial development? (Chapter 7)	*Topics:* Paths to Development *E.g.,* What developmental alternatives to cotton monocropping were conceivable? (Chapters 7 and 8)

that categorical uncertainty became more pronounced over time: while the internal hierarchy of slavery clearly predicted the occupations that emancipated blacks would hold after the Civil War, it became largely decoupled from status attainment in the succeeding decades. Mediating effects, such as the Freedmen Bureau's educational interventions and black migration, also served to curtail the reproduction of antebellum status. By the early twentieth century, the most durable predictor of the kinds of jobs that were available to blacks who had been born in the antebellum South was the legal distinction between those who were free and those who were slaves before 1865.

Chapter 4 extends the analysis of status outcomes to include the region's white population. I probe the question as to whether the class structure of the South changed in the postbellum era and whether different individual and locational attributes predicted who would come to occupy preferred social positions. The analysis in the chapter suggests another source of categorical uncertainty during Reconstruction and beyond. While many Southern journalists and politicians celebrated the expansion of an entrepreneurial middle class at the time, this class actually declined numerically in the proverbial

New South. Moreover, the "decaying" planter class was remarkably persistent, both in its dominance of the top of the wealth distribution and its involvement in the postwar industrialization of the region. The social categories of planters and middling Southerners that were deployed in popular discourse— and within the "New South Creed"—thus had little in common with the reality of class structure following the Civil War.[64]

The next section of the book considers sources of uncertainty in the organizational arrangements that proliferated in the New South with the demise of slavery. Union officials and Southern planters initially attempted to manage postwar instability by maintaining the plantation system, albeit with wage labor rather than slaves. For the planters, a crucial source of uncertainty at the organizational level involved the problem of labor supply. Without formal recourse to coercion and the domestic slave trade, landowners could no longer reliably predict where their workforce would come from and how they could retain black workers on plantations. For former slaves, a parallel source of uncertainty applied to the problem of labor demand—where could they find new economic opportunities without reproducing the exploitative patterns of bondage? Chapter 5 considers why freedmen and women in the postbellum South left the plantation system when their prospects outside of it seemed to be so uncertain.

As the maintenance of plantation agriculture proved increasingly untenable, Southern blacks and whites confronted categorical, as well as classical, uncertainty. Chapter 5 addresses this process with respect to the organizational landscape of Southern agriculture. What forms of agricultural tenure would come to replace the plantation system? How would individual decisions and negotiations influence the predominance of proprietor farming, rental farming, share farming, and wage plantations in the South? Given the interdependence of agriculture and commerce in the South, Chapter 6 extends the analysis to the realm of nonagricultural organizations in the postbellum era. What forms of merchandising would replace the network of cotton factors that had prevailed before the Civil War? How did the spread of capitalist institutions, particularly credit and consumer markets, affect the uncertainty surrounding the commercial and industrial enterprises of the New South?

The final section of the book addresses sources of uncertainty at a regional level. In Chapter 7, I argue that familiar paths to economic development, such as investments in railroad infrastructure, banking, and market centers, produced unpredictable returns for Southern communities in the decades after the war. Confronted with new forms of commerce, boosters faced not only uncertainty in anticipating how much economic and demographic growth to expect from their communities, but also categorical uncertainty in deciding what paths to economic revitalization might be possible. Under conditions of profound change, the most reliable approach for postbellum communities to secure capital investments, attract new residents, and increase the production of local goods was to create organizational forms that were present in other comparable communities, thereby avoiding accusations of idiosyncrasy. By 1900, this produced a remarkable pattern of economic underdevelopment, in which the fates of most small Southern towns were tied to cotton monocropping and a homogeneous pattern of retailing.

The escalating uncertainty observed in the transition from slavery to capitalism in the U.S. South raises the question as to whether a similar process occurred following other instances of emancipation. My concluding chapter summarizes the evidence that we have for the postbellum South and compares it with other postemancipation projects in the Americas. I suggest that the common pattern of gradual emancipation seen in former colonial possessions in the Caribbean and South America has considerable similarity with early efforts to manage uncertainty in the era of Radical Reconstruction. As in the case of the American South, those postemancipation projects soon fell victim to competing claims and mobilization among landowners, workers, and other parties, leading to profound and durable uncertainty in the economies of former slave societies.

CONCLUSION

The interpretation of history has often been a debate between proponents of continuity and proponents of change. During the first half of the twentieth century, the Dunning School dismissed Radical Reconstruction as a political and economic failure. During the second half, the Cliometric School questioned whether the institutions of slavery were as economically backward as one might suppose. This book critically evaluates the continuity of economic institutions in the late nineteenth- and early twentieth-century South. It starts with the assumption that we cannot understand the legacy of American slavery and emancipation without a systematic assessment of the changes in socioeconomic status experienced by both whites and blacks over this period. In developing this assessment, the book employs both interpretive and quantitative methods. The interpretive analyses draw on a large data set comprising over three thousand oral interviews conducted with former slaves by the Works Progress Administration (WPA), as well as letters, memoirs, survey responses, and other narratives from a variety of sources. The quantitative analyses draw from census data and credit reports assembled to analyze individual and organizational outcomes after the Civil War, as well as a systematic collection of labor contracts from the archives of the Freedmen's Bureau.[65]

As one economic historian has argued, "for scholars seeking to understand institutional change and economic performance, the evolution of the South has long been an obvious candidate for study"; indeed, "it would be difficult to read American history without noticing that the South success-fully escaped from both widespread poverty and what the modern eco-nomic development literature considers 'bad' institutions . . . most infa-mously, the disenfranchisement of so many citizens in a country famous for its democratic institutions."[66] While the fulfillment of the South's political and economic transformation would not be realized until a century later, early seeds appeared with emancipation and the reorganization of planta-tion agriculture in the late nineteenth century. The resulting contention among different interests—urban and rural, planter and freedmen, Union and ex-Confederate—would come to render uncertainty a central and en-during feature of life in the South. The most immediate question raised by the end of the Civil War involved the fate of former bondsmen and women. How would they survive, and what institutional rules would structure the way that they were able to earn their livelihood? I turn to this question in the next chapter, which considers the creation of a nominally "free" labor market for African Americans in the postbellum era.

CHAPTER 2

Constructing a Free Labor Market

> Our great effort should be not only to show that free labor can be
> made profitable to the employer, but also to the laborer.... It is the
> duty of the Government to exercise a wholesome guardianship over
> these new-born children of freedom; to guide, direct and protect them,
> at least in their infancy, and to see that injustice and inhumanity are
> not practiced upon them—to make them realize that they are
> freemen.
>
> —James Yeatman, *A Report on the Condition of
> the Freedmen of the Mississippi*

On Independence Day of 1865, less than two months after Lee surrendered
to Grant at Appomattox Court House, James Erwin Yeatman wrote a letter
to the head of the newly founded Bureau of Refugees, Freedmen, and Abandoned Lands.[1] A fervent Unionist, Yeatman had served in the Western Sanitary Commission during the war, helping to secure medical services for
Northern soldiers and wounded ex-slaves in St. Louis. In late 1863, he toured
the Mississippi Valley to assess the education and health of Southern blacks
who had recently been liberated in Union-occupied territory. Yeatman was
impressed by the propensity of freedmen to create independent schools,
often with little more than a Bible, a few books, and a classroom of students
instructed by a literate ex-slave. At the same time, he noted that the freedmen preferred to remain on plantations, often working under old masters,
rather than move into disease-ridden refugee camps where they would face
high rates of mortality. He worried that Southern employers were exploiting the naïveté and economic dependence of freedmen, providing inadequate wages and perpetuating other injustices on workers who had no experience in negotiating terms within an open labor market.[2]

These concerns were reflected in Yeatman's letter. He began with the
lament that the Freedmen's Bureau had "not fixed upon any definite policy,
in regard to the rate of wages to be paid to freed people in the different rebel-
lious states." This was highly problematic, in his eyes, since employers "will
take every advantage of the necessities or ignorance of the poor negro, and
pay him the lowest possible amount, just so it can be called compensation."

Yeatman argued that the dilemma of underpayment was unlikely to be limited to former slave masters: "the tendency everywhere [was] to pay too little," and he had "seen no wages named either by employers, military commandants or others which would be deemed fair and just compensation were they the owner of the negro, and hiring them to labor for others." Yeatman's solution was to fix wage rates for emancipated blacks based on slave hire rates observed in the Southern states before the Civil War, with contracts supervised by agents of the bureau and careful consideration of rations, board, and other costs of living.[3]

The letter was addressed to Oliver Otis Howard, the "Christian general" who served as the head of the Freedmen's Bureau throughout its existence, from 1865 until 1872. During the Civil War, Howard had led Union forces during ill-fated campaigns at Bull Run and Chancellorsville, but later redeemed himself at the Battle of Gettysburg and as the commander of the Army of Tennessee. When the war entered its waning days, Abraham Lincoln appointed Howard to supervise the Freedmen's Bureau. The bureau would issue emergency rations and other necessities, create schools, register marriages, and promote the general welfare of former bondsmen and women. Foremost among the activities of the bureau's commissioners, as W. E. B. Du Bois recalled, was the need "to introduce practicable systems of compensated labor," to secure the rights of freedpeople to choose their employers and provide templates for labor contracts.[4]

Despite—or, perhaps, because of—its immense mandate, the bureau could not intervene in many aspects of the emerging market for free labor.[5] In his reply to Yeatman, General Howard expressed doubt about the ability of government to set wages via centralized administrative fiat. Rather, Howard said he would prefer to have "contracts made as widely possible . . . varying according to the multifarious circumstances of the contracting parties." He deemed it impracticable to offer federal rules of compensation that would cover "the infinite gradation from the able-bodied man to the little child," instead leaving such negotiation to local agents. The role of the bureau, he argued, would be restricted to the monitoring and enforcement of contractual conditions; it was the responsibility of the bureau's agents to do so, and they could "call for military aid if necessary." But more rigid systems of wage setting and worker registration were deeply problematic in his view, "gravitat[ing] to slavery in reality if not in name."[6]

The correspondence between Oliver Otis Howard and James Yeatman parallels a number of modern debates regarding the institutional conditions that structure so-called free labor markets. Do market transitions represent abrupt shifts from the past or continuities with previous economic institutions? To what extent should markets for wage labor be regulated by the state? Who (or what) can establish a fair price for labor? Must price mechanisms be tailored to local circumstances, or can they be applied in broad brush strokes to national markets?

As an antecedent to these questions of political economy, there is also the more rudimentary issue of the role of uncertainty in the market. For Yeatman, the emerging postbellum market for African American wage labor presented a problem of risk. The fair distribution of income in the new labor market was a known quantity, which could be ascertained from the monthly rates paid to slave laborers who were hired out by their masters before the Civil War. The risk to the freedmen was represented by the relatively high probability that employers and federal authorities would substitute the lowest rates of compensation for these fair wages, providing barely enough compensation for emancipated slaves to subsist on. Under General Howard's authority, the bureau was in a position to manage and minimize such risk.

For General Howard, the emerging market for African American wage labor presented a problem not of risk but of uncertainty. The fair distribution of income was not a known quantity, nor did he "deem it expedient [for the bureau] to fix upon a general system of wages."[7] While the bureau could provide standard forms of contract and some federal oversight to approve, register, and monitor contractual conditions, Howard left it to the market itself to dictate the returns on human capital. Worried that employers and former slave owners would conspire to manipulate wage regulation to their advantage, General Howard, like many Northern authorities, was willing to accept uncertainty rather than have Southerners make a mockery of free labor ideology.[8]

THE TRANSITION TO WAGE LABOR

During the nineteenth and early twentieth centuries, social theorists conceptualized the transition to wage labor as one that was fraught with uncertainty, class conflict, and economic upheaval. Writing on the enclosure movement in late feudal Britain, Karl Marx argued that the process that forced peasants from manorial lands simultaneously produced a class of "free and rightless" wage laborers and a class of capitalist landowners. Following the last gasps of German serfdom, Max Weber found that the East Elbian peasants worked under precarious and wretched conditions, with interests often opposed to those of their masters on Prussian estates. Karl Polanyi's influential treatment of the Speenhamland law in England suggested that a true market for wage labor emerged only in fits and starts after the initial phases of the industrial revolution, owing to persistent elements of paternalism in labor regulation. A reading of classic scholarship thus situates the rise of wage labor as a chaotic process, one in which "the economic advantages of a free labor market could [often] not make up for the social destruction wrought by it."[9]

By contrast, current views of labor markets typically take the mechanisms of wage labor for granted, rendering them as socially natural rather than as a product of specific institutional and historical circumstances. Labor markets are described in terms of at-will work arrangements, in which workers are free to choose employers and free to leave when they find better alternatives (or choose not to work at all). Coercion is minimized by assigning the property rights of labor to workers themselves and by removing legal mechanisms that allow employers to exercise violence or threats in the enforcement of labor contracts. Often implicit in this view is the assumption that modern definitions of free wage labor—that is, labor that is nominally at will and unburdened by coercion—can be applied equally well to eighteenth- and nineteenth-century incarnations; and that the essential mechanisms that structure inequality within modern capitalist labor markets—such as investment in occupational skill—can likewise be found across a range of historical contexts.[10]

The emphasis on the modern contours of wage labor may be especially problematic for understanding the value historically placed on the labor of blacks, whose work experiences in the United States were dominated by the institutions of chattel slavery and, at early stages, indentured servitude over a period of nearly two hundred fifty years. Paralleling the tension between classical scholarship emphasizing the disruption wrought by the rise of wage labor and contemporary assumptions emphasizing its continuity with earlier forms of labor organization, an active literature arose in the 1970s to shed light on the valuation of black labor in the U.S. South. Conceptualizations of price mechanisms under slavery derived from two influential (and, in many respects, opposing) arguments. In their provocative and controversial book *Time on the Cross*, the economic historians Robert Fogel and Stanley Engerman advanced the claim that slave pricing in the antebellum South was guided by mechanisms that were largely identical to those that emerged among employers of wage labor in the postbellum era. Evidence for this thesis was located in data that suggested the extensive differentiation of skills in slave markets, the correlation between worker productivity and slave prices, and the relative efficiency of slave plantations. A dissenting view was offered by Marxist historians, led by Eugene Genovese, who contended that the mind-set of the planter class was fundamentally pre-bourgeois, relying on the slave market as a form of conspicuous consumption rather than as a source of a productive labor force. Speculation in slaves occurred as a function of the planters' social prestige more so than considerations of profitability.[11]

While both arguments have shown considerable development—and increased nuance—over the past few decades, neither has mustered a direct and systematic comparison of pricing in the various antebellum markets for slaves and the market for wage labor that emerged immediately after the Civil War. This proves problematic not only for assessing how widely modern mechanisms of stratification were deployed in these nineteenth-century labor markets, but also for assessing the uncertainty that faced black workers, federal monitors, and Southern employers in the postbellum era. If compensation under the Freedmen's Bureau came to reproduce the valuation of labor under slavery, as James Yeatman proposed, then the new labor market would evidence a predictable, path-dependent form of wage allocation. On the other hand, if compensation departed markedly from the logic deployed in the slave markets of the Old South, then workers, regulators, and employers alike would need to grapple with more profound uncertainties regarding the value of black labor.

This chapter examines how the labor market for African American workers that arose immediately after the Civil War was distinct from the diverse markets for slave labor that dominated the Southern economy during the antebellum period. I trace the process of valuation of black labor through four markets in the U.S. South, moving from slave purchases and appraisals within the plantation economy to the antebellum system of "hiring out" to wage setting for black labor under the auspices of the Freedmen's Bureau. Comparative analysis of labor pricing across these markets reveals systematic changes, with slave markets placing price premiums on children and young women and occupational skills emerging as the most salient influence in the pricing of wage labor. This chapter concludes by addressing how the transvaluation of labor occurs when markets for unfree and free workers are governed by distinct institutional conditions.

A COMPARATIVE THEORY OF LABOR MARKETS

A simple typology of labor markets can be constructed based on two underlying dimensions. One dimension considers whether the buyer in a transaction for labor exercises perpetual ownership over his or her workers or whether the transfer of labor power is short term, involving either an employment relationship that is terminable at will or one that is contractually delimited. The other dimension considers whether third parties—either governmental or nongovernmental—monitor the price and conditions under which the transfer of labor power occurs. For the sake of simplicity, the distinctions presented here involve polar opposites, although historical observers have often imagined a continuum of employment relationships

along each dimension. Thus, English workers employed under long contracts in the nineteenth century were said to be "bound like slaves to the
employers," while those hired under short contracts were considered to be
free labor. Similarly, Southern cities in the antebellum period diverged in
their tendency to regulate hired black labor, with some, such as Charleston,
devoting considerable effort to the legal oversight of short-term laborers but
others leaving the management of such affairs to the whims of slave owners
and employers.[12]

Cross-tabulating these dimensions, as shown in Table 2.1, we obtain four
ideal-typical labor markets: (a) the unregulated (or weakly regulated) market
for unfree labor; (b) the regulated market for unfree labor, conducted within
a legal-rational context by third parties such as lawyers, creditors, actuaries,
or the state; (c) the unregulated hire market for labor; and (d) the regulated
market for wage workers. The last market interface corresponds most closely
to what Max Weber termed "formally 'free' labor," wherein the exchange of
labor is subject to a mutual contractual relationship, whether explicit or im-
plied.[13] The contractual nature of the relationship (and its oversight by third
parties) is critical, since it differentiates this market from the unregulated
hire market, which Karl Marx identified as "free and rightless" hired labor.
Free and rightless labor may be found in a variety of historical circumstances,
ranging from the British peasantry removed from their land by the enclosure movement to day laborers in modern capitalist society.[14]

The dimensions in Table 2.1 suggest two trade-offs that have historically
affected a diverse set of markets for labor from the perspective of buyers or
employers. With respect to regulation, the exploitation of labor—especially
in its baser forms—tended to occur most readily when third parties were
unavailable to monitor the terms of exchange and treatment of workers; yet
those third parties may also have been essential to credentialing workers and
managing uncertainty regarding labor availability and replacement. With

Table 2.1. A Typology of Labor Markets

		Third-Party Monitoring and Evaluation	
		Little or None	*Considerable*
Duration of Ownership of Labor Power	*Perpetual*	**Slave purchases**, servile marriage, child servitude, sexual slavery	**Judicial appraisals of unfree labor**, penal labor, debt bondage, serfdom
	Short Term/ At Will	**Unregulated hire market**, day labor, illicit labor	**Regulated wage labor**

Note: Entries in bold correspond to those analyzed empirically in this chapter; other entries are intended to
be illustrative and may appear in different cells depending on the specific legal frameworks and norms of
the society being analyzed.

respect to the time horizon of employment, investment in specific skills and the domination of workers occurred most readily when employers were able to exercise perpetual control over their workforce; yet perpetual transfers of labor power also carried the burden of large sunk costs and considerable risk of laborer mortality or disability in the long run. We now turn to the core question of how these institutional dimensions and trade-offs affected the way that labor was valued in the transition from slavery to capitalism in the U.S. South.

Investment in Occupational Skills

For analyses of wage labor, a common explanation of variation in earnings involves the *human capital* that workers exhibit, as evidenced in their stock of knowledge and occupational skills. Specifically, the process of human capital accumulation under free labor is typified by an opportunity cost that is incurred by the worker (in the interest of acquiring additional education, experience, or training) with the goal of generating future rents that justify that opportunity cost. The logic of human capital accumulation is one in which education or training are typically undertaken early in the life course so that their costs may be amortized over an extended period of time.[15]

In *Time on the Cross*, Fogel and Engerman argue that this idea of investment in human capital applies equally well, if not even more so, to markets for slave labor—after all, "nobody doubts that human beings were a form of capital in slave society." The fundamental difference between slave and free society, according to this account, lies not in the existence of human capital, but in whether employers or workers themselves "hold title to such property rights." Recent studies of markets for unfree labor, such as the New Orleans slave market, have suggested similarly that these were arenas dominated by economic rationality, particularly "a strong incentive for owners to invest in the human capital of their slaves."[16] When human capital is assessed in broad terms, including the health and reproductive capacity of slaves, the ideology of slave owners clearly highlights the importance of investments in this form of capital. But when the concept of human capital is operationalized more narrowly, as an investment in occupational skills or education, it is not at all clear that the logic of human capital theory was widespread in slave societies.

One problem concerns the typical duration of slave ownership. In the antebellum South, the moral ideology of the planter class extolled the paternalism and interpersonal relationships that accompanied the region's peculiar institution of durable bondage. If owners in slave societies viewed their chattel as property to be held over their lifetime, then rents for investments in skills would seldom be realized in the open market for slave labor. In Weber's eyes, the low turnover in slaves alone was sufficient to rule out an equation between chattel slaves and capital. "Human beings (slaves and serfs)," he wrote, ". . . which are used by seigneurial owners as sources of rent are, in the nature of the case, only rent-producing household property and not capital goods."[17]

A related problem in invoking the language of human capital is that durable bondage meant the skills acquired by slaves were often quite specific to particular work arrangements and masters. In the American South, this skill specificity was especially apparent among domestic slaves, whose deference behaviors and relationships to owners would not necessarily extend to other employers, nor to conditions following emancipation. As a matter of exercising control on their plantations, masters offered specialized titles and training as a reward for a slave's talent or loyalty, not as a matter of developing human capital.[18] Where slaves were deployed in the production of staple crops, there was little incentive for slave owners to develop other skills or, for that matter, to view their chattel as investment commodities.[19]

Insofar as long-term slaveholding is entrenched in a society, then, relatively little variation in the value of labor can be explained by the titles that serve as a proxy for occupational skill in other contexts. The absence of third-party monitoring and evaluation likewise generates problems for investments in occupational skill. For skill to generate anticipated rents, potential employers must have some assurance that workers possess the skills they claim and skilled labor must have some assurance that unskilled workers will not move into their occupational jurisdictions. Without these structural conditions—often labeled as credentialing and occupational closure, respectively—material returns to skill investments tend to be diluted.[20] Under chattel slavery, credentialing and closure were weak because occupational training was an idiosyncratic undertaking, remaining largely in the hands of individual slave owners. Owing to high levels of slave mortality and an overwhelming desire among employers to minimize turnover costs, there was little effort to create institutional barriers that regulated movement from one slave occupation to another.[21]

To a slightly lesser extent, this generalization also applied to the hire markets that were highlighted by Yeatman's correspondence. The slave hire markets represented a step toward freedom, insofar as slaves were allowed to choose their own employers, negotiate work conditions, and retain some of their earnings. While skilled labor was often sought after—especially in urban markets for hired slaves—it remained difficult for employers to verify workers' capabilities *ex ante*, given the presence of opportunistic intermediaries, such as slave owners or brokers (e.g., placement agencies).[22]

On the whole, these theoretical arguments suggest that investments in occupational skills primarily affected the valuation of labor in markets that exhibited the joint conditions of regulation by independent third parties (who were in a position to evaluate and protect claims of occupational skill) and short-term control of labor power (which subjected the returns on human capital to regular market exchange and removed investment decisions from paternalistic authority).

Statistical Discrimination

The logic of human capital relies on the differentiation of ability among workers in a labor market, but the logic of *statistical discrimination* relies on the differentiation of ascriptive characteristics (e.g., age, sex, race) that are perceived to be correlated with ability. In the context of free labor markets, the use of statistical discrimination is sometimes justified on the basis of predictions regarding worker productivity that tends to hold on average for a readily observed trait. According to economic theory, employers rely on stereotyping with respect to such traits when labor markets are characterized by imperfect information regarding worker skills and motivations, which are typically unobserved.[23]

Like human capital theory, the theory of statistical discrimination has been applied readily—if implicitly—to markets that deviate from the institutional conditions of formally free labor. As part of their evidence for the capitalist character of slavery in the antebellum South, Fogel and Engerman highlighted age-varying slave prices, which peaked for prime male field hands in their twenties and fell precipitously for younger and older slaves. According to their calculations, this age-price profile correlated strongly with the earnings of slaves over their lifecycle. Moreover, Fogel and Engerman asserted, the lower price of female slaves after the teen years was accounted for by the lower annual earnings of these workers. Rational slave buyers could thus be said to have discriminated statistically by age, sex, and physiology, using observed characteristics as proxies for the agricultural productivity of field labor.[24]

Although there may be some temptation to apply statistical discrimination theory equally to markets for free and unfree labor, the historical record suggests some important differences. One key distinction concerns the role of risk in these transactions. In purchase markets for slaves, buyers can exercise perpetual ownership over labor power. Due to this time horizon of ownership, inferences regarding the ability of slaves assume increased importance. Participants in short-term or at-will contracts tend to have few sunk costs in the employment relationship (at least initially), but slave buyers place a larger investment at risk. As Weber noted, formal rationality in the management of slaves was particularly difficult to achieve, owing to the high level of sunk costs, the exposure of slave labor to "non-economic influences," and the resulting fluctuations in slave valuation. Consequently, if perceived risk is a precondition to statistical discrimination, then such discrimination is likely to be more pronounced in markets for unfree than for free labor.[25]

Another distinction between free and slave labor concerns statistical discrimination against female workers in particular. Almost since their inception, neoclassical theories have emphasized the disruptive role of childrearing and the resulting tendency of women, under free labor arrangements, to choose lines of work that maximized their earnings with this discontinuity in mind.[26] In the context of slavery, historians have pointed to an opposite possibility—that women of childbearing age may have been valued especially highly, insofar as slaveholders had a pecuniary interest in slave breeding.[27] The sexual stereotyping invoked in discussions of slave markets is thus fundamentally different from that in discussions of wage labor markets, with the extent of ownership over labor (literally, including reproduction) representing a key moderating variable.

The time horizon of labor ownership affects statistical discrimination for other demographic categories. In modern free labor markets, child labor is either avoided altogether (due to the regulatory oversight by third parties) or subject to very low wages. As Viviana Zelizer has noted, the cultural shift in the valuation of middle-class children, from "object of utility to object of sentiment," was already complete by the mid-nineteenth century, rendering this population to be "economically worthless."[28] But in slave markets, price discounting at young ages was far more limited. The high valuation of child labor was premised on the future flow of rents expected from adolescent slaves, while the comparable valuation under free labor conditions was largely driven by present productivity. Under slavery, the vacancy chain of openings on a plantation likewise influenced the valuation of child labor. Thus, the Jamaican planter Thomas Roughley wrote that slave children form "the rising generation, from which, in progress of time, all the vacancies occurring in the different branches of slave population are filled up . . . the expectations formed of them are still greater, when contemplated in a future point of view. They are drivers, cattlemen, mulemen, carpenters, coopers, and masons, as it were in embryo."[29]

The regulatory dimension of labor markets may also affect the logic of statistical discrimination. Where third-party oversight of labor markets was absent, there was an additional risk that employers would illegitimately exploit child or female labor. Under antebellum chattel slavery, for example, the sexual exploitation of women often went beyond slave breeding, as masters had intercourse with their female chattel and forced them to bear their children. These acts were formally illegitimate, owing to antimiscegenation sentiments and laws in many Southern states.[30] When hidden from public view, however, such acts of exploitation or intimacy were often tolerated and only infrequently subject to prosecution. Similarly, public norms discouraged the overworking of young slaves (who were to be given light tasks). One Southern state, Louisiana, even briefly banned the sale of children under ten away from their mothers. But the practical effects of these prohibitions on child labor are subject to question.[31] Insofar as the capacity for exploitation is built into labor market pricing, one can expect that unregulated markets for children and young women will display larger price premiums than those found in markets with third-party oversight.

These arguments regarding the operation of statistical discrimination across labor markets suggest three additional propositions. First, we anticipate that price discrimination of workers by sex and age was more pronounced, on average, in markets for unfree than for free labor. Second, considering the value placed on children and women of childbearing ages in particular, the valuation was greater in markets for unfree labor, given the emphasis on demographic reproduction and expected future returns in these markets. Finally, labor markets with limited third-party oversight may likewise have exhibited price premiums for child labor and young women, owing to the greater potential for exploitation (sexual or otherwise) of these vulnerable populations.

From Slavery to Free Labor in the U.S. South

In the United States, the formal emancipation of four million slaves in December 1865 offers a unique historical opportunity to consider the effects of free labor market conditions on the valuation of African American labor in the nineteenth century.[32] Earlier that year, Congress established the Freedmen's Bureau to guide former bondsmen and women on their path from slavery to freedom. The bureau attempted to institute labor market conditions that approximate the ideal of regulated wage labor, as shown in Table 2.1. Labor contracts formed under the bureau's direction were generally of short duration. Available records from the Washington, D.C., and northern Virginia branches, for instance, show a mean contract length of ten months. Longer contracts tended to be applied to child or adolescent apprentices, who by virtue of bureau policy were drawn from the ranks of "orphans, deserted children, and those whose parents are unable, for any reason, to keep them properly." Fewer than 2 percent of the contracts signed in Washington and Alexandria specified durations over a year.[33]

Under the Freedmen's Bureau, employment arrangements could not be terminated at will, and some freedmen feared the contracts would bring a new form of enslavement. Nevertheless, archival evidence suggests some flexibility in contract terms. For instance, Page and Tena Lomax initially signed a contract on September 28, 1865, with James Bryan of Dorchester County, Maryland, agreeing to a three-month term of service with a possibility of a one-year extension thereafter. On December 16 of the same year, the

Freedmen's Bureau received a letter from Bryan's son, noting that the Lomaxs were leaving after the "short trial in consequence of Tiny [*sic*] Lomax's sickness or rather her melancholy on account of separation from her children."[34] Although instances of effective slavery persisted and the meaning of "free" labor continued to evolve, the bureau's insistence on oversight by local superintendents (who witnessed contracts between freedmen and employers) tended to produce the formal conditions of regulated wage labor over the brief period of its existence.

To analyze the valuation of labor under the auspices of the Freedmen's Bureau, I identified and coded all labor contracts that were documented at the bureau's branch offices in Washington, D.C., and Alexandria, Virginia, between August 1865 and March 1867. Despite the urban location of the offices themselves, the contracts covered a large variety of (predominately rural) labor agreements with employers in Virginia, Maryland, and a dozen other states (see Figure 2.1). Only eighteen contracts (fewer than 2 percent of the sample) referenced employment relations within the District of Columbia. Nearly 40 percent of the contracts pertained to labor arrangements outside the Potomac and Chesapeake region, with especially large concentrations in Arkansas and Mississippi.[35] The sample is useful for comparison with antebellum slave markets, given that Virginia and Maryland had served as centers of the slave trade since the early American Republic.[36]

I contrast the postbellum pricing of wage labor with three other labor market interfaces. The antebellum hiring market for slaves in the U.S. South tended to feature short-term work arrangements and limited oversight by independent third parties, placing it in the lower left-hand cell of Table 2.1. As the historian Richard Wade has noted in his early treatment of *Slavery in the Cities*, antebellum hiring generally relied on two mechanisms of exchange: fixed-term (contractual) hiring and flexible-term (noncontractual) hiring. The duration of contractual hiring varied considerably, with some contracts lasting only a few weeks and others, in rare cases, lasting a few years. Examining probate record data for eight Southern states, including Georgia, Louisiana, Maryland, Mississippi, North Carolina, South Carolina, Tennessee, and Virginia, the average term of hire for slaves between the 1830s and the end of the Civil War was approximately eleven months, almost identical to that observed in the wage labor market subsequently regulated by the Freedmen's Bureau. Over 94 percent of these contracts fell in a narrow band, with durations between nine months and a year.[37]

Some Southern cities regulated flexible-term hiring, but these laws tended to serve as controls on the slave population, rather than the exchange process itself. New Orleans, Mobile, Savannah, Charleston, and a number of other municipalities passed badge laws that credentialed a subset of slaves to hire themselves out for specified trades. Charleston, South Carolina, had one of the most sustained set of regulations. Codified in 1806, Charleston's badge

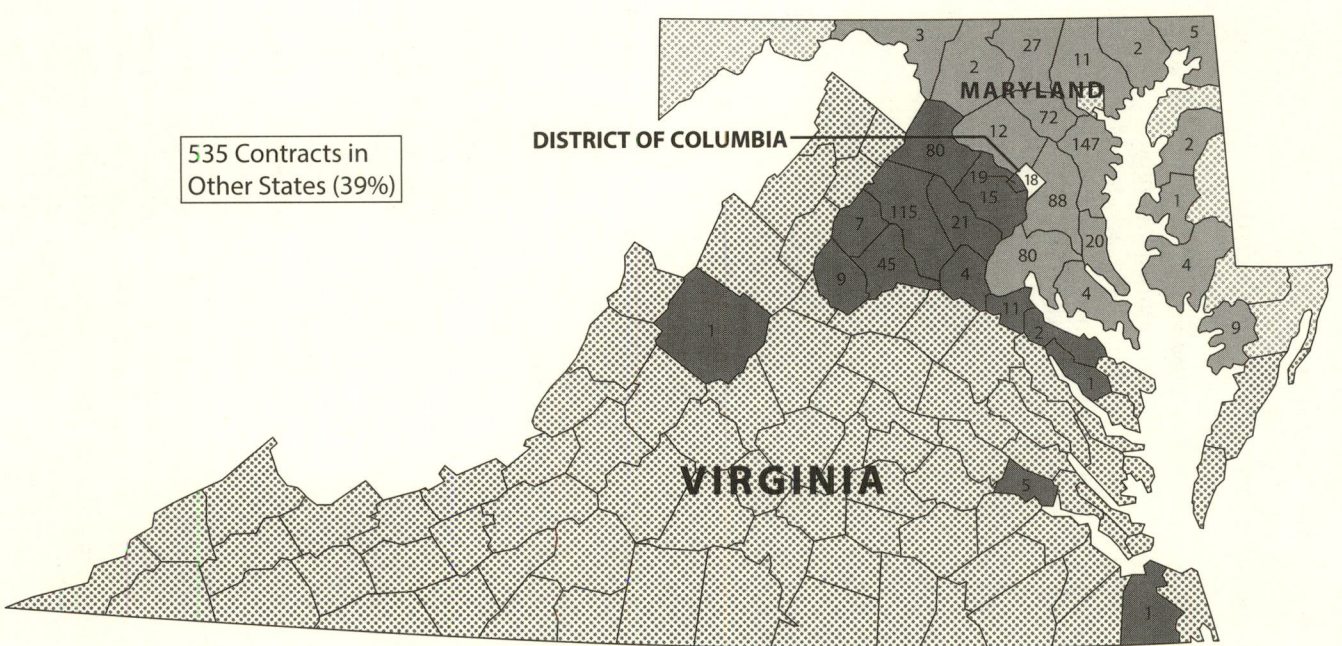

535 Contracts in
Other States (39%)

DISTRICT OF COLUMBIA

MARYLAND

VIRGINIA

3   27   2   5
2   11   2
72
12   147
80
19   18   2
15   88
7   115   21   80   20
45   4   4
9   11
1   2
1

5

9

4

1

Figure 2.1. Spatial Distribution of Employers Signing Contracts in the Alexandria, Virginia, and Washington, D.C., Branches of the Freedmen's Bureau (1865–67)

laws required that slave owners who sought to hire out their slaves pay a tax (commensurate with the occupation of the slaves) and that hired black workers wear a badge—a metal artifact displaying an owner's serial number, a year, and a trade—on their person.[38] However, the badges arguably had only limited regulatory influence on transactions between slave owners and hiring agents. Badge laws served primarily as a means to raise tax revenue from slave owners and to limit slave autonomy, not to produce occupational closure. Most smaller municipalities and rural areas were not in a position to exercise regulatory supervision over the hiring process at all.[39]

The remaining antebellum market for slaves was differentiated into purchases and appraisals, corresponding to the upper-left- and upper-right-hand cells of Table 2.1, respectively. Appraised prices were generally set by third parties when slaves were insured, when a plantation owner passed away, or when legal proceedings required an independent assessment. The market for slave insurance emerged relatively late in the antebellum period and was concentrated in the urban centers of the Upper South. During the 1830s, the Baltimore Insurance Company began to offer policies to a few slave owners in Virginia, with the idea of securing the long-term value of skilled slaves, particularly those who were engaged in risky trades. Valuation in the insurance market was subject to more exacting standards than slave purchases. In the absence of reliable statistics on slave mortality by geography, age, and trade, Baltimore Life was initially resistant to the idea of issuing insurance policies on slaves. Underwriting by the firm was limited to masters who were known not to mistreat their slaves, owing to the problem of moral hazard. To reduce the probability of malfeasance, the firm relied on local insurance agents to monitor the character of slave owners and the value of their insured chattel. As demand for slave insurance increased in the 1840s and 1850s, other Southern companies (e.g., North Carolina Mutual, Greensboro Mutual, Virginia Life), as well as Northern insurers (New York Life, Aetna Life of Hartford, National Safety Life and Trust of Philadelphia), underwrote the value of slaves, adopting similar strictures on the treatment of black laborers.[40] The process of appraising slave values was thus widely conceptualized as a problem of risk.

While the insurance market represented a relatively new interface for the formal appraisal of slaves, judicial sales had regulated prices in the slave trade since the colonial era. In judicial sales, appraisals "were generally made by other planters, that is, by men familiar with market conditions and current price levels" who "exercised considerable care in their evaluations." Following the appraisals, transactions occurred at auction blocks near county courthouses throughout the South.[41] The presence of court-appointed third parties differentiated the institutional conditions of appraisals from slave purchases, which relied on the personal judgments of slave buyers.

Given the high market value of slaves and the information asymmetries between buyers and sellers, the antebellum purchase market was also subject to regulation, as the economic historian Jenny Wahl has emphasized. Much of this regulation was oriented toward legal remedies (e.g., warranties, litigation, restrictive covenants) constraining the ability of slave traders to engage in fraud or misrepresentation. The overarching emphasis of Southern laws governing the sale of slaves was to keep such transactions "private and cheap." Regulation in the purchase market affected the transaction costs of the slave trade, rather than setting the price of labor or terms of exchange directly.[42]

Archival Evidence on the Valuation of Labor

For the antebellum period, extensive archival evidence on slaveholder valuations can be found in public statements regarding criteria used to judge black labor, as well as the letters, circulars, and price tables of slave traders. Tyre Glen, a plantation owner and slave trader living near the North Carolina-Virginia border, developed a price table in the early 1850s that tied valuation directly to the age of male slaves. For instance, his price scale placed a value of three hundred dollars on an eight-year-old slave and exactly thrice that amount on a prime twenty-year-old field hand. Another trader, the Virginian Richard Reid, used a price table that distinguished both age and sex. Late in the life course, when slaves were fifty years or older, Reid's scale heavily discounted the labor of bondswomen, placing their value at half that of their male counterparts. On the other hand, young slave girls were valued closely to boys of the same age (e.g., two hundred dollars for a girl between eight and eleven years and two hundred fifty for a comparable boy).[43] Among children, these criteria were often supplemented by physiological characteristics, such as weight and height.

The archival records provide strong support for the intuition that planters exhibited "an almost universal enthusiasm for vigorous natural increase (and hence capital growth)" and that slaves were priced accordingly. A planter-physician in Georgia wrote in 1857 that slave owners must pay particular attention to the "procreative relationship" of female slaves, "for the raising [of] a family of young negroes on a plantation is an important item of interest in our capital." The care and value placed on childbearing women was a peculiar concern in slave management. In an essay titled "The Policy of the Southern Planter," another slave owner emphasized that "to the breeding women, we give extra clothing, besides favoring them as much as possible in other respects." Among traders and planters, demand for such "breeding women" (i.e., young women who were thought to be fertile) was especially high in the slave labor market.[44]

Attention to skilled trades, on the other hand, was limited in the correspondence of antebellum planters and slave traders. Commenting on a prize-winning essay on slave management, Benjamin Griffin noted that the author "omitted any discussion of the management best adapted to develop manufacturing or mechanical skill in the slave, as there is a general and very proper disposition among slave holders to leave the trades and arts to the white population." Tyre Glen's price table does not refer to skills at all. Richard Reid's papers do identify black mechanics as worthy of especially high valuations, but restrict attention to the occupational skills of this group. The education of slaves was generally thought to be a matter of religious—rather than vocational—instruction. Even then, religious education typically proceeded on the basis of oral transmission, thereby avoiding the thorny topic of slave literacy.[45]

During the Civil War, a profound shift in the criteria used to value black labor was already evident in Union-occupied territory. The District of Columbia, which abolished slavery in April 1862, represented one of the earliest instances of federally mandated emancipation in the Upper South.[46] Many of the able-bodied freedmen were soon employed as military laborers or in government facilities. In an extensive discourse on wages and the possibility of taxation, Lieutenant Colonel Elias Greene, the chief quartermaster for the Department of Washington, revealed a logic of compensation that was quite distinct from that of the antebellum period. Greene wrote that "a vast majority of the colored men engaged in the public service [in D.C.] are employed as teamsters, and laborers, and receive the same pay, as white men similarly employed." Whether or not Greene "made any distinction [between black and white workers] on his rolls," the striking feature of his letter is that he inferred wages based exclusively on occupational skills, rather than the age or physical traits of black laborers. Thus, he asserted that farm laborers tended to receive ten to fifteen dollars per month, waiters were compensated at sixteen dollars per month, barbers, stevedores, and quarrymen averaged from twenty to thirty dollars per month, and a small class of federally employed artisans (e.g., blacksmiths, wheelwrights) received between thirty-five and sixty dollars per month. The survey of occupationally defined wages is complemented in Greene's letter with an emphasis on human capital accumulation. Discussing the development of Freedman's Village, an enclave of emancipated slaves located on Robert E. Lee's former plantation in Arlington, Greene highlights the construction of workshops "where the women and children [may] . . . be taught such occupations, as will fit them for a career of independence, and usefulness, when thrown upon their own resources." During the winter, men could also be taught the "mechanical occupations," comprising the highly skilled artisanal trades of the day. Greene concludes that he would like "to see the same course [of action] pursued throughout the country."[47]

This last point raises the question as to whether the logic of human capital accumulation was limited to a small number of wartime experiments in free wage labor, such as that showcased by the Freedman's Village, or if it spread more widely in the postbellum South.[48] Even more so than the early experiments, the Freedmen's Bureau maintained a strong emphasis on human capital as an investment. Gilbert Eberhart, the Georgia bureau's first superintendent of education, insisted that education for emancipated blacks should *not* be free of charge, calling instead for black communities to provide resources to support their schools and, thereby, asking them to incur an opportunity cost. To a surprising extent, this logic was accepted by former bondsmen. In September 1865, a subcommissioner in Mississippi reported a discussion with an older black worker who "wished to educate his children, thought himself able to pay one dollar per month for school ... and was anxious to have school started." Among bureau agents, such investments were thought to be essential to ensure that emancipated blacks could be self-supporting. These precepts also reflected the importance of what the Reverend Edward Kirk, president of the American Missionary Association, referred to as a "duty" of the free labor ideology, and freedpeople themselves, to produce a group of educated laborers among emancipated African Americans.[49]

Wage guidelines proposed by bureau agents consistently signaled a differentiation of labor value among freedmen by skills and capabilities. Labor regulations issued in the Gulf States in July 1865 dictated a specific premium for skilled trades, stating that "mechanics, engineers and foremen will always receive not less than $5 per month in addition to the first class rates." A circular issued in Georgia around the same time proposed an extensive classification of wage workers by agricultural and domestic skills, with monthly compensation specified for each class. Subsequently, commissioners like Georgia's Davis Tillson vacillated between wage guidelines based on worker skills and a reliance on wage setting in the open market.[50] The adoption of federally regulated wages was ultimately opposed at the top by General Oliver Otis Howard, the bureau's head, who, by July 1865, had decided to leave the returns on occupational skills to the market itself.[51]

The emphasis of the Freedmen's Bureau on ideals such as individualism, achievement, and equality weakened the older practice of ranking black labor largely according to demographic characteristics. As emphasized in his letter to Yeatman, General Howard worried about any effort to set wages for the "infinite gradation from the able-bodied man to the little child." Although the black Southern workforce would continue to encompass women and children, as well as adult men, the criteria used to attribute value to different subgroups had shifted in subtle ways. Officially, the Freedmen's Bureau encouraged employment outside the home for both men and women, as part of its broader war on dependency. In practice, however, assumptions regarding domesticity and masculinity pervaded the judgments of its agents. Freedwomen were far more likely than freedmen to receive rations and other relief from the bureau and able-bodied women with young children were far less likely to receive work. The bureau's leadership also denounced "an apprentice system for children without consent of parent." Child labor did not disappear with emancipation, but its role and value in the postbellum labor market were greatly muted compared to the antebellum market for young slaves.[52]

Quantitative Evidence on the Valuation of Labor

A quantitative comparison of contracts in the antebellum and postbellum eras supports the intuition that there was an abrupt shift in the importance of human capital to the value of labor with the rise of regulated wage arrangements. While the occupations of bondsmen and women explain 0.7 percent (or less) of the variance in labor pricing for slave purchases, appraisals, and hiring, they account for over 5 percent of the variance in wages for the free labor contracts signed under the auspices of the Freedmen's Bureau in the D.C. and Alexandria branches (see Figure 2.2, black bars).[53] Notably, this is not driven by the lack of a complex occupational division of labor under chattel slavery. As economic historians and sociologists have empha-

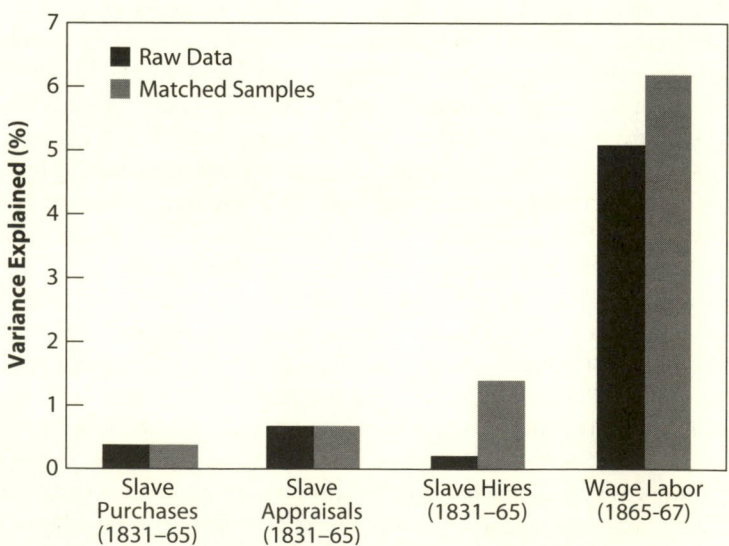

Figure 2.2. Variance (Percentage) in Price of Black Labor Explained by Occupations

sized, midsized and large plantations displayed extensive occupational differentiation in the antebellum period, with status distinctions ranging from overseers and skilled artisans to domestic servants, semiskilled workers, and common laborers (both agricultural and nonagricultural).[54] The probate records collected by Fogel and Engerman reveal seventy distinct occupational labels between 1831 and 1865. Nevertheless, this occupational division of labor does not translate systematically into differential rents on investments in human capital.[55]

The historical comparison of raw price data on black labor should be considered with some caution, owing to selection biases that may affect transactions for either free or slave labor. It is quite plausible that slaves who were hired out during the antebellum era were systematically different than those forced to labor on owners' plantations or households. Similarly, there is no reason to believe that the wage workers sought by employers after the Civil War were a random subset of former slaves. Indeed, descriptive statistics on the four samples suggest variation in demographics and skills across labor markets (see Table 2.2). The proportion of female workers declines from slave labor, to slave hires, to wage labor, and the age distribution of workers becomes less dispersed. The statistics suggest that employers paid more attention to occupational skills, even if only for symbolic purposes,

Table 2.2. Means for Worker and Transaction Characteristics across Labor Markets

	Slave Purchases (1831–65)	Slave Appraisals (1831–65)	Slave Hires (1831–65)	Wage Labor (1865–67)
Workers				
Age (1–10 years)[a]	0.08	0.22	0.09	0.02
Age (11–20 years)	0.35	0.25	0.43	0.31
Age (21–30 years)	0.25	0.22	0.21	0.54
Age (31–40 years)	0.14	0.14	0.10	0.10
Age (41+ years)	0.18	0.17	0.18	0.03
Female	0.39	0.42	0.36	0.18
Skilled labor[b]	0.02	0.03	<0.01	0.22
Physical or mental disability	0.03	0.02	<0.01	—
Transactions				
Price/wage rate ($)[c]	638.21	559.97	54.99	117.55
Period of hire (months)	—	—	11.40	10.38
Number of cases	6,709	51,232	17,158	1,378

[a] Proportions are listed only for those workers with precise ages in the archival records.

[b] All workers with occupational skills that do not involve field work or common labor are defined as skilled in this table.

[c] Nominal prices (in dollars) are listed for slave purchases and appraisals; nominal rates (in dollars per year) are listed for slave hires and wage labor.

under the postbellum regime of free wage labor than in any of the antebellum markets for slave labor.

The sample differences are problematic insofar as the theory of valuation sketched earlier maintains that institutional contexts yield distinct price mechanisms *even when the workers themselves are identical*. Ideally, we would analyze matched samples of workers, involving the same individuals across all four labor markets. Such logical matching is possible for 701 transactions in the probate records, where slaves were subjected to both appraisal by a third party and sale to a slave owner. To complete the construction of matched samples, I used a statistical technique, propensity score matching, to create samples of slave hires and wage laborers that are matched to this subset of probate records.[56]

For the most part, the amount of variance explained by occupations remains similar when samples of workers are matched across labor markets by gender, age, and occupational skills (Figure 2.2, gray bars). A notable exception is the antebellum market for slaves who were hired out. The variation in pricing explained in the matched sample (1.4 percent) is greater than that observed in the raw data (0.2 percent), suggesting that selection biases may reduce the estimated effect of occupational skills in this market. The larger effect of human capital on prices dovetails with historians' claims that the practice of hiring out "contributed to the upgrading of slave labor" and represented an "incipient stage of wages," with returns to skill possibly explained by the practice of allowing hired workers to select their own jobs, the negotiation that ensued between bondsmen and prospective employers, and the greater diversity of industrial and domestic trades that were staffed by hired slaves rather than those who worked directly for their owners.[57]

Further analysis suggests that the timing of skill acquisition over a slave's life course deviates from the pattern anticipated by the logic of human capital investment. In the purchase and appraisal markets between 1831 and 1865, the distribution of slaves in skilled occupations (e.g., artisans, overseers, domestics, and animal handlers) peaked among workers between their mid-thirties and mid-fifties (Figure 2.3). By modern standards, acquisition of skills was delayed, particularly when one considers that the life expectancy of Southern slaves was only thirty-six in 1850. When the same distribution is plotted for Southern blacks based on 1870 census data, a rather different pattern emerges.[58] Apprenticeship tended to occur by age twenty, and thereafter the proportion of free black workers involved in the skilled trades (around 15 percent) was fairly stable until age fifty. The pattern for free labor is thus consistent with the tenets of human capital investment, where skills are acquired early and opportunity costs are amortized over a lifetime.

The effect of demographic characteristics on the price of black labor can be seen most clearly in plots by age category and gender (Figure 2.4).[59] For men, both purchases and appraisals in the antebellum slave market reveal a

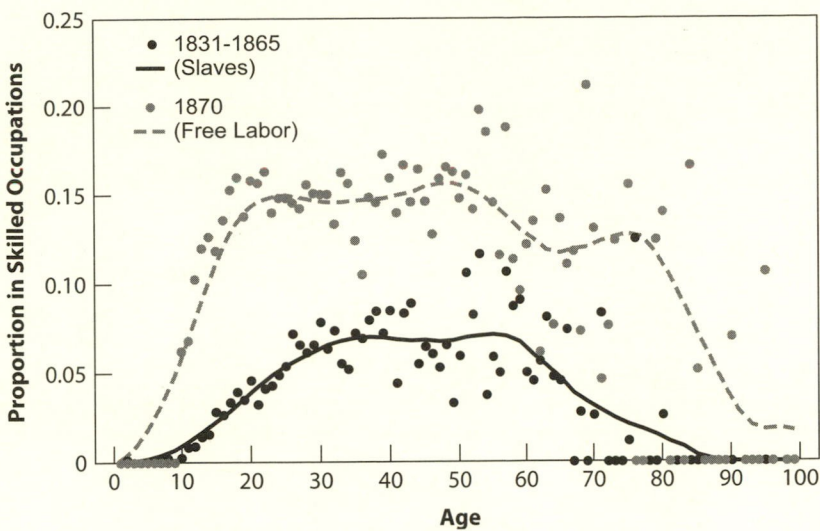

Figure 2.3. Age Distribution of Skilled Black Labor
Notes: Skilled occupations include all work activities aside from unskilled agricultural and general labor. Dots indicate raw averages for blacks of a given age; lines indicate estimates obtained via local polynomial smoothing.

curvilinear trend, with prices rising slightly until these workers reached their twenties and then falling off. In Figure 2.4a, we see a notable deviation between these two markets for black boys under the age of eleven, who were appraised at roughly the same price as slaves in the oldest age category (over forty years), but whose purchase prices reveal a 125 percent price premium over that same category. By contrast, we see discounting for young males in the markets for slave hires and wage labor. In the antebellum South, boys hired on a short-term basis were paid half the rate paid for mature slave hires, and the youngest freedmen in the postbellum period received very low wages (roughly 30 percent) compared to workers over forty.

For black males older than ten, the plot suggests a more muted impact of age on the price of labor in markets with short-term employment contracts as opposed to markets involving chattel slavery. The price for hired or wage labor varies little between adolescence (with monthly rates at slightly under 70 percent of the reference category) and mature adulthood, consistent with the hypothesis that these markets will exhibit weak statistical discrimination by age. We see the same pattern for black women, whose wage and hire rates were relatively flat from adolescence until middle age (Figure 2.4b).

The age-price profile for female slaves was especially peaked in adolescence. While male slaves in their teens and twenties were priced at 80 to 140

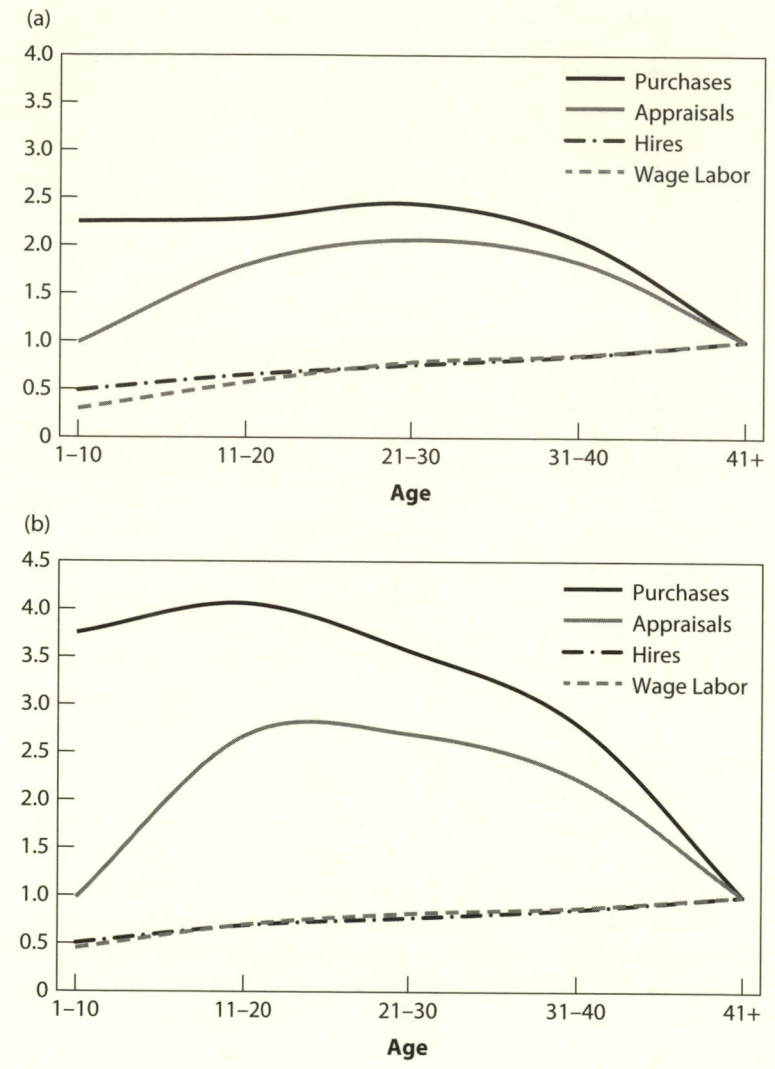

Figure 2.4. Relative Price of Black Labor by Age Category: (a) Male Slaves and Free Laborers, (b) Female Slaves and Free Laborers
Note: Prices are relative to reference category (= 1.0) for slaves or free laborers who are older than forty years.

percent more than mature males, female slaves in their teens and twenties were priced at 170 to 300 percent more than mature females. Although some scholars have questioned the assertion that considerations of slave breeding affected the market for (and demography) of slaves, the estimates shown here reveal a price premium for women who were entering their prime childbearing years. The plots also show a gap between the purchase and appraised prices of female slaves that attenuates over the lifecycle, supporting the argument that exploitation (sexual or otherwise) of girls and young women may have led to price premiums in markets with limited third-party monitoring.

De Jure and De Facto "Free" Labor

On the basis of prices revealed in probate records, price tables, and contracts, the market for free labor that emerged after the Civil War appeared to offer vastly different criteria for the valuation of African American labor than the antebellum market for slave labor in the American South. However, the Freedmen's Bureau contracts reflect the idealized conditions of postbellum labor—that is, the legally regulated (de jure) conditions negotiated under the watchful eye of bureau agents—rather than the de facto conditions that represented the day-to-day experiences of emancipated slaves. Additional historical testimony and complaints to the bureau offer indications that the deviation between the institutionally mandated terms of free labor and the de facto terms was often considerable.

Even in the Upper South, a region that had witnessed an earlier and more pervasive impact of free labor ideology, there were challenges to the doctrine that labor contracts were formed freely between autonomous individuals and that prices were dictated exclusively by the laws of the market. In Elon, Virginia, a group of landowners met on May 31, 1865, to negotiate their own terms of hiring and compensation. They resolved that emancipated slaves would not be hired (and would not be allowed to travel), "without a written pass or recommendation from [their] former master or employer," and that the maximum wage rate would not exceed five dollars per month ("in currency *and* food"). This effort at price fixing attracted the ire of an assistant commissioner for the Freedmen's Bureau, who was alarmed by the possibility of an "iniquitous combination" of employers, especially one that anticipated that their "prices will rule throughout the State [of Virginia], and very likely throughout the South." While the ambitions of these planters were dashed, it is unclear how many other combinations of employers escaped the scrutiny of the Freedmen's Bureau.[60]

In other cases, freedmen were promised fair wages, but were not paid (or were paid inadequately) when their work had been completed. At the end of 1865, the first calendar year in which the Freedmen's Bureau had supervised the new labor market, the superintendent at Amelia Court House in Virginia reported disappointing results. "The Freedmen have been decieved [*sic*] by the employer in nine cases out of ten," he wrote, "that is they did not get what they were led to believe they would get, or [the employer] gave them trouble about getting what had been promised."[61] Deferred compensation was the norm, even under the contractual templates offered by the Freedmen's Bureau. In Washington, D.C., the standard article of agreement first used in October 1865 asked workers to "agree that their employer shall retain one-fourth their month wages until the expiration of their term of service." In a wink to the problem of nonpayment, the standard contract also acknowledged the possibility of "stoppages and arearages" that would need to be "promptly paid at the expiration of . . . service."[62] Outside of territories that had been subject to extensive Union occupation during the war, the majority of contracts did not specify compensation in terms of wages at all. Instead, freedmen and freedwomen were to be reimbursed in terms of crop shares, whose value depended on the quantity and quality of crop sold. In a sample of 345 oral interviews conducted with former slaves across the South, over half (56 percent) reported that they had worked on shares after the war, while slightly over a third (35 percent) reported that they had worked for wages. Slightly under 4 percent reported no compensation at all, suggesting terms that were no different than those of slavery.[63]

Compensation aside, the Freedman's Bureau often took an ambiguous stance on other conditions of free labor. Part of the bureau's mandate was to provide medical care and health care facilities to freedpeople, many of whom had long suffered in war-ravaged zones or refugee camps. But in approving labor contracts, federal agents frequently allowed employers to deny medical assistance to their wage workers in cases of sickness or injury, even though this provision was a standard feature of the model contract favored by General Howard. For instance, examining the contracts signed in the Alexandria, Virginia, branch office between 1865 and 1867, we find that nearly half (43 percent) redacted the benefit of medical assistance.[64] The bureau's position on corporal punishment was also often unclear. Some agents argued that whippings or other forms of physical violence would not be tolerated and entertained affidavits from freedpeople claiming abuse from their employers. But, aside from a few arrests, little effort was made to quell corporal punishment on the part of white employers.[65]

For the Lower South, the question arises whether the de jure and de facto conditions of "free" labor were more pernicious than those in the Upper South. For purposes of comparison, I collected a small sample of 222 Freedmen's Bureau contracts for black wage workers employed in Louisiana, Arkansas, and Mississippi between 1865 and 1868.[66] Employers in these states displayed a conservative attitude toward the rights of wage laborers. Thirteen parishes in Louisiana were exempted from the Emancipation Proclamation of 1863, as federal authorities sought to gain the support of sugar plantation owners by maintaining an emphasis on centralized plantation routine. Following the war, the bureau's assistant commissioner in Arkansas lamented that "wherever the power of our government is not felt through the military arm, the negroes are still held and treated as slaves."[67] In Mississippi, the chaplain of a black regiment reported a widespread view among planters that former slaves who remained on plantations would need to work "as they always had done," a phrase that "was designed to cover both the matters of discipline and compensation."[68] From the perspective of employers, the conditions of wage laborers in these states would thus exhibit little change from those of antebellum slaves.

The wage plantation of Dr. F. G. McGavock, an Arkansas planter, exemplified some of the difficulties faced by the bureau in implementing free labor arrangements in the Deep South. In August 1865, McGavock signed a contract with twenty-six freedmen and women, ranging in age from twelve to thirty-five. The contract stipulated that McGavock pay two-thirds of the workers' wages each month and the (accumulated) remainder at the end of the contract. McGavock would also provide board (at a cost of fifty cents per day), agricultural implements, and a small lot attached to each cabin, which the ex-slaves could use as their personal garden or chicken yard. In return, the freedmen and freedwomen agreed to work from sunup to sunrise when healthy and remain on the McGavock plantation until the end of 1866.[69]

Although the wage contract was witnessed by two officials of the Freedmen's Bureau and authenticated by a third, it became subject to repeated disputes. When the contract was signed, the black workers on the plantation were under the impression that they were engaged for a trial period until Christmas 1865. A number also complained to the bureau (via literate relatives) about routine contractual violations, as workers were denied their full share of rations, received no clothing, or were not paid their wages. Worse, regular reports of violent threats, recourse to whippings, and other forms of inhumane treatment originated from the McGavock plantation. For any freeman or women who left the plantation, McGavock threatened that "he would follow them and bring them back and would put balls and chains on them and feed them on half rations." In February 1866, Captain John Staley, the bureau's superintendent in Memphis, filed a formal complaint about the McGavock plantation with his superiors.[70]

Unfortunately, the state of affairs on the McGavock estate was hardly unique. In his postwar tour of northern Mississippi, James Hawley, the chaplain of a black regiment, found that the planters exhibited three primary concerns, "1. How to control the negro. 2. How to work him hard enough. [and] 3. How to pay him with the least possible expense." While many Southerners were prepared to repudiate coercion when questioned by a union officer, some continued to insist on their right to "knock down" or "shoot a nigger." Hawley thought that many more believed as much, but were too prudent to say so in public. He hoped that the Southern planters would soon learn that "violence is bad economy," that the "stimulus of wages" and federal oversight was enough to restrain idleness, and that the question of compensation was settled with respect to necessity, while remaining open with respect to amount. Though he believed that regulated wage labor would ultimately triumph in the South, Hawley was shocked by the propensity of so many planters to drive emancipated slaves off the plantations merely to spite the free labor ideals of the Yankees. This new habit, he argued, was "a striking commentary on the old pretences of a strong and intense affection between the planter ... and his negroes," challenging "common notions of Southern chivalry and other mythological features of slavocratic history."[71]

While these reports paint a sobering picture of the implementation of "free" labor on the ground, there is little evidence to suggest *formal* contractual differences in the valuation of emancipated slaves in the Upper and Lower South. On paper, wages for freedmen in Louisiana, Arkansas, and Mississippi were actually somewhat higher than those revealed in the contracts from Alexandria, Virginia, or Washington, D.C., perhaps owing to greater demand for labor in the heart of the cotton and sugar belt. Between 1865 and 1867, an average male worker in the sample of contracts for the Upper South signed on for $10.82 per month, while the average male worker in the sample of contracts for the Lower South signed on for $12.47 per month. For women, the respective wages averaged $5.01 and $9.81 per month. Compared to the valuation of slaves, estimates for labor pricing in both regions suggest limited statistical discrimination by age, gender, and the interaction of these demographic variables, particularly for adolescent and adult workers.

The variance in contractual wages explained by human capital, by contrast, was substantial for the Lower South. In the payrolls of wage plantations, workers were ranked by occupational class and ability, ranging from first class foremen to third (and sometimes fourth) class unskilled laborers. This ranking alone explains 45 percent of the variance in wages for the sample of contracts in Louisiana, Arkansas, and Mississippi. The importance of such classification to remuneration may date to the early labor regulations issued by the Department of the Gulf, which dictated a separate wage schedule for male and female hands, based on classes to be "determined by merit and on agreement between the employers and the laborers."[72] It is quite possible, of course, that various ascriptive (i.e., non-merit-based) distinctions came to be linked to these classes in practice, as opposed to assessment of human capital envisioned by the Freedmen's Bureau.

These observations suggest a profound decoupling between the formal (de jure) conditions of wage labor, which conceptualized emancipated slaves as autonomous and uncoerced workers who freely negotiated wages commensurate with their skills and abilities, and the lived (de facto) experience of so-called free labor. During the years after the Civil War, freedpeople were confronted regularly with the possibility that employers would dutifully sign contracts with black workers, only to renege on promised compensation or to resort to practices of physical punishment and intimidation.[73] Nowhere was the disappointment in Freedmen's Bureau more apparent than among those Southern blacks who had been free prior to the war and eagerly anticipated the extension and spread of those privileges. In the Creole community of New Orleans, General Oliver Otis Howard received a polite but questioning audience in November 1865. Members of the Afro-Creole press had trumpeted the possibility of radical political and economic reform, often on the basis of a Caribbean model of slave emancipation. While initially enthusiastic about the Freedman's Bureau, this community had come to view the agency (and Howard) in a more dubious light. By the middle of 1866, when a peaceful procession of blacks was attacked by white reactionaries in New Orleans, attitudes against Howard's agency and its free labor ideology had hardened: one Afro-Creole newspaper simply insisted, "let the Freedmen's Bureau go down."[74]

SUMMARY

What was the fundamental innovation of the free labor market that rapidly—though, in some cases, only nominally—replaced the plantation system of slave labor in the years following the American Civil War? The greatest ambitions of the Freedmen's Bureau held that the rise of free labor would produce a shift in moral order, in which the barbaric and inefficient habit of Southern slaveholding would yield to more enlightened tendencies. Indeed, the civilizing power of the market was touted not only by General Howard (the "Christian general") and his agents, but also by Northern abolitionists, such as the Reverend Edward Kirk, and some African American observers, such as Chaplain James Hawley.[75] In the period immediately after emancipation, many emancipated slaves believed that Southern landowners would change their mind-set and were prepared to negotiate with them in good faith. Whether such hopes were advanced out of idealism or necessity, they were bound to be met with disappointment. Few former slaveholders bought into the moral impetus behind the free labor ideology; instead, the prevalent view among Southern employers was that former slaves would need to work "as they had always done."

A more modest claim for the rise of a free labor market was that it would create a subtle shift in the motivation of employers and workers, primarily owing to the absence of coercion. In his *Wealth of Nations*, Adam Smith argued that the essential problem of unfree labor resided in the misaligned interests of employer and worker. "The experience of all ages and nations," Smith believed, "demonstrates that the work done by slaves, though it appears to cost only their maintenance, is in the end the dearest of any. . . . Whatever work [the slave] does beyond what is sufficient to purchase his own maintenance can be squeezed out of him by violence only." The interests of slave owners were compromised, in this theory, by a love of domination, which led them to "prefer the service of slaves to that of freemen."[76] Even if some of the civilizing tendencies of the market were absent, the removal of coercive means would thus improve the productivity of workers and focus the motivations of employers on pecuniary considerations.

The argument presented in this chapter suggests that, rather than shifts in morality or coercion, other institutional conditions were more salient to the valuation of emancipated blacks. Historically, both free wage labor and other markets tended to involve some element of coercion in which the ultimate source of power for workers was the ability to withdraw labor power, whether by reduction of effort, flight, or legal termination of contracts. The Freedmen's Bureau itself, for instance, acted as much to discipline black laborers as it did to limit recourse to physical punishment among Southern planters.[77] While coercion was certainly diminished under the purview of the bureau, other institutional conditions governing the postbellum labor market—specifically, the duration of ownership over labor power and the oversight of a third (regulatory) party—had a more pervasive influence on the way that labor was priced.

For African Americans, these institutional conditions yielded a new logic of compensation during Reconstruction. In the antebellum era, occupational skills explained relatively little of the variance in the price of Southern slaves, though they accounted for some variation in the wages of equivalent slave hires. Investment in occupational skills occurred relatively late in the life course, and some Southern observers even suggested that masters "leave the trades and arts [entirely] to the white population."[78] Price discrimination by age and gender, on the other hand, was more pronounced in the market for slaves. Under the Freedmen's Bureau, apprenticeship in the skilled crafts tended to occur by the time black workers reached their early twenties and differences in contractual wages were more clearly correlated with those skills. The latter process is consistent with the logic of human capital, in which opportunity costs are borne early in the life course and are justified by subsequent differentials in earnings, while the former is consistent with the logic of statistical discrimination.

The shift in the logic of valuation produced considerable uncertainty in the period immediately following the Civil War, as employers, federal authorities, and freedpeople struggled to understand or influence the allocation of wages. Adding to the uncertainty, the Freedmen's Bureau itself was an unprecedented organization in American institutional life. Never before had a governmental agency in the United States attempted to reform labor and offer economic relief on such a massive scale. The labor policies it would adopt with respect to former bondsmen and women were opaque to outsiders (and, sometimes, insiders too). Once implemented, these policies were decoupled from the realities of the postbellum labor market, in which compensation was often unpaid, delayed, or available only in nonwage form. These initial uncertainties would set the stage for broader questions regarding the status attainment of blacks following their emancipation from the "peculiar institution" of Southern slavery.[79]

CHAPTER 3

Status Attainment among Emancipated Slaves

> The span of time between emancipation and the recovery of the South during the nineties was essentially an interval of upheaval and adaptation to changed circumstances for the Negro laborer. The first five years from 1860 to 1865 witnessed an economic and social revolution from which the Negro emerged as a "free" man. From 1865 to 1880, however, he was largely engaged in finding his place in the American economic system under this changed status.
> —Lorenzo Greene and Carter Woodson, *The Negro Wage Earner*

Writing his final memoir in 1880, the novelist, historian, abolitionist, and former slave William Wells Brown (1814–84) reminisced about a visit to the Norfolk market after the Civil War. Alongside the black men and women managing their market stalls, Brown found the costermongers, or street vendors, hawking green corn, butter beans, squash, snap beans, potatoes, and strawberries. These were the men and women of music, he wrote, since their sales pitch was often delivered in song: "Come sinner get down on your knees, I am g[oing] to glory. Eat [these] strawberries when you please, I am g[oing] to glory." Crowds were attracted as much by the costermongers' narrative and voice as the produce that they had to offer. Brown suggested that this street scene would leave a stranger deeply impressed with the pleasant disposition, urbane manners, and prosperous enterprise of the freed colored people of Virginia.

At the same time, William Brown reckoned that the market scene might give an onlooker pause about some of the opportunities of the black populace in freedom. "The negro is the same everywhere—a hewer of wood, a peddler of vegetables, a wearer of the waiter's white apron," the hypothetical stranger remarks, "freedom has not altered his status." Brown counters this argument Socratically. "Nations are not educated in twenty years," he writes, "... it is only the present generation of negroes who have been able to appropriate any share of the nobler blessings of freedom." For this next generation, Brown does not anticipate a "life among the lowly" colored men and women of the Norfolk market and, instead, hopes for a "very satisfactory future" for the children of freedom, if not for their parents.[1]

How did the uncertainty of Reconstruction affect the occupational opportunities of Southern blacks? The deinstitutionalization of slavery has been studied by a number of intellectuals since the late nineteenth century. In his capacious *Black Reconstruction*, W. E. B. Du Bois conducted a Marxist inquiry into the political potential for greater race and class equality in Southern Reconstruction. Between the two world wars, several large-scale quantitative analyses were deployed under the impetus of the Association for the Study of Negro Life and History, including work by such prominent black scholars as Carter Woodson, Charles Wesley, and Lorenzo Greene.[2] Despite this early flurry of scholarship, however, more recent efforts in social history have often focused on the institution of slavery itself rather than its legacy, while examinations of slavery's consequences have emphasized aggregate, macro-level effects.[3] Lacking longitudinal analysis at the micro level, the degree of continuity or discontinuity in American slavery remains poorly understood for individual blacks emancipated from this institution.

Among sociologists, neglect of the topic is especially surprising, since instances of profound institutional change, such as emancipation, offer an unusual opportunity for students of stratification to interrogate the transformation of structured inequality across institutional regimes. Following such change, the typically strong persistence of status—both intergenerational and intragenerational—may give way to rapid upward or downward mobility. At the same time, formal deinstitutionalization may be accompanied by remarkable stability in underlying conditions channeling mobility processes. According to proponents of path dependence, this institutional stability was reflected in the postbellum South by the employment of ex-slaves on the plantations of former masters, in oppressive sharecropping arrangements, and in other forms of agricultural peonage.

Aside from questions of social mobility, institutional scholars find legacies of formally dismantled institutions to be of interest in their own right. Such legacies hinge on the reproduction of material and cultural conditions from outdated institutions, owing not only to the persistence of socioeconomic status across institutional arrangements, but also to the resulting ambiguity of identity change for persons embedded within them.[4] Particularly for individuals—such as ex-slaves—located in the lowest ranks of socioeconomic status, the subjective sense that new institutional arrangements were merely old wine in new bottles was likely to inhibit productive collective action and reinforce a pernicious cycle of status persistence. Oppositional tactics employed by Southern whites during Reconstruction and its aftermath— including white terrorism, the passage of Black Codes, and the construction of racial segregation—served as institutional supports to this cycle.

In this chapter, I examine the extent to which slavery continued to influence the social status of Southern blacks after emancipation. My specific emphasis is intragenerational, considering samples of blacks who were born before the end of the Civil War, their status within the plantation system of chattel slavery, and subsequent effects of that system on individual socioeconomic attainment. To trace these outcomes, I employ both historical census data and life histories from the Federal Writers' Project, based on interviews conducted with ex-slaves and free blacks during the late 1920s and 1930s. Using quantitative analyses of occupational trajectories, I derive specific implications for the legacy of American slavery and more general inferences with respect to theories of status persistence under conditions of uncertainty. These data place my focus at the intersection, as C. Wright Mills termed it, of history and biography.[5]

Institutional Legacies and Durable Inequality

An institutional legacy refers to the reproduction of material and cultural conditions from a social institution despite the fact that the institution has been formally dismantled (e.g., the ongoing effects of American slavery following the passage of the Thirteenth Amendment). A simple version of such reproduction occurs at the intragenerational level when individuals continue to bear the burden of outdated institutions because socioeconomic status within present institutional arrangements is positively correlated with status under former institutions. The resulting status inequalities are especially durable if they do not necessarily rely on the subjective beliefs of the individuals involved, but are embodied in the organizational forms that channel their mobility processes.[6]

A concrete example of such institutional reproduction can be found in the crop lien and sharecropping systems that emerged during Southern Reconstruction. Prior to emancipation, the majority of the South's four million slaves were employed as unskilled agricultural workers on cotton, tobacco, sugar, and rice plantations. Estimates from probate and plantation records place the percentage of slaves employed in this lowest tier of plantation labor at nearly 70 percent.[7] After emancipation, many of these ex-slaves drifted back to farm work by virtue of necessity. While the Freedmen's Bureau initially adopted agricultural wage work as its prototypical model of compensation, this model was quickly challenged by alternative forms of agricultural tenancy. Already by late 1866, bureau records reveal that about half of the freedmen in Florida were working on shares, as well as nearly three-quarters of the freedmen near Memphis, Tennessee. Even in the sugar plantations of Louisiana, where Union troops had been a regular presence since the early phases of the Civil War, share wages were increasingly common. Between 1865 and 1867, roughly 28 percent of the contracts signed in St. Martin and St. Mary Parishes involved an "interest in profits," rather than wages. More perniciously, by 1867, most of these share contracts also required emancipated blacks to share in the expenses of producing the sugar crop.[8]

Emancipation meant a tremendous increase in the degree to which freedmen and freedwomen controlled their private lives, but, at least for the majority employed in sharecropping arrangements, there was not always a commensurate increase in economic autonomy. Lacking resources of their own, freedmen relied on credit to acquire tools, seeds, livestock, and the like. These arrangements were generally secured by a lien against the crops of the ex-slaves, where the conditions of the lien allowed landlords and merchants considerable authority in dictating the type of crop grown, its quantity, and the method of agricultural production.[9] The debt load imposed by unscrupulous merchants often forced ex-slaves into material penury that placed them in a tier of socioeconomic status similar to that they had experienced as field hands. Even those who were fortunate or talented enough to escape low-status occupations usually spent a period as unskilled laborers accumulating cultural or economic capital. Meanwhile, the authority exercised by merchants and landlords—and effective serfdom of many ex-slaves—meant that the cultural distinction between chattel slavery and "free" labor was likely to seem ambiguous to some.[10] The frequency of physical coercion was reduced under freedom, but even this crucial improvement in the lives of ex-slaves was far from universal. In these respects, sharecropping and lien arrangements could be seen as reproducing material and cultural conditions from the antebellum plantation system.[11]

The possibility of institutional reproduction is present as long as status inequalities under one institutional arrangement translate into inequalities under another arrangement. This pattern contributes to equilibrium in a system of stratification, despite superficial transformation. Three canonical accounts (including structural-functional, Marxist, and neoinstitutional views) have often been advanced to predict durable inequality—or lack thereof—across institutional regimes (see Figure 3.1a–c).

In the explanation advanced by the historical sociologist Charles Tilly, robust categorical distinctions among actors are essential in sustaining status inequality. Insofar as new organizational forms, such as sharecropping arrangements, match old status categories (e.g., slaves and owners) with their own categories of inequality (tenant farmers and landlords), patterns of inequality are likely to be maintained. Thus, structural-functional accounts by historians often assume that there were constraints on status change after emancipation, suggesting that postbellum "racism in slightly new forms performed the same function for the social system that slavery had once served, and racial oppression was essential to the ends of the

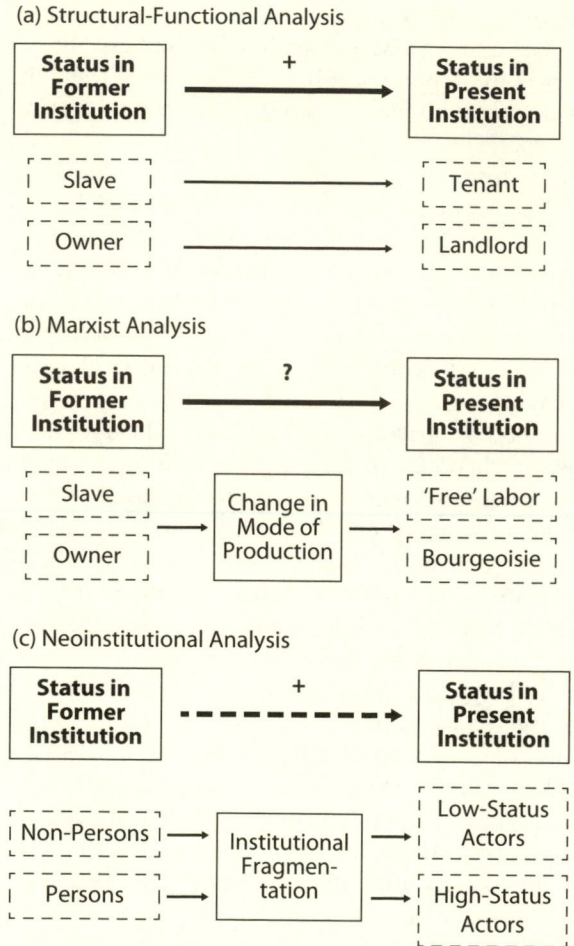

(a) Structural-Functional Analysis

(b) Marxist Analysis

(c) Neoinstitutional Analysis

Figure 3.1. Some Canonical Analyses of Institutional Transformation of Social Status: (a) Structural-Functional Analysis, (b) Marxist Analysis, (c) Neoinstitutional Analysis

system . . . little had changed for the black man, either practically or theoretically." Similarly, sociological arguments reflect on gradations within the slave hierarchy and the tendency of elites to grant privileges in freedom along the same distinctions.[12]

Marxist scholars tend to agree that institutional reproduction rests on robust categorical distinctions, but draw attention to shifts in the means of production that may serve to disrupt these categories across institutional regimes. In this regard, there were fundamental differences in the postbellum situation of the free black laborer, who "owns" himself or herself, and the antebellum slave. Aside from the contractual distinctions noted in Chapter 2, two social dimensions distinguished the self-ownership of free wage laborers from the status of slaves: the capacity for geographic mobility and the potential to invest productive time in pursuits other than work.[13] Geographic mobility allowed some freed slaves to sever ties with former owners and abandon inhospitable areas and conditions in the former slave-holding states, despite the constraints imposed by Black Codes and antivagrancy laws. Substantial interstate mobility, culminating in the Great Migration of the early twentieth century, attested to the popularity of this strategy for many Southern blacks. Another fundamental difference in the two institutional regimes involved the possibility for free blacks to allocate labor time to alternative pursuits, such as education, which could be parlayed into skills or organizational authority that would place them in a different socioeconomic class.[14] Despite the opportunity costs and difficulty of obtaining education, it was widely embraced by former slaves and their children. From a Marxist perspective, the gradational status of blacks within the antebellum regime was not as important to their postbellum occupational attainment as their relationship to the new means of production, mediated via work locale and educational investment (Figure 3.1b).

A third, neoinstitutional perspective on status persistence across institutional regimes questions both structural-functional and Marxist assumptions. Informed by cultural explanations of individualism and agency, neoinstitutionalist concerns with the transition to freedom are driven by the uncertainty inherent in the construction of a new class of "persons" or "actors." In this regard, freed blacks were not simply adjusting to a new legal status or means of production, but were engaged in a more fundamental process of identity reconstruction, navigating tensions between formal equality and functional inequality.[15] The mediating role of identity change implies less stability in status persistence than structural-functionalist accounts might suggest. Thus, scholarship on chattel slavery as a peculiar institution notes that many of its status distinctions did not generalize to the more universalistic standards of free wage capitalism. Some freedmen and freedwomen saw in emancipation the opportunity to point out the hypocrisy of a system of paternalism founded on both Christian ethical codes and harsh physical coercion. The rejection of plantation paternalism and its pattern of personal allegiances among blacks and whites may have weakened the legacy of slavery in the postbellum period.[16]

If processes of identity reconstruction contributed to broader institutional fragmentation, it is also unclear that relationships to the new means of production were as telling as Marxist explanations might propose. To some extent, old and new institutional arrangements existed side by side in the postbellum South, leading to mixed expectations for the free labor force engendered by emancipation. Given such uncertainty, geographic mobility and control over work locale often brought only limited material benefits to blacks—at least within the context of the former slaveholding states. The paradox of symbolic benefit in the absence of material gain could also be seen in the sharecropping system that evolved in the postbellum period. When viewed as a refusal of supervised labor systems that mirrored the overseer system, sharecropping was a victory for ex-slaves. However, share-cropping often transferred wealth systematically from blacks to plant-ers—or, as ex-slave Felix Haywood explained, "freedom could make folks proud, but it didn't make 'em rich."[17] In the neoinstitutional explanation, this material uncertainty is reflected in a loose correspondence between postbellum status attainment and legal status in the antebellum period (see Figure 3.1c).

Factors Affecting Status Disruption

To provide a snapshot of the complexity of slavery's institutional legacy— and potential disruptions to that legacy—I review a number of historical factors impinging on the cycle of status persistence, beginning with the status hierarchy of blacks in the ante- and postbellum South, opportunities for education and migration, and the process of identity reconstruction faced by blacks moving from slavery to freedom. In subsequent sections of the chapter, factors impinging on status disruption are mapped to measures coded from interviews and census records of ex-slaves and free blacks who lived in U.S. states and territories with substantial slaveholdings prior to the end of the Civil War.[18]

Status Hierarchy under Slavery

Status persistence between institutional regimes assumes, first and fore-most, that there was significant status differentiation under former institu-tional arrangements. Early historiographic accounts often assumed, errone-ously, that the occupational structure on Southern plantations was relatively undifferentiated, with most slaves falling into a large class of unskilled field laborers or a smaller class of household servants. Starting with Charles Wes-ley, economic historians began to discover the large number of skilled black artisans and semiskilled slaves supporting the plantation system. More re-cent accounts stress not only that occupational differentiation among slaves on midsized and large plantations was important from a functional stand-point, but also that the Southern planters actively supported such differen-tiation in order to control their slave populations.[19]

At the top of the status hierarchy were the black overseers, or "drivers," chosen for their loyalty to the planters, managerial talents, long plantation tenure, and "imposing physical presence."[20] The drivers enjoyed considerable autonomy in running the day-to-day operations of the plantation, leading to debate among antebellum planters as to whether black or white overseers should be employed in this capacity. Evidence from probate records suggests that the use of black overseers increased until the 1830s, but then declined until the Civil War, possibly due to the Nat Turner uprising (1831) and planter fear of slave insurrection.[21]

Joining the drivers in the elite slave occupations were skilled black artisans—blacksmiths, masons, mechanics, carpenters, and the like—who generally enjoyed better living conditions, vocational education, and autonomy than other slaves. In urban areas, slave artisans were often hired out by their masters, leading to competition with white artisans and occasional antagonism from the general populace. Probate records suggest that around 13 percent of male slaves in plantations were employed in the capacity of skilled craftsmen; the number of female slaves so employed, on the other hand, was negligible.[22]

Between common field laborers and the elite slave occupations of artisans and overseers, there existed a differentiated status hierarchy of domestic servants (e.g., waiters, butlers, cooks, barbers), semiskilled workers (teamsters, coach drivers, gardeners, cloth makers), and unskilled nonagricultural workers (launderers, porters). These strata comprised roughly 13 percent of adult male slaves and 29 percent of adult female slaves on midsized and large plantations. Perhaps more so than the elite slave occupations or ranks of field labor, placement within these middle ranks was subject to ascriptive decisions by masters based on the skin complexions, interpersonal relationships, and personalities of the slaves. Under slavery, status ranks above field hand were perpetuated by marriage patterns. Skilled manual workers, overseers, and to a lesser extent semiskilled workers usually married domestic servants or other high-status slaves.[23] Following emancipation, the institutional peculiarity of some of these ascriptive decisions could render status persistence in the middle range vulnerable to disruption.

From the standpoint of a status attainment model, two other statuses within the slavery regime complicate this hierarchy. One is the substantial number of free blacks in the antebellum South and border states, composing over 5 percent of the black population in 1860.[24] Aside from their autonomy and high prestige vis-à-vis slaves, detailed occupational records from Southern urban centers indicate impressive occupational attainment among free blacks. A census of free blacks from Charleston revealed a number of small proprietors (storekeepers, tavern keepers, milliners) and a large number of skilled artisans; notably, few free blacks went into domestic service compared to urban slaves.[25]

The other complication for a model of status attainment involves slaves who were children at the time of emancipation. Because of the early age at which slaves were put to work—some around age three or four and roughly half by age seven—age itself is not an adequate proxy of childhood under this institution.[26] Rather, a more suitable definition of childhood includes those young slaves who had no occupation assigned to them before emancipation and thus never experienced the working conditions of slavery directly. While accounts of planters themselves suggest that there were benefits to early entry into the slave labor force (in terms of skill formation), the costs of lost childhood and socialization within an antiquated agricultural gang system are hard to ignore. By avoiding this pattern of socialization within the peculiar institution of slavery, some children may have endured its legacy to a lesser extent than their peers who had already spent time working as unskilled agricultural laborers or domestic servants.

Status Attainment after Slavery

After a brief period of celebration, freedmen and freedwomen faced lives characterized by extremely hard work. The Union army encouraged Southern blacks to return to their occupations under slavery as a practical solution to the need for economic relief and to fear among white elites that the Southern economy was unviable without black labor. For agricultural laborers themselves, returning to pre-emancipation jobs was probably not good advice. Many existed in abject poverty, often living meal to meal. Opportunities for blacks to enter higher status occupations were limited in the Reconstruction era, even in the North. Segregationist institutions and cultural norms limited African American status mobility in the late nineteenth and early twentieth centuries. Joel Williamson describes a common reaction among African Americans in postbellum South Carolina, noting that they "searched for perfection within their half of a dyarchical society."[27]

Whites limited African Americans' access to high-status work outside the black community. Southern white elites hired according to informally defined limits of what constituted "black jobs"—typically agricultural labor, semiskilled industrial labor, or domestic service work.[28] For the African Americans who continued to work in agriculture, productivity was severely constrained by the relative lack of tools, especially for sharecroppers who often relied on planter loans. Mobility in the agricultural ladder between wage labor, sharecropping, tenancy, and ownership was frustratingly low in many sections of the postbellum South. Examining retrospective career histories collected from 227 black farmers in Jefferson County (Arkansas), Lee Alston and Joseph Ferrie found that stasis was the norm. Between 1890 and 1938, 94 percent of the respondents who were sharecroppers or tenants in one year would remain in those respective positions the following year.[29]

Strictures constraining black status mobility were not universally successful. The black community included preachers, skilled craft workers, teachers, and a small number of other professionals. Fifty years after emancipation, obstacles to status mobility were somewhat counterbalanced by increased demand for industrial labor during the World War I period. Still, a large portion of jobs blacks gained during the war were lost in peace, and prospects for African Americans occupational mobility did not dramatically improve again until the World War II period.

Education Before and After Emancipation

Planters in the antebellum South recognized the threat that education posed to status persistence among blacks. Following increased abolitionist activity in the 1830s, existing laws against the education of enslaved blacks were strengthened in the slaveholding states. In some areas, it was a criminal offense to teach *any* black, enslaved or free, to read or write. George Albright, a former slave and nineteenth-century politician, explains, "It was only by trickery that I learned to read and write . . . if any slave learned to read and write, he was to be punished with 500 lashes on the naked back, and to have the thumb cut off above the second joint." Official prohibitions against educating blacks and widespread planter hostility toward learning among slaves limited literacy to a very small fraction of the Southern black population at the time of emancipation.[30]

Northern attempts to develop an educational infrastructure in the South began before the Civil War was over. The Union army trained teachers, confiscated rebel homes as schools, and sought to instruct ex-slaves, as General William Sherman put it, in "the rudiments of civilization and Christianity." While some of these efforts may have been driven by moral concern, the Union's military use of ex-slaves as soldiers was severely limited by illiteracy and federal officials saw education as a means of control, as well as enlightenment. Handbooks distributed by the Freedmen's Bureau were designed to help the recently emancipated by instilling strong work ethics and ideologies of disciplined docility in their readers. Attention to these federal initiatives has also sometimes concealed the fact that the earliest, and most effective, efforts to create new schools during the 1860s were launched by African Americans themselves. In Mississippi, for instance, private black schools were founded during the Civil War in Grenada, Meridian, Natchez, Raymond, and Vicksburg, as well as in numerous smaller towns and abandoned plantations.[31]

Following the Civil War, the Freedmen's Bureau undertook a more systematic effort at institutional intervention, which was matched, with varying degrees of effort, by the development of public systems of primary education among Reconstruction governments. Even at its height, this system of public education reached only one-tenth of black children and suffered considerable setbacks with the restoration of Southern elites in the 1870s.

Government efforts were dwarfed in many areas by the grassroots formation of schools by freed African Americans, many of whom worked as builders and teachers without pay.[32] Maria Jackson's story reveals that, for Southern black families, obtaining education was a struggle, wrought with pragmatic compromise: "[My brothers and sisters] learned right well in school. Us other children had to help Daddy in the field." Nevertheless, public education could be counted as one of the successes of Reconstruction; by the 1890s, black literacy nationwide had risen to nearly 40 percent.[33]

Among the first generation of blacks who had been born under slavery, there was considerable variation in educational outcomes. Interviews with former slaves in the 1920s and 1930s suggest that very few (fewer than 1 percent) had a formal education under the antebellum regime. More received schooling during the postbellum period—including primary education (39.3 percent), vocational school training (0.8 percent), and college (4.2 percent). During both periods, some blacks began a formal education but had to stop prematurely due to personal or social circumstances. This was especially true in the antebellum regime, where masters and legislatures vacillated in their opinions of educating slaves and the seasonal demands of plantation labor could limit schooling to certain times of the year. Other Southern blacks received an informal education (outside a school environment) from literate blacks or whites who had no teaching credentials (19.4 percent, combining antebellum and postbellum experiences).[34]

Well-publicized debates raged in the late nineteenth century concerning the most effective forms of education for black status attainment. Booker T. Washington famously advocated a system of practical, industrial education, claiming that "the opportunity to earn a dollar in a factory now is worth infinitely more than the opportunity to spend a dollar in an opera house." Fearing that Washington's approach would lead to abject proletarianization, W. E. B. Du Bois countered with proposals for college education, emphasizing the "talented tenth" among blacks.[35] Even today, these debates are unlikely to be settled with the data at hand. What can be hypothesized, however, is that education—of *any* sort—served to substantially disrupt the legacy of the antebellum regime.

Empirical investigations using census data support the intuition that the transmission of impoverished human capital from slaves to their descendents weakened in the decades after emancipation. In 1880, literacy rates among blacks who had been born in slaveholding states remained markedly lower than literacy among blacks born outside the South. While differences in literacy continue to be observed for the children of this antebellum generation, the gap in educational attainment narrowed considerably for the following generations. By 1920, the difference in the literacy rate between children whose families had moved out of the South, but whose grandparents were born in slavery, and children whose grandparents were not born in slavery was a mere 3 percent, controlling for other variables.[36]

Migration

The geographic mobility of blacks following emancipation served as a second disruption to the reproduction of the antebellum regime. In a path-breaking analysis, Carter Woodson traced three waves of Southern black migration following emancipation: one resulting from the immediate disruption of the plantation economy during the Civil War, a second, westward movement following the restoration of reactionary white governments during the late 1870s, and a third movement, the Great Migration to the North, peaking during World War I when wartime industries were understaffed and foreign immigration was reduced to a trickle.[37] Many Southern elites actively tried to stop migration using persuasion, accommodation, and legalized detention. At least as late as 1916, cases exist wherein black agricultural workers were forcefully prevented from seeking better prospects through migration.[38]

Du Bois recognized benefits to migration, in terms of developing a pan-African American identity. The aims of migrants themselves—and migrant aid societies in the North and West that assisted them—were far more concrete. John Mathews described to interviewers why he relocated repeatedly across the Cotton Belt: "When [the] end of the year come there was nothing to pay the [farm] hands. I got work at a saw mill and made enough for us to live on. When the bulldozers tell me to move, I move."[39] Still facing profound discrimination in the postbellum South, other blacks saw migration as a form of collective action, the only way to "elevate [themselves] to a higher plane of true citizenship." Meanwhile, some black leaders, such as Frederick Douglass, considered migration an abdication of rights and a failure to leverage the sheer number of blacks in the South to economic and political advantage.[40]

Patterns of migration reflected the embeddedness of freedpeople in communities that formerly supported slavery, as well as their ongoing economic dependency on former masters in those areas. As emphasized by modern students of collective action, individual advantage and collective disadvantage often existed side by side. At the individual level, interstate migration following emancipation may have severed subservience to local white elites, and blacks migrating outside the bounds of the former confederacy may have encountered reduced discrimination.[41] At the same time, this exit strategy could cripple more fundamental civil rights reform in the South for decades to come.[42]

Some descriptive evidence regarding migration patterns can again be gleaned from census data and the narratives of former slaves and free blacks who lived in the South during the antebellum era. Among blacks who were interviewed by the Works Progress Administration (WPA) during the Great Depression, roughly 11 percent reported interstate migration—whether coerced or voluntary—under the regime of slavery. Following the Civil War, nearly half reported interstate migration, and by the 1930s about 14 percent had left the Southern states that once composed the Confederacy.[43] Census data suggest broad similarities. In 1880, shortly after the end of Radical Reconstruction, about 45 percent of blacks who resided in a slaveholding state in 1860 had moved to a different state, with the majority of migrants (a third of all blacks born in slave states and territories) living outside the boundaries of the former Confederacy. In total, approximately half a million blacks emigrated from the South between 1870 and 1910.[44]

Reconstructing Identities

The attention placed by economic historians on material conditions among emancipated blacks has sometimes slighted the parallel process of cultural reconstruction—how ex-slaves came to terms with their change in identity from slave to freeman or freewoman. As emphasized by theories of path dependence, this dynamic may be intimately tied to underlying status persistence. A slave who had languished as a field laborer in the plantation economy and was driven into peonage after emancipation may have questioned the meaning and value of identity change. In many cases, though, the cycle of reproduction was broken insofar as ex-slaves' valuations of their identities became decoupled from the material conditions of life, instead emphasizing more abstract principles of freedom.[45]

Identity reconstruction among ex-slaves occurred in a climate of stigmatization, as Southern whites questioned the social and economic usefulness of the freemen and freewomen. Freedom was an attribute still considered unnatural for Southern blacks, leading to a discrepancy between what Erving Goffman has referred to as idealized and actual social identity. Strategies for managing this discrepancy took on a number of forms among ex-slaves. Some engaged in wholesale rejection of the planter regime, its status hierarchy, and violence. Lydia Jefferson, a former house slave from Louisiana, felt like she came out of "a black hole into [the] sunlight" after emancipation; the "treatment what some of [the] slaves got dat I's see with my own eyes was awful." Jefferson expressed this view even though her own existence on the plantation had been one of relative privilege, at least compared to field hands. Other ex-slaves expressed the ambiguity inherent in weighing ante- and postbellum identities. Talking to an interviewer, Andy McAdams noted, "Well son, I'se expected lots different from freedom than what we got ... news came one day that we were free and that [same] day they opened the gate and set the dogs after us—just like you would a bunch of wild cattle that you were going to turn loose in a large pasture to graze or rustle for their living." McAdams recognized that his personal suffering might be accompanied with collective benefits for Southern blacks as a whole: "Us old slaves has had a hard time of it but it has been worth all our hardships cause, look at the Negro people today. . . . our people progressed along to where they don't have to suffer the hardships we did trying to learn what our white people wanted us to do."[46]

PATTERNS OF SOCIAL MOBILITY

I tracked changes in the social status of Southern blacks using interviews from the WPA Federal Writers' Project. Following pilot projects conducted at Fisk University, Southern University, and Prairie View College in the late 1920s, the Federal Writers' Project sought to develop a more comprehensive biographical portrait of ex-slaves. Between 1936 and 1940, this led to the collection of life histories from over three thousand former slaves and free blacks in twenty-five states, as well as a large amount of secondary materials, such as bills of sale from the antebellum South and obituaries of ex-slaves.[47]

In many respects, the WPA interviews provide a unique data set for tracking black status mobility in the nineteenth century. Before 1870, U.S. census records did not identify most Southern blacks by name or occupation; slave schedules simply enumerated characteristics such as number and age of slaves owned by particular masters. Other potential sources of data on status mobility—such as conscript records for the Union army—do report former occupations, but are obviously conditioned on particular status outcomes for ex-slaves. Consequently, despite the caveats noted in Appendix A, the WPA archives include the most representative data available on intragenerational black mobility between the antebellum and postbellum regimes. The interviews from the WPA are complemented below by a representative 1 percent sample of records linking the 1880 and 1860 censuses.

Quantitative Evidence on Status Attainment

Extending a class schema developed by sociologists Robert Erikson and John Goldthorpe, I sorted detailed occupational descriptions of freedmen and women into seven status distinctions under the slave regime and nine status distinctions following emancipation (see Table 3.1).[48] Examining the postbellum rankings, two departures from modern status hierarchies can be noted. First, even low-skill nonmanual occupations (class VIII) were

Table 3.1. Occupational Status Attainment of Sampled Blacks, During Slavery and Afterward

Pre-1865			Post-1865[b]		
Status	Unweighted %	Weighted %[a]	Status	Unweighted %	Weighted %
Slave					
I. Unskilled agricultural	22.8	36.6	I. Unskilled agricultural	12.1	12.0
II. Unskilled manual/domestic	10.9	7.4	II. Unskilled manual/domestic	18.5	16.9
III. Semiskilled agricultural	2.3	1.7	III. Semiskilled agricultural	29.5	29.4
IV. Semiskilled manual	2.8	3.6	IV. Semiskilled manual/skilled domestic	21.1	19.0
V. Skilled domestic	22.9	6.7	V. Proprietor farmer	3.1	3.3
VI. Skilled manual (artisan)/driver	1.6	6.6	VI. Skilled manual/supervisor of unskilled or semiskilled workers	7.8	9.4
Free or child of slaves			VII. Small proprietor/supervisor of skilled manual workers	1.2	1.5
VII. Free black	2.1	5.5	VIII. Low grade professional/nonmanual worker	6.0	7.5
Child of slaves (no occupation)	34.6	31.9	IX. Official/high grade professional/ proprietor	0.7	1.0
Total (N)	1,400[c]			1,392[d]	

[a] Weights are based on the geographic distribution (1860 census) and occupational distribution (Olson 1992 sample) of southern blacks.

[b] Percentages based on a pooled sample of all jobs held by respondents (2,298 job positions).

[c] Seventy-one cases contain incomplete data on status within the antebellum regime.

[d] Eight additional cases contain incomplete data on status within the postbellum regime.

considered to be of relatively high status. As in today's developing countries, clerical and other lower-end, nonmanual occupations had not yet been deskilled by technology in the late nineteenth century. White-collar workers thus enjoyed a high degree of autonomy and developed idiosyncratic skills that were difficult to replace.[49] Second, there is considerable differentiation in the ranking of agricultural occupations, particularly between independent farm proprietors (class V), sharecroppers and rental farmers (placed in class III), and common farm laborers (class I). This differentiation reflects the autonomy offered by farm ownership during the postbellum era, as opposed to the exploitive character of sharecropping and the similarity of supervised agricultural labor to fieldwork under the slave regime.[50]

Unsurprisingly, many emancipated slaves in the WPA sample came to be employed as agricultural workers, sharecroppers, or farm proprietors (44.7 percent after weighting). Another large group (36 percent) found work as unskilled or semiskilled manual or domestic laborers, including cooks, maids, launderers, railroad workers, and the like. Considering the longevity of these former slaves, a key methodological question is whether the small number who were able to enter elite occupations (especially as professionals or officials) is representative of the black population as a whole. Due to the time period covered (1865–1930s), no strict basis of comparison is available. However, analyses of census records around the middle of the period provide indications as to whether substantial bias exists. In 1890, the top ranks of socioeconomic status—professionals and officials—composed merely 1.1 percent of the black working population.[51] The percentage in the weighted WPA sample is almost identical (1.0 percent), with no significant departure from the population parameter under random sampling.

Table 3.2 provides a descriptive cross-tabulation of antebellum status and highest achieved postbellum status among the sampled freedmen and women. The diagonal of the mobility table suggests considerable status persistence among emancipated blacks, with each antebellum status generally being linked to disproportionate odds of representation within a comparable postbellum status.[52] By the same token, upward mobility into the ranks of professional and nonmanual workers tends to be relatively rare for blacks formerly employed as slave field hands, domestics, or semiskilled laborers, while downward mobility into the ranks of unskilled and semiskilled wage laborers is typically avoided by former slave artisans, as well as blacks who were free in the antebellum South. All of this suggests some empirical support for a structural model of status persistence across these institutional regimes.

Preliminary conclusions in this regard must be tempered by a number of caveats. First, the destination states considered in the mobility table combine occupations held immediately after the Civil War (often under former masters) with later occupational outcomes. This tends to conflate short-term status stability with what may be long-term fragmentation of status structures.

Table 3.2. Status Mobility of Sampled Blacks between Antebellum and Postbellum Regimes

Antebellum Status	Weighted Number	Postbellum Status (Highest Achieved)								
		I	II	III	IV	V	VI	VII	VIII	IX
Slave										
I. Unskilled agricultural	509	17	49	197	101	29	52	20	43	1
II. Unskilled manual/domestic	103	1	18	38	18	5	6	2	16	0
III. Semiskilled agricultural	24	2	0	10	4	3	2	0	1	0
IV. Semiskilled manual	50	0	7	5	27	2	5	0	4	0
V. Skilled domestic	93	1	13	15	34	3	16	3	7	1
VI. Skilled manual (artisan)/driver	92	0	0	1	19	6	44	0	19	3
Free or child of slaves										
VII. Free black	77	0	8	10	10	0	21	0	21	8
Child of slaves (no occupation)	443	11	67	148	111	19	33	3	46	6
Total (*N*)	1,392[a]									

[a] Row totals need not sum to number of cases due to rounding associated with case weights. Dark gray shading indicates that observed count exceeds expected count by a ratio of at least 1.4; light gray shading indicates that expected count exceeds observed count by a ratio of at least 1.4. Shading is limited to cells with an expected count of at least one observation.

Second, the pattern is complicated by the appearance of new classes during the postbellum period, such as independent farmers and a black petty bourgeoisie. For instance, supervisors and small proprietors (class VII) were drawn disproportionately from entrepreneurial blacks who were once unskilled field workers. Third, the simple cross-tabulation does not address other factors affecting mobility patterns during the postbellum period, including education, migration, and gender.

Multivariate models that control for the aforementioned factors reveal that some features of status under slavery had substantial effects on the jobs held by blacks after the Civil War. In particular, those blacks who were free in the antebellum period had significantly higher occupational prestige than those who had been slaves.[53] Figure 3.2 plots the relative probability of

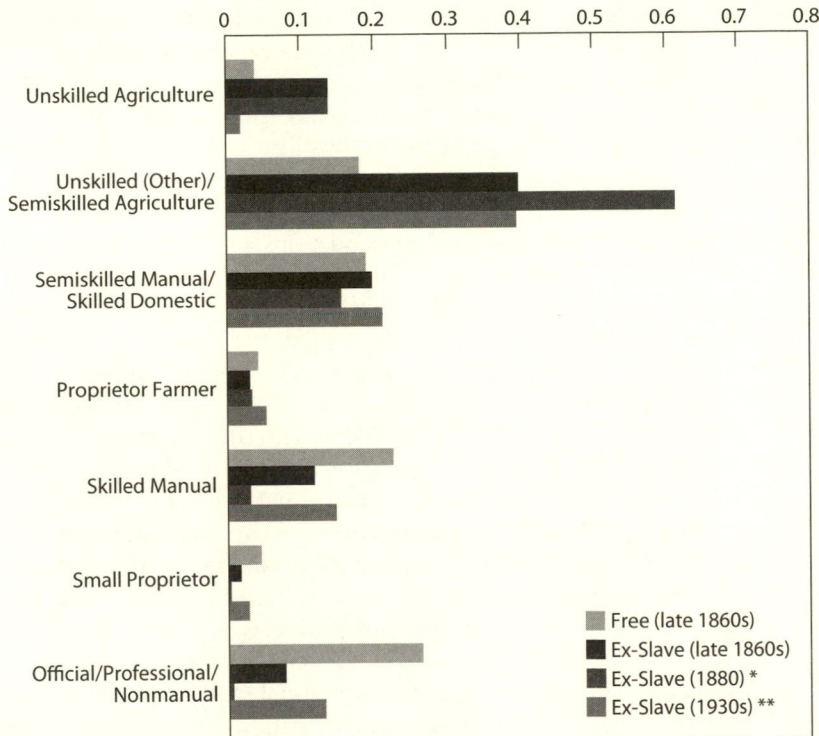

Figure 3.2. Predicted Probability of Occupational Status for Free Blacks and Former Slaves in the Postbellum U.S. South
Notes: Predictions are for a black male born in 1845, based on the equation shown in note 53. Data are coded from interviews with former slaves by the Works Progress Administration (WPA), with the exception of (*), which is taken from IPUMS linked 1860–80 representative sample of census records. Estimates in the 1930s (**) are based on highest occupational status achieved over the life course.

different occupational outcomes for a black male born in the South in 1845. Immediately after the Civil War (in the late 1860s), the estimates show that former slaves tended to be overrepresented in unskilled occupations and semiskilled agriculture, while blacks who were free in the antebellum period were overrepresented among skilled artisans, small business proprietors, professionals, and nonmanual workers. This pattern reflected several advantages on the part of free blacks. They did not face the public identity adjustment that former slaves underwent during emancipation, having already established an autonomous sense of self that they could present to employers, authorities, and other members of society. Blacks who had been free in the antebellum South were also much more likely to have accumulated wealth and belong to communities with established social support networks.[54] Moreover, the occupational mix among free blacks before emancipation is likely to have provided further advantages over those blacks who toiled under slavery.[55]

In the decades after emancipation, some former slaves were able to shift out of employment as agricultural laborers and enjoyed modest improvements in their likelihood of farm proprietorship, nonmanual work, or involvement in artisanal trades. Even these gains in occupational status were not unambiguous or linear. Conducted soon after the end of Radical Reconstruction, the 1880 census revealed very few Southern-born blacks who worked in middle-class or white-collar occupations.[56] The setback was especially pronounced for ex-slaves. According to the estimates shown in the figure, a thirty-five-year-old former bondsman had only a 4 percent chance of reaching a position in an occupational rung above that of independent farmer in 1880. This reversal seems to disappear, however, as the career histories of these former slaves are observed into old age. By the 1930s, when most of the interviewees in the WPA sample were in their seventies or eighties, the distribution of the highest occupational status over their life course begins to resemble—but does not yet reach—that achieved immediately after the Civil War by blacks who had been free in the antebellum era.[57]

Status outcomes immediately following emancipation were a function of position within the occupational hierarchy of slavery. Slave artisans and craft workers, in particular, enjoyed better prospects than the majority of ex-slaves who had been employed as field laborers. As shown in Figure 3.3, the odds that a slave employed as a skilled manual worker would attain a high level of occupational status after emancipation were more than six times those of a field slave. Since slave artisans were often hired out for wages before 1865, their more favorable status attainment following slavery may have reflected their relative autonomy and experience with the marketplace, as well as their technical abilities. Status persistence beyond the antebellum regime was also evident for household servants and other slave occupations, revealing an ordered hierarchy that differentiated these statuses from unskilled agricultural labor.[58]

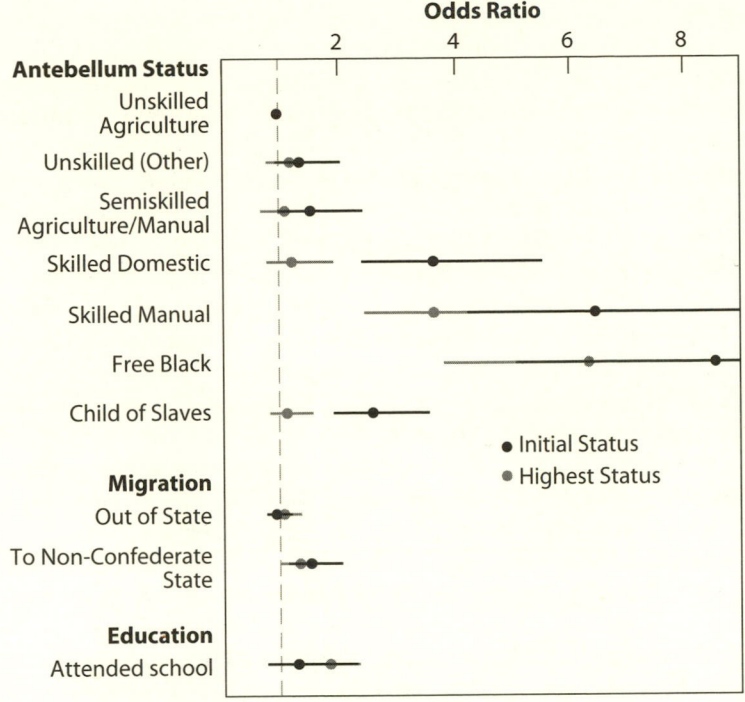

Figure 3.3. Odds Ratios from Model Predicting Postbellum Occupational Status of Blacks Formerly Residing in U.S. Slaveholding States
Notes: 95 percent confidence intervals are shown as black (initial status) or gray (highest status) lines. Models include controls for gender and age. Unskilled agricultural labor (fieldwork) is the reference category for antebellum status (odds ratio = 1.0).

The children of slaves, who had not yet been assigned an occupation under the slave regime, enjoyed some occupational advantages over those who were employed in unskilled trades on the plantation or in urban slavery. While children were certainly not exempt from the effects of slavery, the estimates in Figure 3.3 suggest that they tended to fare better in their initial job prospects after emancipation than adults who had labored in low-status slave occupations. This effect of childhood holds independently of a freedperson's chronological age, suggesting that enculturation in the routines of slave labor per se had adverse consequences that could persist well beyond the antebellum regime. These consequences may have included lowered expectations for fair labor contracts and submissive work habits—for example, reluctance to make suggestions or negotiate with powerful others.[59]

Education under the antebellum regime did little to change intragenerational patterns of occupational inheritance. As shown in the figure, receiving schooling (whether formal or informal) within the planter regime provided only limited benefit for status attainment outcomes immediately after the Civil War. This could result from the sporadic nature of such education or the fact that socialization within the older institutional arrangement simply did not offer the adaptability needed following emancipation. For older ex-slaves, it is also possible that the benefits of such education—often received under clandestine circumstances—were counteracted in the late antebellum period by the active hostility of many planters and efforts at "reeducation."[60]

Black migration served to disrupt the effects of status persistence to a greater extent. While interstate migration through the mid-1860s provided little improvement in status outcomes, exodus from the former Confederate states presented more promise to former slaves. Those who left for the North or West were roughly one-and-a-half times as likely to achieve a higher occupational status than those who stayed.[61]

For blacks remaining in the South, the Reconstruction era generated a great deal of political and economic uncertainty. The Black Codes that were passed under every Johnsonian state government in 1865 and 1866 restricted the movement of former slaves, effected the servitude of black children (under the label of "apprenticeship"), and excluded blacks from some forms of property ownership and skilled trades. In certain instances, the Black Codes also included restrictions on the ability of white employers to recruit black laborers who were already under contract elsewhere, under antienticement statutes.[62] The codes were challenged by the Freedmen's Bureau and Northern military authorities, and in 1867 radical Republicans in Congress passed the Reconstruction Act, removing civilian government in every former Confederate state but Virginia. The following years of Radical Reconstruction brought new opportunities for freedmen, but also deep resentment from conservative white Southerners. As shown in Figure 3.4, the short-term impact of Radical Reconstruction on status attainment among blacks who remained in the South was negligible. Based on the 1880 census, the odds of occupational advancement for blacks in states with longer periods of radical Republican rule (such as South Carolina) were no different than those of blacks in states where conservative Democrats quickly regained control of state legislatures (e.g., North Carolina).[63] But, over their life course, the impact of Radical Reconstruction on blacks who had been born in chattel slavery seemed to be more telling. Long after all Southern state legislatures had reverted to rule by conservative whites (by April 1877), the highest occupational status of blacks who lived in states with extended periods of radical Republicanism was significantly greater than those who lived in states with only brief periods of progressivism on black civil and economic rights.[64]

Examining the highest status attainment of respondents during the post-bellum period (Figure 3.3), several important differences from initial occupational attainment can be noted. While the status distinction between free

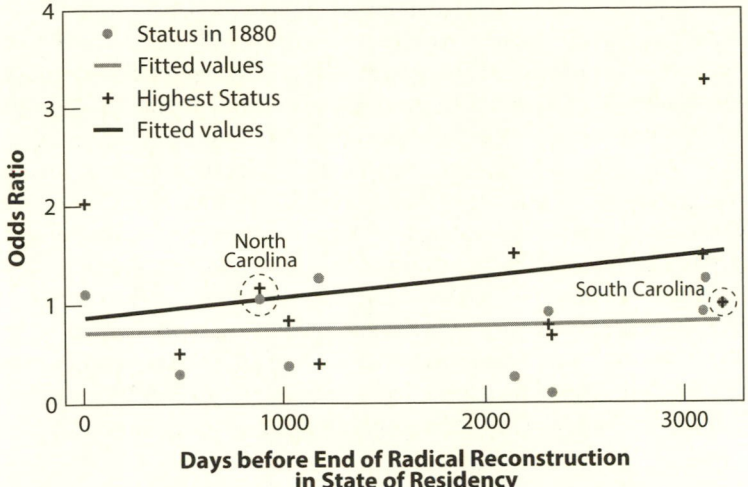

Figure 3.4. Effect of Duration of Radical Reconstruction on the Odds That Southern Blacks Achieved a Higher Occupational Status (by State of Residency)
Notes: Duration of Radical Reconstruction is defined as the difference between the readmission of a state in the Union and the date when conservative Democrats reestablished control in state legislatures. South Carolina is the reference state for status attainment (odds ratio = 1.0).

blacks and slaves prior to 1865 continued to have telling effects, status persistence based on the occupational slave hierarchy weakened considerably. Former slave artisans and craft workers, whose skills generalized across institutional arrangements, had clear status advantages, but other high-status slave positions (e.g., household service) offered no durable advantage compared to common field labor. For domestic and semiskilled workers, the institutional reproduction of the slave regime appeared to be limited by the fact that many of its status distinctions were rooted in particularistic traits (deference behavior, relationships with masters) that became less salient following emancipation. In the long run, categorical uncertainty increased as these distinctions under slavery had little capacity to predict the occupations that former slaves would come to hold or even the set of occupations that might be available to them.

Another source of discontinuity in status attainment was that education and investment in human capital, which had been deemed largely irrelevant by white elites under slavery, came to affect black upward mobility. As Du Bois and Washington had emphasized, schooling—whether rooted in formal college education, vocational training, or informal apprenticeship—was an institutional intervention that would benefit blacks in the long run.

To be truly effective, however, such schooling had to be decoupled from the older educational mechanisms of the antebellum South, which were ad hoc at best and often rooted in the paternalistic ideology of the planters. Although blacks faced barriers to professional employment throughout the postbellum period, education brought a host of cumulative advantages over the life course, including increased access to academic and vocational knowledge, as well as a lower likelihood of victimization in labor contracts. Educational opportunities ranged widely, from Hampton-model institutions designed to create more productive agricultural laborers to black-run schools that were oriented toward academic achievement (but which often suffered severe resource shortages). Despite this variability in quality, emancipated slaves embraced education and were generally rewarded in their efforts in doing so. Blacks who attended school after the Civil War were nearly twice as likely to attain a higher occupational status as those who did not.[65]

SUMMARY

For the last generation of blacks born under American slavery, the legacy of this institution evidenced both persistence and disintegration in the decades following emancipation. Status distinctions between free blacks and slaves under the antebellum regime continued to influence occupational attainment in the postbellum era. Slaves who were emancipated after reaching adulthood evidenced socioeconomic scars for years to come compared to children who only glimpsed the conditions of the slavery regime. But other features of the slave regime disintegrated over time. Except for those who learned skills in manual trades, occupational status within the system of slavery carried few durable occupational advantages or disadvantages in the late nineteenth century.

Mediating factors, such as migration and education, also served to disrupt institutional reproduction after 1865. Emigration was consistently defamed by Southern elites as a move away from home to dangerous territory, outside the protective arms of paternalism.[66] But former slaves who confronted disenfranchisement and economic exploitation in the South often found better opportunities outside the former confederacy. At the same time, there was generally an absence of benefits for those migrating *within* the confederacy, particularly for black adults. This could be accounted for by a number of institutional factors. By the early 1880s, blacks encountered antivagrancy laws throughout much of the South. New arrivals to a formerly Confederate town could expect to be jailed or forced into penitentiary labor if they failed to immediately find work. Moreover, blacks who migrated within the South were those who were most harshly persecuted; they often had to leave home in a hurry, regardless of employment prospects at their destinations.[67]

Educational opportunities during Reconstruction helped to offset the forced illiteracy of the slavery regime. The success of such education in garnering new economic opportunities for freed blacks was all the more impressive considering that formal schooling in the antebellum period had been largely ineffective. The analyses in this chapter thus suggest that substantial barriers to status mobility among blacks were produced by the legacies of slavery, but they do not support the contention that mobility processes were equivalent across the two regimes. Rather, the findings imply that mobility among freedmen and freedwomen depended on many of the same factors determining mobility in contemporary America. Freedmen and freedwomen needed opportunities for education; the resources to move to areas in need of skilled labor; information about job opportunities they could reasonably trust; a childhood free of hard labor and physical abuse; and, ideally, work experience that drew on technical skills.

With respect to canonical explanations of institutional transformation and social status, the findings in this chapter suggest qualified support for all three perspectives (see Figure 3.1). In the immediate aftermath of the antebellum regime, status structures evidenced recalcitrance and developed consistent mappings between categories of inequality under slavery and freedom. This substantiates an account of durable inequality across these regimes. Mediating characteristics—such as labor mobility and investment in human capital—also exercised some influence on initial status attainment among newly emancipated blacks. Consistent with Marxist accounts, these features of the means of production within free wage capitalism became central influences on the mobility regime over time. Simultaneously, institutional fragmentation contributed to loose coupling of social status across the regimes in the long run. While some details of this process are particular to the deinstitutionalization of slavery, the general pattern is one familiar to neoinstitutional scholars. When regulatory changes lead to the formal dismantling of one institutional regime, the beliefs and norms that supported that regime often linger, contributing to conflicting expectations and fragmentation of authority systems.[68] Such patterns of partial reproduction were reflected in the Reconstruction and Restoration eras during the latter half of the nineteenth century.

These complex patterns of mobility among former slaves also suggest why the uncertainty surrounding status attainment remained so enduring. The first few years of emancipation raised questions about the compensation of freedpeople in an emerging labor market, with the assumption that they would continue to inhabit the occupational roles that they had held as slaves (Chapter 2). The primary source of uplift for former slaves was exit from the South, much as it had been during antebellum times. With the retreat of the Freedmen's Bureau and beginning of Radical Reconstruction, the rules of status attainment seemed to change again. Southern blacks witnessed some of their peers rising to high political office, to ownership of land and businesses, and to select professional occupations, such as teaching and ministry. While this raised hope among freed blacks, their everyday reality also included oppositional tactics from Southern whites and violence from paramilitary groups, such as the Ku Klux Klan. Blacks were left to wonder what occupations or trades were truly possibilities for them and which ones invited threats to life or livelihood.[69]

The benefits of Radical Reconstruction for black status attainment were mixed. Judged on the criterion of socioeconomic advancement, Reconstruction did little to improve the immediate fate of Southern-born blacks. By 1880, those African Americans who lived in Southern states with long periods of Republican rule fared no different in occupational status than those who lived in states where Conservative Democrats quickly reasserted control over state government. And the opportunity among former slaves to practice a skilled trade or own a small business seemed worse than it had been during the turbulent years after the Civil War.

In the long run, the fate of African Americans who were born under slavery improved slightly, but was no less uncertain. Over a lifetime, the most stable predictor of occupational status for Southern blacks born before the Civil War was whether they had been slaves in the antebellum era. It remains unclear whether such differences were generated by the greater capacity of free blacks to accumulate resources in the antebellum period, the difficulty encountered by former slaves in constructing a new identity, variation in skin tone (i.e., color stratification), or the greater likelihood that free blacks had a white or mulatto parent. Even these advantages were challenged by the evolving system of racial classification in the South—particularly, the *Plessy v. Ferguson* case—and the proliferation of Jim Crow laws from the 1880s onward.[70]

The epigraph at the beginning of this chapter suggests that it was the African American laborer in the South who had to contend most directly with categorical uncertainty, with "finding his place in the American economic system under [the] changed status" of freedom. In the next chapter, I extend this perspective to address the evolving class structure of the postbellum South and the uncertainty it generated for all of its residents, whether white or black, immigrant or native.

CHAPTER 4

Class Structure in the Old and New South

> The line is marked. On one side lies the planter class, on the other the poor. Individuals may pass over the line, but the transition is abrupt. There are no intermediate resting-places.
> —Milton Clapp, *Southern Quarterly Review*

> [T]he rise of the middle class has been the most notable thing connected with the white population of the South since the war.
> —John Spencer Bassett, *South Atlantic Quarterly*

Mark Twain begins his first novel, *The Gilded Age* (coauthored with Charles Warner), with a colorful rendition of rural life in the antebellum South. The fictional hamlet of Obedstown, Tennessee, offers a caricature of preindustrial and, in many respects, precapitalist society. When a mail carrier arrives bearing a single letter from the outside world, the town's populace of men, consisting exclusively of yeoman farmers dressed in homespun jeans, bearing dilapidated straw hats, and chewing tobacco, gathers around. The farmers appear to be largely self-sufficient—their goods are locally produced and the light load of the youthful carrier suggests only limited integration with national, much less international, markets. Class distinctions among these poor whites are subtle, though the mention of a few titles ("judge," "squire") implies the presence of a small aristocracy. A lackadaisical ethos permeates the gathering. Hands are placed firmly in pockets (except when they are used to adjust the tilt of straw hats). No one seems to be in a particular hurry to accomplish anything.[1]

Despite the slow pace of life in Obedstown, at least one resident—the town's postmaster, Squire Hawkins—holds higher aspirations. He has acquired seventy-five thousand unimproved acres in the hope that natural resources and industrial development will lift the land's value. During the antebellum era, Hawkins's entrepreneurial ambitions are repeatedly dashed and he dies penniless. His last words to his children instruct them to "never lose sight of the Tennessee Land," as the real estate passes on to them.[2]

The aftermath of the Civil War seems to offer new prospects to the Hawkins family. Squire Hawkins had been seen as a speculator and a dreamer in the conservative Old South, but the idea of an enterprising class was given legitimacy by the political forces of the postbellum era. Hawkins's son and daughter are able to take their plans to Washington, D.C., where they seek to entice federal support for an industrial college on the Tennessee land, among other business schemes. It is the beginning of the Gilded Age.

While Twain and Warner's novel is primarily a morality tale cautioning against the pitfalls of avarice, it also offers a standard narrative of economic development. Institutional transformation propels a change in the structure of premodern society, from one in which communities are largely populated by yeoman farmers to one in which an emerging middle class can seek to profit from a diverse array of nonagricultural businesses. Similarly, a number of historians have closely linked industrial development and capitalist modernization with the influence and expansion of an entrepreneurial class. Focusing on the case of late eighteenth-century England, Reinhard Bendix argued that the emerging entrepreneurial class successfully confronted a hostile aristocracy and traditional workforce in order to establish a thriving ideology of entrepreneurship and a secure position for its small businesses. Social historians have documented the vitality of an urban class of proprietors in a variety of other industrializing contexts, including the antebellum U.S. North, the postbellum South, and postrevolutionary France. More abstractly, scholars since Alexis de Tocqueville have proposed that the conditions of modern capitalist society are beneficial to the formation of autonomous enterprise and thus the prospects of an entrepreneurial class whose fortunes are tied to those businesses.[3]

Other commentators have been less convinced of the vitality of an entrepreneurial middle class in the transition to capitalism. Karl Marx, most famously, predicted that small entrepreneurs would occupy a tenuous position in capitalist society, one that would be eroded in the polarized relationship between haut bourgeoisie and working proletariat. C. Wright Mills, echoing this claim, suggested that "the industrialization of America, especially after the Civil War, gave rise not to a broad stratum of small businessmen, but to the captain of industry."[4]

Despite a considerable lineage in the social sciences, the impact of economic modernization on the size and coherence of the middle class remains unclear. To what extent is capitalism associated with an expansion in the numbers of small business owners? How are other factions of the middle class, such as white-collar employees, affected by capitalist transformation? What is the fate of the older classes of yeoman farmers and planters in the wake of these changes? This chapter examines these questions for the population of the American South during the latter half of the nineteenth century, suggesting how accounts of structural modernization and Marxist perspectives on middle-class decline must be amended to take the uncertainty of institutional change into account.[5]

THE MIDDLE CLASS

Although the concept of the middle class is a central term in the social science lexicon, the process of middle-class formation has typically been ceded to historians as a subject of scholarly inquiry. As recently as the early 1990s, a review by Melanie Archer and Judith Blau suggested that social science theories have largely treated the emergence of a middle class as a residual phenomenon, instead favoring a "two-class" model that emphasizes tensions between an elite and a laboring proletariat.[6] Like Clapp, the editor of the *Southern Quarterly Review* who denied the existence of a Southern middle class during the antebellum period, social scientists have often fallen back on dichotomized conceptions of class history. Recent treatments have enriched theoretical understanding of the foundations of class, but social scientific analysis of middle-class emergence has arguably made only limited progress beyond the classic statement of Mills in *White Collar*.[7] Scholars seeking an account of the rise of the middle classes will find them mostly in community-based social histories, focusing on specific urban contexts or institutions that were supportive to the development of a petit bourgeois consciousness. Influential studies include Stuart Blumin's work on middle-class formation in the large seaboard cities of the Northeastern United States, Leonore Davidoff and Catherine Hall on the creation of "middling" institutions in Britain, Lynne Feldman on the painstaking effort of blacks to carve out a middle-class community in segregated Birmingham, and C. Vann Woodward on the rise of an entrepreneurial class in the urban New South.[8]

Historical scholarship has offered rich insights into middle-class organization and culture, but takes a slightly different perspective than that adopted by sociologists and economists. Following E. P. Thompson's pioneering study of the English working class, a common emphasis in historical studies concerns the appearance of a self-interested class consciousness or a perception on the part of others that a class does (or does not) exist. This perspective privileges the opinions and behaviors of historical observers. In contrast to this conceptualization of class-for-itself (or, in Karl Marx's terms, *Klasse-für-sich*), social scientists tend to be inclined toward descriptions of class-in-itself (*Klasse-an-sich*), offering summaries of characteristics that may be linked systematically to a class, apart from self-awareness or self-promotion.[9] In the sociological perspective, class formation is ultimately dependent on awareness of position, but meaningful distinctions in the objective relationship of individuals to the means of production (via investments in human and financial capital) typically constitute a precondition to such awareness.

A central dilemma in scholarship on middle-class formation is that there is not *one* middle class, but many middle classes. Archer and Blau identify four distinctive occupational groups that appear in the literature on the history of the middle class, including skilled artisans, retailers and shop-keepers, a petite bourgeoisie of (nonretail) business owners, and the "new" nonmanual white-collar class of clerks, managers, officials, and other employees of bureaucratic organizations. Furthermore, one can add the established professions of the nineteenth century—such as physicians, lawyers, and civil engineers—as well as quasi-professionals—such as teachers, nurses, journalists, and the like.[10] Although all of these occupational groups could lay claim to being part of the middle classes, it is not immediately evident what basis of social commonality is shared among them. Are the historical boundaries of the middle class marked by income and wealth? By education and cultural capital? Or by self-conscious efforts to associate and organize in view of shared collective interests?

To simplify matters somewhat, this chapter relies on a basic differentiation of the middle classes into two groups: one defined by a propensity toward small business proprietorship (the "entrepreneurial" middle class) and another defined by a propensity toward nonmanual employment in large organizations (the "bureaucratic" middle class). Viewed historically, the entrepreneurial middle class subsumes master artisans, small manufacturing proprietors, independent professionals, service proprietors, and store-keepers. The bureaucratic middle class includes clerks, white-collar employees, military and government officials, quasi-professionals, and salespeople. Farm proprietorship and employment are conventionally excluded from both definitions, thus distancing the middle classes from yeoman farmers, agricultural laborers, and slaves, as well as the landed gentry that dominated the antebellum South.

The Structural Perspective on Middle-Class Emergence

Few social historians now subscribe to the intuition that capitalist institutions are a *necessary* precondition to the formation of a middle class.[11] Still, there is a broad consensus among a number of scholars that capitalist institutions provide an infrastructure for the expansion of organizing activity and for middle-class advancement. This structural view extends to the American South, where a common contention among historians remains that "slavery functioned to keep the South's middle class small and its domestic market thin."[12] Accordingly, from this view, it is only with the end of slavery that protocapitalist institutions allowed the Southern middle class to flourish.

In organizational terms, the structural argument has been articulated lucidly by the sociologist Arthur Stinchcombe. He begins an influential essay by emphasizing that "one of the classic problems in organizational analysis is to describe the kinds of populations in which the transition process from 'traditional' to 'modern' can take place—in which, in other words, special-purpose organizations can be invented and built." Insofar as those organizations are built by autonomous individuals (or entrepreneurial groups) rather than states, the process he describes bears on the emergence of an entrepreneurial class, as well as the middling clerks, managers, and white-collar professionals that those organizations employ. Stinchcombe focuses on the structural conditions that enhance *organizing capacity*—that is, the likelihood that individuals in a society will create formal organizations. In his account, critical variables affecting organizing capacity include (a) urbanization, (b) literacy and numeracy, (c) banking and a money economy, and (d) political upheaval.[13] To this list, we might add the existence of (e) free labor markets, which have been identified by both Stinchcombe and Weber as an important structural feature of capitalism. While these variables represent general conditions affecting organizing capacity, they lead to a number of specific predictions concerning the formation of a middle class in the American South.

Following in the footsteps of Max Weber, Stinchcombe recognizes urbanization as an essential component of the transition to modern capitalist society. Weber's ideal type of the city was one in which the basis of urban growth shifted from military to economic foundations, where authority was legal-rational rather than traditional or charismatic, and where groups were differentiated by class rather than family lineage.[14] The rise of an urban economy is thus one of the most rudimentary requirements for middle-class formation. As societies move from self-sufficient farming and close-knit agrarian communities to specialized occupations in far-flung cities, new enterprises emerge within a highly differentiated division of labor. The smaller ventures—for example, bakeries, butcher shops, restaurants, taverns, law offices, and the like—are initiated by an entrepreneurial middle class, while the larger organizations—such as banks, factories, and city government—employ a bureaucratic middle class in clerical and managerial positions. The differentiation of organizational forms, in turn, attracts new waves of middle-class migrants to urban centers.

With the exception of coastal cities such as Charleston, Mobile, Savannah, and New Orleans, the relative lack of urban centers in the Old South before 1850 posed a substantial barrier to middle-class formation. There is some debate among historians as to the timing and influence of urbanization on the emergent middle class during the second half of the nineteenth century. Jonathan Wells suggests that urban social structure was already developing in the antebellum period, noting that "opportunities to attend school, hear a lecture, participate in a debating society, or join a library were rife in southern towns by the 1850s" and that "work on the part of middle-class southerners to industrialize and urbanize was bearing considerable fruit" by that decade. Don Doyle, on the other hand, locates the rise of the urban South and of a new business class in the 1880s, following Radical Reconstruction.[15] Some census figures place even the urban takeoff of the New South in doubt. When the urban population is defined as inhabitants living in settlements with more than twenty-five hundred inhabitants, the South lagged behind not only the industrialized Northeast between 1850 and 1900, but also the Midwestern states and Western frontier. Whereas nearly 40 percent of the Midwestern and Western population was urban by 1900, substantially less than 20 percent of the South's population lived in urban places.[16] If urbanization is the critical variable fostering organizational development, then these figures would lead us to anticipate a comparatively small Southern middle class at the turn of the century.

Like urbanization, literacy is considered to be a basic historical correlate of middle-class existence. Small entrepreneurs had to be literate in order to write orders for goods, manage inventories, extend credit, and enter into contracts. Independent professionals required literacy for their schooling and to keep up with the latest developments in law, medicine, or engineering. Bureaucratic professionals, by definition, were expected to follow and generate systems of written organizational rules.[17] In the middle classes, perhaps the only exception to this pattern was found among skilled artisans and proprietors of small manufactories. Even in these occupations, enterprises benefited considerably from the human and cultural capital of literate owner-managers.[18]

Although the technical functions of literacy and numeracy come to mind most readily, historians and sociologists have also called attention to their rhetorical function for the middle classes. Newspapers, public libraries, and the periodical literature represent an important source of bourgeois ideas and solidarity in early capitalist societies. Advocacy for literacy and education often became a cause célèbre among the middle classes, especially when it was opposed—as it often was in the antebellum South—by a landed gentry. Aside from its function as an enabler of middle-class enterprise, education offered a way to demarcate and legitimate the position of the petite bourgeoisie between a lower class of common laborers and an upper class of agrarian elites. Numeracy offered similar symbolic benefits to the middle classes. For instance, the use of double-entry bookkeeping as an accounting method did as much to legitimate the enterprise of a merchant or trader as it did to ensure the valuation and verification of profit. This was true, especially, when the audiences for such accounts were themselves members of literate and numerate classes.[19]

Debates about the impact of literacy on middle-class development in the South largely parallel those for urbanization. In Jonathan Wells's thesis of antebellum class formation, the founding of schools, academies, and colleges exploded in the three decades *prior* to the Civil War, a rich literary culture emerged (especially among middle-class women), and intellectual exchange between North and South solidified class solidarity across sectional divisions. Similarly, Jennifer Green has found that the military schools that developed in the South during the 1840s and 1850s often served as a "launching pad for the professional careers of nonagricultural, non-elite" men, particularly through their vocational and scientific training. Historians have documented earnest attempts at public schooling in the antebellum era, even in areas—such as South Carolina—where such efforts were ultimately thwarted.[20]

Other scholars have a less positive view of educational opportunities during the antebellum period. Edward Ayers notes the weak tradition of public schooling in the antebellum South—for whites, as well as blacks—and lack of political support for educational institutions. In his perspective, one of the heralded accomplishments of the New South was the school reform that began in the 1880s.[21] As of yet, the historical record has been unclear as to whether this expansion in educational effort served to differentiate the middle class *in particular* (on the basis of human capital investments) or contributed to the educational uplift of *all* factions of Southern society.

Systems of credit and banking constitute a third institutional support to the middle class. Historically, small proprietors have relied on credit for loans and trade finance with suppliers, importers, and commission merchants. Trade finance, in particular, created a substantial need for credit in early modern economies, owing to the scarcity of hard currency, inefficiencies in transportation and communication networks (which introduced substantial lags into commercial transactions), and seasonal fluctuations in agricultural production (which exacerbated those lags even further). As a consequence, many small shopkeepers and manufacturing proprietors could survive economically only by buying materials and finished products on credit.[22]

While the fortunes of a few large enterprises—and the bureaucratic middle class they employed—were tied to distant banks or wholesalers, the viability of other businesses relied on local financial infrastructure. Considering small manufacturing proprietors in the Carolina Piedmont, for instance, David Carlton and Peter Coclanis emphasize that their options for financing fixed capital investments and the procurement of raw materials in the postbellum era tended to depend "on their own resources" and "on the ad hoc personal networks they were able to construct . . . in a highly personal financial environment." Not surprisingly, members of the Southern middle class were especially vocal proponents for local bank creation, composing part of a larger nineteenth-century movement in favor of "internal development."[23]

The character of capital allocation among the entrepreneurial middle class also distinguished them from the landed gentry and yeoman farmers in agrarian society. Much of the economic well-being of farm proprietors was vested in physical capital, such as land, livestock, agricultural implements, and farm structures. By contrast, the capital allocation of the petite entrepreneur required more flexibility. Liquid assets or short-term credit were needed among shopkeepers, master artisans, and physicians to maintain store inventories, procure raw materials, stock medical supplies, and the like. The existence of monetary exchange and banking greatly simplified these transactions.

Considering Stinchcombe's fourth structural condition, it is hard to claim that there is a general correlation between political upheaval and the viability of the middle classes. Nevertheless, political revolutions in agrarian society have often favored the entrepreneurial petite bourgeoisie. Revolutions challenge vested interests—particularly those of the landed aristocracy—and generate resources for new organizations. Small merchants and manufacturing proprietors are well positioned to take advantage of commercial opportunities in the aftermath of political upheaval, while the fate of larger bureaucratic organizations hinge on their relationship with the ancien régime.

Perhaps the strongest theoretical rationale in favor of a positive effect of political revolution on an entrepreneurial middle class may be found in ecological theories of social organization. An extensive body of scholarship emphasizes the inertia that tends to limit organizational change and the resulting tendency of organizational forms to be imprinted by the social circumstances that existed when they were first created.[24] In the face of structural inertia, the proliferation of new organizations—and the entrepreneurs who found them—is most likely to occur under conditions of dramatic institutional change, such as political revolutions. Reshaping existing interests and resources into new opportunity structures, revolutionary periods "transform broad and cumulative social and economic change into bursts of organizational activity." Some organizational scholars qualify this proposition further, arguing that political turbulence is especially favorable to small-scale entrepreneurs who are able to move quickly to exploit new resources, rather than to bureaucratic enterprises that focus on the efficient utilization of resources. Given this argument, the economic prospects of middling entrepreneurs should improve under conditions of political upheaval.[25]

Free labor markets offer a final structural antecedent to the rise of an entrepreneurial class. For Stinchcombe, the mobility of resources is a crucial factor driving the formation of new organizations. Some of this mobility is generated by the capitalist institutions discussed above, such as systems of banking—which encourage the mobilization of capital—and urban economies—which promote the liquidity of real estate. The emergence of formally free labor is equally critical, insofar as it allows entrepreneurial elements to arise from social groups that were once tied to owners (in chattel slavery) or to the land (as in postbellum restrictions on labor, such as debt peonage).[26]

The rise of free labor markets may also have indirect repercussions on the prospects of small business owners. As Weber proposed, free labor is one of the key conditions for the formal rationality of capital accounting in business enterprise. While unfree labor arrangements such as slavery or indentured servitude ostensibly allow for greater control of workers, they also impose a need for more capital investment (e.g., in the purchase of slaves) and greater risk to capital than free labor markets. In Weber's analysis, the use of unfree labor was prevalent historically "in agricultural production on a large scale ... or in very simple industrial processes," in addition to household use.[27] Where petite bourgeois enterprise relied on a small number of workers to supplement owner-managers and their kin, the emerging free labor markets of the postbellum South appeared to offer a more flexible source of labor.

The Marxist Perspective on Middle-Class Decline

If the general thrust of structural arguments is to assert the expansion of the middle class with capitalist modernization, the thrust of Marxist arguments is to claim the decline of artisanal and entrepreneurial elements under the same conditions. The widely cited Marxist thesis concerning the proletarianization of the entrepreneurial middle class suggests that "the lower strata of the middle class—the small tradespeople, shopkeepers, and retired tradesmen generally, the handicraftsmen and peasants—all these sink gradually into the proletariat, partly because their diminutive capital does not suffice for the scale on which modern industry is carried on, and is swamped in the competition with the large capitalists, partly because their specialized skill is rendered worthless by new methods of production."[28] For the United States, France, and Germany, statistical data in support of this contention suggest a decline in self-employment since the 1880s, albeit with some reversals over the past four decades. While the fate of the petty bourgeoisie in late capitalism remains an open question, its decline in early capitalism is one of the more robust findings of Marxist analysis.[29]

On its surface, the thesis of proletarianization appears to apply well to the postbellum South. In 1880, around 75 percent of manufacturing workers were employed in small workshops spread throughout the region. During the following two decades, industrial development contributed to the emergence of large-scale production, including sawmills and turpentine camps in the coastal plains, cotton mills in the Black Belt, and coal and iron mines in Appalachia. With postbellum growth in productivity outstripping that of New England during the early nineteenth century, industrialization seemed to threaten the proprietors of small, inefficient manufactories. At the same time, integration with foreign and national markets flooded the South with cheap, nonlocal goods and exposed its petite bourgeoisie to competition from firms operating at greater scale and efficiency.[30]

Despite these changes in the business environment, an open question is whether the entrepreneurial middle class actually *declined* during the post-bellum period or whether it simply faced new institutional challenges—ones that were equally detrimental, in a Marxist perspective, as those evident in the plantation economy. Skilled artisans, for instance, already faced prole-tarianization before the Civil War, given threats by planters and industrialists to substitute slave artisans for unruly whites.[31] And if the postbellum mer-chant was subject to the whims of large Northern wholesalers and manufac-turers, then much the same could be said for the relationship between the antebellum merchant and the planter elite. Worse, some critics of antebel-lum planter hegemony, like Milton Clapp, argued that the high degree of economic autonomy among Southern plantations (each with "its own smiths, its own carpenters, its spinners, its weavers") suppressed the emer-gence of an entrepreneurial middle class, whereas the large estates of other nations furnished employment to nearby tradesmen and merchants.[32]

Operational Definition of Class Membership

A systematic evaluation of the structural and Marxist arguments requires information on class composition during the transition from slavery to cap-italism. The primary data for this chapter are taken from the five censuses spanning the period from 1850 until 1900.[33] The analysis focuses on class composition in the Lower South, subsuming the states of Alabama, Geor-gia, Louisiana, Mississippi, and South Carolina. Some historians, including Woodward, have suggested that a thriving middle class first emerged in the Lower South in the decades after the Civil War. By comparison, Stuart Blu-min locates the formation of a middle class in the more industrialized Northeast in the three decades before the Civil War; and Whig Party activ-ism in the Upper South had likewise created conditions that were condu-cive to antebellum middle-class emergence.[34] The nineteenth-century Lower South thus offers the most nascent stage of middle-class emergence covered by available microdata.

The chapter defines middle-class membership on an occupational basis (see Table 4.1). Individuals are considered to be members of the entrepre-neurial middle class when they are likely proprietors of small independent businesses or partnerships and derive their income from nonagricultural pursuits.[35] To assess the construct validity of the definition, I use a 1 percent sample of labor force participants in 1880 (ages fifteen and older) and match it to records on business ownership, drawing on the Dun *Mercantile Agency Reference Book*, the most complete listing of business enterprises at the time. As shown in Figure 4.1, the odds of nonfarm proprietorship are relatively high in the occupations designated as "entrepreneurial"—nearly five times those observed among bureaucratic occupations (e.g., clerks, white-collar

Table 4.1. Occupations in the Middle Class(es)

Artisans and manufacturing proprietors	Independent professionals
Baker	Architect
Blacksmith	Dentist
Boat maker	Engineer (civil)
Book/newspaper publisher	Lawyer
Bookbinder	Physician/surgeon
Boot/shoemaker	Veterinarian
Brewer or maltster	
Butcher	Military or government employees
Clock/watchmaker	
Confectioner	Quasi-professionals
Cooper	Actor/artist
Distiller/refiner	Auctioneer
Dressmaker	Author
Engraver	Barber
Gilder/goldsmith	Clergy
Gun/locksmith	Designer/draughtsman
Harness/saddlemaker	Journalist
Jeweler	Musician
Marble/stonecutter	Nurse/midwife
Mechanic or machinist	Photographer
Miller	Teacher
Printer/lithographer	Undertaker
Shipwright	Other quasi-professional
Tailor	
Tanner	Salespersons
Upholsterer	
Wheelwright	Service proprietors
Other artisan or proprietor[a]	Billiard or bowling saloon keeper
	Boarding-house keeper
Clerks or white-collar employees	Hotel keeper
Banker/broker	Livery-stable keeper
Bookkeeper/accountant	Restaurant keeper
Clerk	Saloon keeper
Manager/company official	
Other white-collar employee	Storekeepers or wholesalers
	Commercial broker
	Trader or dealer (any set of goods)

[a] Includes makers of agricultural implements, artificial flowers, blinds, brooms, brushes, cabinets, candles, carpets, carriages, cars, cordage, doors, hats, organs, patterns, pianos, pumps, sails, sashes, shirts, soap, steam boilers, stoves, tinware, tools, trunks, and woodenware.

employees, salespeople, government officials, quasi-professionals), six times those observed among agricultural, manufacturing, and service laborers, and almost twelve times those observed among farm owners.[36] This supports the use of this occupational definition as a proxy for entrepreneurial propensity outside the agricultural sector.

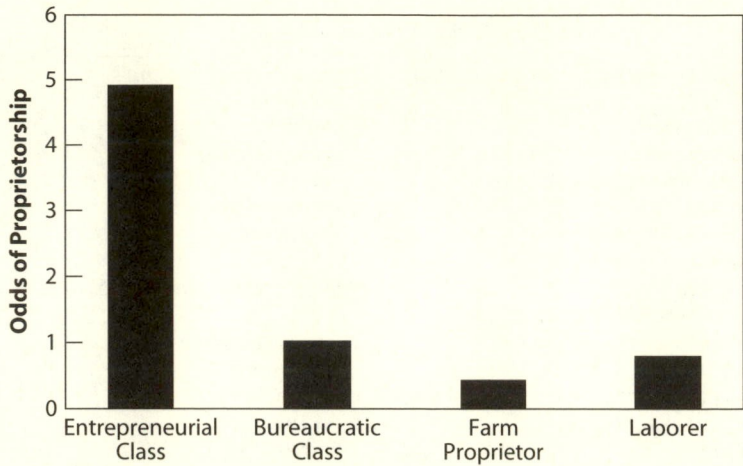

Figure 4.1. Odds of Nonagricultural Business Proprietorship by Occupational Class, U.S. Lower South (1880). © 2011, Elsevier.
Notes: Analysis based on 20,124 labor force participants (age fifteen or older) and 321 observed instances of (nonfarm) business proprietorship. Estimation of odds ratio controls for age, gender, and race. Bureaucratic (white-collar) middle class serves as the reference category (odds ratio = 1.0).

Members of the bureaucratic middle class are defined as either nonmanual employees of large organizations, such as banks, railroads, insurance companies, the military, or government, or service sector employees who are differentiated from common laborers, but have not attained the autonomy of independent entrepreneurs. In particular, the latter part of the definition differentiates between the established professions (medicine, law, engineering, and the like), which afford their occupants an opportunity for independent practice, and the quasi-professions (teaching, nursing, ministry), which tend to position their occupants as employees of organizations or congregations.[37]

Attributes of the Middle Classes

Table 4.2 summarizes the literacy and wealth of the Southern middle class in the antebellum and postbellum eras, comparing the resources maintained by this group with those held by farm proprietors and by common laborers.[38] During the antebellum period, the entrepreneurial middle class was only weakly differentiated from its bureaucratic counterparts on these dimensions. Given bureaucratic reliance on systems of written rules, employees of large enterprises and quasi-professionals tended to be significantly more literate (99.5 percent) than small proprietors (95.9 percent).

Table 4.2. Average Literacy and Wealth of Occupational Groups among White Adults in the Lower South

	Antebellum Period (1850–60)			Postbellum Period (1870–1900)		
	Literacy (%)	Value of Real Estate ($)	Value of Other Property ($)	Literacy (%)	Value of Real Estate ($)	Value of Other Property ($)
Entrepreneurial middle class	*95.89*	*1,874.85*	*3,864.36*	*95.42*	*1,581.70*	*1,116.39*
Artisans and manufacturing proprietors	93.23	430.27	838.37	93.64	598.62	260.19
Independent professionals	99.55	4,728.07	6,565.57	98.08	2,688.88	1,359.25
Service proprietors	96.00	1,437.33	1,929.57	94.67	2,127.50	575.00
Storekeepers and wholesalers	98.99	3,149.77	8,365.64	96.75	2,140.36	2,108.12
Bureaucratic middle class	*99.54**	*1,184.66*	*2,217.39*	*97.40**	*491.07***	*254.08****
Clerks and white-collar employees	100.00	821.38	1,264.50	97.70	442.42	205.76
Military and government	96.43	737.68	2,440.00	95.62	703.44	608.36
Quasi-professionals	99.60	603.57	1,676.37	96.82	519.69	245.03
Salespeople	—[a]	—	—	99.04	—	—
Farm proprietors	*85.81****	*2,664.73**	*6,292.88****	*81.95****	*1,269.26*	*671.13****
Laborers	*87.18****	*216.59****	*281.73****	*76.63****	*158.90****	*82.01****
Agricultural laborers	85.46	253.43	371.99	72.60	54.26	66.36
Manufacturing laborers and apprentices	93.76	470.89	540.98	87.44	308.84	130.29
Service laborers	85.14	74.75	112.82	76.23	306.06	90.11
F-test (across classes)	67	22	48	349	31	53
Total sample size	8,897	8,924	5,140	23,899	5,885	5,885

Source: Integrated Public Use Microdata Series, 1 percent samples.

Note: For purposes of comparability, all samples are limited to white adults, age twenty and older.

[a] Fewer than twenty observations in these cells.

p < .05. ***p* < .001 (two-tailed tests, comparisons to entrepreneurial class).

But the factions of the middle class cannot be distinguished on the basis of average financial capital, considered in terms of either real estate or other assets. Owing to the high level of asset variance within each group, the differences reported in the table ($1,875 versus $1,185 for real estate and $3,864 versus $2,217 for other property) are not statistically significant.[39]

With respect to laborers and farm proprietors, the Southern middle class occupied a predictable position in the status hierarchy. On average, members of the middle class were more literate than both laborers and farmers, possessed less land and other property (including slaves) than the yeoman farmers and planters, and owned more property than the laborers. On the basis of this distribution of education and financial capital, it seems appropriate to speak of an objective position for "middling sorts" during the antebellum era, consistent with qualitative evidence on class formation before the Civil War. However, this class position would have necessarily combined a diverse set of occupations, owing to the weak differentiation among entrepreneurial and bureaucratic elements at the time.

In the postbellum era, the distinctive positions *within* the middle class became more apparent. The entrepreneurial and bureaucratic middle classes were now clearly differentiated, with the small proprietors controlling land and liquid assets in pursuit of entrepreneurial profit and nonmanual employees exhibiting a higher level of literacy in the service of large enterprise. With the demise of chattel slavery, the financial resources of the entrepreneurial class also placed them above farm proprietors in mean liquid assets ($1,116 versus $671) and marginally higher in real estate assets ($1,582 versus $1,269).[40] Statistically, this process of class differentiation is reflected to some extent in F-tests for the microcensus data, which compute the ratio of between-class variability over within-class variability (see Table 4.2).[41] In contrast to its antebellum birth as a vague component of "the middling sorts," the entrepreneurial class appeared to achieve a cohesive class position in postbellum Southern society. On average, members of the postbellum entrepreneurial class had also amassed more assets than any other major occupational class, including farm proprietors.

Using the historical census, it is difficult to trace the effects of these resources on other forms of status attainment within the middle class, though there is some evidence as to how class status was perpetuated across generations. Pooling the data from 1850 until 1880, we can readily identify the higher rates of school attendance and literacy among the children of household heads who occupied middle-class positions. In nineteenth-century Southern households headed by members of the bureaucratic or entrepreneurial middle classes, some 15 percent of school-age children were attending school during the year that the census was conducted and, during the postbellum period, 75 percent of those children over nine years of age were literate.[42] By contrast, in households headed by members of other classes, only 10 percent of their children were attending school at the time of census collection and 49 percent of the older children were literate. Although the data do not permit a more fine-grained investigation into the intergenerational transfer of human capital, it seems clear that members of the middle class were able to pass educational privilege on to their progeny, potentially sharpening class boundaries.

Size of the Middle Classes

While the analysis of literacy and financial capital suggests greater certainty regarding the composition of the Southern middle class over time, a descriptive analysis of class size reveals a surprising trend. During the antebellum period, artisans, independent professionals, and other proprietors constituted around 15 percent of the white adult labor force in the Lower South (see Table 4.3). Although the size of this entrepreneurial middle class was substantially smaller than that represented in the rest of the United States (around 19 percent), it did not vary significantly between 1850 and 1860. In the two decades after the Civil War, however, the Southern entrepreneurial class *declined* as a proportion of the labor force, to 13.3 percent in 1870 and 10.6 percent in 1880. By the end of Reconstruction, this decline was evident in every faction of the entrepreneurial class, including artisans and manufacturing proprietors (which were merely $5.12 / 8.51 = 0.60$ of the proportion in the labor force they were in 1860), independent professionals (0.64), service proprietors (0.54), and storekeepers and wholesalers (0.82). Despite a modest rebound in the prevalence of the Southern entrepreneurial class by the turn of the century, it remained proportionately smaller than it was before the Civil War. Meanwhile, national statistics suggest that the entrepreneurial middle class was a relatively stable feature of the occupational structure in other parts of the United States, with little difference in labor force proportion between 1850 and 1900.

    A devil's advocate might counter that the postbellum trend toward middling entrepreneurship would be most pronounced not among whites but among blacks who, having shed the shackles of slavery, found that they had to develop their own businesses in a capitalist—yet segregated—society. In this vein, C. Vann Woodward asserted that "enough of a Negro middle class had emerged in the [eighteen] eighties to reflect faithfully the New-South romanticism of the white middle class, with its gospel of progress and wealth." Despite such pronouncements, census data tracking the rise of a black entrepreneurial middle class during the late nineteenth century are rather equivocal (Table 4.4). Restricting attention to free blacks in the antebellum period, one finds that the small number of these respondents in the South often worked as proprietors, a statistic that is supported by city censuses from the same period.[43] The size of the entrepreneurial class of blacks

Table 4.3. Size of Occupational Groups as Percentage of White Adult Labor Force, United States 1850–1900

	Rest of United States	Lower South					Rest of United States
	1850	1850	1860	1870	1880	1900	1900
Entrepreneurial middle class	*19.60*	*14.35****	*15.89*	*13.35****	*10.56****	*11.87***	*19.12****
Artisans and manufacturing proprietors	14.27	7.86	8.51	5.99	5.12	5.43	12.44
Independent professionals	1.31	2.15	2.31	2.29	1.49	1.43	1.17
Service proprietors	0.71	0.72	0.80	0.61	0.43	1.31	1.92
Storekeepers and wholesalers	3.31	3.62	4.27	4.46	3.52	3.70	3.59
Bureaucratic middle class	*4.65*	*6.05****	*8.33****	*10.18****	*8.58****	*13.72****	*18.09****
Clerks and white-collar employees	2.33	2.89	4.76	6.22	4.86	6.51	8.69
Military and government	0.53	0.54	0.58	0.88	0.81	1.02	1.39
Quasi-professionals	1.69	2.50	2.78	2.88	2.67	3.74	5.33
Salespeople	0.10	0.12	0.21	0.20	0.24	2.45	2.68
Farm proprietors	*44.65*	*59.58****	*44.20****	*39.43****	*44.34****	*37.22****	*19.20****
Laborers	*30.81*	*19.78****	*31.52****	*36.96****	*36.43*	*36.60*	*42.79****
Agricultural laborers	5.45	4.85	12.57	25.10	22.54	20.22	11.29
Manufacturing and construction laborers	7.81	5.48	5.07	4.00	4.48	7.92	10.79
Service laborers	17.55	9.45	13.88	7.86	9.41	8.46	20.71
Other	0.29	0.23	0.07	0.09	0.10	0.59	0.79
Total sample size	47,621	4,285	5,720	7,025	8,320	13,049	230,883

Source: Integrated Public Use Microdata Series, 1 percent samples.

**p < .01. ***p < .001 (two-tailed tests of difference in proportion, comparison for italicized entries to column to the left).

Table 4.4. Size of Occupational Groups as Percentage of Black and Mulatto Adult Labor Force, United States 1860–1900

	Rest of United States 1860 (Free)[a]	Lower South 1860 (Free)[a]	Lower South 1860 (All)[a]	Lower South 1870[a]	Lower South 1880	Lower South 1900	Rest of United States 1900
Entrepreneurial middle class	*5.90*	*27.17****	*(10.81)****	*1.57****	*1.51*	*1.94***	*3.34****
Artisans and manufacturing proprietors	5.09	20.11	10.69	1.44	1.36	1.51	2.28
Independent professionals	0.07	0.54	0.01	0.01	0.02	0.02	0.10
Service proprietors	0.37	2.72	0.05	0.02	0.04	0.20	0.57
Storekeepers and wholesalers	0.37	3.80	0.06	0.10	0.09	0.21	0.39
Bureaucratic middle class	*4.22*	*4.35*	*0.07****	*1.15****	*1.66****	*3.82****	*7.46****
Clerks and white-collar employees	0.17	1.09	0.02	0.65	0.54	1.72	2.95
Military and government	0.07	0.00	0.00	0.10	0.08	0.09	0.84
Quasi-professionals	3.91	3.26	0.06	0.39	1.04	1.93	3.54
Salespeople	0.07	0.00	0.00	0.01	0.00	0.08	0.13
Farm proprietors	*6.94*	*10.33*	*0.18****	*11.46****	*19.79****	*27.47****	*15.58****
Laborers	*82.33*	*57.61****	*88.93****	*85.80****	*76.98****	*66.42****	*73.38****
Agricultural laborers	14.96	5.98	60.30	64.55	43.18	38.30	21.20
Manufacturing laborers	4.21	16.85	5.93	1.88	1.84	3.05	4.80
Service laborers	63.16	34.78	22.70	19.37	31.96	25.07	47.38
Other	*0.61*	*0.54*	*0.01*	*0.02*	*0.05*	*0.35*	*0.25*
Total sample size	*2,967*	*184*	*10,819[a]*	*17,640*	*11,767*	*16,870*	*18,891*

Source: Integrated Public Use Microdata Series, 1 percent samples.

[a] Based on oversample of free blacks in 1860 and blacks in 1870. Occupational distribution for all blacks in 1860 uses Olson's (1992) probate sample.

** $p < .01$. *** $p < .001$ (two-tailed tests of difference in proportion, comparison for italicized entries to column to the left).

in the Lower South (27 percent of the free black labor force) was significantly larger than that found in the rest of the United States (around 6 percent). Adding information on slave occupations from plantation records, the percentage of all Southern blacks involved in artisanal activity (e.g., blacksmiths, mechanics) in 1860 hovered around 11 percent.[44]

Following the Civil War, the percentage of blacks involved in artisanal activity declined substantially, and there was little change in the percentage of independent professionals, service proprietors, and storekeepers. Even by the turn of the century, only 2 percent of the Southern black labor force could be classified as members of the entrepreneurial middle class, while slightly more (over 3 percent) of the black labor force in the rest of the United States could be placed in this category. If blacks represented the bellwether of an emerging entrepreneurial class in the New South, then the relative prevalence of this class must clearly be questioned when enumerated on an occupational basis. Entrepreneurial opportunities for blacks in the late nineteenth and early twentieth centuries were limited, tended to be associated with high rates of business failure, and offered few paths to upward mobility.[45]

From the standpoint of the historical literature, these demographic trends are puzzling. While scholars have discussed the rise of a "third estate" comprising the middle class in the New South, the numerical prevalence of that class can be substantiated only for white workers in white-collar occupations. With growth and bureaucratization, large enterprise—including railroads, insurance companies, and manufacturing firms—employed an expanding army of clerks and managers in the South, as they did in other parts of the United States. The era of Radical Reconstruction also induced a boom in the presence of military personnel and officials. Between 1860 and 1900, the ranks of these middling occupations within large organizations nearly doubled, from 8 to 13.5 percent of the white adult labor force.[46] The postbellum expansion of the bureaucratic middle class was far more modest among blacks. Even in 1900, the percentage of Southern blacks employed in white-collar occupations was smaller than the percentage of free blacks who were so engaged in 1860 (in the South or, for that matter, the rest of the nation).

Meanwhile, the middling entrepreneur—envisioned by Mark Twain and others as the archetype unleashed by the unfettered capitalism of the Gilded Age—was in decline, falling from 16 to 12 percent of the Southern white labor force over the same period. Inspection of occupational titles in the antebellum census records suggests that a small number of these entrepreneurs had been tied directly to the plantation economy, either as slave traders or as cotton factors and brokers operating as intermediaries for the planter class.[47] But the scale of decline was too large and too widespread to be explained by the disappearance of these individuals alone. The erosion of the middling entrepreneurs must therefore be traced back to broader capitalist transformations, rather than the immediate effects of slave emancipation.

Institutional Conditions and the Entrepreneurial Middle Class

In the nineteenth-century American South, the correlates of class membership suggest partial support for a structural theory of entrepreneurial middle-class expansion and partial support for a Marxist theory of decline. Figure 4.2 displays odds ratios predicting whether a labor force participant could be classified as a member of the entrepreneurial middle class, based on individual characteristics, capitalist infrastructure in a given county of

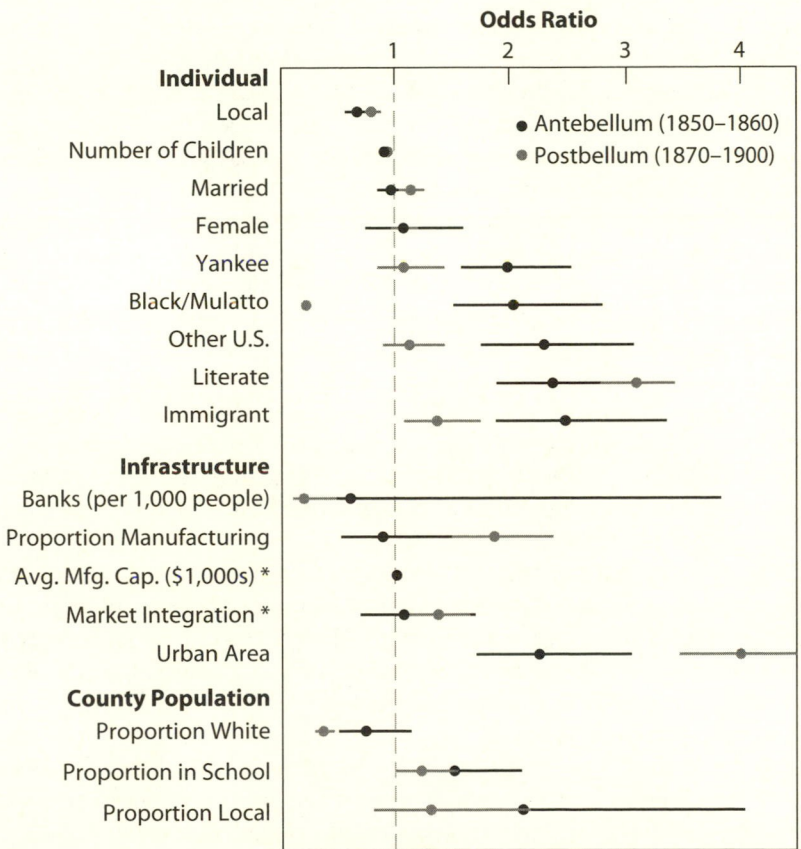

Figure 4.2. Odds Ratios from Model Predicting Membership in Entrepreneurial Class, U.S. Lower South (1850–1900). © 2011, Elsevier.

Notes: 90 percent confidence intervals are shown as black (antebellum) and gray (postbellum) lines. All models include controls for age, age squared, year, and state of residency. Estimates for manufacturing scale and market integration do not include data for 1850.

residence, and demographic features of the population in that county.[48] Consistent with Stinchcombe's structural theory, urbanization was a clear predictor of the size of the entrepreneurial middle class in a region, though the magnitude of this association was different in the antebellum and postbellum eras. Before the Civil War, the prevalence of the entrepreneurial class in towns with twenty-five hundred or more inhabitants was twice that of rural areas, while after the Civil War it spiked to a ratio of four times that of rural areas. These findings support the contention by some historians that the urban centers of the Old South were weak incubators for small proprietors. Don Doyle, for instance, notes that plantation agriculture in the Old South relied only on a few entrepôts for shipping cotton, rice, tobacco, and sugar. In this economic system, urban services were concentrated in the hands of factors, middle-man merchants and wholesalers who inhibited—rather than propelled—the development of towns and cities.[49] In the New South, more diversified entrepreneurial activity thrived in urban centers, a trend that continues to this day in metropolitan areas such as North Carolina's Research Triangle and Atlanta.

In further support of a structural theory of entrepreneurial class expansion, literacy increased the likelihood of membership in the class by a factor of two before the Civil War (and slightly more afterward). The ability to read and write in some language was a persistent requirement for small business proprietorship. Structurally, this would seem to have been a propitious development for the entrepreneurial class in the New South, as school reform was soon matched by improvements in educational expenditures and literacy. As discussed in Chapter 3, the possibility of educational uplift into a middle class was embraced by black leaders, in particular, whether as a means of expanding the ranks of skilled artisans and small proprietors or developing the "talented tenth" of college-educated freedmen.[50]

The remaining infrastructural variables suggest that the evidence for other aspects of the structural and Marxist theories of entrepreneurial class development is mixed. Dovetailing with Marx's concern about the pernicious effects of banks on the lower middle class, the data reveal that local banking infrastructure did not encourage entrepreneurial propensities during the antebellum period and was actually detrimental to middling entrepreneurship following the Civil War. In the antebellum era, cotton planters and their intermediaries were at the center of an elaborate financial network, linking banks, wholesalers, importers, and manufacturers. With the collapse of this system in the 1860s, the South faced severe shortages of credit and currency, though these were soon addressed by the boom in private banking and expansion of credit markets (see Chapter 1). For middling entrepreneurs, a specific problem nevertheless arose due to the altered character of banking following Civil War interventions. As Richard Sylla has documented, the creation of a national banking system tended to "restrict loan output in local markets" and encouraged the movement of bank funds to "lumpy investments in railroads and large-scale industry." These historical developments correspond broadly to the "centralization" of capital that Marx anticipated.[51]

The Marxist argument fares less well in its other predictions. The average scale of manufacturing enterprise in Southern counties did not have a negative relationship with the prevalence of an entrepreneurial middle class, nor the fate of artisans in particular. Indeed, one might argue that many of the typical middling businesses of the late nineteenth-century South could coexist comfortably alongside the largest manufacturing enterprises of the day, such as textile mills, iron works, and tobacco factories. Industrialization, assessed as the proportion of county economic output that was produced by manufacturing as opposed to agricultural enterprise, had no significant relationship with middling entrepreneurship in the antebellum period and, following the Civil War, seemed to encourage the expansion of this class. The integration of credit markets was also correlated with the presence of an entrepreneurial middle class in the postbellum era. For instance, the estimates shown in Figure 4.2 suggest that a county where all businesses were rated by a mercantile agency for purposes of long-distance trade with Eastern wholesalers (e.g., in New York, Boston, Baltimore, etc.) had a 36 percent higher incidence rate of middling entrepreneurs than a county where none of the businesses had such credit ratings.[52]

Some of the most nuanced transformations in the antebellum-postbellum transition involve the implications of political upheaval and the formation of a free labor market for the demographic characteristics of the entrepreneurial middle class. As suggested previously, the end of slavery did not invariably lead to entrepreneurial opportunities for African Americans in the Lower South. During the antebellum period, respondents who identified as free blacks or mulattos in this region were *twice* as likely to be members of the entrepreneurial class than their white counterparts. After the Civil War, African Americans in the South were *one-fifth* as likely to be members of the entrepreneurial class. To a considerable extent, this difference may be attributable to the pernicious effects of discrimination and Jim Crow in the post-Reconstruction period, which limited the white clientele whom black entrepreneurs were able to cater to, as well as their access to physical sites of business and financial capital. As Nicole Etcheson has discussed, "Southern whites did not just want blacks to labor; they wanted blacks to labor for *them*, not become independent proprietors. Whites stifled attempts at independent economic activity by means of laws and petty fines designed to cripple entrepreneurship."[53] Institutional constraints aside, free blacks in the antebellum era often possessed business skills, social networks, and other resources that blacks emancipated after the Civil War lacked, following a lifetime of slavery.

Political upheaval during Reconstruction and beyond also served to dampen the prospects of entrepreneurs from other regions in the Lower South. The influx of immigrants, Yankees, and other nonregional natives had served as a regular conduit of entrepreneurial ventures during the antebellum era, with individuals originating from these areas being two (or more) times as likely to be members of the entrepreneurial class as regional natives.[54] Individuals in the Lower South who continued to reside in the state of their birth ("locals") were especially unlikely entrepreneurs, perhaps owing to a lack of exposure to new business ideas or the experience and social networks needed to fulfill them. In regions such as the nineteenth-century South, which are handicapped by a tradition of extractive industry and export agriculture, migrating merchants, manufacturing proprietors, artisans, and other small entrepreneurs were potent importers of new organizing routines and resources.[55]

Following the Civil War, geographic mobility offered fewer advantages toward membership in the entrepreneurial class. As the historian Ted Tunnell has noted, some Southerners had viewed prototypical Yankees, especially those from New England, "through clouds of prejudice" before the Civil War—the Northerner migrants were seen as "small-minded, acquisitive creatures ... lacking the manly virtues of southern planters."[56] But it was the defeat of the Civil War that truly stoked the fires of resentment. Editors for Southern Democratic press popularized the epithet "carpetbagger" at the start of Radical Reconstruction to denigrate outsiders who were thought to be seeking political or economic opportunity in a prostrate land. Despite popular claims to the contrary, the carpetbaggers who came South were overwhelmingly of middle-class origin, establishing small enterprises rather than outposts for Northern investors. Moreover, in an institutional context where Southern whites had become resistant to the economic encroachment of outsiders, migrants from other parts of the United States no longer evidenced significantly higher rates of entrepreneurial activity than regional natives.

The postbellum incidence of middling entrepreneurship was also attenuated among immigrants and other ethnic minorities. In Southern cities such as Charleston and Mobile, Jewish, German, and Irish immigrants had been active in developing entrepreneurial ethnic enclaves during first half of the nineteenth century. Between 1800 and the 1820s, the Jewish population of Charleston outnumbered that of New York City and was especially prominent in mercantile pursuits.[57] In the aftermath of the Civil War, even progressive Southerners revealed considerable xenophobia against such "foreign" elements. Henry Grady, the editor at the *Atlanta Constitution* during the 1880s, put the prejudice succinctly in his famous New South speech, when he argued that "one northern immigrant is worth fifty foreigners" in the pursuit of Southern economic development.[58]

Institutional theorists remind us that myth and ceremony are as important to organizing processes as functional requirements or objective resource constraints.[59] Much the same could be said for the fate of social classes. Even in the face of declining prevalence, there is considerable qualitative evidence to suggest the emergence of a self-conscious and self-interested entrepreneurial middle class after the Civil War. By the 1880s, members of the middle class were playing a prominent role in local and state government, especially in thriving centers such as Atlanta and Nashville. Associations of middling business owners proliferated. Participation in chambers of commerce and boards of trade provided an important organizational basis for the solidarity of the entrepreneurial class. Simultaneously, the idea of a postbellum black middle class was promoted by an educational reform movement directed at African Americans in the cities of the New South.[60]

In the closing decades of the nineteenth century, newspaper boosters were also vocal in spreading the gospel of a New South that was built with the sweat of urban entrepreneurs and values of the middle class.[61] Although Henry Grady was perhaps the most well known of these proponents, his ministry was soon carried forth by other journalists, as well as Southern politicians such as Joseph E. Brown and Benjamin Hill. Along with a myriad of young Southern progressives, these postbellum writers and politicians helped create the New South Creed, an ideology of racial harmony and economic progress rooted in the leadership of a petite bourgeoisie. Despite the rise of Jim Crow and the meager numbers of middling entrepreneurs in the South, the creed was widely accepted as fact by 1900, sustaining the appearance of the entrepreneurial middle class as a then dominant feature of Southern society.[62]

The Planters and Yeoman Farmers

If the South's middle-class proprietors and artisans were in decline during the postbellum era, what was the fate of planters and yeoman farmers in the New South? The deterioration of the planter aristocracy was taken as a matter of course in early historical treatments of the aftermath of the Civil War. In his influential text on the *Origins of the New South*, C. Vann Woodward recognized that there were a "few survivors of the old planter class" who were able to prosper within the new order. For the most part, however, even the leadership of the region's conservative political factions, such as the Redeemers, "were of middle-class, industrial, capitalistic outlook, with little but a nominal connection to the old planter regime." Woodward went on to argue, more boldly, that "no ruling class of our history ever found itself so completely stripped of its economic foundations as did [the old planter class] of the South in this period."[63]

The thesis of decline among the South's planter elite is attractive because it accords with the narrative promulgated by Henry Grady and other Southern boosters, arguing that the emerging protocapitalist institutions of the region would readily push aside the class that had relied so heavily on chattel slavery and that was unable—or unwilling—to adapt to the changed circumstances of the New South. But, viewed in conjunction with recently available census data, the thesis raises thorny questions. If the middling proprietors of small workshops and manufactories were themselves in decline, who was responsible for the region's rapid postwar industrialization?

The sociologist Dwight Billings has argued persuasively that the industrial origins of the New South lay not in the middle class, but among the planters. Studying the ownership of North Carolina textile mills between 1865 and 1884, Billings found that over half of the manufacturing proprietors were either bona fide members of the planter class or "prominent agrarians." A previous generation of historians, such as Eugene Genovese, had argued that the class structure of the antebellum South positioned the slaveholding planter class in opposition to industrialization. This conflict is not apparent after the Civil War. Biographies of influential planters reveal men who were "conservative in [their] attitude toward social change but progressive in terms of whatever had to do with improving the material accommodation of life," including the development of "canals, railroads, forests, building, and industrial processes."[64] Postbellum planters thus began to constitute an investor class, with interests in manufacturing, banking, or transportation. While the typical farm proprietor was unlikely to pursue business opportunities outside the domain of agriculture (see Figure 4.1), the planter elite was central to the new logic of Southern industrialization.[65]

A second challenge to the thesis of planter disruption involves the evidence on wealth and landholding in the census records. If the economic foundation of the planter aristocracy was indeed shaken irrevocably by the demise of chattel slavery, then we would expect a dramatic shift in the top echelons of the South's wealth distribution in the years following the Civil War. This shift would entail both a transformation in the class origins of wealth holders, from planters to merchants and professionals, and a transformation in the nativity of the elite, from individuals born in the South to those born in other parts of the country. The evidence on geographic origins weighs in favor of a weak pattern of disruption. Considering nativity in a systematic sample of white adults in the Lower South in 1860, one finds that 84 percent of the individuals among the top one percent of wealth holders were born in the eleven Southern states that would come to compose the Confederacy. While there is a slight drop in the proportion of these Southern natives by 1870, to 72 percent among top wealth holders, the statistical significance of the change is modest.[66] Even during Radical Reconstruction, there is little indication that Yankee carpetbaggers migrating from the Northeast had come to dominate the pinnacle of the Southern wealth distribution.[67]

A more nuanced pattern can be seen in the occupational distribution of wealthy white males in the Lower South (Table 4.5). Before the Civil War, plantation proprietors represented over three-quarters of the Southern financial elite, with large holdings in real estate and slaves. By 1870, the proportion of planters had dropped to less than half of the elite (42 percent), with substantial losses in both land values and other wealth (particularly, the assets that had been invested in human property). Nevertheless, the trend toward the economic decline of the planters is more equivocal when two other features of the census data are considered. First, the postbellum elite includes a large group of rentiers (22 percent of the Southern aristocracy), composed of individuals with substantial landholdings who are not working and with limited access to liquid wealth. This agrees with the intuition that some of the former planters were transformed into a rentier class, owing to the disruption of the Civil War and the organizational transformation of Southern agriculture (toward farm tenancy and leasing).[68] Accounting for the rise of rentier capitalism, the planters and passive landholders continued to make up nearly two-thirds of the wealthiest Southerners in the years after the war.

Table 4.5. Occupational Composition of the Top One Percent of Wealth Holders, U.S. Lower South

Occupational Group	Percentage of Elite	Real Estate Holdings (median in dollars)[a]	Other Property (median in dollars)[a]
Antebellum period (1860)			
Planters	77	25,575	60,165
Rentiers[b]	9	25,000	52,300
Merchants	7	26,500	50,000
Professionals	4	24,000	60,000
Official or quasi-professional	2	—	—
Other	1	—	—
Postbellum period (1870)			
Planters	42	12,000	3,635
Rentiers[b]	22	13,000	1,000
Merchants	20	10,000	7,500
Professionals	8	11,000	2,755
Official or quasi-professional	6	13,310	3,500
Other	3	17,000	2,500

Note: Analysis limited to white population, age fifteen or older.

[a] Personal property includes value of slaves in 1860. Medians for wealth are not reported for occupational groups that have fewer than five observations.

[b] Individuals out of the labor force or with no known trade.

Another subtlety in the census data involves the nominal loss of wealth between 1860 and 1870. On the one hand, it is clear that the Civil War and emancipation wreaked havoc on the assets of the planter aristocracy, with the median value of landholdings divided in half and median value of other wealth falling by a devastating 94 percent. Yet it is also clear that equally dramatic losses were suffered by well-to-do merchants and professionals (see Table 4.5). When the relative wealth of these groups is considered, the postbellum fate of the planters does not seem nearly as dire. Examining patterns of landholding within five counties in the Alabama Cotton Belt, the historian Jonathan Wiener found that 43 percent of the planters with the greatest wealth in real estate continued to be found among this elite group in 1870. The rate of planter persistence compared favorably to that found in the antebellum period, when 47 percent of the wealthiest planters in the Alabama counties in 1850 remained among the elite in 1860.[69]

The statistics thus provide some support for John Hope Franklin's thesis of persistence in the postbellum status structure, in which "the most highly respected member of society . . . and indeed the most powerful in many ways, was still the planter." Of course, there were many regions of the South—particularly, the upper Piedmont and Mountain South—where the planter class was never a dominant presence. Even in the antebellum period, the upcountry areas were more likely to be the province of small farms, run by yeoman farmers with relatively few slaves.[70] Like the planters themselves, traditional perspectives have often positioned this class of farmers in opposition to capitalist development. Among the Southern Agrarians, a conservative faction of Southern writers active in the 1920s and 1930s, there was the romantic view that the nineteenth-century yeomanry composed a "great body of free men" who "had hardly anything to do with capitalists and their merchandise."[71] These white farm proprietors were the rural, self-sufficient producers whom Mark Twain portrayed in his description of Tennessee before the Civil War.

By most historical accounts, the precapitalist yeoman farmers of the Piedmont were challenged as much by modernization in the New South as the planters of the Cotton Belt. The economic and personal disruption posed by the Civil War alone was enough to push many from land ownership to tenancy. In the antebellum period, the slaveholding yeomen had held a considerable amount of their wealth in human property—around half of all assets for farmers who possessed as few as two slaves—as well as much of their productive labor force. Moreover, as Stephen West has argued, "The new relations of commerce and credit undermined older patterns of self-sufficiency and local exchange and went hand in hand with the growth of markets towns in the southern upcountry." As rural economies were integrated with national markets, both logistically and financially, the fate of the white yeoman seemed precarious.[72]

Despite the challenges posed by the new capitalist order of the South, the yeoman farmers persisted through Radical Reconstruction, much as their planter counterparts in the low country and Cotton Belt. In 1860, farm proprietors constituted 44.2 percent of the white adult labor force in the Deep South. Following a mild contraction during the immediate aftermath of the war, the farm proprietors again stood at 44.3 percent of the labor force in 1880.[73]

In contrast to the planter class, the numerical persistence of the yeomanry came at considerable cost. Part of the cost was evident in their financial assets, as white farmers found themselves sliding downward in the wealth hierarchy, particularly relative to the middling entrepreneurs of the South's growing urban centers. The postwar crop lien system, accompanied with a singular rush toward cotton cultivation, exacerbated these financial woes, with small farmers obtaining agricultural supplies and personal necessities on credit, and then desperately hoping that cotton prices would allow them to retain some of their earnings.[74]

The more subtle cost to the South's yeoman farmers was cultural. Insofar as the future of the New South was associated with commercial and industrial development, the rural middling farmer was increasingly characterized as a reactionary impediment to capitalist modernization. The populist agrarian insurgencies of the 1880s and 1890s did not help matters, cementing a perspective in the eyes of Southern townsfolk that the rural white farmer was anxious about his postwar status and hostile to the new economic order of the region. In contrast to the virtues ascribed to the antebellum yeomanry—integrity, independence, self-respect, and the like—the labels that accompanied the rural white farmer by the closing decade of the nineteenth century were far less favorable—poor, uncouth, "white trash," and, perhaps most derisively, "redneck."[75]

SUMMARY

In many respects, the institutional transformation of the American South after the Civil War seemed to offer fertile conditions for an entrepreneurial class that would displace the South's antebellum planter elite and yeoman farmers. The demise of chattel slavery and its substitution by a (nominal) free labor market was conducive to the rise of petite bourgeois elements among both black and white Southerners. The spread of public education during Reconstruction advanced the literacy and numeracy required for small business proprietorship. Increasing geographic mobility exposed Southerners to new business ideas, commercial values, and consumption needs. Meanwhile, the political upheaval of the Reconstruction era threatened the old status quo of the planter aristocracy and yeomanry.

Despite the promise of the New South, it remained largely unfulfilled with respect to the prevalence of the entrepreneurial middle class. The proportion of artisans, small manufacturing proprietors, independent professionals, and storekeepers declined, rather than increased, between 1860 and 1900. Suffering from discrimination, segregation, and a lack of adequate resources and business skills, few emancipated blacks were able to engage in business proprietorship. Local resentment of Northern and other nonregional business interests limited the entrepreneurial activities of these migrants compared to the antebellum era. Southern entrepreneurs also failed to constitute a cohesive political coalition that could take advantage of the turmoil following the Civil War and expand the commercial membership of the class. Some elements of the petite bourgeoisie aligned themselves with the remnants of the planter elite, forming the Redeemers, a faction of conservative Democrats. Others, known pejoratively as Scalawags, joined an opposing coalition of freedmen and Northern entrepreneurs.

Meanwhile, the old classes of the planter elite and yeoman farmers persisted to a remarkable extent during Radical Reconstruction. A number of planters remained at the top of the wealth hierarchy and took an active interest in the South's gradual turn away from an agrarian economy. The "plain folk" who had populated rural white society in the antebellum era continued to represent a large fraction of the labor force.[76] Paradoxically, this persistence was accompanied with growing status anxiety among the agrarian classes and, perhaps less paradoxically, growing derision from the middle-class inhabitants of the South's urban centers.

These dynamics in the class structure of the South suggest another potent source of uncertainty. In newspaper accounts and booster rhetoric, the promoters of the New South insistently proclaimed that whites and blacks would enjoy the prospect of becoming members in an expanding category of middle-class entrepreneurs, especially as the old class categories of yeoman farmers and the planter elite faded into the background. Even among Northern migrants and foreigners, who were disparaged as carpetbaggers, the New South Creed suggested a growing set of opportunities for middle-class advancement. This narrative, which persisted well into the twentieth century, was decoupled from the reality of the class structure of the postbellum South. In the decades after the Civil War, entry into the entrepreneurial middle class represented an attractive yet elusive goal for white and black Southerners.

CHAPTER 5

The Demise of the Plantation

The great problem of cotton culture just now is the growing scarcity and worthlessness of our laborers. I am a Northern man, an ex-federal officer—have paid wages and treated my hands with the utmost kindness for the last three years, but find a growing dislike [among freedpeople] to being controlled by or working for white men.

—Planter in Montgomery County, Texas

[My former master was] so mean he never would sell the man and woman and chil[dren] to the same one. He'd sell the man here and the woman there and if they's chil[dren], he'd sell them some place else. . . . I stays with Miss Olivia till '63 when Mr. Will set us all free. I was 'bout 17 year[s] old then or more. I [was] going [to] find my mama.

—Former slave born on a farm near St. Louis, Missouri[1]

In the late 1860s, a firm of Boston brokers conducted an extensive survey of economic conditions affecting the production of cotton. Based on circulars received from correspondents in every state of the former Confederacy, the company of Loring and Atkinson sought to pinpoint the challenges and opportunities that planters faced in the post–Civil War South.[2] In their report, an adverse impact of emancipation itself on crop production was quickly dismissed, for "slavery was an economic mistake" and former slaveholders "would not have slavery again if [they] could."[3] Other problems, such as the crop failure of the 1867–68 growing season, were treated as idiosyncratic and unlikely to be repeated again. Among needed improvements for Southern cotton cultivation, Loring and Atkinson briefly touched on the desire for better fertilizers and technology, investments in the education of young freedmen and women, and the possibility of relying on immigrant labor, primarily from Europe and China.[4]

According to the report, the greatest source of uncertainty for the plantation economy lay in African American labor and, particularly, the tenuous connection established by the Freedmen's Bureau between contracted wage workers and large-scale agricultural enterprise. A correspondent from DeKalb County, Georgia, lamented the "scramble for labor" that he observed, which encouraged some employers to "persuade negroes to break their contracts," whereby "the moral force of contracts is weakened, and labor thus becomes uncertain." Many Southern planters were baffled by the propensity of freedmen to leave former masters and plantations, with white commentators often resorting to prejudicial views of economic irrationality on the part of emancipated slaves. A Mississippi planter claimed that blacks were "a wonder-seeking, credulous, improvident people, sometimes leaving neighborhoods *en masse*, deserting comfortable homes for something better." Another planter from Texas declared that black workers "love change, and a month's work at a place," while "white people love home . . . as the spot from which issue all their money and comforts."[5]

As economic sociologists have often emphasized, contracts are a relatively weak device for regulating exchange relationships, in the absence of interpersonal trust and other noncontractual bases of social order.[6] While the contractual templates monitored by the agents of the Freedmen's Bureau sought to resolve one form of uncertainty—*how* workers were to be paid after the Civil War—they could not resolve others, such as *whom* those workers would choose as their employers and *what* forms of labor and social organization they would gravitate toward. A planter from Jefferson County, Arkansas, summarized his view of the problem succinctly: "It is not the price of the labor, but the uncertainty of it that makes it so objectionable."[7]

In this chapter, I consider how uncertainty among planters and former slaves contributed to the demise of the Southern plantation, once the cornerstone of large-scale agricultural production in the United States. My argument suggests that there is limited support for exogenous explanations of plantation demise, which emphasize damage from the Civil War or pressures from population growth. Organizational dynamics, especially challenges from alternative forms of labor organization and interdependencies with midsize farms, played a more pivotal role. The most crucial influence involved the decisions made by emancipated slaves in the plantation system with respect to their incentive structures and the reconstruction of their familial networks. My findings thus lead to a perspective on plantation decline that brings former bondsmen and women back in as agents of grassroots insurgence and change.[8]

THE PLANTATION AS AN ORGANIZATIONAL FORM

Using a broad organizational definition, the term "plantation" refers to any large agricultural unit (five hundred acres or more) that is oriented toward the production of a commodity crop, owner-operated (rather than rented or tenant farmed), and heavily reliant on hired or enslaved labor.[9] In the American South, the plantation form had emerged by the early eighteenth century as "the basic unit of capitalist agriculture." It achieved its peak in 1860, when roughly one-third of all Southern cropland was concentrated in large agricultural estates. Nevertheless, just one decade later, informed observers predicted that "a time may come . . . when the cotton plant, instead of being grown in great continuous fields, a hundred or more acres together, will be cultivated as in a garden."[10] By 1880, the plantation system had practically ceased to exist, with less than 1 percent of farms and only 8 percent of cropland in the Cotton South being operated under this model. Although census enumerators and social scientists would continue to use the term "plantation" well into the twentieth century, this nomenclature came to denote decentralized, sharecropped, and tenant-farmed enterprises that were fundamentally different from the centralized plantation form of the nineteenth century.[11]

On initial inspection, the disappearance of the plantation form in Southern agriculture appears to have a straightforward explanation: namely, that it was a natural consequence of exogenous factors such as the U.S. Civil War and the emancipation of four million slaves. Closer scrutiny reveals that the plantation system initially staved off these threats and was successfully undermined only by mobilization among former slaves who sought to reunite families or find alternative job opportunities, as well as competition from alternative forms of agricultural tenure.[12] An analysis of the internal and organizational demography of the plantation system is thus crucial to understanding its disruption and provides a window on social processes that may threaten organizational forms more generally.

Explanations for the Demise of Organizational Forms

One basic explanation for the demise of organizational forms is that exogenous institutional conditions (such as regulatory reforms or normative changes imposed by outside agents) drive the disappearance of certain templates for organizing human activity. Understandings of the decline of American plantation agriculture frequently invoke this narrative, with the Thirteenth Amendment to the U.S. Constitution serving as the pivotal event for the elimination of this peculiar institution. Since the late eighteenth century, Southern plantations had come to rely heavily on forced labor, and consequently emancipation appeared to pose severe threats to the system of large-scale agriculture. Regional statistics suggest broad consistency with this argument: in 1860, the average, owner-operated farm in the U.S. South and border states comprised well over three hundred acres, an outlier compared to both the densely populated Northeast and sparsely populated West (see Figure 5.1). By 1880, the scale of Southern farms had

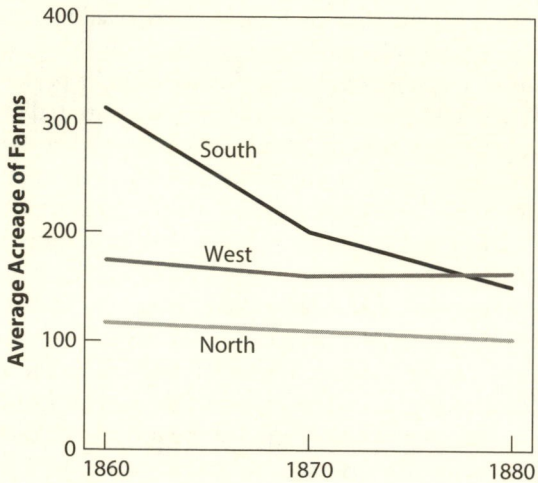

Figure 5.1. Change in Average Farm Acreage by U.S. Region, 1860–80. © 2004, The University of Chicago Press.

Notes: The South and Border region includes Alabama, Arkansas, Delaware, District of Columbia, Florida, Georgia, Kansas, Kentucky, Louisiana, Maryland, Mississippi, Missouri, Nebraska, North Carolina, South Carolina, Tennessee, Texas, and Virginia. The West includes California, Dakota, Iowa, Minnesota, Nevada, New Mexico, Oregon, Utah, Washington, and Wisconsin. The North includes Connecticut, Illinois, Indiana, Maine, Massachusetts, Michigan, New Hampshire, New Jersey, New York, Ohio, Pennsylvania, Rhode Island, and Vermont.

fallen in line with the rest of the country, with most of the remaining variation accounted for by population density.[13] The emancipation of Southern blacks and the demise of the plantation appear to play a crucial role in this general pattern of institutional convergence.

Nevertheless, more detailed examination questions the direct connection between slave emancipation and the disappearance of plantation agriculture. As the economic geographer Charles Aiken has highlighted, "The Southern plantation was not destroyed by the fall of slavery, and slavery was not the critical element that defined the plantation."[14] The plantation form had become so firmly institutionalized by the mid-nineteenth century that most planters sought to reestablish the system on the basis of fixed wage payments between 1865 and 1866. Lacking familiarity with alternative forms of agricultural tenure, planters believed that they could "go right on like we always did," including the use of ex-slave work gangs.[15] Prima facie, the resulting *wage plantation* system could be readily adapted to free black labor. Out of economic necessity, many black laborers continued initially to work on plantations under wage agreements. Descriptions of antebellum and postbellum plantations emphasized similarities in their organizational structures, pointing to continuity in such practices as housing workers in old slave quarters, providing them with rations comparable to those received under slavery, and allocating quota rewards for crop production.[16] Parallels between the two organizational forms were encouraged by outside authorities, including the Freedmen's Bureau, despite underlying shifts in the salience of human capital and statistical discrimination in the postbellum labor market. Given the initial persistence of plantation agriculture in the years following the Civil War (and the mobilizing effort required of former slaves to challenge it), a direct causal link between formal emancipation and the demise of the plantation seems historically untenable.

An alternative exogenous explanation for the disappearance of the plantation system addresses the impact of material resource conditions that supported the organizational form. During the aftermath of the Civil War, the devastation imposed on human life, livestock, cropland, and farm implements appeared to pose a fundamental threat to traditional Southern agriculture.[17] Sherman's infamous March to the Sea and other Union incursions had left many Southern plantations in ruins. Between 1860 and 1870, the (former) slaveholding states suffered an aggregate decline of sixty-one million dollars in livestock and farm machinery values, a sum that would amount to billions today. During the same period, working animals—horses, asses, mules—declined by nearly one-third in the cotton states.[18] These immediate consequences from the war called the viability of large-scale agriculture into question, given the reliance of plantations on extensive tracts of arable land and, by historical standards, complex agricultural technology.

While this account seems plausible, an examination of geographic heterogeneity in plantation prevalence following the Civil War offers only modest support for the intuition that war damage impacted the persistence of the organizational form. Figure 5.2 plots the change in the number of plantations relative to all agricultural units between 1860 and 1870 at the county level. Medium-gray areas on the map denote relatively stable plantation counties—that is, those in which the density of plantations in 1870 (as a percentage of all farms) did not differ from the density of plantations in 1860 by more than ±0.5 percent. Black and light-gray areas denote decreased and increased prevalence, respectively. Some of the patterns of decline appear to follow those of major Union incursions in the South—such as the zones observed in the lower Mississippi River valley and in northern and central Virginia. In other cases, the pattern deviates considerably from Civil War campaigns. Upper Georgia evidences stable (and, in a few counties, even *increased*) plantation prevalence, despite the extensive Atlanta campaign.

The spatial variation suggests that an emphasis on short-term declines in carrying capacity—such as those affecting the cropland, farming machinery, and livestock on which the plantation system was constructed—should be complemented by attention to long-term contractions in the resource niche

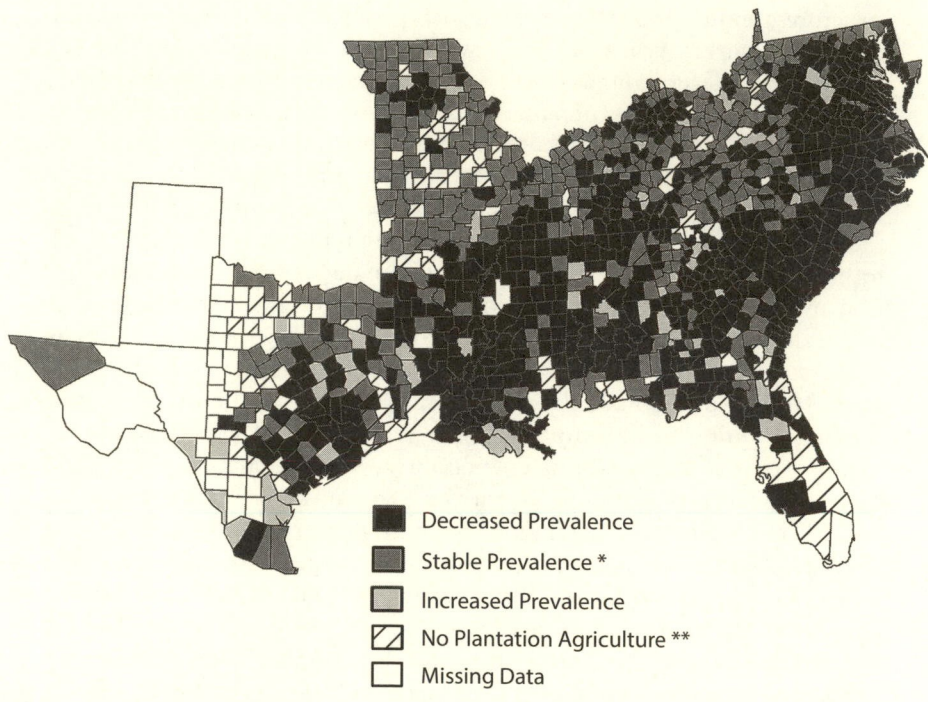

* Change in Prevalence No Greater Than ±0.5% of All Agricultural Units

** Counties without Plantations in 1860 and 1870

Figure 5.2. Change in Plantation Prevalence in the U.S. South, 1860–70. © 2004, The University of Chicago Press.

Notes: For stable prevalence*, change is no greater than ±0.5 percent of all agricultural units. No plantation agriculture** indicates counties without plantations in 1860 and 1870.

of the plantation. As the sociologist Edgar Thompson noted in his early scholarship on economic frontiers, a major long-term threat to the plantation involved human population growth. The Southern farm was uncharacteristically large by national standards, averaging 315 acres of improved cropland by 1860. Arguably, this model of Southern land tenure was incompatible with population growth, which favored a less expansive system of farming.[19] Some social historians have even suggested that the development of Southern urban centers, such as Charleston, was inhibited in the antebellum era by their dependence on the plantation economy.[20] Following the economic frontier thesis, the decline of large-scale agriculture might be traced to Southern urbanization that was postponed until after the Civil War, representing a contraction in the plantation's resource niche because of alternative land allocation.

Internal Demography and the Demise of the Plantation

In direct contrast to accounts that emphasize the "top-down" influence of exogenous changes in institutional arrangements or material resource conditions, micro-level analyses of the internal demography of organizational forms question how participants are likely to react to those external forces— for example, *what* would former slaves do with their newfound freedom? These "bottom-up" explanations allow a greater role for agency in the analysis of threats to organizational forms, encourage consideration of counterfactuals to observed historical patterns, and render uncertainty a central feature of the analysis.[21]

From a social movement perspective, a key element in the analysis of internal demography is the threshold, or tipping point, where a critical mass of participants decides to abandon an organizational form and seeks out alternative arrangements. Threshold phenomena apply when the costs and benefits of supporting the alternative arrangement vary depending on how many other participants make the same choice.[22] In the postbellum South, for instance, the defection of agricultural laborers from wage plantations in small numbers may have incurred relatively little individual cost, as alternative opportunities in nonagricultural employment were readily available. If moderate numbers of laborers left the wage plantations, individual mobilization costs could rise as the pool of nonagricultural workers became saturated and few alternative agricultural opportunities presented themselves (particularly, given the economic and social difficulties associated with land acquisition among free blacks). Following large numbers of defections from the plantation system, the mobilization cost could again fall, as plantation owners were forced to abandon the wage plantation altogether in favor of alternative forms of land tenure, such as sharecropping.

Four generic types of tipping-point outcomes can be illustrated using the empirical pattern observed for Southern blacks abandoning the plantation system as well as several hypothetical counterfactuals. In the observed pattern (Figure 5.3a), the plantation was gradually abandoned in favor of experiments with sharecropping and other forms of land tenure during the period of Radical Reconstruction.[23] This outcome can be contrasted with a counterfactual pattern (Figure 5.3b), where the plantation system is subject to rapid displacement, possibly due to revolt among ex-slaves (as some Southern whites feared) or federal reparations encouraging proprietor farming (the "forty acres and a mule" solution hoped for by many emancipated Southern blacks). Alternatively, it is equally plausible that the wage plantation system would have survived emancipation (Figure 5.3c), if exodus from the plantations failed to achieve the critical mass required to sustain alternative agricultural arrangements. Finally, institutional fragmentation

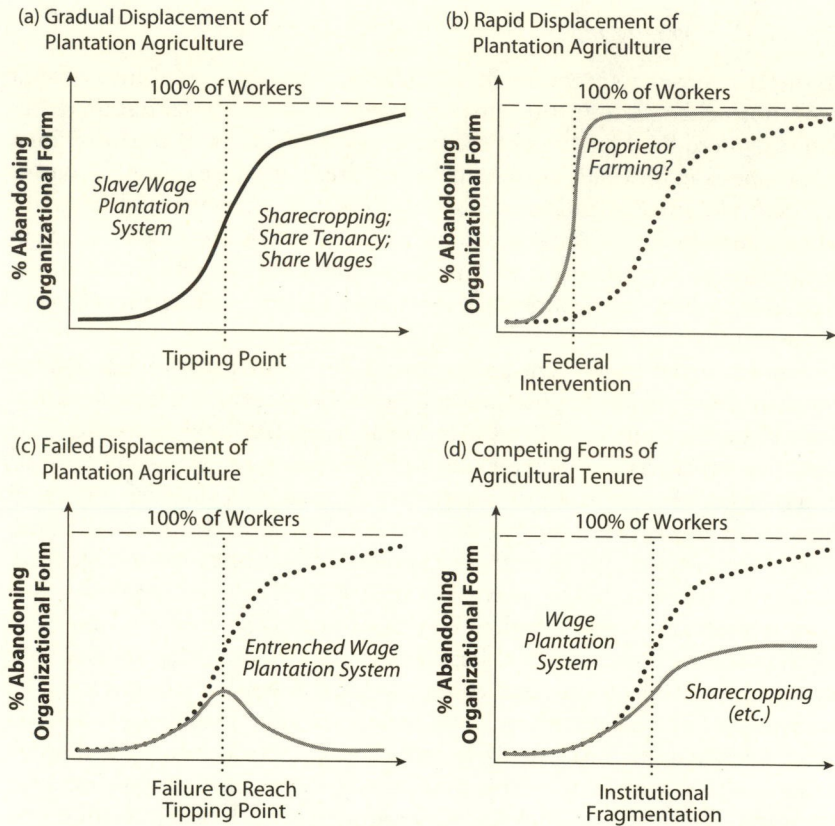

Figure 5.3. The Tipping Point in Internal Plantation Demography and Counterfactual Patterns: (a) Gradual Displacement of Plantation Agriculture, (b) Rapid Displacement of Plantation Agriculture, (c) Failed Displacement of Plantation Agriculture, (d) Competing Forms of Agricultural Tenure. © 2004, The University of Chicago Press.

(Figure 5.3d) could have occurred if the costs of abandoning the plantation system increased after sharecropping had achieved critical mass, leading to the sustained existence of both competing forms of land tenure.

Given these plausible counterfactual patterns, an examination of internal demography should address the mechanisms supporting one outcome (gradual displacement of the plantation form) rather than the others. Drawing from research on social movements, two mechanisms can help to account for this pattern of decline: one based on differential incentives among organizational participants, and the other based on the effects of social networks.

A well-established literature examines the mobilization costs and benefits that participants bear in undertaking insurgent action.[24] In the case of the wage plantation, the costs to free blacks for *not* abandoning the form can be identified readily. A common explanation for black emigration from large-scale agriculture was that white planters, used to relying on forced labor, failed to provide adequate reimbursement for retaining their workforce. As discussed in Chapter 2, labor contracts were routinely broken by white landowners, and other antimarket practices—such as collusion over wage payments—were common. Moreover, the postbellum plantation form suffered from what the organizational sociologists Michael Hannan and John Freeman have termed *structural inertia*, retaining many of the features of its antebellum counterpart. The gang system of labor was still widely used after emancipation and overseers were simply given new titles such as "supertender," "manager," or "agent."[25] Physical punishment of laborers, though less than that experienced under slavery, often persisted. More fundamentally, many freeman and freewomen associated the very idea of labor-intensive, large-scale agriculture with chattel slavery and sought to distance themselves from any organizational form exhibiting these features. Contemporary observers emphasized "the desire of the [black] laborer or freedman to be entirely independent of the white men."[26]

Still, the emancipated slave faced daunting obstacles in leaving the plantation. Some of these involved immediate constraints, such as antivagrancy laws limiting black migration. Of greater theoretical importance, from a social movement perspective, there was no alternative form of land tenure available to free blacks at the close of the Civil War. Tenant farming as an organizational form was virtually unknown in the antebellum period and land ownership remained elusive for the great majority of emancipated blacks.[27] Like many incidents of insurgent action, it can therefore be argued that the displacement of the plantation form required a critical mass of defectors.

Because employment opportunities for emancipated slaves differed by human capital and antebellum status, several classes of early defectors may be identified. Black artisans (e.g., blacksmiths, carpenters, masons) had enjoyed some advantages in the antebellum period—even competing successfully against white craftsmen—and continued to witness strong demands for their skills outside the plantation system. Other manual workers on plantations were desired in a variety of postbellum industrialization projects. Planters were particularly concerned about competition from railroads, which tended to draw laborers from large-scale agriculture. In their postbellum report on cotton production, Loring and Atkinson estimated "that hands representing 50,000 bales are working on railroads in [southwest] Georgia, beside which the large number of new railroads being built in other parts of the South, are constructed chiefly by black labor."[28]

The availability of such nonagricultural employment suggests that early exits from the plantation occurred primarily among artisans, manual laborers, and field laborers prepared to abandon agricultural work. Ex-slaves who had held other antebellum positions, such as domestics, were likely to venture cautiously into an uncertain labor market. The aggregate effect of this differential attrition among former slave classes is that the tipping point for the displacement of plantation agriculture would have been approached in the years following the Civil War but probably not reached (see Figure 5.4a). Even if the free labor market had been able to accommodate all of the skilled and semiskilled manual workers from the plantation system, this number would only have been about 16 percent of the total plantation workforce.[29] A more conservative figure would be based on the amount of manufacturing activity in the American South, which accounted for only 6.5 percent of total employment by the turn of the century. Considering internal demography alone, another mechanism is required to explain the displacement of plantation agriculture and appearance of alternative forms of land tenure.

A crucial element of success for new organizations or social movements is the presence of preexisting network ties connecting potential members to others within the organization and an absence of ties between those potential members and individuals or organizations posing conflicting commitments.[30] By the same token, individual organizations—and, more generally, organizational forms—are threatened when the balance of network ties connects their members more strongly to actors outside the boundaries of the organization than within. In this respect, an important, but underanalyzed, microstructural component of the demise of the Southern plantation

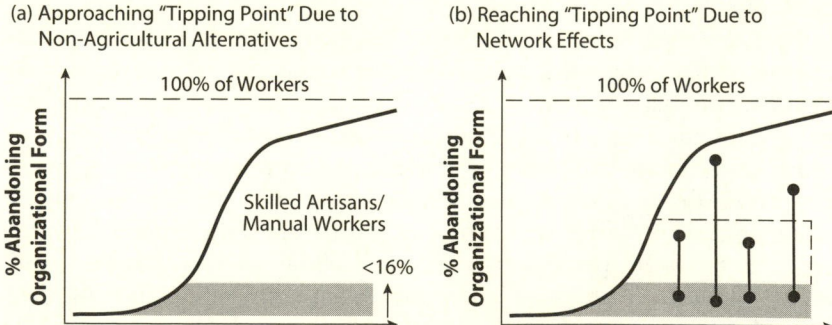

Figure 5.4. Social Movement Effects and the Tipping Point in Plantation Agriculture: (a) Approaching Tipping Point Due to Nonagricultural Alternatives, (b) Reaching Tipping Point Due to Network Effects. © 2004, The University of Chicago Press.

system is that it had originally been developed with very little regard for the familial networks of slaves. Large numbers of nuclear slave families were broken due to the sale of some family members by planters, as well as the migration of planters themselves. Some social historians speculate that "a central tension between slaves and their owners [may have] had its origins in the separation of work and kinship obligations." Although kin sometimes remained on nearby plantations after familial disruption, many slaves reported that close relatives were in distant or unknown locations.[31]

As former slaves left their plantations in the postbellum era to reconstruct familial networks, two possible outcomes may be anticipated. On the one hand, if network ties occurred exclusively between ex-slaves on different wage plantations, the aggregate effect would simply be migration (and temporary disruption) among plantations. On the other hand, if familial networks bridged an existing group of defectors (particularly, those who had already entered nonagricultural employment) with those remaining on wage plantations, then network effects could trigger further abandonment of the organizational form (Figure 5.4b). According to this structural explanation, the tipping point in the abandonment of plantation agriculture was reached due to the combination of a core group of defectors and the reconstruction of familial ties between those defectors and individuals who were slower to abandon the plantation system. Conversely, when plantation owners limited family disruption among their slaves, this social support may have posed a countervailing influence on decisions to leave the plantation.[32]

Organizational Demography and the Demise of the Plantation

An emphasis on the internal demography of organizational forms leaves a crucial question unanswered: why do forms disappear altogether, when they could continue to exist alongside new organizational arrangements? For the postbellum Southern economy, this translates into a question about institutional fragmentation, given the potential for an equilibrium involving both tenant farming and wage plantation forms (see Figure 5.3d). Using extensive information on individual costs and benefits, threshold models of internal demography may be able to identify when such institutional fragmentation can occur.[33] Analyzing whether the process leads to the competitive exclusion of one form or another, however, often requires information at a higher level of analysis, particularly the demography of other organizations.

Organizational theorists emphasize competition within a resource niche as a predominant factor influencing the viability of an organizational form. Although organizations in a population are subject to competitive pressures throughout their history, these pressures tend to grow geometrically with density in the population.[34] When do these ecological dynamics contribute to the demise of an organizational form? For the plantation in particular, older theories of ecological succession do not provide a satisfactory organizational explanation, since they relate the changing nature of land tenure to the population density of *individuals*. Edgar Thompson, for instance, traced the early predominance of large plantations growing cash crops, followed by the appearance of yeoman farmers and smaller, subsistence farms. He noted that in the advanced stages of plantation economies, large-scale agricultural holdings increasingly become carved up into tracts farmed by peasants or former bondsmen. Interestingly, this pattern of ecological succession affects plantations *despite* a number of competitive advantages that might be garnered from their large size, considering capital indivisibilities, division of labor, and market power.[35]

Explaining the phenomenon at an organizational level calls for attention to the major forms of agricultural tenure at the time of the Civil War, their respective niches, and the economies of scale accruing to each (see Table 5.1). Two considerations address why the plantation form was threatened by other agricultural producers, despite its apparent economies of scale. First, some historians have argued that economies of scale in Southern agriculture were curvilinear, accruing primarily to agricultural units of intermediate size (those employing between eight and twenty-five working hands) rather than plantations or small family farms. Diseconomies of scale tended to apply to the largest agricultural holdings, possibly owing to limits of administrative capacity on the part of plantation owner-managers.[36] By virtue of this argument, the postbellum plantation form could have been undermined by the growth of midsized agricultural producers in the South.

Second, if the competitive success of plantation agriculture was tied not only to its scale but also its level of crop diversity, then there is a clear

Table 5.1. Competitive Positioning among Agricultural Forms in the Postbellum Cotton South (1880)

Organizational Form	Crop Niche	Economies of Scale	Labor Organization	Mean Crop Diversity[a]	N
Small family farm (<100 acres)	Subsistence crops	–	Personal/family labor	0.407	7,493
Medium-size farm (100–499 acres)	Cash and subsistence crops	++	Hired wage labor	0.514	1,210
Wage plantation (500+ acres)	Cash crops	+	Hired wage labor	0.506	77
All cases					8,780

Source: Data are from Ransom and Sutch (1999).

[a] Crop diversity varies from 0 (for a monocropped farm) to 1 (for a farm that maximizes crop diversity), calculated using Shannon diversity index. Cases are weighted for sample representativeness. Analysis excludes small wage farms that have less than 100 acres in crops and improved land but employ more than twenty-six weeks of hired labor per year (*N* = 990), as well as large farms that have 500+ acres of crops or improved land, but are rented or tenant farmed (*N* = 13).

possibility that dediversification in the lean years following the Civil War may have led to a blurring of boundaries with other producers. Records on individual farms from the 1880 census suggest that the crop diversity of plantations and medium-sized farms was almost identical (Table 5.1). Farm operators identified acreage for cotton, corn, and up to four other crops (e.g., tobacco, rice, potatoes, etc.). As seen in the table, small family farms were only slightly more specialized in crop allocation, while the niche width of midsized farms and plantations was virtually equivalent.[37] Moreover, the land allocation of midsized farms and plantations in the Cotton South was almost identical following the Civil War, with 33 percent and 35 percent of arable land, respectively, being devoted to the cotton crop. From the perspective of agricultural production, this begs the question as to whether the postbellum wage plantation continued to represent a distinctive organizational form relative to its competitors during the postbellum era.

While distinctions in production outputs yield the most typical boundaries for organizational forms, economic sociologists have also identified labor organization as another dimension to be considered in describing competition between forms. From this perspective, the most salient threat to the wage plantation may not have involved midsized farms, which adopted a largely congruent model of hired gang-system labor, but a variety of smaller tenancy forms, ranging from sharecropping to farm ownership. As emphasized by economic historians, these arrangements represented radical alternatives to the plantation in the postbellum period because they could count on a reliable and price inelastic supply of family labor. In effect, "the [small] size of farms was largely determined by the acreage which the family could cultivate," while all larger agricultural enterprises had to invest extensively in the recruitment and monitoring of hired wage labor.[38]

The ecology of alternative forms of labor management was a crucial pull factor influencing the abandonment of the plantation among former slaves. In regions of the South where small plots of land became readily available for sharecropping or rental farming, the demise of the plantation form was likely to be hastened. This dynamic reflected the more general difficulty sustained by larger-than-family farms in retaining their wage labor force during the late nineteenth and early twentieth centuries. Regions experiencing growth in family farms were also likely to witness the emergence of economic institutions, such as country general stores and agricultural creditors, which supported small-scale tenancy. Conversely, the legitimacy of wage labor arrangements could be sustained when midsized producers in a region thrived. Not only did these producers rely on supervised wage labor, like the postbellum plantations, they also employed a similar external network of importers, wholesalers, and middlemen known as cotton factors. In contrast to a perspective that emphasizes crop production, an emphasis on labor organization thus holds that wage plantations and midsized farms could function as complementary organizational forms, while smaller farms represented a greater competitive threat.[39]

PLANTATION ECOLOGY

I conducted an analysis of farm ecology between 1860 and 1880 using both aggregated and disaggregated census data. The aggregated data derive from the reports on agriculture for the eighth, ninth, and tenth U.S. census, which provide the size and tenure distribution of agricultural establishments, the value of farm machinery and livestock, and the amount of "improved" (arable) cropland, all at the county level. These data are supplemented with information on human demography and manufacturing from other census reports.[40]

Because the aggregated data conceal heterogeneity in such organizational characteristics as labor requirements, crop diversity, and the sociodemographic background of owners, I also examined a systematic sample of farms from the 1880 manuscript census to develop a profile of the postbellum plantation in the final period of its existence. The sample includes 11 percent of all farms drawn from seventy-three representative counties throughout the South, comprising 11,202 farms in all.[41] I employ these data in aggregated form to track the demise of the plantation form between 1860 and 1880.[42]

I identified the number of plantations in each county as a key indicator of the viability of the plantation economy.[43] Considered relative to all farming establishments, the prevalence of plantations decreased on average by over 50 percent between 1860 and 1870, from 3.8 percent to 1.8 percent of agricultural units in former slaveholding counties (Table 5.2). Further decreases are evident in the following decade, with plantation prevalence dropping to an average of 1 percent of agricultural establishments in the Cotton South. The statistics also reveal considerable destruction of fixed capital assets between 1860 and 1870 (almost ninety-three thousand dollars per county, on average), population growth, and loss of arable land—all of which could pose ecological constraints on the persistence of plantation agriculture. Developments affecting the labor force of Southern plantations seemed more propitious, at least on the surface. Relatively few blacks emigrated from the South after the Civil War (net population growth of 172 per county, on average), although many relocated from rural to urban areas. Foreign immigration also provided a small "reserve army of labor," since planters sought immigrants as replacements for ex-slaves on the plantation system.[44]

Figure 5.5a presents factors predicting changes in the number of plantations in 1,090 Southern counties between 1860 and 1870.[45] Plantations were generally more likely to survive in counties where there was a growing free population. In conjunction with other evidence on the ecology of the

Table 5.2. County-Level Statistics for Plantation Agriculture and Related Ecological Measures

Variable	Mean/Proportion	Standard Deviation	Minimum	Maximum
Prevalence of plantation agriculture				
Ratio of plantations to all farms (1860)	0.038	0.065	0.000	0.558
Ratio of plantations to all farms (1870)	0.018	0.040	0.000	0.434
Ratio of plantations to all farms (1880)[a]	0.010	0.024	0.000	0.214
Environment (1860–70)				
Change in cropland (1,000s acres)	−38.424	105.716	−1,376.288	341.916
Change in free population (1,000s)[b]	4.934	11.064	−11.818	279.788
Change in fixed capital (livestock and farm machinery) ($1,000s)	−92.701	326.091	−2,184.398	1,470.679
Organizational density (1860)				
Farming establishments	634.442	401.044	1.000	2,365.000
Manufacturing establishments	26.783	64.160	0.000	1,232.000
Labor demography				
Black population (change in number of blacks, 1860–70) (1,000s)	0.172	2.464	−18.055	40.508
Foreign population (change in number, 1860–70) (1,000s)	0.102	2.014	−17.884	56.395

[a] Based on stratified sample of seventy-three Southern counties, weighted by region to represent the Cotton South.

[b] Excludes immigrant population.

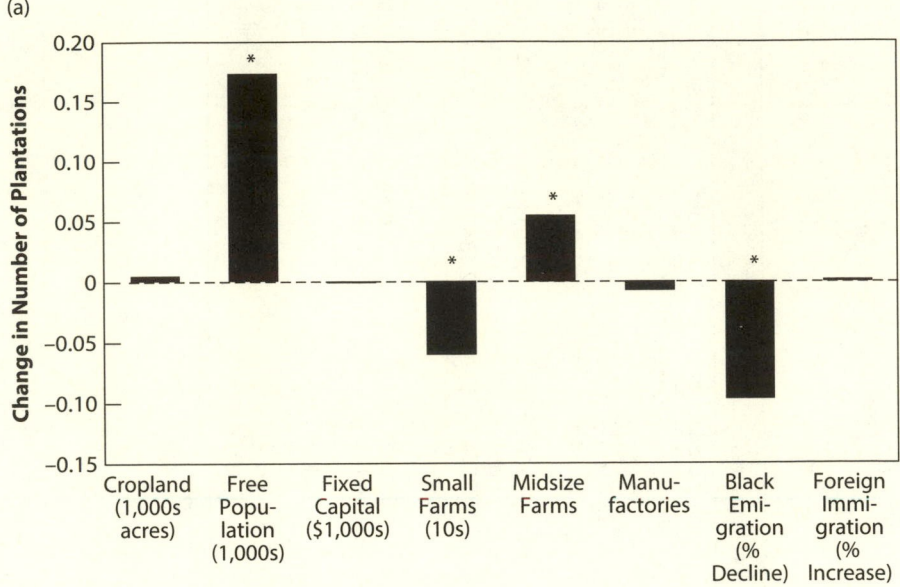

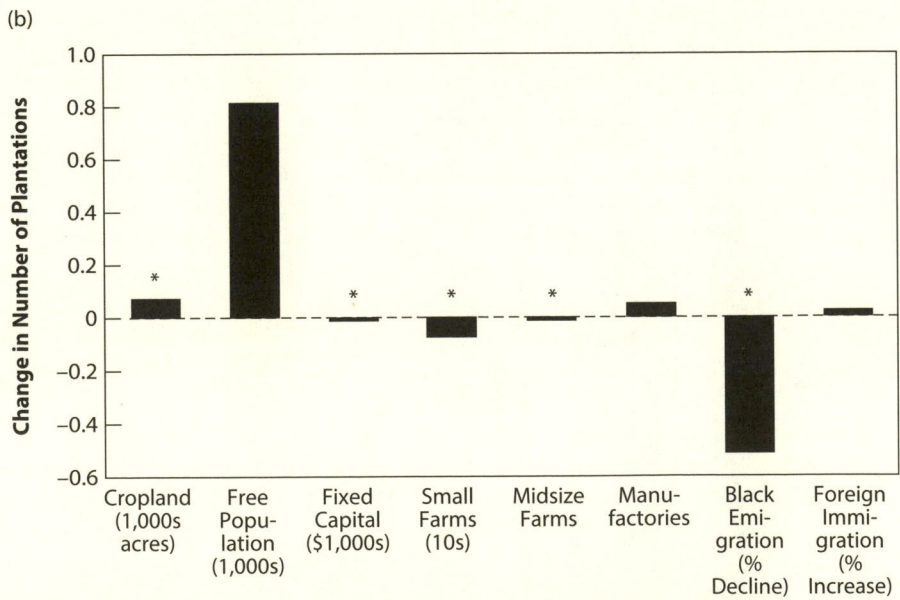

Figure 5.5. Factors Influencing the Number of Plantations in Southern Counties: (a) Effect in All Southern Counties, 1860–70, (b) Effect in Selected Southern Counties, 1860–80.
Note: *Statistically significant at $p < .05$ (one-tailed test).

plantation, this finding challenges the economic frontier hypothesis, which positions the organizational form predominately in underpopulated regions.[46] Instead, the positive correlation reflects the wage plantation's need for a relatively large agricultural and commercial labor force.

The county-level data also highlight two significant organizational dynamics. First, we can see that declines in the plantation form tended to be exacerbated when a county had a proliferation of smaller family-owned or sharecropped farms (less than one hundred acres in size). In particular, the estimates suggest that a county would lose one plantation for every 160 small agricultural enterprises that developed in the region. This process of "creative destruction" dovetails with the argument of labor historians, who emphasize the tendency of the wage plantation and small-acreage sharecropping or rental farming to constitute competing alternatives from the perspective of freed blacks at the end of the Civil War. Choice of alternative forms of agricultural tenure, in this respect, did not just draw labor away from larger agricultural units, but also led to labor unrest and pressure for the reorganization of the plantation form into smaller tenant plots.[47]

While the plantation form was threatened in regions with growing numbers of small producers, it persisted in regions experiencing growth in midsized farms (100–499 acres). From the standpoint of competition over crop output, this result seems surprising, given the scale advantages exhibited by midsized agricultural units and their substantial niche overlap with plantations. Nevertheless, the survival of the plantation form in the postbellum era was often driven far more by the problem of avoiding the delegitimation of a particular form of labor organization than success in the commodity markets for cotton and other cash crops. Ex-slaves in a region who saw substantial numbers of medium-sized farms relying on wage labor may have been more likely to accept this arrangement on the plantation as well, rather than considering the possibility of nonwage contracts.[48]

Destabilization of the plantation form was strongly associated with the emigration of black workers from a county, driven by movement from rural to urban areas in search of alternative employment, as well as hopes of reuniting with family members in other counties or states. For every 10 percent of a county's black population that migrated elsewhere, estimates suggest that one antebellum plantation would disappear by 1870. The presence of foreign immigrants did little to prevent plantation decline. Contemporary accounts from planters themselves underscored the unreliability (and small numbers) of Chinese, Swedish, German, Dutch, and Irish farm workers who were induced to work on Southern plantations during the postbellum era.[49]

Figure 5.5b presents corresponding statistics for the 1860 to 1880 period, using aggregated microcensus data from a more limited set of counties.[50] A number of similarities and differences between these estimates and those calculated for the 1860 to 1870 period are worth noting. First, the availability of cropland represented a carrying capacity constraint that had a slightly greater impact on plantation persistence over the long term than in the years immediately following the Civil War. Second, after 1870, the growth of midsized agricultural units began to be *negatively* associated with plantation persistence. Although the viability of these farms tended to legitimate the use of wage labor on plantations in the immediate postbellum period, their ongoing proliferation later became a source of competition in both the labor and output markets.[51] Finally, the impact of labor demography (especially the emigration of former slaves) continued to have a significant relationship to plantation persistence. The next section examines the underlying mechanisms of plantation abandonment among individual black workers during the first few years following emancipation.

Departures from the Plantation System

The internal demography of the plantation system was analyzed using 1,508 Works Progress Administration (WPA) interviews with former slaves who reported on their activities during and after the Civil War. In these interviews, representing approximately half of all ex-slave narratives collected by the WPA, respondents indicated when they left the plantation system and whether they ever returned as wage laborers.[52] Responses on timing were grouped into segments, as shown in Table 5.3. For purposes of analysis, those slaves escaping the plantation during the Civil War were considered as exiting during the first annual segment, between 1864 and 1865.

Figure 5.6 plots survivor functions tracking the proportion of sampled African American laborers remaining on plantations over time. The solid line provides the estimate for the average ex-slave (i.e., when all sociodemographic characteristics are held at their mean values). The function generally matches estimates of turnover offered by historical observers, ranging from 40 percent to 50 percent in the period shortly after the Civil War. Writing in a Memphis newspaper, one planter argued that 1.3 million plantation slaves had been actively employed in cotton production in 1860, but that no more than eight hundred thousand free blacks were so employed (under wage contracts) within a few years after the Civil War.[53] Because reports concerning exits from the plantation system are likely to be influenced by observer characteristics, I also provide separate estimates for the sample of respondents queried by white interviewers and the sample queried by black interviewers. The plot suggests that departures from plantations may have been underreported to white interviewers, leading to a discrepancy of 11 percent in estimates of workforce retention by 1870. The following analyses control for the confounding influence of interviewer effects.

Table 5.3. Individual-Level Statistics for Internal Demography of Plantation Workforce

Variable	Mean/ Proportion[a]	Number of Respondents	Description
Exit from plantation system			
Left during war	0.072	1,508	Approximate time given by ex-slaves when they first
Left upon emancipation	0.090		left their former owner(s); right-censored after 1870
Left within one year	0.376		
Left within one to two years	0.081		
Left within two to five years	0.163		
Stayed (until right-censoring)	0.218	▼	
Demographics			
Gender	0.489	1,505	Male = 0; female = 1
Age	13.130	1,492	Age in 1865
Status under slavery			
Child of slaves	0.279	1,353	Unemployed child of slaves
Artisan/overseer	0.090		Skilled manual worker (e.g., blacksmith) or slave driver
House servant	0.148		Skilled domestic (e.g., cook)
Semiskilled field/chores	0.220		Semiskilled agricultural (e.g., teamster) or domestic
Unskilled field hands	0.263	▼	Unskilled agricultural
Social networks			
Reported on fellow ex-slaves leaving plantation	0.169	1,508	No report = 0; report = 1
Time delay until fellow ex-slaves left	1.160	255	Left by/upon emancipation = 0; left within two years = 1; left afterward/stayed = 2
Married during slavery	0.070	1,508	Single = 0; married = 1
Broken family	0.210	1,508	Nuclear family intact = 0; family broken = 1
Reported conditions on plantation			
Experienced abuse	0.278	1,508	No reported abuse = 0; inadequate food; some reported punishment = 1; reports of physical violence (e.g., whippings, forced sex) = 2
Witnessed abuse of others	0.303	1,508	No reported abuse = 0; observed physical violence = 1
Interviewer characteristics			
Race	0.246	1,433	White = 0; minority = 1

[a] Weighted based on gender-stratified occupational distribution of slaves (1860).

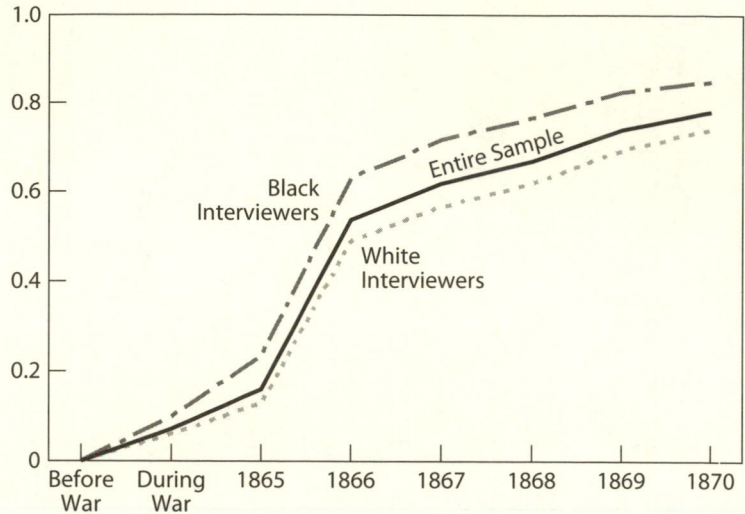

Figure 5.6. Estimates of Cumulative Turnover (Proportion of Workers) from Southern Plantations. © 2004, The University of Chicago Press.
Note: Estimates consider only exits from plantations; laborer mortality and rehires are not addressed.

Based on the WPA interviews, Table 5.4 lists the principal reasons given by former slaves for leaving their plantations. In only a small number of cases did exogenous circumstances such as the destruction of a plantation, a failure to convert to wage labor arrangements, or a planter's decision to abandon plantation agriculture force ex-slaves off the plantation. Considering the remaining respondents, 37 percent found that economic necessity (or coercion) required that they stay on the plantation after emancipation, while over 51 percent left the plantation by choice.[54] Since causal inference hinges on whether worker turnover is driving the decline of wage plantations or whether the decline of wage plantations is driving turnover, in subsequent analyses I remove the eighty-four cases from the WPA sample in which ex-slaves noted that they were forced off the plantation by exogenous "push" factors (e.g., Union destruction of planter estates).

The reasons provided by slaves who left the plantation prove instructive in sorting out the subjective salience of differential incentives, norms, and networks in the abandonment of this organizational form. Interestingly, relatively few former slaves emphasize status or income differentials between the plantation system and the emerging market economy of the New South (8–9 percent), contrary to the expectation of some economic historians.[55] While a number of slaves left the plantations during the Civil War to join the Union army, the material and status-based incentives of nonplantation labor proved

Table 5.4. Primary Reasons Given by Emancipated Slaves for Leaving the Plantation

Reason	Unweighted (%)	Weighted (%)
Social networks	*22.9*	*21.6*
Reunite family	20.7	19.6
Left to marry	2.2	2.0
Conditions on plantation	*18.6*	*18.9*
Cruelty/dislike of master	17.6	17.7
Broken promises	1.0	1.2
Relative social status	*7.8*	*9.4*
Better opportunities in army	3.3	5.1
Better opportunities on other plantation	0.6	0.5
Better opportunities elsewhere	3.9	3.8
Exogenous factors	*11.7*	*11.4*
Forced by circumstances	9.6	8.4
Forced by master	2.1	3.0
Other reason (unspecified)	*1.5*	*1.4*
Stayed (various reasons)	*37.6*	*37.2*

Note: Based on reports from 720 respondents. Weights are calculated from gender-specific occupational distribution of slaves (1860).

uncertain in the postbellum period. A far more typical reason for the abandonment of plantation labor was normative in character, relating to the unreformed brutality of the wage plantation form. A number of former slaves reported having cruel or unscrupulous masters and wage contract conditions that were routinely violated (19 percent); these individuals were inclined to abandon plantation agriculture even if they lacked better opportunities elsewhere. The most common motivation guiding the decision to leave was related to family formation (22–23 percent), as many ex-slaves left the restrictive confines of the plantation to reunite broken families or to marry.

I corroborated these results using a behavioral analysis of the abandonment of plantation agriculture among all WPA respondents (see Figure 5.7a).[56] As noted in the exploratory analysis, these specifications are subject to strong interviewer effects, with respondents being more likely to tell white interviewers that they delayed leaving the plantation system. Differential incentives by occupational status account for some variance in exit rates. In particular, artisans, semiskilled laborers, and field hands left the plantation system at between 1.31 and 1.42 times the rate as house servants, which posed clear problems for the sustainability of plantation agriculture. On the whole, however, status comparisons between plantation and non-plantation labor account for only a small part of the motivation for labor turnover.[57]

Paralleling the responses enumerated in Table 5.4, reactions to living conditions in the plantation system were another important influence on the

(a) Impact on Leaving, without Effect of Social Networks

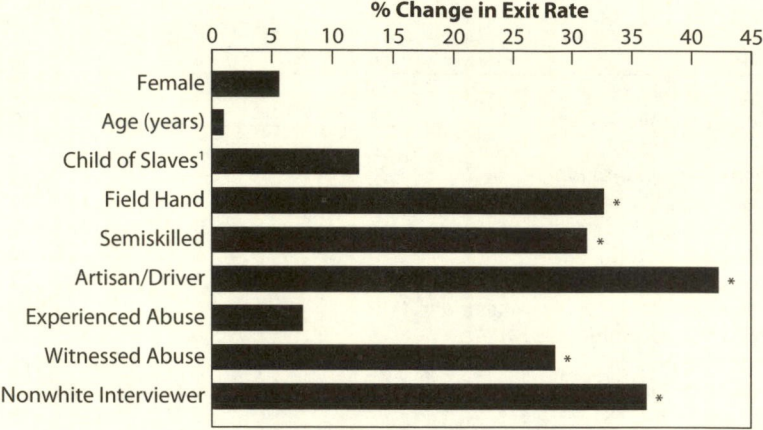

(b) Impact on Leaving, with Effect of Social Networks

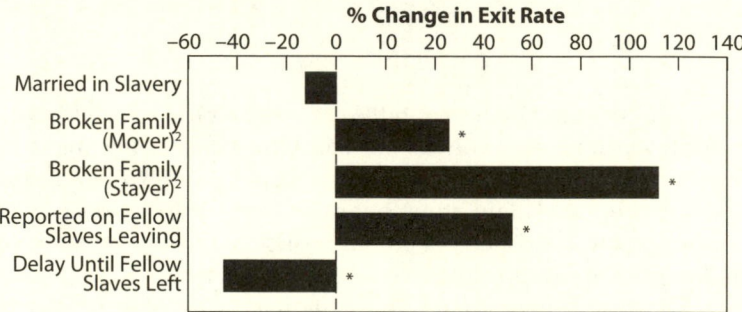

Figure 5.7. Factors Influencing Exit Rate from Plantation System among Emancipated Blacks: (a) Impact on Leaving, without Effect of Social Networks, (b) Impact on Leaving, with Effect of Social Networks
Notes: (1) Reference category is house servants. (2) "Movers" have an exit propensity (θ) equal to one based on attributes shown in panel a; "stayers" have a propensity equal to zero. *Statistically significant at $p < .05$.

exit process. The effect was contextual rather than self-directed, as former slaves were especially sensitive to abuse directed at their fellow laborers. This dovetails with the idea that physical violence, poor rations, and inadequate shelter served as signals of structural inertia, even when former slaves did not suffer the consequences themselves.[58] In conjunction with the findings for social status, the results suggest that the core movement away from the wage plantation was initiated by (a) former slaves in "unreformed" plantations (i.e., organizations incorporating structural elements from the antebellum system) and (b) former slaves with low status relative to opportunities in the postbellum labor market (artisans, semiskilled workers, and field laborers). The exit rate from the wage plantation tended to be especially high for the small group of skilled artisans.

How can one account for the mobilization of the large number of former slaves who initially stayed in the plantation system? A number of local network influences seemed to increase the rate of exits (see Figure 5.7b). With the exception of marital status, strong network ties contributed substantially to the plantation laborers' decision to stay or leave. Those ex-slaves whose nuclear families had been broken due to the sale of family members or migration of masters evidenced a high rate of exit from the plantation system (at least 1.46 times the rate of those with intact nuclear families). Based on this dynamic, the postbellum plantation system would have suffered destabilization even if competitive conditions had been favorable and its incentive systems were aligned with those of the free labor market. Because the system was developed on the assumptions that its labor force had no right to geographic mobility nor to familial integrity, the removal of these restrictions posed severe structural problems for the plantation form. As former slaves migrated in search of family, the need for more flexible labor arrangements became clear.

Another notable feature of the impact of familial networks is that the effect held to a greater extent for stayers than for movers.[59] Former slaves with low thresholds for plantation abandonment were motivated readily by status comparisons between plantation and nonplantation labor, as well as negative reactions to the structural inertia of the plantation form. But those ex-slaves with few alternative economic opportunities in the postbellum era were taking a leap of faith in exiting plantation work arrangements. Contrary to prior social theory questioning the mobilizing role of strong ties for late movers, broken family ties could serve as a crucial catalyst in this respect.[60]

Weak ties also played some role in defections from the plantation. Those laborers reporting knowledge of plantation abandonment among their fellow ex-slaves left at a much higher rate than those not reporting on such local knowledge. Moreover, laborers exited the wage plantation at one-half to one-third the rate when a large number of other ex-slaves on that plantation stayed. Despite the magnitude of these bandwagon effects, neither evidences any significant interaction with non-network thresholds. Strong tie influences thus remain the principal factor differentiating movers from stayers.

ALTERNATIVE FORMS OF AGRICULTURAL TENURE

How does the mobilization of former slaves from the plantation bear on the ecology of competing agricultural forms? Our discussion thus far has largely considered these mechanisms in parallel, with the only micro-macro link being that the decision of slaves to abandon the plantation weakens that form and has implications—albeit ones not currently specified—for the viability of alternative arrangements. To draw out the effects for Southern agriculture, we must address how choices of agricultural tenure brokered between free blacks and Southern landowners in the postbellum period contributed to a cycle of "creative destruction" that hastened the demise of the plantation form.

For the sake of simplicity, the agricultural forms that emerged in the postbellum period can be arrayed on a single dimension, reflecting how many inputs workers provided and, correspondingly, how much autonomy they could expect to exercise under each form of land tenure (see Figure 5.8). At one extreme, one finds the wage plantation form, where workers simply provided labor and operated under direct supervision. At the other extreme, we locate proprietor farming, where workers became farm owners, providing land, livestock, tools, management know-how, and labor, while operating under a relatively high level of autonomy. On the continuum in between, various "share farming" forms were defined as arrangements in which workers provided not just labor, but also some combination of management know-how and, possibly, livestock and tools—with all inputs being reimbursed based on crop shares. In "rental" arrangements, laborers provided all inputs aside from land, which was secured through a nonshares contract.[61]

As underscored by the analysis of the internal demography of the plantation, few emancipated blacks preferred the wage plantation as a form of land tenure. At the same time, structural impediments and the opposition of white landowners also rendered proprietor farming an unlikely goal for many freemen and freewomen. Consequently, the majority of black farm operators settled for sharecropping or share tenancy (54.5 percent by 1880), while about half that number opted for rental agreements (25.7 percent). The distribution of tenancy choices thus reflected the well-known compromise between emancipated blacks, who wished to throw off the shackles of plantation gang labor, and white landowners, who "discouraged any sign of black independence that might have suggested a move toward social or economic equality."[62]

The empirical effects of tenure choice on organizational ecology are sketched on the right-hand side of the figure. Each arrow from a tenure choice to a particular organizational form indicates that the conditional probability of establishing that type of farm is at least 10 percent, given the tenure choice. Thus, share farming arrangements contracted by Southern blacks were largely limited to the development of small tracts of land (92 percent of these cases). Rental farming agreements also generally involved small agricultural holdings (88 percent), but in 11 percent of these cases black farmers were able to secure the use of midsized farms, which typically involved the hiring of some wage laborers. Access to larger agricultural

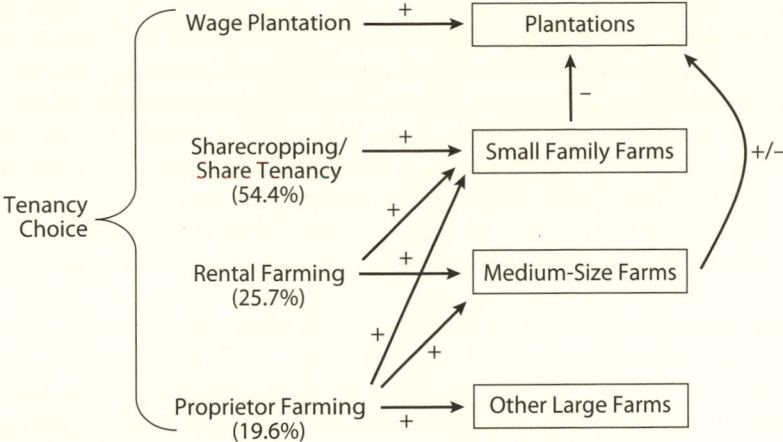

Figure 5.8. Individual Tenancy Choice and Organizational Ecology in Southern Agriculture. © 2004, The University of Chicago Press.
Note: Percentages correspond to tenure distribution of Southern blacks in the 1880 microcensus (see Reid 1981: Table 3.1).

holdings was most likely in the case of outright ownership—70 percent of black agricultural proprietorships entailed small family farms, but 19 percent involved midsized establishments and 10 percent involved large farming units.

The figure underscores the unanticipated consequences of white resistance to the upward mobility of former slaves on the agricultural tenure ladder. By limiting black land ownership, Southern whites eliminated one crucial avenue whereby wage labor on larger agricultural units could have been legitimated, particularly if it involved emancipated blacks working for other emancipated blacks. Instead, most former slaves had to be satisfied with low-acreage share farming agreements. This in turn stimulated the need to break the wage plantations into smaller tenancies and generated uncertainty about the categories of agricultural forms that would exist in the years after emancipation. The same mechanisms that supported short-term persistence in the status structure of the plantation system (see Chapter 3) also hastened the demise of its central organizational form.

SUMMARY

This chapter has suggested that common historical explanations are inadequate to account for the disappearance of plantation agriculture in the postbellum period. Exogenous institutional explanations—proposing a straightforward relationship between the elimination of slavery and the disappearance of the plantation—do not address the initial persistence of the plantation form under wage labor arrangements. Exogenous material explanations—focusing on damage from the Civil War or trends in urbanization—fail to explain much of the variance in plantation prevalence at the local level. Moreover, contrary to theories that position this form of agriculture on a sparsely populated, resource-rich frontier, the Southern plantation was *most* likely to persist in areas where these material conditions seemed unfavorable, such as counties with a limited influx of capital for agricultural reconstruction or with a growing population.

In lieu of these accounts, the decline of the plantation can be explained by reference to the organizational and internal demography of the organizational form. Over the long term, ecological mechanisms emphasizing interdependencies between plantations, midsized farms, and smaller agricultural producers address much of the variance in regional plantation decline. In the short term, these mechanisms are complemented by dynamics affecting the internal demography of the plantation itself. Following long-standing appeals by social movement theorists for more analysis of grassroots movements that challenge organizational arrangements, incentive structures, networks, and norms among former slaves constituted a fundamental test of the wage plantation.[63]

The decision to abandon the plantation was not one immediately engendered by emancipation, with almost half of WPA respondents waiting more than a year to make the decision to leave. This is unsurprising from a sociological perspective, given the nature of plantations as total institutions. Most plantation slaves had lived in closed societies, subject to limited contact with the outside world and habituated routines imposed on them by planters and overseers. Upon emancipation, initial release from the plantation may have led slaves to feel "marvelously alive to the liberties and pleasures of civil status," followed by uncertainty or anxiety as to their new role in Southern society. High-status slaves (overseers and skilled artisans), in particular, risked "moving from the top of a small world to the bottom of a large one."[64]

Attitudinal and behavioral analyses of emancipated slaves suggest that normative reactions played a substantial role in the destabilization of plantation agriculture. The plantation form suffered decline in the postbellum period due to its incongruence with the emerging free market for black labor and the unwillingness (or inability) of planters to modify the incentive and authority structures of the plantation. Structural inertia had accumulated among Southern plantations since the early 1700s, ensconced in organizational routines and racialized status hierarchies. The rigidity of the plantation system inhibited a successful transition of this form to wage labor arrangements and, ironically, initiated uncertainty about the future organization of Southern agriculture.

Simultaneously, white resistance to upward status mobility among freed blacks contributed to uncertainty regarding the alternatives to plantation agriculture. It was only through the gradual "constriction of possibilities" in the years after emancipation that share farming emerged as the most viable option for commodity crop production in the postbellum South.[65] Social networks among emancipated slaves served as a key impetus to mobilization toward alternative organizational arrangements. The plantation had been developed on the assumption that its workforce was geographically immobile unless moved or sold by plantation owners and that kinship ties among slaves could be largely ignored in allocating and exchanging slave labor. When these assumptions were challenged by emancipation, large numbers of former slaves migrated in search of family members, guided by bits of news from kin or other members of the black community. The new agricultural forms created to replace the wage plantation also tended to have a foundation in familial networks, as black sharecroppers and rental farmers largely recruited labor on the basis of kinship ties.[66]

These findings have several implications beyond the substantive example of the Southern plantation. Most important, understanding challenges to organizational forms requires detailed attention to the activities and perceptions of their participants. The postbellum plantation is perhaps one of the clearest historical examples where the actions of an otherwise disenfranchised and subjugated minority could have far-reaching consequences for the decline of a form of social organization. But most organizations generate choices between exit, voice, or loyalty for their members that can lead to rapid abandonment of forms, fundamental restructuring, or organizational stability.[67] In this chapter, I have focused primarily on the alternatives of "exit" and "loyalty." Qualitative accounts from the postbellum period also reveal that the option of "voice" was frequently employed by former slaves, as they confronted former masters with new demands and developed cultures of resistance.[68] Which outcome prevails is likely to depend on the specific context confronting individual members, as well as the broader institutional frameworks that yield alternative incentive structures, norms, and organizing templates.

This chapter also points to the importance of understanding geographic variability in the decline of organizational forms. Aggregate data often disguise regional pockets of persistence in organizational populations, owing to heterogeneity in resource and institutional environments. Separating the impact of these structural factors from more idiosyncratic factors associated with a region (e.g., a local cultural identity supporting certain types of organizational forms) remains difficult. Well into the twentieth century, one could find ethnographers assigning the label of "plantation counties" to certain locales in the American South. Indeed, one Arkansas observer noted in 1942 that "the plantation is as deeply rooted today as at any time in the history of the South."[69] That this label persisted, despite a fundamental restructuring of the underlying organizational form, underscores the uncertainty of individual and collective identities in the aftermath of American slavery.

CHAPTER 6

Credit and Trade in the New South

"Well, Atwater and Lambeth here had a big company store. After we got our land broke in the spring (in other words, we started a crop) we could come down here and say, 'Now Mr. Atwater, we want a ton of fertilizer 'til middle of November 'til we sell some cotton.' We could buy it on credit. They furnished everybody for fertilizer, almost, around here."

[Interviewer:] "What if you had a bad crop one year and couldn't pay? What would happen?"

"That's the reason that Atwater and Lambeth went broke. [laughter]"
—Interview with John W. Snipes by Brent Glass,
November 20, 1976[1]

John Snipes was born into farming. Shortly after he got married at the tender age of seventeen, his father helped him to settle into a tenant house in Chatham County, North Carolina. Snipes began to raise four or five acres of cotton in 1919. He and his wife also diversified by planting a little corn, raising a pig, and, occasionally, cutting down oak trees to make cross ties, the beams that supported railroad tracks. As was the case in many rural Southern households, there was very little money to go around. Lacking the cash to pay wages for agricultural labor, Snipes and his wife worked the farm themselves. Market goods, such as flour, coffee, and sugar, could be purchased only sporadically, either on credit or following the bulk sale of cotton or lumber. Credit was especially important in advance of the growing season, when Snipes—and his father before him—had to obtain fertilizer, seed, livestock, and other agricultural necessities. It was through this process of exchange and debt that Southern firms like Atwater and Lambeth came to hold "thousands of little old mortgages," many of them collateralized by no more than an old mule or cow and the promise of a bumper crop.[2]

The economic history of the New South has often been characterized as one in which predatory merchants, secure in their local monopolies over the provision of agricultural inputs and household goods, are able to charge usurious interest rates to the farmers and sharecroppers to whom they extend credit. In turn, those farmers and sharecroppers are drawn into a trap of debt peonage, in which an increasing amount of effort must be devoted to commodity crops (particularly, King Cotton) in lieu of agricultural self-sufficiency.[3] While there is certainly a kernel of truth to this argument, it ignores the broader uncertainty that was inherent in the networks of trade and credit that connected rural farmers to country stores and urban wholesalers. When John Snipes left farming in 1929 to seek employment in a cotton mill, he cited the boll weevil and low Depression-era cotton prices as the primary culprits, not indebtedness. Meanwhile, Atwater and Lambeth, the general store with "thousands" of mortgages, was truly in the grip of a credit trap. Having sold fertilizer to so many farmers on credit, it could not service its own debt to its suppliers and went bankrupt in the 1930s. Asked about the fate of the company decades later, a local mill supervisor said simply, "Guano broke them."[4]

This chapter is concerned with the "downstream" uncertainty faced by suppliers and investors in dealing with enterprises such as Atwater and Lambeth. In supplying fertilizer or other goods to country stores and their customers in the New South, how did wholesalers hope to manage risk and uncertainty? And why were they so often unsuccessful? In seeking answers to these questions, I suggest that we obtain a different perspective on the economic underdevelopment of the postbellum South than one that focuses on only the "upstream" market faced by small farmers who sought to obtain goods on credit through rural furnishing merchants.[5] While farmers took on risks in producing for the market, many were negotiating with store owners who were embedded in the same local networks and communities as themselves. Consequently, farm foreclosures and distress sales were relatively infrequent. Merchants would even carry farm families out of compassion or familiarity, in some instances over a period of years.[6]

The uncertainties surrounding the trade among country merchants, manufacturers, and wholesalers were more profound. Often separated by distances of hundreds of miles, their exchange relationships had little recourse to the social devices used to manage uncertainty within Southern communities. After the Civil War, moreover, these relationships had to bridge the sectional division between the North, where many wholesalers were concentrated in the large seaboard cities, and the South, where many country stores and manufactories were located in the hinterland. The physical and social distance between suppliers and Southern businesses created a need for new institutions to govern the flow of commerce. Although these institutions did emerge in the postbellum era, they ultimately proved inadequate to manage the economic uncertainty of merchants and, in some respects, may have even exacerbated it.

TRADE AND UNCERTAINTY

At first glance, a key source of uncertainty for suppliers appears to have been the sheer complexity of marketing and shipping goods to the South. By the late postbellum era, the trade networks of the region moved to the steady beat of "drummers," traveling salesmen who connected urban wholesalers with country stores and rural settlements. Census figures provide one suggestive, albeit crude, indicator of the growing importance of this occupation to the region's economy. In 1860, salesmen constituted a negligible sliver of the Cotton South's population, representing one-fifth of 1 percent of the white adult labor force (see Table 4.3). The proportion remained essentially flat through Radical Reconstruction, before exploding between 1880 and 1900. By the turn of the century, the drummers' share of this labor force had increased tenfold, to 2.5 percent of all white adults employed outside the home.[7]

Despite its rapid expansion, the enterprise of the drummers itself was not as haphazard as it might seem. The central offices of wholesaling companies often dictated both the territories and product lines that the drummers would cover. The rise of modern marketing aided the cause of the salesmen, with advertising first appearing in national magazines during the 1860s, followed by an explosion in the number of registered brand names and trademarks, from 121 in 1871 to 1,138 in 1875. The institutionalization of credit rating practices ostensibly allowed drummers to determine which country merchants were reasonable risks and which ones were unlikely to repay their debts. A status hierarchy rapidly emerged. Some well-heeled salesmen traveled in luxury, offering free cigars to customers and dealing with only the oldest and most established stores; others called on more modest establishments, at the edge of town or in rural areas.[8]

A more tenacious root of uncertainty involved the diverse nature of the businesses that the drummers were hoping to sell to. Atwater and Lambeth, the aforementioned general store in Chatham County, North Carolina, provides a case in point. The store itself advertised a product line that ranged "from the cradle to the grave" (and, indeed, did offer both cradles and caskets). In addition, the proprietors ran three other enterprises, including a sawmill, a grist mill, and a cotton gin. With so many lines of trade, one observer could only comment incongruously that "they were big for a little old place."[9] Such a broad portfolio of products and services was not unusual in the South. Toward the end of the nineteenth century, another fairly typical general store in Alabama had ties to over one hundred sixty suppliers in nineteen states.[10]

From the perspective of any given supplier, the involvement of many Southern stores in a wide array of trades created two sources of uncertainty. First, the risks undertaken by each store could not be compartmentalized to a particular industry or product line. Instead, suppliers were subject to uncertainty about how much inventory and effort was committed to the products and raw materials that they carried, as opposed to those carried by other wholesalers. Second, the risks undertaken by each store could not be compartmentalized to a particular supplier. While a wholesaler might anticipate the probability that a country store would default in making payments to them, it could not readily ascertain the probability that the store would default in making payments to *other* suppliers. The calculation of risk for any given downstream tie between the wholesaler and a country store—a crucial ingredient in rational credit rating—could thus be contaminated by the uncertainty associated with a set of other supplier relationships unknown to the wholesaler.

Because the degree of uncertainty in these downstream ties hinges to a large extent on the ability of suppliers (and other audiences) to categorize Southern businesses in different trades, I focus next on the issue of classification in the nineteenth century. Difficulties in classification proved especially problematic for the trust and credit that had to be extended to these businesses in an economy that was still largely wed to annual crop cycles and where cash was scarce in the aftermath of the Civil War.

CLASSIFICATION AND CREDIT

Uncertainty in Classification

Classification plays a ubiquitous role in identifying and evaluating organizations in modern society. Phone books, newspapers, and the Internet offer classified listings of businesses and services, guiding our consumption activities, job searches, and appraisal of local amenities. Trade directories, catalogues, and reviews offer more specialized categorical schema, with functions ranging from the rating of dining establishments and enumeration of distinct investment opportunities to the differentiation of artistic genres and producers. Government agencies and academics rely on Standard Industrial Classification systems, which emerged around the time of World War II in the United States and abroad to assist in the collection of official statistics and the development of industrial policy.[11]

If we turn the clock back to the early or mid-nineteenth century, however, we find little in the way of such systems of organizational classification. In the United States, the first Census of Manufacturers in 1810 aggregated households and establishments by the kinds of goods they produced, but did not identify individual enterprises or attempt to categorize activities that fell outside of manufacturing. Trade directories at the time were crude. By the 1840s, large urban centers such as Boston, Charleston, and New York City had directories of businesses and voluntary associations, which enumerated organizations, their locations, and their functions.[12] For the vast majority of individuals populating smaller communities, though, organizational classification required personal inspection of the goods or services provided by an enterprise, direct contact with the proprietor, or hearsay about an organization via social ties. Even in cities, the spatial agglomeration of organizations into retail districts yielded an important heuristic for identifying their form and function.[13]

The problem of uncertainty was widespread in classifying business enterprise in the nineteenth century. Although commercial specialization, particularly for wholesalers, had become prevalent in urban centers since the colonial period, retail proprietors in more rural areas continued to engage in diversified trade, offering an eclectic variety of product lines and services.[14] On first contact, customers, suppliers, and creditors dealing with these enterprises faced considerable uncertainty as to how much inventory or labor was devoted a particular line of business and, in some cases, whether such commitments were stable throughout the year or subject to seasonal variation. From the perspective of historical contemporaries, these unfocused pursuits also raised questions about the character and capacity of the business proprietors who were involved in them. As the historian Rowena Olegario has noted, "The inability to remain in one pursuit was as much a danger as was the lack of enterprise[;] business writers warned against the perils of tying up capital, time, and energy in outside ventures."[15]

Classification of some enterprises was even more difficult, given their adoption of inherently ambiguous identities. The term "sundries"—suggesting miscellaneous products, odds, and ends—dates to the mid-eighteenth century and was soon adopted by business proprietors who had extended their inventory or services in an undefined way (e.g., "drug store and sundries"). This ambiguity was encouraged by distribution practices at the time, given that wholesalers often added miscellaneous free goods to shipments as a marketing strategy. For instance, Thomas D. Clark describes a characteristic case from the late nineteenth century in which a merchant transacting with Blackwell's Durham Tobacco Company "was given ten 25-pound boxes of soap with an order for the same amount of tobacco."[16] Lacking detailed contextual knowledge about an enterprise's clientele and suppliers, some observers could only guess as to the lines of business it was engaged in.

Even before the Civil War, such ambiguity posed difficulty for the multiple audiences that were seeking to partner with Southern businesses. Bankers, commission merchants, importers, and manufacturers all sought to evaluate these enterprises on a slightly different basis. Would a firm be able to repay its loans to a bank or serve as a good investment for buyers of promissory notes? Would the firm be able to pay for raw materials and other goods that were shipped to it? Would it be able to deliver finished goods following a lag time of weeks or months? When the trade of a business proprietor or an enterprise could be classified unambiguously, answers to these inquiries tended to be remarkably similar. In 1860, one agency assembled separate ratings of over two thousand businesses in the Cotton South for financial investors, for buyers, and for suppliers. The ratings were very highly correlated among these audiences as long as the evaluated business could be categorized clearly by outside observers. For those businesses that pursued "miscellaneous" lines of trade, the consensus in ratings declined.[17]

In the antebellum South, uncertainty in classification was mitigated to some extent because merchandising operated through the factorage system, in which cotton factors and merchants with an intimate knowledge of the hinterland operated as brokers with Northeastern wholesalers. Formal reports on businesses tended to be limited to those located in a few large Southern cities, such as Charleston, Mobile, and New Orleans.[18] Given the small number of Southern enterprises and trades that were followed by Northern interests without recourse to the factorage system, business classification tended to be fairly clear (see Table 6.1). Nearly 90 percent of credit-rated businesses fell tidily into a single industry category. Although this statistic undoubtedly does not reflect the hodgepodge of activities pursued by many plantations, country stores, manufactories, and households in the interior of the Cotton South, it does reveal how much that uncertainty was managed by informal means—that is, through commodity factors and "respectable letters" from other intermediaries—rather than formal reporting.[19]

This clarity in business classification quickly broke down, however, as Northern business interests sought more information on enterprises in the South following the Civil War. Partially as a function of the expanding set of businesses that were being evaluated, partially as a function of entrepreneurs who were hedging against the economic tumult of Reconstruction, correspondents indicated that many Southern proprietors were engaged in multiple trades by 1870—nearly three times the number who reported doing so before the war. Providers of goods, services, and credit faced a growing problem of uncertainty, insofar as their ability to assign calculable risk to any given enterprise was impaired by not knowing to what extent the fate of that enterprise hinged on a specific industry. Worse, in subsequent

Table 6.1. Classification of Businesses in the Cotton South, Based on R. G. Dun Credit Reports (1860–1900)

	1860 (%)	1870 (%)	1880 (%)	1889 (%)	1900 (%)
Single trade/industry	88.9	78.6	76.8	75.7	76.7
Multiple trades	5.8	16.4	15.7	15.5	13.5
Ambiguous trade (etc.)	4.4	3.9	6.4	7.3	8.2
Multiple and ambiguous trades	0.9	1.1	1.0	1.5	1.6
Number of businesses	2,213	16,035	26,386	34,449	42,313

Note: All classifications are taken from entries in the July editions of R. G. Dun's *Reference Book*. For 1889, coincidence with the decennial census data was not a consideration (owing to the destruction of the 1890 census) and sampling was timed for the sake of completeness of the Dun archives in the Library of Congress. Duplicates and records without business classifications have been removed for purposes of analysis.

decades, an increasing number of businesses in the Cotton South were being labeled by correspondents as having ambiguous lines of trade. In the 1880 credit reports, the classification of 6.4 percent of all firms was marked with an etcetera ('&c.), denoting an ambiguous product line or service for an enterprise, increasing to over 7 percent in 1889 and 8 percent in 1900.[20] In the postbellum era, customers and suppliers for Southern businesses thus found that their business classifications were often challenged by categorical uncertainty, in which not only was it difficult to decide how much of a commitment a proprietor was making to a particular line of trade, but the category defining that line of trade itself was left open-ended.

With the growth of advertising, issues in the classification of Southern enterprise also became increasingly visible. While businesses that devoted all (or much) of their effort to a single type of product could distribute simple yet convincing circulars or testimonials, those with a broad range of products presented more dense catalogues, retail lists, or lengthy advertisements in magazines or newspapers (Figure 6.1). In a three-page advertisement in 1896, Lummus Cotton Gins, a manufactory based in Georgia, highlighted the virtues of its standard gins, focusing on such features as the "Lummus Patent Stationary Carder," its double brush belts "made of [the] best oak-tanned leather," and brush heads that "cannot come loose." By comparison, a five-page list from S.R. White and Brothers in 1885, a machine shop based in Virginia, juxtaposed a description of its "Stonewall Cotton Gin," with plows, shellers, fan mills, and an assortment of other implements. Interested parties were urged to request a much longer (120-page) catalogue from the company.[21] Such instances of product diversity need not have been problematic if multiple product lines were especially likely among large manufactories or merchants. But the available data from postbellum credit reports suggest that there was very little association between the assets held by Southern businesses and the different lines of products or services that they offered.[22]

(a)

Figure 6.1. Advertising Circulars for Two Producers of Cotton Gins: (a) Producer Emphasizing Single Product Type, (b) Producer Emphasizing Multiple Product Types
Sources: Figure 6.1 (a) Item B0043, Lummus Cotton Gin advertising pamphlet, Advertising Ephemera Collection. Figure 6.1 (b) Item A0259, S. R. White and Brothers advertising pamphlet, Advertising Ephemera Collection. Items are from John W. Hartman Center, the David M. Rubenstein Rare Book and Manuscript Library, Duke University.

(b)

Uncertainty in Credit Transactions

The problem of classification was especially salient for the correspondents who were charged with evaluating the credit worthiness of businesses on behalf of mercantile agencies. Mercantile agencies operated by "classifying people [and firms], putting them into boxes tagged 'failure' or 'success,' 'winner' or 'loser'" and they were paid "a premium for clear distinctions and bold contrasts."[23] In his treatise on credit evaluation, Peter Earling, a leading authority on mercantile credit during the late nineteenth century, warned that "no matter how great a man's ability, he can not hope to master every calling[;] to select *the* vocation suited to our special ability, is the most important step in a man's career."[24] Contrary to other domains that have been studied by scholars of organizations and markets—such as art, films, gastronomy, and stock picking—the principal objective in nineteenth-century credit rating "was to minimize risk, not to encourage it as a source of growth or innovation."[25]

Antebellum business transactions suffered from fundamental gaps in information and trust. Local stakeholders could gain knowledge about a business through physical inspection or through their social networks, but audiences located at some distance had to rely on less reliable sources, such as letters of reference or reputational hearsay. The information gap was acute for providers of credit, who often offered loans or financed trade without the benefit of direct contact.[26] Inadequate data for business loans, in the modern sense, represented only a minor part of this information gap. Given the lack of efficient transportation and communication networks, any business transaction involving goods or services delivered at a distance could impose a need for credit assessment. This need was compounded by the scarcity and lack of standardization in hard currency during the early Republic. With economic expansion in the South (and "old" Southwest), financiers and wholesalers in the large Northeastern seaboard ports were especially hard-pressed to obtain informative assessments of merchants and manufacturers in the hinterland.[27]

Around the middle of the nineteenth century, systematic credit reporting depended on local correspondents (often attorneys) who offered information on businesses in their own communities. This form of credit reporting was pioneered by the New York firm of Griffen, Cleaveland and Campbell in 1835 and the Mercantile Agency of Lewis Tappan in 1841. At the Mercantile Agency, it was refined further under the stewardship of Robert Graham Dun, who replaced Tappan as a partner in the mid-1850s.[28] By 1859, the R. G. Dun Mercantile Agency had enjoyed some early successes in taming the uncertainty of credit transactions. The agency had 1,195 subscribers requesting credit information in New York alone and branch offices in more than a dozen cities in the United States, Canada, and United Kingdom. But the business information provided by the agency suffered from a major weakness: credit reports could be obtained only by subscribers who called on a "confidential clerk" at the agency about a particular enterprise. There was no comprehensive volume summarizing the activities and credit ratings of a range of businesses. In response to demand, the Mercantile Agency issued its *Reference Book* in February 1859, covering more than twenty thousand businesses, listed by name, line of business, and credit rating.[29]

Given its format, Dun's *Reference Book* soon became a business standard for linking the evaluation of an enterprise to its classification. As Roy Foulke noted in his retrospective on the history of R. G. Dun, this was a volume "which contains the names of all active commercial and industrial business enterprises in every city, town, village, and hamlet in the United States, together with two symbols, one before, and one after each name. The symbol which appears before each name indicates the line of business activity, and the one which follows indicates the estimated financial investment in the business and its general credit worthiness." The simple format was especially useful for wholesalers, who often required rapid checks on the credit worthiness of country merchants who would appear unannounced on their doorsteps.[30]

Dun's system of credit evaluation did not emerge fully formed in the late 1850s. A detailed examination of the *Reference Book* over time suggests that its evolution can be periodized into three distinct classification regimes: (a) an antebellum schema, which offered an early and (largely) mutually exclusive classification of trades (1859–61); (b) a postbellum schema, which recognized the importance of businesses that combined multiple trades in the Reconstruction era (1864–early 1880s); and (c) a "modern" schema, which combined features of the antebellum and postbellum approaches, persisting until the adoption of the Standard Industrial Classification (SIC) codes in the mid-twentieth century (late 1880s–1950).

Classification Regimes at R. G. Dun

Shortly after producing the first volume of the *Reference Book*, Dun adopted a new approach to the 1860 volume that would divide its contents by industry groups.[31] Six industrial categories were advanced for this purpose, including shipping and commission merchants; silk, cotton, and woolen goods; boots and shoes; hardware, founders, metals, and house furnishings; booksellers, publishers, and stationers; and hats, caps, furs, and straw goods. The volume also added private bankers, who had not been covered by the inaugural volume. This subdivision was designed primarily to appeal to subscribers who specialized in one of the industry groups and thus only wanted to purchase that part of the *Reference Book*.

Table 6.2 shows the distribution of credit-rated businesses in the *Reference Book*'s listings for the Cotton South, using a similar subdivision by industry groups.[32] In 1860, much of the attention of Dun's correspondents in the South was devoted to shipping and commission merchants (including cotton factors), which composed over 28 percent of the listings in the *Reference Book*. Notably, these were also the largest and most trusted merchants operating in the region, with nearly forty-four thousand dollars in mean capital assets and a good credit rating on average.[33] The only other trade group attracting comparable attention involved the drug, dry goods, grocery, and general stores that served both urban areas and much of the countryside. Along with the commission merchants, these firms were essential intermediate nodes in the supply chain linking Northeastern wholesalers and rural farmers. Given the importance attached to the South's factorage system, it is unsurprising that Dun reporters applied so much of their effort to evaluating the credit of enterprising middlemen in the antebellum economy.

Despite this focus, Dun's antebellum schema for credit rating still proved to be too inclusive. Recognizing "that even under his elaborate classification system many country merchants defied clear classification," Dun soon excluded small traders and "adapted the present work to that class of merchants who grant credit as bankers, money-lenders and wholesale dealers." The number of firms covered in the book declined nationally from over 31,000 to 25,260 in 1861, reflecting a more limited scope for the Mercantile Agency. With the onset of hostilities in the Civil War, Dun suspended the production of the *Reference Book* entirely in 1862 and 1863. As the end of the conflict appeared in sight during the following year, the Mercantile Agency prepared to issue a new version of the book, delivering copies to subscribers in September 1864 and reissuing the volume with some corrections in January 1865.[34]

The postbellum schema that emerged revealed a number of fundamental changes. Coverage in the *Reference Book* had been extended substantially, to 123,000 firms nationally around the end of the war and a staggering half million by 1872. Dun also devoted more attention to estimates of capital worth, seeking a substantive financial basis for evaluating businesses. Most notably, the postbellum schema was increasingly geared toward large specialized wholesalers (and their "jobbers"), leading Dun to call for classification "without such rigid discrimination in the markings."[35] The correspondents at the Mercantile Agency now referred to some two hundred trades in classifying business organizations, including such categories as general store, tan yard, saw mill, and tailor.

The shift in the scope and focus of credit evaluation was especially evident in the postbellum South. After the Civil War, commission merchants composed a rapidly disappearing segment of the businesses evaluated by

Table 6.2. Major Trade Groups and Credit and Assets for Businesses in the Cotton South, Based on R. G. Dun Credit Reports (1860–1900)

Trade Group	1860			1870 and 1880			1889 and 1900		
	%	Average Credit[a]	Average Assets ($)[b]	%	Average Credit[a]	Average Assets ($)[b]	%	Average Credit[a]	Average Assets ($)[b]
Shipping and commission merchants, cotton factors	28.2	Good	43.8	5.0	Good	76.4	2.2	Good	99.0
Clothiers, textile goods, textile mills	4.7	Fair	20.9	3.8	Fair	16.5	3.9	Poor	26.6
Leather goods	8.0	Fair	18.2	3.4	Fair	11.0	1.9	Poor	17.2
Furniture, housewares, hardware	9.2	Fair	35.9	3.6	Fair	20.7	3.2	Fair	21.2
Booksellers, publishers, stationers	2.2	Fair	29.9	1.2	Fair	10.8	1.8	Poor	11.5
Drug stores, dry goods, general stores, grocers	28.1	Fair	24.3	49.8	Fair	11.6	59.5	Poor	10.4
Other	19.7	Fair	16.1	33.3	Fair	20.1	27.5	Fair	23.8
Credit-rated businesses		2,047			36,346			59,846	

[a] Dun's qualitative interpretation of mean credit score, with "good" credit ≈ 2.5, "fair" credit ≈ 3.0, and "poor" credit ≈ 3.5.

[b] Mean of capital assets for businesses within trade group, reported in $1,000s. For 1860, Dun did not provide assessments of pecuniary strength, and assets were estimated using credit rating and other firm characteristics.

Dun, declining to 5 percent of all enterprises in the *Reference Book* in 1870 and 1880 and a mere 2 percent toward the end of the nineteenth century (Table 6.2). This fate is well illustrated in the declining fortunes of Amedee Couturie, a Louisiana commission merchant specializing in liquor and wine imports. Couturie thrived in the antebellum and early postbellum period, even becoming embroiled in New Orleans politics. But by the 1880s, his net worth had been cut in half (from nearly one million to less than half a million dollars) and his credit rating was reduced. In explaining the devaluation, a New Orleans credit reporter wrote that "business with him for several years past has been on a downward grade, as it has been with a majority of [the] French importing houses." The reason for this decline was that "the firms here who sell to the interior [are] importing direct them-selves or through the general agents in [New York]."[36]

In lieu of these once-prosperous middlemen, Dun reporters in the Cot-ton South devoted more of their energies to the evaluation of modest busi-nesses, particularly country storekeepers, who represented roughly half of all entries in 1870 and 1880 and nearly 60 percent by the turn of the century. As the historian Edward Ayers has pointed out, these establishments "served as small cogs in a large and complex machinery of trade"; their proliferation exacerbated the problem of classification noted earlier, since "markets con-verged in even the most solitary country store, which traded in everything from eggs grown by a local farmwife to cast-iron stoves manufactured in Massachusetts to harnesses tanned in St. Louis."[37] Another third of credit-rated businesses fell into a category that included an eclectic set of trades, with most falling outside the industry subdivisions that had been used be-fore the war. Correspondents thus faced the challenge not only of rating more businesses involved in multiple and/or ambiguous trades, but also of rating businesses that had fewer assets, had less consistent credit histories, and that operated in a broader array of industries than those evaluated be-fore the war.[38]

The postbellum classification schema was well suited to the ill-defined industry boundaries of the Reconstruction era. By the mid-1880s, however, Dun subscribers increasingly wanted categories at a higher level of aggrega-tion, "so they could address circulars and draw off lists of names for the use of traveling salesmen."[39] In March 1885, the *Reference Book* added a column for "Trade Classification," which sorted businesses into one of twenty-six cat-egories. The new categories were indicated symbolically (e.g., * for general stores, ˥ for lumber dealers and saw mills) and supplemented the existing detailed classification. Some hybrid forms did not fit comfortably into the higher-order categories, and other businesses (such as turpentine dealers) could not be mapped to them at all. Still other industries dealt primarily with perishable goods or machinery that required special expertise in distri-bution. In some of those instances, forward integration by manufacturers substituted for "jobbers" and, thus, the need to manage downstream uncertainty. Despite these caveats, Dun's schema became highly institutionalized.[40]

The institutionalization of credit evaluation and classification at the Mercantile Agency was evident, more generally, in several changes between the end of the Civil War and turn of the century. The elaboration of the classification system from a single level of fine-grained industrial categories to a two-tier schema increasingly meant that credit correspondents had to consider the logical coherence of business functions in the enterprises they analyzed. In the Cotton South, around four-fifths of businesses involving multiple trades straddled the symbolic trade classifications that were adopted in 1885. On Robert Dun's insistence, reporters at the credit agency were also subject to more training in the task of credit and industrial classification. At the end of the Civil War, his correspondents were typically unpaid locals—most often attorneys, bank cashiers, or merchants—with limited experience in credit reporting. In the succeeding decades, these correspondents were gradually replaced by a cadre of professional reporters, who journeyed over wide-ranging circuits, accumulating experience in credit reporting and exposure to business enterprise in diverse regions. As an infrastructural support to their activities, the reporters could count on a growing number of branch offices that opened in the New South and, starting in the 1870s, the diffusion of mechanical typewriters among them. Though the South was not virgin territory for R. G. Dun, the two decades after the war witnessed substantial expansion of its credit rating efforts in that region, including the founding of eighteen branch offices in former Confederate states.[41]

A more subtle facet of institutionalization involved public acceptance of business classification into nominal (industry) and ordinal (credit) categories. Between mid-century and the 1880s, the morality behind Dun's schema was subject to regular attack, as the press and courts debated the "inquisitorial" (and potentially libelous) nature of credit rating agencies. The problem of legitimacy was pervasive in the antebellum South. Although Southern storekeepers relied extensively on generous credit and terms from Northeastern wholesalers, many residents were hostile to the inquiries advanced by Yankee credit-rating agencies. Before the Civil War, Southern businesses were especially suspicious about the Mercantile Agency, since the firm's founder, Lewis Tappan, was an influential abolitionist. A Norfolk paper ran a report from a local attorney who "declined Tappan's offer [to spy] on his neighbors, a role, he said, which even a slave would scorn." In turn, Tappan's convictions prevented the agency from undertaking much coverage of the South before the late-1840s.[42]

In the postbellum era, opposition to credit rating reached its height in 1876, with the publication of *The Commercial Agency "System" of the United States and Canada Exposed* by Thomas Meagher (also known as Charles Maynard), a disgruntled former employee of Robert Dun. Partially in response to such confrontation, the Mercantile Agency's approach to classification and credit rating evolved considerably until the 1880s. These changes seemed to bear fruit with a marked decline in journalistic and legal challenges during the closing decades of the nineteenth century. In 1882, federal courts established that credit reports were privileged communications, and in 1896 they were given copyright protection, defined as the intellectual property of the seller, not of the subject or purchaser of those reports.[43] Although they had a distinct legal status from the credit reports, the ratings published in credit reference books were also increasingly protected by legal contracts, limiting the ability of subscribers to loan them out and requiring that the books be returned to R. G. Dun after a specified time. By the final decade of the nineteenth century, Peter Earling would declare that the Mercantile Agency was "a permanent institution with the American business-public, and has come to stay."[44]

Table 6.3 summarizes the effects of institutionalization on credit evaluation between the 1850s and 1900. The success of institutionalization appeared to be predicated on four properties: (a) categories in Dun's classification system became sufficiently detailed so that it became clear when the boundaries of trade groups were being violated; (b) individuals applying the classification system were trained specifically for this purpose; (c) there

Table 6.3. The Impact of Institutionalization on Credit Evaluation of Southern Businesses at R. G. Dun and Company

	Antebellum Schema (1859–61)	Postbellum Schema (1864–85)	"Modern" Schema (1885–1900)
Classification system	Single-level taxonomy; effort to create mutually-exclusive trade categories	Single-level taxonomy; accommodation of hybrid and ambiguous firms	Multilevel taxonomy; ability to identify hybrids involving unrelated trades
Correspondents	Untrained local attorneys, merchants, and bank cashiers	Untrained local attorneys, merchants, and bank cashiers	Professional traveling credit reporters
Branch offices	Few (two in the Cotton South before the Civil War)	More (high rate of branch founding in the 1870s)	Numerous (ten in the Cotton South by 1890)
Legitimacy challenges	Pervasive (reluctance to enter slave South; local opposition to Yankee "espionage")	Many (including law suits and exposés by the press and former insiders)	Few (the Mercantile Agency is seen as a "permanent institution")
Effort to manage	Risk	Classical uncertainty	Categorical uncertainty

was a proliferation of organizations that promoted or drew on the classification system; and (d) the classification system was no longer viewed as being subject to legal or moral reproach. As highlighted by recent perspectives on institutionalization, the process thus drew on multiple foundations, including the gradual protection of credit classifications in law and jurisprudence (a regulative foundation), the acceptance of the schema by professionals and arbiters of business ethics (a normative foundation), and the intuitive understanding of those categories by credit reporters and other business audiences (a cognitive foundation).[45]

As the credit rating system became more institutionalized, it was also being deployed to manage more extreme forms of uncertainty surrounding business in the American South. In the antebellum era, the Mercantile Agency devoted much of its effort to evaluating well-established commission merchants in the region, categorizing their activities in single lines of trade and ascribing risk based on personal acquaintance and credit history. The era of Radical Reconstruction witnessed greater challenges for Dun's credit reporters, who confronted not only a less stable political economy, but also smaller businesses in a greater array of industries with more enterprises that were engaged in multiple trades. Dun's system of classification evolved accordingly to accommodate businesses that were hybrids of two or more industries. In the 1880s, the businesses that were rated by Dun continued to diverge from the heavily capitalized commission merchants, but the agency also rated more businesses with poor credit and those engaged in ambiguous lines of trade. In an effort to manage categorical uncertainty, the agency relied increasingly on professional credit reporters and a two-tiered system of classification that would suggest whether the trades pursued by a proprietor were unrelated or fell within a related group of trades.[46]

The Effect of Uncertainty on Credit Rating

Credit evaluations serve as a useful quantitative trace of the uncertainty affecting Southern firms and Northern business interests in the region over the latter half of the nineteenth century. In summarizing the credit worthiness of an enterprise, correspondents were instructed to consider factors such as capital assets, the "nature, extent and hazard of business," the character and qualifications of proprietors, and firm strengths and weaknesses.[47] At the Mercantile Agency, firms were ranked into seven credit categories, ranging from A1, for a respected firm with unlimited credit, and 1 or 1.5, for firms with strong credit ratings, down to 2 or 2.5, indicating good credit, 3, indicating fair credit, and 3.5, indicating an undesirable credit report. The distribution of ratings was highly skewed, with many businesses receiving low ratings (over half in the Cotton South) and only a few receiving strong or unlimited credit endorsements (less than 2 percent at a rating of 1.5 or higher). After the war, 20 percent of Southern businesses in the *Reference Book* received no credit coverage from a Dun correspondent. Subscribers were instructed to consult with a clerk in a branch office when encountering such "blank" ratings, thus incurring additional transaction costs.

Using the entire sample of Mercantile Agency entries for the postbellum Cotton South, Figure 6.2 graphs estimates of credit rating and coverage by the type of trade classification applied to individual businesses. Considering Dun's detailed industry descriptors, each firm was assigned to one or more of the 219 categories of trades identified in the *Reference Book*. Approximately 83 percent of the firms in the period between 1870 and 1900 were listed with only one explicit category, slightly over 15 percent were listed with two, 1 percent with three, and only 0.05 percent were associated with four categories. *Hybrid* businesses were defined as any firm that combined more than one trade.

The estimates suggest that hybridity generally posed problems for Southern firms being evaluated by credit reporters. As shown in Figure 6.2a, the probability of a fair (or higher) credit rating for a sole male proprietor running a grocery store that was involved in another trade was less than 0.24, compared to 0.27 for a proprietor running a comparable store classified exclusively in the grocery category. With respect to credit coverage, the hybrid firms were also more likely to be scrutinized by Dun's correspondents. A male grocer's business had a 5 percent chance of not receiving coverage, holding all other firm characteristics at their means (Figure 6.2b). If that grocer was involved in another trade, the chance of noncoverage decreased to a little over 3 percent. In conjunction with the trend toward diversification across trade categories, as seen in Table 6.1, this suggests that many Southern business establishments would have received more negative ratings and more intensive attention in the postwar years than the single-trade businesses that were predominant before the war.[48]

Two other sources of uncertainty affected the credit evaluation of businesses after the war. Credit reporters assigned *ambiguous* businesses to a residual category, in addition to one or more explicit industry categories. In the postbellum era, the classification of roughly 9 percent of all firms in the Cotton South was marked with an etcetera ("&c."), denoting an ambiguous product line or service for a multiproduct enterprise.[49] After 1885, credit reporters also attempted to ascribe higher-order categories to firms in order to identify those in related lines of business. *Boundary violations* occurred when a hybrid organization had multiple lines of business that could not be mapped to a single trade group. In the Cotton South, roughly 8 percent of all firms exhibited these violations of Dun's industry boundaries.[50]

Ambiguity in the categorization of a business had a negative and highly significant correlation with its credit rating, suggesting that reporters who

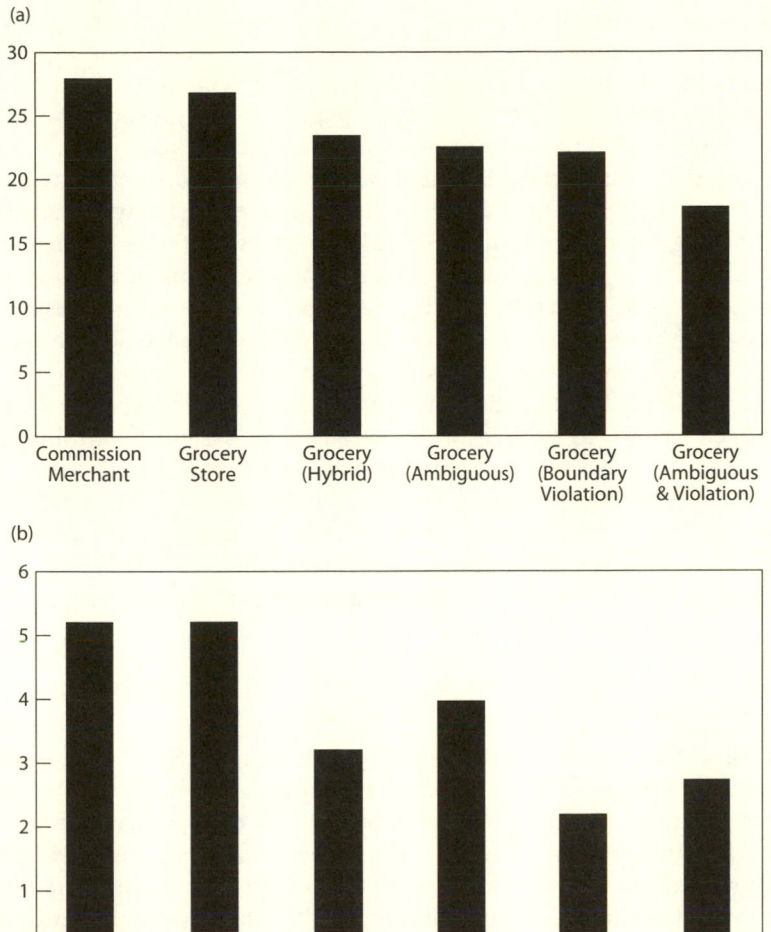

Figure 6.2. Estimates of Credit Rating and Coverage by Type of Trade Classification: (a) Percentage of Firms in the Cotton South Receiving a Fair Rating (Dun Rating of 3 or better), (b) Percentage of Firms in the Cotton South Receiving No Credit Coverage
Note: All estimates are based on a male-owned sole proprietorship, with other firm characteristics held at their means.

encountered firms engaged in unspecified lines of business were inclined to lower their evaluations. Similar devaluation was evident for boundary violations of trade groups. Using the preceding grocery store example, the probability of a fair credit rating can be estimated at 0.23 for this business when it was flagged as ambiguous and 0.22 when it violated the trade groups introduced in 1885 (Figure 6.2a). Violations of industry boundaries were especially likely to be noted by credit reporters. When the grocer engaged in another trade that straddled industry boundaries (e.g., drug and grocery store), then the likelihood of receiving a credit rating increased to 98 percent.[51]

From the perspective of Southern business proprietors, the postbellum trend toward diversifying their trades thus meant less certainty in obtaining credit and greater monitoring by outside observers, particularly when lines of business were ambiguous and when combinations of those businesses did not fall neatly into related industries. Moreover, the types of businesses that credit reporters encountered in the New South were likely to be judged more critically than those that were evaluated in the antebellum era. As noted previously, much of the Mercantile Agency's attention before the war had been devoted to trade involving the factorage system. Controlling for business assets, business classification, and proprietor characteristics, the commission merchants and cotton factors at the center of that system continued to enjoy a small ratings premium after the war. By that point, however, the bulk of credit reporting had turned to retail establishments, such as the dry good stores, general stores, and groceries that populated much of the interior of the Cotton South.[52]

Variability and Utility of Credit Ratings

On the surface, the credit reporters who traveled in the South displayed assurance in their assessments, especially as their evaluations and heuristics became institutionalized in American business. But closer examination suggests that such certainty among correspondents was itself misplaced. Over the course of the postbellum era, the ratings filed at R. G. Dun and Company reveal considerable variability, especially when correspondents analyzed a firm that was engaged in multiple trades or that was categorized ambiguously. And the success of those credit ratings in predicting crucial outcomes, such as business failure, proved increasingly elusive. There is little indication that Dun reporters themselves were aware of these problems. Indeed, the efforts at Dun can be seen as an early historical stage of business quantification, in which the correspondents were charged with responsibility for "uncertainty absorption," providing assessments to investors, suppliers, and customers that seemed more authoritative than the reality of trade in the postbellum South would reasonably support.[53]

A simple indicator of uncertainty among credit reports involves the variance in ratings for a particular type of business, once readily observed attributes (such as assets) are controlled for. Robert Dun's own exhortation to his employees was that "there should be a constant effort to keep the credit marking [of firms] in close relation to [their] capital marking."[54] Despite this effort at the economic rationalization of credit reporting, the typical Southern business involved in a single trade deviated from the average for its asset class by nearly half a credit point. For example, Dun's 1882 *Reference Book* recommended that businesses with two thousand to ten thousand dollars in assets be assigned a credit rating of 3, 3.5, or 4. In the Cotton South, the average business in that asset class would have tended toward one of the more extreme ratings in the range (either 3 or 4). Moreover, among Southern businesses involved in multiple trades, the variance in credit ratings increased by at least 10 percent, while the variance for businesses involved in ambiguous lines of trade increased by at least 7 percent.[55] Along with the trend toward problems in business classification by the late nineteenth century, this suggests that fine-grained distinctions in the credit worthiness of Southern businesses would have been subject to considerable uncertainty among credit reporters and clerks, heavily influenced by either soft information on firms or random error.

Variability in ratings aside, the widespread dissemination of Dun's *Reference Book* in the New South should have simplified the thorny task faced by investors, suppliers, and customers in evaluating the state of Southern business. During the antebellum era, inquiries about any particular firm involved a trip to the branch offices in Charleston or New Orleans (or Dun's New York City headquarters), where a clerk would read material from the Mercantile Agency's handwritten ledgers to a subscriber. The ledger entries themselves contained information on the character, capacity, and experience of business proprietors, though these assessments were subject—at least in popular view—to numerous omissions and inaccuracies. The language used to describe firms was often shrouded in ambiguity in an effort to avoid accusations of libel. Considering the transactions costs involved and the imperfect quality of information on antebellum Southern enterprise, the use of the ledgers suggested far less certainty about creditworthiness than that evidenced in the aftermath of the Civil War.[56]

The public function of Dun's postbellum schema for credit rating was to convert the opaque and hard-to-access information in the ledgers into clear-defined evaluations of businesses. The handwritten credit ledgers maintained by Dun reporters required that proprietor name(s), location, and industrial classification be entered first, followed by entries on assets, credit evaluation, and activities, often over a period of successive months and years. The narrative format rendered some assessments of credit (e.g., "has credit for wants") and assets ("doing but little") to be far more vague than others (see Table 6.4). The *Reference Book* compressed these evaluations into sharp categories and encouraged comparison with other enterprises in a locale or an industry. It also pruned the credit records of personality characterizations

Table 6.4. Sample of Entries in New Orleans Credit Ledger

Proprietor Name	Location	Classification
Fred'k Schmidt	New Orleans	Gro. & Bar

Mar '72: Married, of good character and habits, and considered an honest, clever, good man. Industrious and hardworking. Keeps a stock of about $2 to 3,000, and can get credit for small amounts.

Mar '73: Doing a good business in his line. Has stock on hand worth about $5,000.

June '73: Stock $3 to 6,000. Credit good for wants.

Jun '75: In business several years. Of good character, doing good business, and has credit for wants. Generally estimated worth $8 to 10,000.

Dec '75: In close saving and economical. Doing a small, safe business. Owns the property he occupies. Bought in '67 for $5,500, now clear. Has in business about $1,500 and doesn't buy large. Fair pay, regarded good for a moderate amount. Means in all about $7,000.

Jul '76: In a good location and apparently doing a fair trade. Has a good stock. Owns real estate worth $5,000. Is considered a good and economical man and has credit for fair amounts. Is pretty fair pay. Estimated worth $7 to 8,000.

Jul '77: Has a very nice store. Not very large, but well filled. Said to be doing a fair trade. Owns real estate and is a good, economical man. Pays very well. Estimated worth $6 to 9,000.

Sep '77: Owns his store. Cost formerly $5,500, worth now only $2,500. Has a stock of about $1,500. Pays well and enjoys fair credit. Means altogether estimated at $4,000.

Jan '79: Does small, close business. Pays well. Has good credit.

Mar '80: No change. Is doing a good, living business. Pays promptly. Is in good credit, and regarded good for his engagements. His estimated worth $2 to 5,000.

W. Winkleman	New Orleans	Saloon

Mar '72: Formerly kept the "Half Way House" where he failed. Afterwards undertook the grocery business, which he then left when he married a widow who kept saloon. She is worth fully $12–15,000. The building belongs to her. W. is worth of himself $3–4,000. He has always been considered honest and prompt in his payments, and gets credit for his wants.

Jul '73: Doing but little and considered rather slow. Is thought to change about too often.

Jul '74: Out of business.

Source: Louisiana, Vol. 15, p. 64, R. G. Dun & Co. Collection, Baker Library, Harvard Business School.

(e.g., Frederick Schmidt's description as "an honest, clever, good man") that may have seemed at odds with the scientific aspirations of credit reporting. As one scholar of credit rating has noted, the credit ratings reported in the massive reference books have often been portrayed as "the epitome of efficient and rational economic information" whose "development is said to have initiated the systematic use of quantitative statistics to communicate creditworthiness."[57]

By converting the soft information in the ledgers and oral reports into the hard categories of the *Reference Books*, however, the Mercantile Agency did not necessarily improve the utility of the credit information that it provided to many subscribers. In contrast to other agencies, candor had never been a distinguishing feature of the narratives provided by R. G. Dun and company.[58] The ratings issued in the books shortly after the Civil War continued this trend, coding many financially precarious firms as no worse than "fair" (or leaving evaluations blank) in an effort to avoid legal challenges. Even after following Bradstreet into the rating book format, the Mercantile Agency initially viewed this information as a mere supplement to the oral reports delivered by clerks at branch offices. The advertisements of Dun and prefaces to the *Reference Books* urged subscribers to supplement examination of the typeset books with visits to branch offices for "full and detailed reports."[59]

Kelly Patterson, an economic sociologist, has examined a complete sample of *Reference Book* entries during the 1870s for New Orleans and Charleston, the two coastal cities that served as the hub of Dun's activities in the South. Analyzing nearly ten thousand businesses operating in these urban centers, Patterson found that credit reporters had a decreasing propensity to downgrade the credit rating of businesses or assign undesirable credit scores, particularly as railroad failures and the Panic of 1873 placed the Southern economy into a tailspin. While downgrades and poor evaluations were common in 1871 and 1872, affecting over half of the rated enterprises in these cities, they declined to just over 40 percent of rated enterprises between 1873 and 1875, and, furthermore, to under 20 percent of rated enterprises during the late 1870s. The legitimacy challenges faced by R. G. Dun and Company led credit reporters to soften their credit evaluations over time.[60]

At the end of Radical Reconstruction, perhaps the most damning indictment of the "hard" information provided in the *Reference Books* was its limited ability to predict the insolvency of proprietors to whom credit was provided. Business failures ranged from legal interventions, in which assets were seized by law enforcement, to abandonment, in which business proprietors escaped town, leaving their creditors behind. During the 1870s, Patterson estimates that between 2.5 and 4 percent of the firms rated by Dun failed each year in New Orleans or Charleston. At the beginning of the 1870s, the ratings issued by Dun successfully predicted the failure of businesses in these cities, with each half-step decrease in credit rating (e.g., from 2.5 to 3) being associated with a 12 percent increase in the hazard of failure. But by 1877 and 1878, the period in which Dun faced the greatest scrutiny, its credit ratings in these urban Southern locales were no longer significantly correlated with failure. As Patterson highlights, the quality of credit ratings eroded just at the moment when economic and political uncertainty generated the greatest need for information and critical appraisals of Southern enterprise.[61]

SUMMARY

The trade networks of the South witnessed a remarkable transformation in the years following the Civil War. While the "planter's alter ego," the cotton factor, returned after the hostilities between North and South and, in some cases, had maintained a "business as usual" attitude during them, the changing nature of social and economic relationships would quickly undermine his role in the Southern economy. Taking advantage of the region's expanding railroad system, opportunistic suppliers pushed their salesmen deeper into the interior of the South, bypassing the cotton factors who congregated in the port cities. Improved communication allowed sellers in rural markets to follow the price movements of cotton without relying on the factors as brokers. And credit markets expanded outside of urban centers, pushed by the crop lien system on the one hand and the diffusion of systematic credit rating on the other.[62]

The development of credit markets was a key ingredient in this transformation.[63] Robert Dun's Mercantile Agency created one of the first general schemata for classifying and evaluating business enterprise in the American South. At an early stage, Dun's system evidenced limited institutionalization along a number of dimensions, including the rudimentary nature of his industrial taxonomy, the training of his correspondents, the organizational infrastructure available in the South to support their activities, and the acceptance of his classifications and evaluations by the general public. Within the span of a mere thirty years, the Mercantile Agency and its reference books had become a permanent institution in American business. Professional correspondents replaced amateurs, branch offices proliferated, and legal assaults on the credit rating system ebbed. By the end of the century, the trade groups constructed by Dun and his agents were well established and affected the fate of Southern firms that violated them.

Despite the organizational success of Dun's system, its effects in taming the economic uncertainty of trade in the New South were less definitive. The evolution of credit reporting at Dun sought to replace prejudice and hearsay with rationality in business assessment. But a considerable number of the Southern firms evaluated by Dun's reporters fell into more than one of the lines of trade identified by the firm and, in the decades after Radical Reconstruction, a small but increasing proportion were classified ambiguously. The enterprises that were hard to classify suffered devaluation and higher variability in their credit ratings, even after correspondents took account of business assets, industry, proprietor demographics, and other characteristics. The Mercantile Agency's growing reliance on arbitrary trade groups often exacerbated uncertainty and contributed to the limited predictability of credit ratings during the times of greatest economic turbulence.

Other demographic and organizational changes added mightily to the uncertainty of credit markets in the postbellum era. While the risks of farm management in the antebellum era were largely concentrated in the hands of planters and yeoman farmers, the postbellum spread of farm tenancy created a new class of poor white and black croppers and rental farmers who sought access to credit markets. These credit markets were characterized by unpredictable and often usurious interest rates, as well as opaque and often predatory lending practices, especially for African Americans in the South.[64] Outside of agriculture, the changing face of artisans and shopkeepers augmented uncertainty in the Southern credit markets. The antebellum economy of the Lower South had featured around one thousand black business owners, many of whom were concentrated in supportive business communities of free mulattos and who had access to considerable assets. After the war, these free people of color were joined by newly emancipated slaves who sought to make their way in business, but who had far fewer assets and less social capital and who were less likely to be literate.[65]

Uncertainty in the trade networks of the New South was generated by both these new categories of entrepreneurs and new categories of business organization. Much of the historical literature has attended to the "upstream" uncertainty that confronted croppers and consumers who sought to secure loans, agricultural supplies, or other goods from local merchant-landlords during the postbellum era. This chapter has argued that an equally (if not more) prominent source of uncertainty originated in the "downstream" relationships of wholesalers and investors to these merchants and their clientele. Economic development in the region was hampered when outsiders could not make sense of Southern businesses and the credit risks that they posed.

CHAPTER 7

Paths to Development

> The old South rested everything on slavery and agriculture, uncon-
> scious that these could neither give nor maintain healthy growth. The
> new South presents a perfect democracy, the oligarchs leading in the
> popular movement—a social system compact and closely knitted, less
> splendid on the surface, but stronger at the core—a hundred farms for
> every plantation, fifty homes for every palace—and a diversified
> industry that meets the complex need of this complex age.
> —Henry W. Grady, 1886 New South speech to the
> New England Club[1]

In the years leading up to the American Civil War, Irwinsville and Hawkinsville, Georgia—two hamlets separated by fifty miles in the state's Wiregrass
region—shared a pastoral and preindustrial existence. The south Georgia
piney woods around Irwinsville were populated primarily by subsistence
farmers. From Hawkinsville, "one could walk through twenty miles of un-
broken forest [to] . . . the site of present-day Eastman, without passing a
house."[2] During the postbellum period, the development of these rural settlements and their surrounding regions diverged noticeably. The population in Hawkinsville nearly doubled in the decade after 1870, rising from
813 to 1,542 residents, while Irwinsville experienced a meager increase of 56
residents (20 percent) over the same period. These growth patterns were
paralleled by differences in business culture. The northern Wiregrass region
around Hawkinsville adopted a prototypical pattern of industrial development, yielding a New South economy that emphasized lumber, sawmills,
and railroads over tenants and neo-plantations. Meanwhile, the southern
Wiregrass near Irwinsville remained tethered to a yeoman farming economy, unresponsive to the ambitions of the emerging New South.[3]

How can we explain variance in local development under conditions of
uncertainty? As the examples of postbellum Hawkinsville and Irwinsville
suggest, development trajectories are not merely a function of capital accumulation and labor supply, but reflect more subtle distinctions of place.
Following periods of political or economic upheaval, local revitalization
may be especially sensitive to distinctions drawn by risk-averse residents,

investors, consumers, and entrepreneurs.[4] In the field of human ecology, scholars have long sought to account for such place distinctions in community structure, encompassing not just the distribution of the human, but also the organizational, population. In times of economic stability, places that evidence a distinctive character and portfolio of organizations may thrive. Conversely, under conditions of uncertainty, those that deviate from social expectations may suffer the indignity of stagnation.[5]

In this chapter, I offer a historical approach to understanding local development that underscores the idiosyncrasy of places and how such idiosyncrasy may be assessed in terms of local organizations. I analyze the postbellum South between 1870 and 1880, a time window that offers a context in which a large number of locales were exposed to similar conditions of institutional change and economic hardship. From a research design perspective, this setting offers another important advantage as well: the postbellum South was remarkably self-contained. As historians have documented, virtually all of the residents in Southern towns and villages came from the region itself. In the late nineteenth century, Northeastern cities experienced a surge of foreign immigration and Western towns served as hosts to a diverse mix of cultures, but Southern counties competed with each other for residents and workers. Place distinctions were therefore likely to be strongly influenced by the culture of the New South.[6]

Using a combination of U.S. census and Dun Mercantile Agency records, this chapter assembles information on the demographics, economic geography, and organizational composition of counties across the five Southern cotton states. The analyses below leverage these data to augment conventional economic explanations of regional performance, seen in terms of indices such as capital investment and gross product, and seek to offer a novel organizational framework that can inform understandings of development under conditions of environmental change. Whereas recent theories of local development suggest that places should stand out, differentiated by a creative class of individuals or the distinctive urban core of organizations they help to create, I find that idiosyncrasy proved inimical to economic and demographic development in the more uncertain milieu of the Reconstruction South.[7]

MODELS OF DEVELOPMENT

Following the example set by Henry Grady, the idea of local boosterism has long accompanied the rise of the purported New South. While Atlanta had borne witness to extensive destruction during the Civil War, its entrepreneurial spirit and diversified economy in the postbellum era led to frequent comparisons with thriving cities in the North and West. With the support of Northern investment, Birmingham began to exploit nearby deposits of limestone, coal, and iron to become the center of the emerging Southern steel industry. In the interior of the Upper South, smaller boomtowns such as Roanoke seemingly arose out of nowhere, buoyed by a combination of railroad construction and industrialization. Boosters began to refer to these places as the "magic cities" of the New South.[8]

Efforts to decode the ingredients of such "magic" patterns of growth have preoccupied not only urban boosters, but also social scientists. The most influential models have identified paths to development that combine features of local geography, the allocation of investments, and the spatial reach of networks and markets. Some models posit a mutualistic division of labor between settlements, while others view each urban place as an economic unit that is in competition with others for resources and reputation.[9] Below, I review three perspectives on local development—including central place theory, theories of spatial monopoly, and the dual-sector model of economic growth—and apply them to the locales of the Lower South in the 1870s and 1880s. In a marked departure from the rhetoric of boosters, as well as many existing treatments by historians, this section reviews the evidence on the applicability of these theories for a wide variety of settlements and counties, not just those that became highly urbanized or served as examples of success in the New South.

Market Centers

An established scholarly tradition views settlements as centers of markets, systems of exchange based on price or barter that are geographically constrained by the ability of buyers to travel to obtain goods or services, as well as by the ability of sellers to deliver those goods or services. While conceptions of modern markets are sometimes aspatial, conceptions of precapitalist and early capitalist markets tend to place special emphasis on the problems posed by distance for transport and communication. In this view, the commercialization of households is seen as a function of distance from settlements, with a high dependence on market exchange among those families who live in or close to town and an orientation toward subsistence production among those who live farther away.[10] The perspective seems especially well suited to understanding urban development in the postbellum era, given Edward Ayers's contention that "the South's towns and cities existed largely as trading centers, their fates dependent on the fortunes of their hinterlands and their connections with railroads."[11]

Central place theory was originally proposed by the geographer Walter Christaller to explain the tiered arrangement of different-sized settlements in southern Germany, and it was subsequently elaborated by sociologists and economic geographers.[12] In Christaller's ideal-typical formulation, a

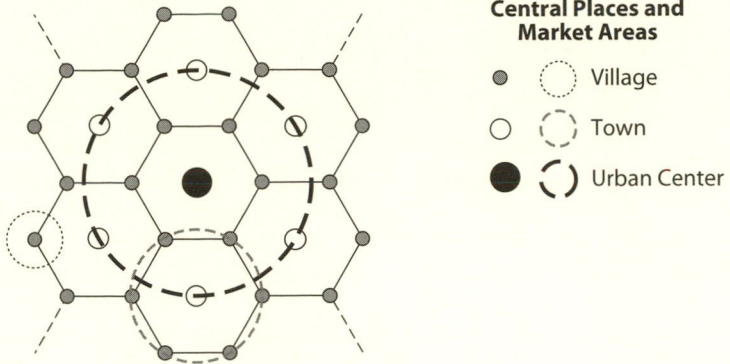

Central Places and Market Areas

◉ ⟨Village⟩

○ ⟨Town⟩

● ⟨Urban Center⟩

Figure 7.1. Ideal-Type Central Place Hierarchy

number of settlements in each tier serve as tributaries to a larger settlement, known as their *central place*. For instance, a set of six villages, each equipped with a minimal capacity to provide goods and services, might surround a larger town, which could offer some basic retail establishments (see Figure 7.1). In turn, a set of such towns might surround an urban center, which offers specialized retail stores, banking, and wholesaling facilities (and so forth). Assuming a homogenous distribution of the populace across a region, the tiered arrangement ensures that markets for specialized goods and services (referred to as *thresholds* in the theory) are sufficiently large to support their production or sale in central places. By the same token, central place theory argues that communities benefit when they are spatially arranged into these hierarchies, which help to optimize the regional distribution of commodities, transportation, and administrative services.[13]

From the perspective of the theory, community growth hinges on the spatial arrangement and scale of other communities in a given region. If there are additional settlements of a similar scale nearby, then a community will suffer due to competition with a proximate central place. If there are too few proximate settlements at a smaller scale, then a community will lack tributaries for its specialized services and goods. If there is no larger settlement within a reasonable distance, then a community will lack access to higher-order wholesaling and financial services. With respect to economic and demographic development, the mechanisms underlying this perspective are thus ones of logistical and market infrastructure.

Using business organizations to identify market centers in the postbellum South, Table 7.1 summarizes the distribution of settlements by central place type and business density. In Christaller's version of the theory, a central place at each level of the hierarchy is defined as a settlement that serves its own population and the population of $m - 1$ smaller settlements, where

Table 7.1. Distribution of Settlements in the Cotton South, by Organizational Density and Central Place Type

Type	Examples	1870			1880		
		N	Business Density[a]	Population (1,000s)[b]	N	Business Density[a]	Population (1,000s)[b]
I. Regional metropolis	New Orleans (LA)	1	736+	191.4	1	977+	216.1
II. Primary commercial	Charleston (SC), Mobile (AL)	2	504–735	40.5	4	471–976	36.8
III. Secondary commercial	Augusta (GA), Vicksburg (MS)	6	212–503	16.5	9	175–470	11.6
IV. Urban cotton center	Huntsville (AL), Shreveport (LA)	19	71–211	4.9	28	82–174	3.3
V. Rural cotton center	Dalton (GA), Tuskegee (AL)	54	39–70	1.6	86	41–81	1.8
VI. Town	Prattville (AL), Tupelo (MS)	170	14–38	—	245	15–40	—
VII. Village	Graham's Cross Roads (SC)	484	4–13	—	659	5–14	—
VIII. Hamlet	Williams' Station (AL)	1,497	1–3	—	2,356	1–4	—
Total		2,233			3,388		

[a] Count of credit-rated business establishments in settlement.

[b] Mean population of settlement within central place type; reliable population figures are not available for smaller settlements.

m varies depending on whether the functions in question involve marketing, transportation, or administrative infrastructure. The table employs Christaller's predicted parameter for business markets ($m = 3$) and categorizes every settlement in the Cotton South in 1870 and 1880 by its count of business establishments. As a result, we observe roughly $m - 1$ times the settlements at the second level of the hierarchy (primary commercial centers) as we do at the first level (featuring the regional metropolis of New Orleans); and we observe $m - 1$ times the settlements at the third level (secondary commercial centers) as we do at the first and second combined; and so forth.[14]

With a population that exceeded two hundred thousand inhabitants in 1880 and over two thousand credit-rated businesses, New Orleans was considered to be the regional metropolis in the hierarchy, despite its westward location within the Cotton South. Charleston and Mobile, the other primary ports of the South during the antebellum period, retained their importance as commercial centers, though they were increasingly challenged by secondary centers in the interior, such as Atlanta, which enjoyed access to five rail lines in 1865 and fifteen by 1900. Atlanta's entrepreneurial culture was reflected in the rapid growth of businesses in the city, from slightly over three hundred firms in 1870 to nearly nine hundred in 1880. Smaller settlements also proliferated in the New South, with the addition of over one thousand new post office locations between 1870 and 1880 alone, each hosting an average of two and a half new business enterprises.[15]

Given this general classification of settlements by central place type, the implications for economic and demographic growth within particular counties can be stated rather simply. We expect counties to develop more rapidly when settlements in those counties and adjacent counties conform to the central place hierarchy, such that the smaller settlements are adequately served by larger settlements and larger settlements are surrounded by a sufficient number of smaller settlements requiring their specialized services. For each county in the Cotton South, I examined the sample of settlements in that focal county, its neighboring counties, and the neighbors of those neighboring counties. Settlements were then assigned to four distinct categories based on Table 7.1—including hamlets (class VIII), villages (class VII), towns (class VI), and cotton centers (class V or larger)—and deviations from the expectations of central place theory were calculated.[16] Figure 7.2 plots the fraction of counties in 1870 and 1880 that deviated from those predictions at different probability levels.

By this standard, a fairly large number of Southern counties fell neatly into a central place hierarchy during the postbellum period. In 1870, 55 percent of counties (and their surrounding territory) had less than a 2 percent chance of deviating significantly from the hierarchy of settlements outlined in Table 7.1; in 1880, the fraction of counties conforming to central

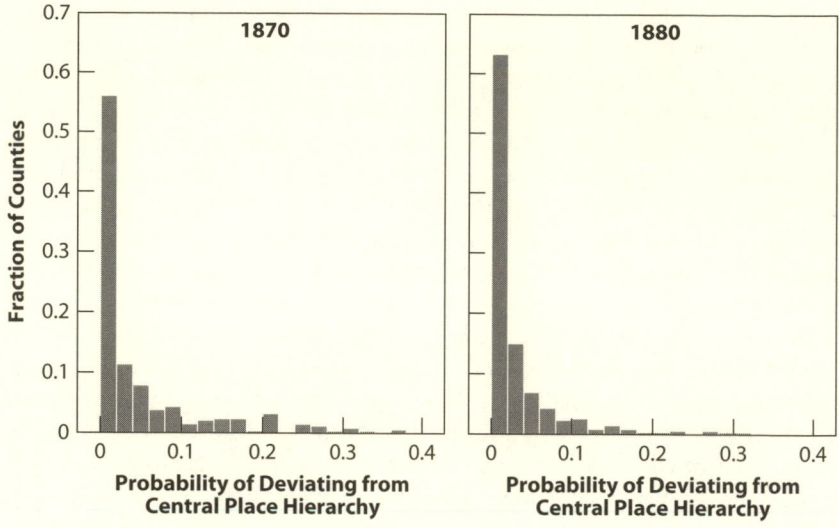

Figure 7.2. Deviations from Central Place Hierarchy among Southern Counties, 1870 and 1880

place theory at this level increased to 63 percent. On the surface, the arrangement of settlements over time thus suggests an evolution toward a tiered hierarchy that improved the efficiency of trade in the Cotton South and ensured that even the rural populace had access to higher-order goods and services (provided, of course, that they could afford to pay for them).

Detailed examination of the geography of settlements in the Cotton South reveals a more complex reality. Within counties, settlements large and small were often clustered near railways, navigable rivers, and other urban centers, leaving underserved hinterlands with little in the way of businesses. Consider the case of Autauga County in Alabama. In 1870, the county contained one larger town (Prattville), a village (Autaugaville), and four small hamlets (Independence, Indian Hill, Mulberry, and Vernon). Surrounding counties included six cotton centers, eight additional towns, thirty-four additional villages, and 111 additional hamlets. Comparing this distribution to that of the Cotton South as a whole, the settlements in Autauga and surrounding counties seem to conform well to the expectations of a central place hierarchy.[17] Visual inspection of a historical Autauga map, on the other hand, suggests that many of its settlements were arrayed close to the southern border of the county, where the Alabama river flowed and larger urban centers, such as Selma and Montgomery, were relatively close (see

Figure 7.3). The piney woods in the center and northern end of the county were marked by a dearth of urban infrastructure, save for the moribund hamlet of Kingston, which had once served as the county seat but became little more than a ghost town after the Civil War.[18]

If such geographic deviations from central place theory are evident for those Southern counties that fall in the left tail of the distributions plotted in Figure 7.2, then aberrations are even more likely for the remaining counties in the long right tails. This is consistent with the claim, advanced by some historical geographers, that the distinct economic conditions of the antebellum South—rooted in slavery and a colonial urban system—hindered the subsequent emergence of commercial centers in a spatial pattern that would readily conform to central place theory.[19] Whether the spatial pattern of settlements in the postbellum South actually proved inimical to regional economic and demographic growth will be tested later in this chapter.

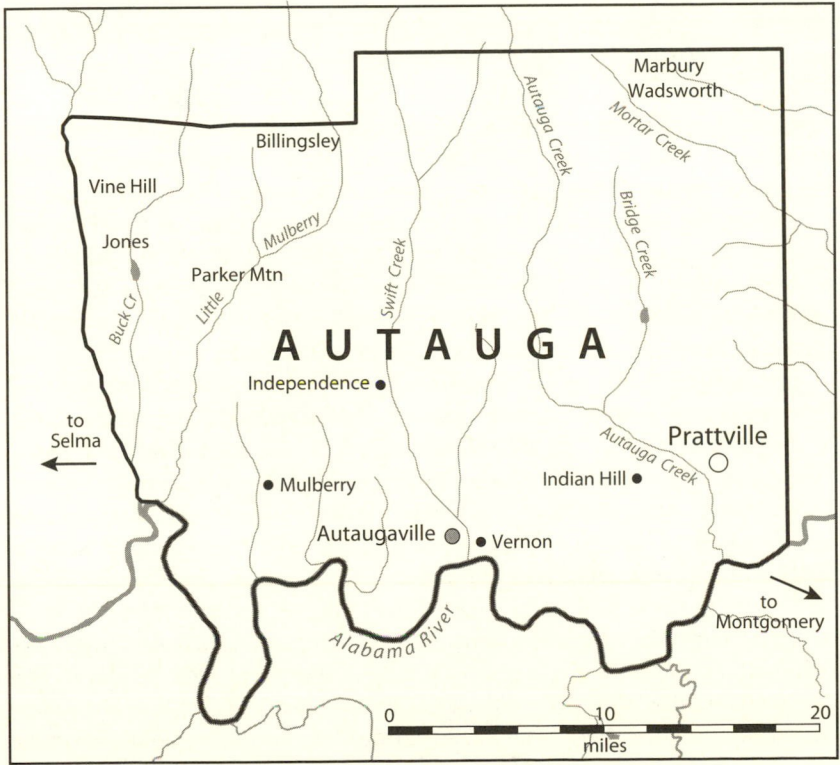

Figure 7.3. Map of Autauga County, Alabama

Spatial Monopolies

Theories of firm location offer an alternative view of potential barriers to the economic and demographic development of communities. Demand maximization approaches explain the location decisions of businesses and their infrastructural supports (e.g., railway stations) in terms of spatial markets covering some segment of a larger market area. While economic geographers have noted that optimal locations allow firms to maximize price and effective demand, they also acknowledge that this could have negative welfare implications for residents and communities, particularly when transportation networks are limited and the organizations in question offer critical financial or retail services.[20] Whereas central place theory assumes that settlements or suppliers are able to maintain a monopoly over a hinterland without adverse consequences, theories of spatial monopolies take those adverse consequences as their primary point of departure.

A provocative version of this argument was advanced by the economic historians Roger Ransom and Richard Sutch in their account of Southern economic development. Cataloguing the locations of rural general stores during the postbellum period, they found that over half of the post office addresses they identified featured only a single store. The widespread existence of such territorial monopolies did not bode well for community residents and farmers, they argued, since the general stores not only offered important commodities, but were often the only source of short-term financial credit. Under these circumstances, the price of credit was usurious and proved a barrier to local development. More generally, Ransom and Sutch's account suggests that the existence of spatial monopolies among crucial organizational forms in a settlement generates conditions that are ripe for the exploitation of residents and inimical to community growth.[21]

The argument in favor of the deleterious effects of territorial monopolies rests on several important assumptions. One is that the average distance between suppliers would have typically exceeded the range that farmers (or other customers) would have been able or willing to travel in order to compare prices or loan terms. In the Cotton South, for instance, Ransom and Sutch estimate that the *minimum* average distance between general stores in 1880 would have been at least 5.5 to 9 miles, representing a round trip that would require much of a day by ox-drawn wagon. Another assumption is that the merchants operating these country stores were *increasingly* in a position to exploit the advantages of their spatial monopolies. While the initial postwar success of country merchants seemed to offer access to commodities that had heretofore been limited among the Southern rural populace, it was the consolidation of market power and unwillingness of new general stores to enter existing merchant territories that would provide a basis for exploitative pricing. Finally, the argument hinges on the idea that

the disappearance or absence of general stores did not pose a greater problem to economic development than the monopolies that were established
by many proprietors. Ransom and Sutch acknowledge that many general
stores indeed went out of business, but point to their inability "to carve out
a territory of influence" as a primary culprit.[22]

To some extent, these assumptions can be questioned based on the available quantitative evidence. Table 7.2 cross-tabulates the distribution of general stores across locations in the Cotton South with the availability of local
railway infrastructure. A reasonably large number of rural locations—722 (31
percent) in 1870 and 1,122 (33 percent) in 1880—conform to the ecological
preconditions of a theory of spatial monopoly, involving isolated locations
with a single general store and no railway stations. This statistic falls short,
however, of the 54 percent identified by Ransom and Sutch. With the rebuild-
ing of railway lines after the Civil War, many areas with one or no general
stores (composing roughly 10 percent of all rural locations) allowed residents
to travel rapidly to other locations, where they could access the goods and
services of competing merchants.[23] Transacting with general store proprietors
in towns with railway access generally brought price advantages to customers
as well. While merchants in more isolated locales had to factor in high over-
land shipping costs over dusty Southern roads, those near railroad stations
could offer a wider array of goods at lower prices (or higher margins).[24]

Another third of rural locations in 1870 featured locally competitive
markets, with more than one general store in a settlement and, in some

Table 7.2. Distribution of General Stores and Railway Stations in the Cotton South,
by Locations

	1870		1880	
	All Locations	Rural Locations	All Locations	Rural Locations
No general store or railway station	643	643	600	600
No store, but railway station	158	158	81	80
One store and no railway	722	722	1,122	1,122
One store and railway station	65	64	116	116
Two stores and no railway	232	232	393	392
Two stores and railway station	47	45	100	100
Three+ stores and no railway	293	286	570	566
Three+ stores and railway station	170	152	447	411
Total	2,330	2,302	3,429	3,387

Sources: General store locations from R. G. Dun and Co. (1870–80). Data on railroad stations from the *Official Railway Guide* (Allen and Burns 1869/1880).

Note: Locations correspond to post office addresses and/or railway stops. Rural locations are defined as those that lie outside of commercial and urban cotton centers (see Table 7.1).

cases, railway access to other locations as well. In certain respects, the most problematic markets for rural residents were not the ones that hosted a monopolistic country store, but ones that did not attract a general merchant or railway station at all. Some 28 percent of rural locations fell into this category in 1870, though that percentage had fallen substantially to 18 percent by 1880. More generally, the evolution of the spatial distribution of stores over time proves instructive. The propensity of some merchants was to move into territories that were not served by any existing country stores, as Ransom and Sutch predicted. But many others chose to set up businesses in areas that already hosted one or more merchants. As a consequence, the percentage of rural locations with local competition among general stores *increased* from 31 percent to 43 percent between 1870 and 1880, while the percentage of territorial monopolies remained relatively stable. There is little structural evidence of the consolidation of market power by merchants over the decade.[25]

Case studies of particular regions also question the conclusion that the geographic dispersion of merchants invariably produced territorial monopolies. Nuanced examinations of credit ledgers and geographic analysis of store locations have repeatedly found more rivalry between merchants than anticipated in Ransom and Sutch's account.[26] Considering the explosive growth of general stores in Alabama during the 1880s, for instance, Louis Kyriakoudes notes that there was a pattern of lower-order urbanization, in which numerous general stores clustered in emergent market towns, particularly those that were served by railways. Other historians, such as Michael Wayne, have argued persuasively that the basis for merchant power in the postbellum era was the crop lien system, not the spatial arrangement of country stores.[27]

Dual Sector Model of Development

In addition to the spatial location of urban centers and the presence of firm monopolies, a third factor often linked to development in protocapitalist societies is investment in manufacturing. An influential dual-sector model of development, advanced among others by Nobel Prize winner Arthur Lewis, locates the "take-off" of backward economies in their transition away from subsistence agriculture. Consistent with neoclassical principles, this perspective posits that labor is attracted from regions with subsistence economies to those with opportunities for wage labor, particularly those with above-average wages resulting from industrial investment. As long as the supply of labor from the subsistence sector is high (in theory, unlimited), then wage increases will remain modest and the returns to investment in the industrial sector will remain high, fueling a virtuous cycle of regional economic development.[28]

Early efforts by entrepreneurs and boosters to create industrial centers in the Cotton South conform superficially to the assumptions of this model. Prattville, mentioned earlier in this chapter as a town in Autauga County, serves as a useful case study of industrialization. The town had been founded in the late 1830s by Daniel Pratt, a transplanted New Englander who established a manufactory to produce cotton gins. In the late antebellum period, Pratt's firm became the largest gin manufacturer in the world, shipping to locations as far away as Mexico and Russia. Prattville itself began to adopt Yankee pretensions as the "Lowell of the South."[29] By 1870, with a population of over thirteen hundred residents, Prattville was the central place of Autauga County, servicing such settlements as Autaugaville, Indian Springs, and Vernon. Based on the Lewis model, its economic growth might have been expected to continue unabated, drawing on a rural labor pool of around ten thousand county residents, many of whom were still involved in subsistence agriculture.

On closer inspection, though, Prattville may be the exception that proves the rule. While Daniel Pratt was credited as Alabama's first industrialist, his enterprise was heavily dependent on the welfare of regional agriculture. Other organizations in town—including a sawmill, foundry, gristmill, and store—catered mostly to the local hinterland. The Civil War pushed Pratt's business empire to the brink of collapse, as it did with most other enterprises in the community. The Yankee ethos of Prattville also appears to have been only skin deep. Just prior to the war, non-Southerners accounted for a mere 7.4 percent of the community's free population. Prattville's businesses drew to a considerable extent on industrial slave labor; and Pratt himself became an ardent supporter of the peculiar institution. In the immediate postbellum period, as a consequence, Prattville struggled with the same social and economic uncertainty that was affecting communities across the Cotton South.[30]

The experience of Prattville underscores the problem faced by Southern communities in pursuing a development strategy based on manufacturing during the era of Radical Reconstruction. With existing forms of manufacturing enterprise still tethered to antebellum dependencies and practices, industrial development during the 1870s has been described by historians as "only the spottiest and most halting kind." In the Cotton South, the amount of county gross product that was generated by the output of manufacturing businesses grew listlessly from 17.5 percent in 1870 to 19 percent ten years later. Even in 1880, roughly three-quarters of manufacturing employment in the South was located in small workshops rather than in factories.[31] Despite the presence of a dual-sector economy, with a large pool of workers in subsistence (generally, agricultural) labor and some Northern capitalists who were interested in developing Southern industry, manufacturing failed to take off in the years after the Civil War.

LOCAL DEVELOPMENT UNDER UNCERTAINTY

Perhaps the most glaring omission in conventional models of local development is uncertainty. The idea of a central place hierarchy as a driver of development assumes that businesses and towns in a region have reliable information on the distribution of the populace in the hinterland, and that
this populace has reliable information on the goods and services that businesses and towns are able to provide.[32] Similarly, the pernicious effect of
spatial monopolies hinges on the assumption that business proprietors
have information that allows them to maximize household demand for
their goods, while minimizing competition from other firms. And the dual
sector model of development presumes not only a robust, categorical distinction between the subsistence and manufacturing sectors, but also the
ability of workers and investors to anticipate the value of wages and output
from those sectors.[33]

The assumptions are dubious under any circumstances, but especially so
when there is profound change in economic institutions. The uncertainty
of the postbellum era was self-evident to even the most ardent of the New
South boosters. In an oration to an audience in Virginia in June 1889, only
six months before his death, Henry Grady waxed poetically that "in the day-
break of the second century of this republic[,] the fixed stars are fading from
the sky and we grope in uncertain light ... established ways are lost, new
roads perplex, and widening fields stretch beyond the sight."[34] More con-
cretely, the uncertain road of development was reflected in the physical appearance of New South towns. Rather than build edifices out of brick, residents in boomtowns like Roanoke were more likely to put up temporary
wooden structures. Saloons and companies devoted to land speculation
proliferated more than other businesses. Atlanta, the intellectual heart of
the New South movement, was noteworthy for its hospitality businesses,
with more than three thousand rooms in hotels and boarding houses in
1881. These businesses reflected a "get rich and get out" mentality among
some Southern entrepreneurs and residents.[35]

An alternative narrative of development shifts the focus of attention to
the problem of organizing businesses and community institutions under
conditions of uncertainty. Where would postbellum entrepreneurs and investors find templates for initiating new ventures? What kinds of communities would prove attractive to current and potential residents? What paths of
development would allow communities to imitate and learn from the experience of others? Given the insularity and close-knit culture of the Cotton
South, the answers to these questions would most likely be found in the
norms of community structure that emerged among the urban centers of
the region itself.

Norms of Community Structure

Sociological approaches to local development have called attention to the consequences of social organization (and disorganization), particularly as they relate to the ability of communities to develop shared norms of behavior and progress. Drawing from the early work of the Chicago school, classic ecological research tended to highlight *informal* organization—networks, neighborhood associations, spatial arrangement of housing, and so on—and analyze individual-level outcomes rather than development in communities as a whole. Newer incarnations of these ecological approaches have focused more resolutely on aggregate outcomes and the distribution of formal organizations. In one influential text, Michael Hannan and John Freeman ask, "Why are there so many (or so few) kinds of organizations" in a locale? The question is of both theoretical and practical importance, because variety in organizational forms may offer a "repository of alternative solutions" to local problems.[36]

How does a community's portfolio of organizational forms affect local development? Existing studies suggest that the causal link between organizational diversity and outcomes related to economic development, demographic growth, and civic engagement need not be straightforward. What seems more important than diversity, in certain respects, is that the various organizations that emerge in a community are viewed as appropriate and integrative by community members and outsiders.[37] While explicit norms of community structure—including zoning ordinances, urban renewal guidelines, and building codes—are of recent historical vintage, implicit norms also govern the ecology of preindustrial locales. As soon as transportation and communication networks emerge to a point that permits the comparison of different regions, individuals begin to form cognitive prototypes that differentiate *typical* and *idiosyncratic* locales. In preindustrial society, these schemata build on the basic organizational structure of rural agrarian villages and intimate new types of organizations that should emerge at each stage of development.

During the postbellum era, popular rhetoric among writers and boosters regarding the rise of a New South offered a similar creed regarding the appropriate steps to transform agrarian settlements into industrial centers. As Mark Wetherington suggests in his history of the northern Georgia Wiregrass region, the idea of a common path to development began to displace a variegated model of communities as railroad depots, market centers, mill towns, or tourist traps: "with the passage of time and cotton's ascendancy, communities became less distinct in character" and were marked by "a unity of form: weather-beaten stores, dusty gins and warehouses, dilapidated black 'bottoms,' and elegant 'White Ways,' the Victorian and neocolonial neighborhoods of the town elite."[38] Commentators ridiculed communities

(a) Perfect Nested Hierarchy

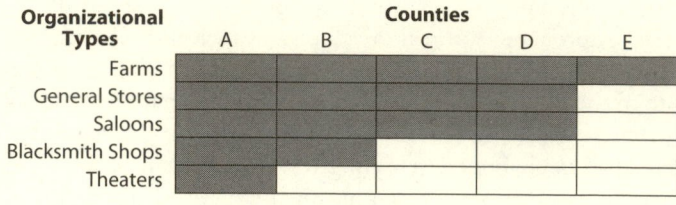

(b) Nestedness with Idiosyncrasy

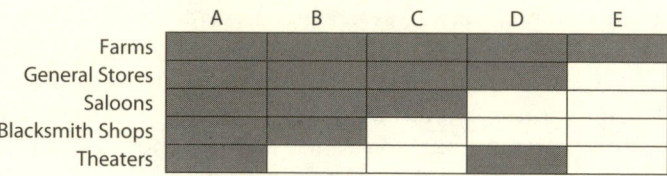

Figure 7.4. Two Patterns of Organizational Demography across a Set of Hypothetical Counties: (a) Perfect Nested Hierarchy, (b) Nestedness with Idiosyncrasy

that skipped stages in a normative sequence of development. In their cautionary tale about the Gilded Age, Mark Twain and Charles Warner drew a satirical portrait of Obedstown, a fictional Southern hamlet that boasted little more than a few scattered houses, a blacksmith, a general store, and a lethargic population in the antebellum period, yet which sought to attract an industrial college after the Civil War.[39]

These qualitative intuitions can be developed further by considering the hypothetical nineteenth-century counties shown in Figures 7.4a and 7.4b. The five counties (labeled A through E) are cross-tabulated with the organizational types found in those counties (gray cells indicate the presence of at least one organization matching a type). In the county-organization matrix shown in Figure 7.4a, we see a strong norm governing the appearance of new organizations at each stage of development. All of the locales feature farms, and most also have general stores and saloons. A smaller subset features blacksmith shops; and only one county has managed to attract a theater, a rarity in the late nineteenth century. This pattern of organizational form emergence across counties, termed a *nested hierarchy*, conveys an implicit social norm, in which rare organizational types only appear once a county has attained a given level of organizational diversity.[40]

Figure 7.4b illustrates a violation of this norm. The counties (A-E) are arrayed in the same order from left to right, with county A being the most diverse in organizational forms and county E being the least diverse. But now, county D features a theater even, though it lacks more rudimentary organizational forms, such as a saloon or blacksmith shop. When organizational types in a locale deviate substantially in this fashion from the prototypical order of form emergence, we label them as *idiosyncratic*. Under conditions of uncertainty, these locales tend to violate taken-for-granted standards governing organizational composition and attract accusations of illegitimacy from outside observers.[41]

To what extent did Southern counties on the whole evidence a clear pattern of community structure during Reconstruction? Using the approach to idiosyncrasy introduced above, I prepared a matrix that cross-tabulated all of the counties in the Cotton South with all of the types of businesses that were located within them (Figure 7.5).[42] The matrix displays a typical pattern of nestedness, with businesses concentrated toward the top and left of the matrix. Hospitable counties—that is, those with a high carrying capacity for

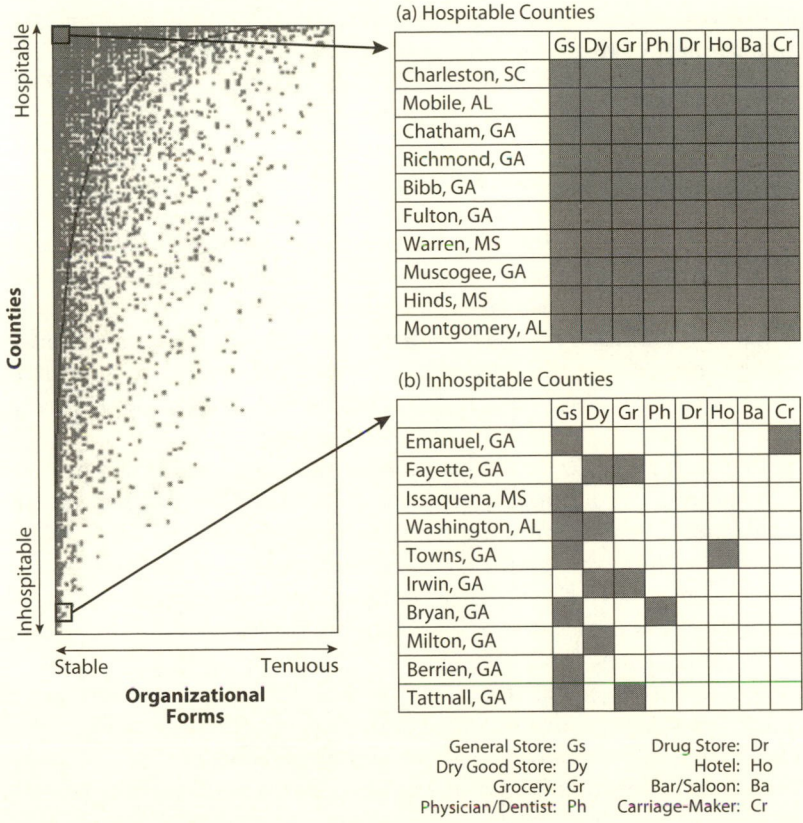

(a) Hospitable Counties

	Gs	Dy	Gr	Ph	Dr	Ho	Ba	Cr
Charleston, SC								
Mobile, AL								
Chatham, GA								
Richmond, GA								
Bibb, GA								
Fulton, GA								
Warren, MS								
Muscogee, GA								
Hinds, MS								
Montgomery, AL								

(b) Inhospitable Counties

	Gs	Dy	Gr	Ph	Dr	Ho	Ba	Cr
Emanuel, GA	■							■
Fayette, GA		■						
Issaquena, MS		■						
Washington, AL		■						
Towns, GA						■		
Irwin, GA								
Bryan, GA			■		■			
Milton, GA			■					
Berrien, GA	■							
Tattnall, GA	■		■					

General Store: Gs   Drug Store: Dr
Dry Good Store: Dy   Hotel: Ho
Grocery: Gr   Bar/Saloon: Ba
Physician/Dentist: Ph   Carriage-Maker: Cr

Counties (vertical axis: Hospitable / Inhospitable)
Organizational Forms (horizontal axis: Stable / Tenuous)

Figure 7.5. County-Organization Matrix for the Cotton South, 1870: (a) Hospitable Counties, (b) Inhospitable Counties

businesses—feature all of the frequent organizational forms, including general stores, dry good stores, groceries, and the like. Inhospitable counties, by contrast, only feature a subset of these forms, most commonly general stores. The figure suggests a pattern of business development where general stores tended to appear first in these counties, corresponding to a long-standing insight among historians that these enterprises "frequently marked the beginnings of towns" in the postbellum South.[43] They were followed by dry good stores and groceries, and succeeded by slightly less common forms, such as physician offices, hotels, and carriage-makers. There are, unsurprisingly, also a number of counties that deviated considerably from the idealized pattern, as suggested by the scatter of businesses toward the right-hand side of the matrix.[44]

Mechanisms and Scope Conditions

To clarify the effects of idiosyncrasy, we can consider the mechanisms that link this concept to economic and demographic development, as well as the scope conditions that delimit its application. In the neoclassical theory of regional development, economic output is represented as a function of local technical infrastructure, the pool of available labor, and a region's stock of financial capital.[45] This basic framework is built on assumptions of complete knowledge about the use of such resources and their consequences. During times of uncertainty, when institutional change makes probabilities and outcomes unknown to local supporters, the neoclassical model is thrown out of order. An ecological framework linking local place distinctions to organizational growth patterns reassembles the pieces. In particular, it connects two developmental processes to the ecology of local organizations: (a) the capacity of a locale to imitate others that have already passed through a particular stage of development and (b) the ability of a locale to attract and retain residents and investors.

Consider first the benefits that accrue from social learning when communities are able to imitate other locales. Communities can generate new organizational activities and structures rapidly if they follow norms of local development observed in other typical communities.[46] Conversely, idiosyncratic communities must find their own paths to development, often on the basis of trial-and-error learning. The inability to imitate other locales is especially problematic in the face of environmental uncertainty.

Such conditions impact the decisions of residents and investors, as well. While communities with a variety of organizational forms allow for more effective matching between workers and jobs, these benefits accrue only when the organizational composition of a locale matches the taken-for-granted assumptions of potential residents.[47] Speculators and entrepreneurs are also more likely to find a match for their financial interests when the organizational landscape conforms to norms found in the wider society. When communities are idiosyncratic by this standard, investors tend to wonder about their economic prospects and propriety. This seems especially true of the postbellum South, where local investors preferred "relatively 'safe' industries, thereby biasing the southern industrial economy against the pursuit of a broadly based and innovative development."[48]

These arguments must be qualified by a number of scope conditions. First, the concept of idiosyncrasy depends on the assumption that members of a society are enculturated with taken-for-granted schemata regarding the organizational composition of locales. According to this assumption, individuals learn from an early age to expect that some resilient organizational forms are found in even the smallest of settlements, while rare and fragile forms are limited to the largest urban centers. The formation of such cognitive schemata may be challenged under certain conditions. For instance, if substantial numbers of foreign immigrants enter a region, the expectations they bring regarding community structure may derive from the culture of their homeland rather than the culture of their new society. Alternatively, in circumstances of especially prolonged turmoil and transformation, members of a society may develop norms that are based on largely random patterns of community structure, rather than ones that are well patterned. A strong version of the thesis only holds, therefore, when (a) the majority of community residents (and potential residents) are raised in the same regional culture and (b) patterns of community structure within that region are unlikely to occur by random chance.[49]

Another scope condition to the organizational theory sketched here concerns the types of locales for which developmental processes can be reliably predicted. In rural areas, cognitive schemata suggest generic rules concerning the types of organizations that inhabit these locales and the frequency with which they appear. As settlements increase in population and organizational density, deviations from norms of community structure become more acceptable. Large urban centers offer distinctive mixes of organizations and amenities that defy easy typification. As Harvey Molotch and his colleagues have noted, it is these "holistic qualities that make Chicago the 'city of the broad shoulders' rather than, like Paris, 'the city of light.'"[50] Consequently, arguments regarding idiosyncrasy are more likely to hold when (c) patterns of organizational structure are examined in locales that have not attained the demographic scale of cities.

The Effect of Idiosyncrasy on Economic and Demographic Growth

I examined the effect of idiosyncrasy on local development using data sources at two levels of analysis: business organizations and counties. For both levels, I sought to develop a complete enumeration of these units in the Cotton South during the two census years following the American Civil War (1870 and 1880). Processes of economic and demographic development were then evaluated in terms of growth measures and differences between the decennial waves.

For both theoretical and empirical reasons, I restricted the sample of organizations to nonfarm businesses. Businesses are most closely tied to the development outcomes examined in this chapter, including the production of goods and services, employment opportunities, and capital stock. While a broader sample of organizational forms would add churches, voluntary associations, public agencies, and the like, the analysis of this broader sample would also call for elaboration of the basic theory and its conception of development. Moreover, the data on the prevalence of business organizations during this period are far more reliable than that for other organizational forms. Some attempts were made at the time to collect similar data for nonbusiness organizations (e.g., churches in the 1870 census), but these data are available on only a sporadic basis. Finally, I exclude agricultural enterprises (e.g., farms) because they were ubiquitous features of the organizational landscape in Southern counties during the postbellum period. Their inclusion does not contribute to variation on the measure of idiosyncrasy.

County-level data—subsuming indicators of economic and demographic growth, composition of the population, and geographic area—were collected from the federal census and supplementary sources. The 1870 wave includes a total of 346 counties (or, in the case of Louisiana, parishes) in the five cotton states. Due to its large population size and lack of comparability with other counties, I removed Orleans Parish (LA), the site of New Orleans, from further analysis. At the other extreme, three counties (Colquitt County, GA; Greene County, MS; and Jones County, GA) were sufficiently undeveloped in 1870 as to lack *any* credit-rated business organizations whatsoever. After removing these outliers, the data include 342 counties, which were also sampled in 1880. Table 7.3 provides an overview of available measures and descriptive statistics for these two time periods.

I assessed the growth of postbellum counties in terms of three outcomes. *County gross product* serves as a general indicator of economic development. This variable is operationalized by summing the value of manufacturing output produced over a given year with a broad measure of the value of farm output (including crops, forest products, home manufactures, and animals slaughtered or sold for slaughter). A second economic indicator— *capital investment*—is measured as the investment of fixed capital in a county, including the value of farm implements and machinery, buildings, and investments in manufacturing equipment.[51] Demographic growth is indexed by the *aggregate population* of a county.

Given the scope conditions of the theory of development, initial estimates restrict attention to the 316 counties in the Cotton South that lack

Table 7.3. Descriptive Statistics for Counties in the Cotton South

Variable	Description	Mean 1870	Mean 1880	T Test
Outcomes				
Gross product	Sum of manufacturing and agricultural output in $1,000s (census)	1,139.25	979.25	***
Population	Aggregate population of county in 1,000s (census)	12.39	15.82	***
Capital investment	Investments in farm machinery, implements, buildings, and manufacturing in $1,000s (census)	186.34	198.64	ns
Demographic variables				
White	Percentage of population that is white (census)	54.75	52.87	***
Immigrant	Percentage of population that is foreign-born (census)	0.96	0.73	***
Male	Percentage of population that is male (census)	49.43	49.97	***
Local population	Percentage of population that was born in same state as county (census)	80.48	85.03	***
Racial diversity	Index of qualitative variation across racial categories (census)	0.60	0.59	ns
Economic variables				
Wage rate	Annual wages paid in manufacturing and agriculture in $/population (census)	16.04	—	
Return to capital	County gross product/capital investment (census)	13.29	—	
Total capital stock	Value of farm machinery, implements, buildings, land, and manufacturing capital in $1,000s (census)	1,224.93	1,340.69	**
Organizational variables				
Manufacturing	Output of manufacturing firms as percentage of gross product (census)	17.44	19.10	ns
Bank	Whether county has at least one bank (Dun)	0.12	0.28	***
Railroad station	Whether county has at least one railway station (*Official Railway Guide*)	0.49	0.65	***
Competitive GS market	Percentage of settlements in county with more than one general store (Dun)	37.75	46.07	***
Central place hierarchy	Probability that settlements in county and surrounding counties deviate from central place hierarchy × 100% (Dun)	5.38	3.00	***
Business density	Number of business establishments in county (Dun)	50.96	80.39	***
Idiosyncrasy	Deviation of county from prototypical pattern of development (Dun)	3.22	4.44	***
Geographic variables				
County area	Area in square miles (Historical U.S. County Boundary Files)	680.04	647.88	***

Note: $N = 342$. T tests identify significant differences in means between years (*ns* indicates nonsignificant).

**$p < .01$. ***$p < .001$ (two-tailed tests).

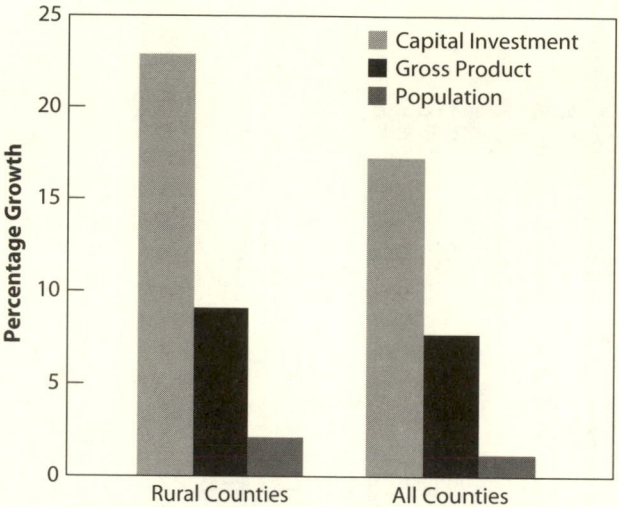

Figure 7.6. Effect of a Decline (One Standard Deviation) in Organizational Idiosyncrasy on Capital Investment, Gross Product, and Population in Southern Counties, 1870–80

large settlements (i.e., commercial or urban cotton centers). As seen in Figure 7.6, avoiding organizational idiosyncrasy in these rural counties was essential to the growth of capital investment, economic output, and aggregate population.[52] Given a decrease of one standard deviation in idiosyncrasy between 1870 and 1880, a county is estimated to have experienced a growth of over 24 percent in invested capital, over 9 percent in gross product, and over 2 percent in population.[53] Conversely, those counties that attracted a more idiosyncratic mix of business organizations were penalized in the uncertain economic and political environment of Reconstruction. For Cameron County in Louisiana, the locale with the largest increase in idiosyncrasy over the decade (nearly four and a half standard deviations), the estimates suggest a decline in county gross product that was more than 40 percent, a nearly 10 percent decline in county population, and a complete depletion of fixed capital investment in farming and manufacturing.[54] Notably, these effects are observed even when controlling for changes in the number of businesses in each county. For economic growth and capital investment in particular, there was no significant difference between a county hosting a "factory town" dominated by a single enterprise and a county that hosted a large and growing number of businesses.

Extending the analysis to include those counties that have a commercial or urban cotton center has some impact on the effect of idiosyncrasy (Figure 7.6). While the magnitude of the effect on capital investment and economic output declines slightly, these estimates remain highly statistically significant. Meanwhile, the effect on demographic growth decreases to a point where this association is statistically insignificant. The change in magnitude is consistent with the scope conditions of a theory of development under uncertainty, which posit that idiosyncrasy is less problematic for regions with larger settlements.[55]

Figure 7.7 considers the effects of other changes in organizational infrastructure during Reconstruction. Southern counties that located an increasing amount of activity in manufacturing generated a higher gross product and more capital investment, consistent with dual sector models of economic growth. The implication of manufacturing investment for development more broadly was somewhat ambiguous, since industrialization did not tend to promote local population growth. There was also not a significant positive association between economic growth and the development of financial institutions or railroad networks in a county. Indeed, the estimate plotted in the figure suggests that counties attracting railroads between 1870 and 1880 experienced a 16 percent decline in county gross product and a 47 percent decline in the capital invested in manufacturing and agricultural

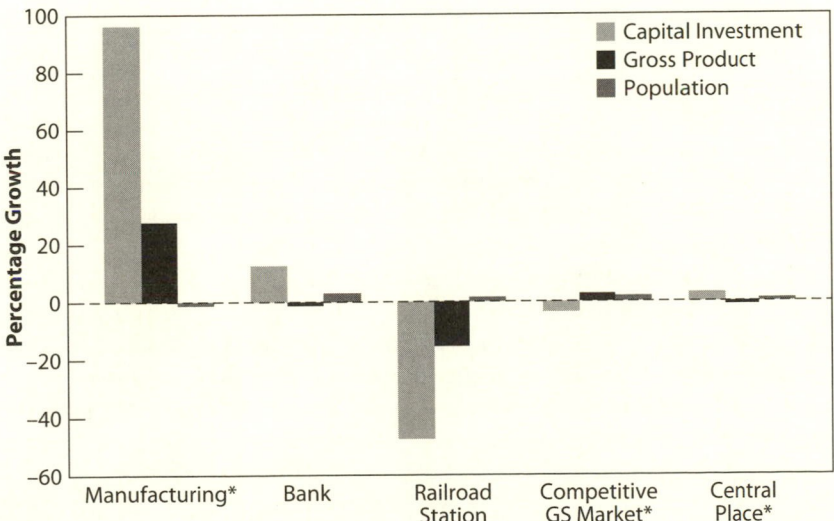

Figure 7.7. Effect of Changes in Organizational Infrastructure on Capital Investment, Gross Product, and Population in Southern Counties, 1870–80
Notes: *Estimates reflect the effect of a one standard deviation increase in county manufacturing output (as the percentage of total output), percentage of settlements with a competitive general store (GS) market, or degree of conformity to central place hierarchy. Remaining estimates reflect the effect of adding a bank or railroad station in a county that did not have one previously.

pursuits. This may be attributed to a number of factors, including the large amounts of capital outlays diverted to railway infrastructure, the symbolic nature of some railroad construction efforts, and the fall of many Southern railways into receivership following the Panic of 1873.

To consider the impact of spatial monopolies, I also identified settlements in each county with less than two general stores as subject to monopolistic conditions. An aggregate measure was then constructed by enumerating the percentage of settlements in that county existing within the spatial monopolies of store merchants. As seen in Figure 7.7, the presence of spatial monopolies among merchants had no appreciable impact on economic or demographic development. By the same token, there was no indication that the degree of conformity among a county's settlements to a central place hierarchy affected the ability of Southern counties to grow their economies or populations.

Several other statistical features of local development during Reconstruction are worth noting. In terms of economic output, demographic growth, or capital investment, Southern counties benefited when they had larger nonwhite (particularly African American) or immigrant populations. This is unsurprising, given the enormous reliance of the antebellum South on enslaved black field workers, domestics, and artisans and the efforts of the planter elite in the postbellum period to substitute immigrant laborers in agricultural pursuits.[56] Racial diversity also appeared to offer a positive benefit to economic growth, perhaps owing to the emergence of distinct ethnic enclaves or entrepreneurial cultures. Among African Americans, however, new centers of business activity, such as Durham, North Carolina, and Washington, D.C., tended to be located in the Upper South, gradually overtaking the older fonts of black enterprise in Charleston, South Carolina, and New Orleans.[57]

The unusual institutional circumstances and uncertainty of the period caution against efforts to view Southern development exclusively in terms of conventional neoclassical models of development. For instance, there is no empirical support for the contention that higher-than-average wages in a locale served to attract workers and their families. In explaining such deviations from ideal-typical wage-maximizing behavior, economists have suggested that antienticement and other restrictions on black worker mobility had a substantial impact on labor market outcomes, while historical sociologists have called attention to the diverse set of motives that guided the migration of emancipated African Americans, aside from pecuniary concerns.[58] Owing to technological progress, typical neoclassical models of growth also tend to hypothesize a positive trend in economic development, even in the absence of expansion in labor supply or capital investment. But in the volatile context between 1870 and 1880, when prices for cotton declined precipitously and agriculture and merchandising were subject to profound organizational changes, Southern counties with stable populations and capital investment could expect a *decline* of as much as 46 percent in the value of their economic output.[59]

Summary

As the economic sociologist Alejandro Portes has pointed out, scholars have increasingly come to realize that organizations and institutions should occupy a central role in our conceptual analysis of development processes. Both economists and sociologists regularly subscribe to this view in discussing national development, but the insight has been slow to trickle down to the analysis of communities or regions.[60] And while much recent policy attention, following Robert Putnam, has been directed at the role of organizations in promoting the civic life and cohesiveness of communities, attention to the effect of organizational composition on regional economic and demographic growth has sometimes been ignored.[61] To fill this gap, this chapter has introduced an organizational framework to understand how the composition of organizations within and across locales can influence local capital accumulation, migration patterns, and economic output.

Applying this framework to data from Southern counties in the aftermath of the Civil War, the findings suggest a fairly pervasive impact of organizational composition on the economic and demographic growth of communities, though one whose effects vary in their magnitude depending on the outcome studied. The idiosyncrasy of these counties—that is, their tendency to deviate from taken-for-granted sequences of business emergence—strongly affected their level of economic output and capital investment, but exercised a more modest effect on population growth. To some extent, this pattern may be due the fact that residents, local investors, and small entrepreneurs responded strongly to regional norms of community structure, while migrants (particularly, those that originated from outside of the region) were less inclined to evaluate communities on this basis. In the context of Reconstruction, this intuition coincides with accounts that associate an influx of newcomers with Northern "carpetbaggers." While the common narrative also emphasizes the role of Northerners in capital investment, this conception of capital inflow is now disputed by many historians. Edward Ayers, for instance, suggests that most of the capital supporting manufacturing in the postbellum period was local and that "Northern capital played only a small role in building the Southern factories" until 1900. Other historians point specifically to the conservatism of local investors and the "intricate links between enterprise and community" in the postbellum era.[62]

Alternative perspectives on development (including central place theory, the theory of spatial monopolies, and dual-sector models) are divorced from the sociological analysis of formal organizations in a community. They tend to eschew uncertainty in favor of assumptions about the perfect information that consumers, investors, and entrepreneurs hold regarding local markets. Empirically, they perform poorly in explaining the trajectories of development in the postbellum South. Investment in manufacturing, for instance, was far more sluggish than a dual-sector model of development might suggest. And while census data suggest a clear correlation between the growth of manufacturing and indicators of economic development, there is little evidence that Southern workers migrated efficiently between locales with low wages and subsistence agriculture and those with high wages and more extensive manufacturing industry.

In proposing an organizational framework for studying local development, this chapter seeks to complement, rather than replace, conventional economic models of growth. Even under conditions of uncertainty, there is still a basis for the neoclassical model, which conceptualizes regional growth as a function of capital and labor inputs and computes capital accumulation as a function of return on capital.[63] Nevertheless, this parsimonious account misses the organizational texture that affected economic development in the postbellum South. Much of this texture existed in interacting fields of local organizations and the social rules that governed those fields. The rules took on mundane, yet familiar, forms: the appearance of a physician in a county was expected to be followed closely by the appearance of a drug store to fill prescriptions; the appearance of a hotel was often followed by the appearance of a bar or saloon to entertain out-of-town visitors.[64] When locales hosted businesses that conformed to such rules, they enabled residents and business owners to engage in the taken-for-granted rituals of daily life, though the broader trajectory of the New South remained indeterminate.

CHAPTER 8

Emancipation in Comparative Perspective

> Before the rebellion, it was accounted the very extreme of Anti-Slavery
> fanaticism to believe in the possibility of immediate emancipation
> without social ruin. The wisest Anti-Slavery men of the day, whether in
> this country or in Europe, assumed it almost as an axiom that there
> could be no transition from slavery to freedom without an apprentice-
> ship, or some other arrangement that should deaden the shock. . . .
> When it had become a generally accepted fact that Slavery must come
> to an end, the idea still adhered that the emancipation must be
> gradual in order to be safe.
> —Editorial in the *New York Times*, February 25, 1864[1]

Even among Northern journalists and politicians, there was widespread
panic at the idea that the American Civil War would end without the proper
means to manage the uncertainty of the South's transition from chattel slavery. By February 1864, when Union-occupied Memphis held a convention
initiating the reorganization of Tennessee's state government, the convention's policy of "immediate and unconditional emancipation" drew some
stunned responses. Earlier discussions of emancipation had touted the pecuniary benefits that might apply to states that agreed to slowly free their
slaves. Abraham Lincoln's special message to the Border States, in March
1862, emphasized the gradual nature of emancipation and the resulting capacity of employers to substitute white for enslaved labor. The following
year, Maryland's Governor A. Bradford insisted that "emancipation shall
only be so gradual so as to guard it against the evil consequences that must
necessarily result . . . from too sudden a change in any system of labor that
is of indigenous growth." But in the waning years of the war, Unionists in
Maryland, Louisiana, Arkansas, Florida, and Missouri were moving toward
"the end of Slavery without delay."[2]

Given Northern apprehension surrounding immediate emancipation,
many of the institutional devices that were deployed by Union authorities
during and after the war only offered gradual freedom to ex-slaves, in effect if
not in name. As one leading scholar of the Freedmen's Bureau has noted, its
agents could be "accused of being concerned primarily with reestablishing

social and economic order . . . more often than not align[ing] themselves with white Southerners or simply fail[ing] to take into account the aspirations of former slaves." For the majority of Southern blacks, the presence of Northern agents initially meant a compulsory system of labor that substituted wages for the whip.[3] In wartime Louisiana, for instance, General Order 91 (November 1862) prohibited corporal punishment, but also discouraged Union officials from giving rations to unemployed freedmen or allowing movement outside the plantations without written passes. Given the ongoing social control of blacks under these guidelines, the resulting labor market could accurately be referred by the hybrid nomenclature of a "slave-wage system."[4] Efforts at managing uncertainty even assured some conservative white Southerners of the virtues of emancipation. On May 16, 1865, a commentator in the *Macon Telegraph* suggested that gradual emancipation was not desirable at all; it was better to "turn [the slave] loose at once, and he would in a few months or a year, find his level and his true situation and interests." Such purported freedom was to be accompanied by "rigid police and patrol laws . . . so as to maintain order and the right of property." Under this system of supervision, the commentator concluded more darkly, "Sambo would soon learn that he must labor or starve."[5]

Overlooking its specific racialized tone, the mind-set behind this statement was not exclusive to the American South, but could be found among elite members of European ancestry in a variety of societies undergoing the transition from slavery to capitalism. This final chapter considers the South's process of emancipation in comparative perspective. To what extent did other nations and colonies in the Western Hemisphere deploy similar devices in managing the uncertainty of institutional transformation after slavery? How "immediate" was the end of slavery in those contexts? And when and how did initial concerns around *classical uncertainty* (e.g., the difficulty in inferring wages for familiar forms of plantation labor) devolve into struggles around *categorical uncertainty* (e.g., the difficulty in determining what categories of labor were possible for former slaves)?

The perspective of this chapter is, in the words of Charles Tilly, one of "big structures, large processes, and huge comparisons."[6] An attempt to generalize across processes of emancipation in a number of societies is fraught with the peril of doing violence to the history of any particular case. Just as no two slave societies were the same, one can argue that local paths to emancipation reflected numerous and nuanced gradations. In the Caribbean islands alone, stretching from the Bahamas in the north to Trinidad in the south, there were notable variations in geography, topography, population growth, dependence on the sugar crop, planter power, and ties to colonial empires that affected both the character of slavery and the extent to which freedom was extended in its aftermath. These variations have been studied with analytical payoff.[7] My goal here is to sketch some broad similarities that link the emancipation of blacks in the American South with processes of emancipation in other New World societies that relied on chattel slavery. Given the exceptionalism often attributed to the American South, this comparison calls for some empirical abstraction.

THE PROCESS OF EMANCIPATION

At a glance, the process that brought about the emancipation of African Americans in the Southern states was fairly unique in the Western Hemisphere. Only the U.S. South and Haiti witnessed full-blown warfare directed toward the goal of emancipation. Only the U.S. South had governmental monitors supervising the process so extensively, initially through the Freedmen's Bureau (until the early 1870s) and, more indirectly, through a federal military presence that persisted in some quarters until the end of Radical Reconstruction. Moreover, the American South was one of very few cases of emancipation initiated in the nineteenth century where there was no effort made to compensate former slaveholders for their loss of chattel property.[8]

But to what extent was the process of emancipation in the American South truly exceptional? When the transition from antebellum slavery is framed through the lens of uncertainty, a number of parallels stand out between it and other instances of emancipation in the Western Hemisphere (see Table 8.1). The great majority of these cases involved an initial effort to manage the uncertainty of emancipation using governmental intervention. Outside of the Southern case, the mechanisms for reducing uncertainty tended to fall into three categories.[9] Programs of *gradual emancipation* linked the timing of manumission to a slave's age, birth cohort, and/or a future calendar year, ensuring that bondsmen and women would continue to be exploited by slaveholders for a specified duration, slowing the influx of freed slaves into the population, and providing dominant ethnic groups (especially, those of European ancestry) assurances that social order and hierarchy would be maintained. The first instance of gradual emancipation in the New World, adopted by Pennsylvania in 1780, allowed masters to hold slaves born before that year until their deaths; another generation of children born to slave mothers could be held until their twenty-eighth birthday.[10] As the epigraph at the beginning of this chapter suggests, gradual emancipation was widely promoted as an approach to managing the uncertainty of slavery's demise in the South. While Lincoln himself abandoned the idea of the "gradual abolishment of slavery" in the early years of the war, it was implemented de facto through some of the measures of the Freedmen's Bureau. The policy of "binding out children," in particular, meant that black youth in many parts of the South would not be emancipated

Table 8.1. The Process and Timing of Emancipation in the Americas, 1777–1888

Location	Process	Compensation to Slaveholders	Beginning	End
Argentina	Gradual	Yes	1825[a]	1854
Bolivia	Gradual	Yes	1825	1831
Brazil	Gradual	Yes	1871	1888
British colonies	Gradual	Yes	1833	1838
Central America	Immediate	Yes	1824	
Chile	Gradual	Yes	1811[a]	1826
Colombia	Gradual	Yes	1840s[a]	1852
Cuba	Gradual/partial		1870	1886
Dutch colonies	Gradual or immediate	Yes	1863	1873
Ecuador	Gradual	Yes	1840s	1852
French colonies	Immediate	Yes	1848	
Haiti	Revolution		1804	
Mexico	Partial	Yes	1829	1837
Paraguay	Gradual	Yes	1825	1862
Peru	Gradual	Yes	1821	1854
Puerto Rico	Gradual/partial	Yes	1870	1873
Uruguay	Partial	Yes	1842[a]	1854
Venezuela	Gradual	Yes	1821	1854
United States				
Connecticut	Gradual		1784	1809
District of Columbia	Immediate	Yes	1862	
Massachusetts	Immediate		1780	1783
New Hampshire	Gradual		1783	1857[a]
New Jersey	Gradual		1804[a]	1846[a]
New York	Gradual		1799	1827
Pennsylvania	Gradual		1780	1847
Rhode Island	Gradual		1784	1840s
Vermont	Immediate		1777	
U.S. South	Supervised		1862	1870s

Sources: Fogel and Engerman (1995: 33–34) and Rodriguez (1999).

[a] Indicates ambiguity depending on sources or definition. Fogel and Engerman place different dates on emancipation in Argentina (starting in 1813), Chile (1823), and Colombia (1814). There were numerous earlier efforts at emancipation in Uruguay. The New Jersey legislature initially adopted a program of gradual emancipation in 1786. In New Hampshire and New Jersey, slavery disappeared definitively only with the Thirteenth Amendment.

until they reached adulthood and that programs of so-called apprenticeship would produce effective bondage in the years after the Civil War.[11]

Across slave societies, a second mechanism that managed uncertainty among slaveholders was *partial emancipation*, which involved the freeing of only certain segments of the enslaved population or elimination of certain practices of bondage.[12] Partial emancipation could have pernicious effects on bondsmen or women who were unlucky enough to live in a particular region or have a particular status. For instance, protests from Texan slaveholders led infamously to an exemption of that territory from Mexico's antislavery edict in 1829. When a new Mexican president, Antonio López de Santa Anna, finally pushed for an end to the exemption under a unified constitution in December 1835, American settlers in Texas initiated a war of secession.[13] At the end of another war of secession, three decades later, the text of the Thirteenth Amendment contained a crucial caveat that exempted those who were convicted of a crime, whether real or fabricated, from its prohibition on slavery and indentured servitude. Between the 1870s and World War II, this exemption contributed to the re-enslavement of tens of thousands of blacks in the convict leasing systems of the South.[14]

While partial emancipation was not nearly as common in the Americas as programs of gradual emancipation, it was sometimes combined with other approaches. In Cuba, slavery was disassembled iteratively through legal measures that combined age-targeted aspects of gradual emancipation with aspects of partial emancipation that targeted institutionalized features of slavery. Thus, the Moret Law (an initial step toward Cuban abolition in 1870) freed young children and elderly slaves, while also banning the use of whips against those who remained in bondage. It was succeeded in 1880 by the creation of *patronato*, an apprenticeship system with some provisions for wages; the prohibition of stocks and chains in 1883; and the true abolition of slavery in 1886. As in the case of the American South under Union occupation, Cuban slavery was removed only in fits and starts over a period of several years.[15]

A third mechanism desired by slaveholders in managing the impact of emancipation was *compensation* for their loss of human property. Such reimbursement could be full or partial, and could be combined with programs of immediate, partial, or gradual emancipation. In 1833, the British Parliament enacted a scheme of compensated, gradual abolition for all of Britain's colonies, whereby field hands would be freed after six years and other slaves would be freed after four years. Parliament simultaneously created a twenty-million-pound fund—representing roughly one-twentieth of Britain's total national product at the time—to indemnify slave owners in the British West Indies for their economic losses. A Parliamentary Return published in March 1838 revealed awards to more than thirty thousand slaveholders, with nearly 64 percent of the compensation going to former slave owners in two British colonies, Jamaica and British Guiana. In other slave economies, such as Venezuela, the state created new taxes that were used to purchase the freedom of individual slaves over a period of many years via compensated manumission.[16]

A notable feature of nearly all these compensation schemes is that they were designed exclusively with slaveholders in mind. With the exception of a few small experiments (and, usually, without legislative sanction), the nations of the Western Hemisphere made no provision for compensation to former slaves themselves. The early process of emancipation in the South followed a similar course.[17] When slaves were freed in Washington, D.C., in April 1862, the Emancipation Act signed by Lincoln provided for treasury funds that could be deployed to compensate slaveholders for their loss of chattel, provided that slaveholders remained loyal to the Union. Compensation was disbursed for the emancipation of nearly three thousand slaves on this basis. Since fewer than a thousand residents of Washington owned slaves, this act was arguably symbolic, offering an exemplar to assuage the economic misgivings of the slaveholding planter elite in states in rebellion.[18] In the year thereafter, Lincoln worried about the constitutionality of the Emancipation Proclamation, owing to its lack of a provision for compensation. During the Thirty-Seventh Congress (1861–63), this aspect of emancipation was actively discussed in Washington, with most congressmen being in favor of full compensation to slaveholders.[19]

The arduous path to African American freedom in the South could thus be characterized as one that was not so unusual at all, one which (at various times) mixed institutional elements of gradual, partial, and compensated emancipation that had been deployed throughout the Americas. In institutional theory, the term "bricolage" has been applied to describe such combinations, particularly when existing ideas are redeployed in a novel context or seek to address new problems.[20] The policies of the Freedmen's Bureau itself were hardly uniform across time or space, but reflected acts of bricolage, in which agents adapted "to local circumstances and crop conditions in trying to negotiate agricultural contracts that promised fair wages in return for steady work." For instance, the initial labor contracts signed in Georgia in 1865 and 1866 continued to rely on an antebellum conception of blacks as gang laborers, who had to agree to terms with former masters as a collective entity. By 1867, the Georgia contracts were evolving and increasingly "appeared to be vehicles for asserting black individuality," with most now being signed "between individual heads of black households and employers."[21] Whether intentional or not, the bureau's approach in Georgia signified a form of partial emancipation, where the legal construction of ex-slaves as autonomous agents in a capitalist labor market was delayed for a number of years.[22]

In comparative perspective, the lengthy duration of governmental supervision in the effort to manage economic and political uncertainty in the South was also not unusual. If we take the period of federal monitoring as beginning with the first instance of emancipation in Washington, D.C. (April 1862) and continuing to the withdrawal of remaining federal troops at the end of Radical Reconstruction (the summer of 1877), then the process of supervision took fifteen years. Considering the other states and colonies in the Western Hemisphere, the average duration of emancipation was over three decades (Table 8.1). In some instances, moreover, closer examination reveals that purported cases of "immediate" emancipation were not so immediate after all. The initial transition toward the abolition of slavery in Saint-Domingue (later Haiti) began shortly after the French Revolution, in the early 1790s. It would not firmly be institutionalized until 1804, when Haiti declared its independence from France. Even in the unique Haitian case, where the end of slavery came "from below"—as a matter of slave insurrection—rather than "from above"—as a matter of governmental fiat—the process of emancipation was drawn out and subject to repeated efforts by French authorities to manage uncertainty in their Caribbean colony.[23]

Managing Uncertainty

A central argument of this book has been that the early economic struggles of emancipation in the American South revolved around problems of classical uncertainty: how contracts could assign a wage to workers who had never participated in a free labor market; how one could predict whether ex-slaves would stay on the plantation or in the households of former masters; how much the communities of the New South stood to gain if they rebuilt economies that were no longer appendages of the plantation system. This uncertainty was reflected in the smallest of social and economic transactions. As late as December 1867, agents of the Freedmen's Bureau continued to observe unrealistic expectations regarding wages among many freedmen, suggesting "the confusion and uncertainty that attended conditions of labor."[24] Employers were equally susceptible to false expectations, often rooted in antebellum practices and social structures. As emancipation shook the institution of the Southern household to its core, there was fundamental bewilderment among elite families as to why they no longer exercised as much authority or coercive license over the black domestics in their personal sphere.[25] Throughout the region, the transition from slavery meant that all Southerners—white and black, poor and wealthy, rural and urban—were unsure as to what the future would bring.

A source of continuity (as well as ongoing oppression) in the institutional transformation of the South lay in the familiar categories of action and social roles that were invoked immediately after the Civil War. While the war bared deep rifts between North and South, one thing that many whites in both regions agreed on is that blacks would continue to toil primarily as agricultural laborers and domestic servants; and they agreed, furthermore, that the large-scale plantation would continue to be cornerstone of the cotton economy. As in slavery, black women would continue to perform much of the reproductive labor in affluent white households, caring for children, washing clothing, and performing chores that were devalued in the broader economy.[26] Native-born planters and rentier capitalists would continue to make up a large proportion of the wealthiest landowners in the South, despite modest encroachments from merchants, carpetbaggers, and other factions. And the return of King Cotton also meant that "his chief retainer," the cotton factor, would return briefly to the center of the urban wholesaling market.[27]

This initial continuity in categorical inequality was repeated in instances of slave emancipation throughout the Western Hemisphere. In the British colonies, the 1833 Act of Emancipation institutionalized the continuity by requiring that former slaves work as apprentices for former masters in their existing occupations. Only after these "apprentices" had provided 40.5 hours of uncompensated work per week, did it become possible for them to seek out wage labor or new occupations. These changes introduced economic uncertainty, but it was primarily a matter of degree rather than a qualitative break with the past. Some apprentices used their overtime to engage in small-scale entrepreneurship (in handicraft, retail trade, and the like). The introduction of new opportunities for wage labor also meant a potential expansion of buying power on the part of ex-slaves, though plantation shops were in a structural position to capture much of this income. On the whole, the British Act of Emancipation functioned primarily to maintain the plantation system and its established hierarchy of slave occupations, rather than to prepare former slaves for freedom.[28]

The process of emancipation was similar among other colonial powers. In Suriname, a period of apprenticeship began under gradual emancipation in 1863 and lasted for ten years.[29] Although it was instituted three decades after the British Act, the process and problems of apprenticeship in the Dutch colony reflected the experience of the British Caribbean. Dutch policy preserved the plantation system, primarily by obligating ex-slaves to continue working on large-scale agricultural estates, albeit with wages set by colonial law. Uncertainty arose because former bondsmen and women now had some flexibility in choosing their employers and because employers had flexibility in paying wage premiums above and beyond the legal minimum. But, with respect to the demography of the labor force and the conditions of work, the general impact of apprenticeship was to generate an economy in Suriname that reproduced the categorical inequality from the last decade of slavery in the first decade of freedom.[30]

In many slave societies in the New World, the institutional devices used to manage the uncertainty of emancipation were invoked as well to manage new flows of laborers who might substitute for slaves. Before the abolition of slavery in Cuba, planters on the island began to import large numbers of indentured and contract laborers from China, totaling around 125,000 workers by 1874.[31] The contracts issued to these bound workers assumed a form that mirrored aspects of those issued to freed slaves in the U.S. South after the Civil War, including a fixed term of service (typically eight years in the case of Cuba), reimbursement that included a small wage combined with food and clothing, a specified number of days off work every year, and some stipulation of medical treatment. While early generations of Chinese migrants to Cuba were ostensibly free to pursue other opportunities after a period of indenture, an 1860 regulation required Chinese workers who completed their term to sign another contract (either with the same or with a different master) or face deportation. These constraints notwithstanding, the workers—often referred to historically as "coolies"—were not slaves, but fell into a third category that was clearly positioned in the social status hierarchy between free and unfree labor.[32]

Even in the British colonies, the ongoing reliance on servile labor was not the only institutional device deployed to reduce uncertainty. Both apprenticeship and the coolie system allowed planters to maintain a direct monopoly over worker labor supply. But indirect monopolies were established as well, by limiting the opportunities of workers to seek alternative sources of livelihood or consumption.[33] Planters in the colony of Antigua skipped apprenticeship entirely in favor of the immediate emancipation of slaves. The small size of the island and dominance of the sugar crop was combined with an antiemigration ordinance (in 1836) to ensure that freed blacks had little choice but to toil on Antigua's sugar plantations. Long after apprenticeship had disappeared in the British Caribbean, the reproduction of planter power in Antigua continued on the basis of an indirect monopoly over its workers.[34]

Despite continuities between slavery and the period of emancipation in many New World societies, the institutional breach was usually sufficient to generate uncertainty around wages, worker retention, and some possibility of economic activity outside the plantation system. This characteristic form of uncertainty was not invariably found in other societies making the transition from slavery. In the Portuguese possession of São Tomé and Príncipe, less than two hundred miles off the West African coast, slavery was replaced by perpetual indenture in 1875. Before World War I, roughly seventy thousand indentured workers were imported, mostly from Central Africa, in order to supply the thriving cocoa plantations of the island. Because there was no simple way to exit the colony and because the children of indentured servants were also born into indenture, the British historian William Clarence-Smith has suggested that "the only effective change after the 'abolition of slavery'... was that employers were compelled to pay their workers." Even in this one respect, mobilization among the planters of São Tomé and Príncipe soon removed most economic uncertainty from emancipation. Labor regulations issued in 1880 specified the exact amount that men and women were to be paid in their first two years of indenture, as well as the increase in pay thereafter. Unlike the instances of emancipation in the Western Hemisphere, the "modern slavery" of São Tomé and Príncipe eliminated even classical uncertainty from economic transactions, at least until the early twentieth century, when planters began to entice workers away from other plantations by paying wages that were substantially different from the legislated minimum.[35]

The Escalation of Uncertainty

A second argument in this book is that efforts to manage the uncertainty of emancipation in the U.S. South ultimately fell short, as the federal intervention of the postwar period gave way to emergent institutions that mixed indigenous traditions and prejudice with elements of capitalism. In some respects, the resulting uncertainty was propitious for those who had felt the burden of slavery most acutely. Among the first generation of freedmen and women, social positions in the antebellum South were only weakly associated with status attainment following Radical Reconstruction. With the exception of the categorical distinction between free blacks and slaves, the internal hierarchy of the old plantation system did not prove exceptionally durable in its effects on black inequality. By the late 1860s and 1870s, the plantation system itself was rapidly being displaced by alternative forms of agricultural tenure and contract, including sharecropping, tenancy, and rental arrangements. As a result, predicting the position of the freedman and woman in Southern society seemed a far more uncertain exercise in 1880 than it had been at the close of the Civil War.[36]

The prospects for the future were no more certain among the white populace or the businesses that they owned. The creed of the New South, promulgated by Henry Grady and his successors, confidently maintained that the demise of slavery would be associated with the rise of an entrepreneurial middle class, the fall of the planter elite, and the industrialization of the region. By 1880, however, the ranks of small artisans, manufacturers, shopkeepers, and service proprietors among the white adult labor force were thinner than they had been in 1860, while the ranks of agricultural laborers had expanded substantially. Farm proprietors composed a relatively stable faction of the adult white population, but their role in Southern society was increasingly denigrated by townsfolk seeking to embrace a more urban vision for the region. Outside of agriculture, business owners were embedded in networks of credit and trade that far exceeded the complexity of the antebellum factorage system, with its small number of interpersonal relationships among planters, factors, and wholesalers. The institutional spread of credit agencies sought to manage the uncertainty of doing business in the postbellum South, but was thwarted by the growing multiplicity and ambiguity of trades that enterprises were engaged in.[37]

The escalation of uncertainty was reflected in contestation around social categories: what positions were available to blacks and whites in the New South, what merits or costs would be associated with those positions, what organizational forms should agricultural and other businesses take on, and what paths to economic development were possible for Southern communities. Many of the features of categorical uncertainty were undoubtedly specific to the institutional transformation of the American South. But some notable parallels could be observed in other societies undergoing the transition from slavery.

Following the end of chattel slavery, one common source of categorical uncertainty involved the economic role of women. It is now widely understood that enslaved black women in the New World were expected to perform the same arduous field labor as their male counterparts, in addition to domestic and reproductive duties. Among white women, the conception of a "weaker sex" had, at least by the nineteenth century, allowed for some exemption from harsh agricultural and manual labor (aside from frontier regions were male labor was in limited supply). This exemption did not extend to black female slaves. Whether one looked at the cotton fields of the South, the cane fields of the Caribbean sugar islands, or the livestock pens of Jamaica, one was likely to find female slaves working alongside bondsmen.[38]

During periods of gradual or supervised emancipation, uncertainty regarding the female labor supply was managed to a considerable extent by third parties. In the British Caribbean, the system of apprenticeship ensured that former bondswomen would continue to hold many of the same backbreaking occupations that they had under slavery. With full emancipation, it was far less clear as to what categories of work would come to define the lives of black women. After visiting the British West Indies, one correspondent mused in 1861 that "the effect of freedom was to abolish almost entirely the labour of women in the cane-fields." For Afro-Caribbean women, new work trajectories could lie in full-time housekeeping and child rearing, in domestic service, in cultivating small agricultural holdings, or in marketing the goods from home production.[39]

Even with growing uncertainty around work trajectories, one could argue that the conditions of labor for black women had drastically improved compared to those conditions under gradual or supervised emancipation. Data from the United States paint a more nuanced picture. The Freedmen's Bureau had pursued an equivocal approach to the employment of former bondswomen, both encouraging it in its "war on dependency" and discouraging it through the actions of its agents.[40] Nevertheless, an inspection of labor contracts, as well as census data, suggests that the employment prospects for black women appeared to be steady or improving during the postwar years. In the contracts signed by ex-slaves in northern Virginia and Washington, D.C., skilled occupations were more commonly allocated to black women than black men.[41] Average occupational income among black women in the United States—while still substantially lower than that of black men or white women—also appeared to make considerable headway during the 1860s and 1870s. Once Radical Reconstruction ended, alongside federal supervision in the South, black women experienced deepening inequality. Between 1880 and 1930, the gap in average occupational income between black women and white men grew steadily in the United States. The categorical uncertainty surrounding former slaves and the daughters of slaves—who fit neither the feminized expectations placed on white women nor the hypermasculine expectations placed on black men— would increasingly lead them into devalued occupations.[42]

A second example of escalating uncertainty with cross-societal generalizability could be found in the domain of race relations. In the American South, supervised emancipation brought a tenuous truce, in which the Freedmen's Bureau persuaded ex-slaves to remain in hierarchical work relationships with former or new masters, and the Reconstruction Acts established the military control that would allow black males some semblance of political participation. The institutional supports to this truce featured an array of state-level policies aimed at improving the status of former slaves and integrating them into Southern society, including provisions for "like and equal" public schools in Arkansas (1873), the integration of public schools, inns, theaters, and railways in Florida (1873), provisions for the equal treatment of black and white customers in South Carolina (1870) and Mississippi (1873), and labor laws supporting the priority of workers' wages over other liens against Southern employers (1868–72 in various states).[43] The incomplete institutionalization of these policies and the notorious effort to dismantle them after Radical Reconstruction led to fundamental uncertainty about the possibility of black enfranchisement and harmonious race relations in the South. The uncertainty was reflected in the residential and labor segregation of the Jim Crow era, the elimination of initiatives aimed at public education, and, perhaps most acutely, the "festival of violence" against blacks in the form of lynching and white terrorism.[44]

The South was hardly alone in this pattern of escalating uncertainty in race relations following a period of supervised emancipation. The state of New York commenced gradual emancipation on July 4, 1799, agreeing to free female children of slaves at the age of twenty-five and male children at the age of twenty-eight. In 1817, all slaves born before 1799 were freed, and in 1827, slavery was fully abolished. In the years that followed, New York City became a center of not only the national abolitionist movement, but also simmering racial tensions. These tensions exploded in the summer of 1834 in an eight-day riot featuring the worst display of violence that the city would witness before the Civil War. The riots began when antiabolitionists broke up an integrated meeting of blacks and whites celebrating the anniversary of slavery's abolition; they ended with the widespread destruction of black homes, churches, schools, and small businesses. To the shock of progressives, these events had "demonstrated that [racial] amalgamation was as much a psychological trigger point in the North, as in the South."[45]

On the surface, the categorical uncertainty of postemancipation race relations in the United States was based on a very different racial hierarchy than that found in other former slave societies of the New World. The institutionalization of the "one-drop rule" in the United States sought to construct a rigid dichotomy between whites and blacks, as did the norm of racial segregation.[46] In the Caribbean and Latin America, by contrast, a more nuanced racial hierarchy developed, based on a continuum of skin tone, ancestry, culture, experience, and achievement.[47] Nevertheless, with full emancipation, the graded hierarchy did not serve to mitigate uncertainty and, perhaps, even exacerbated it in the domain of race relations. West Indian blacks, for instance, maintained considerable enmity toward mulattos, who were seen as collaborators of European planters and imperialists under colonial rule. The West Indian–born pan-Africanist Edward Wilmot Blyden went so far as to denounce marriage between "genuine Negroes" and colored people of mixed-race ancestry as a form of miscegenation.[48] While slavery (and, later, apprenticeship) had once functioned to produce a robust separation of blacks and free colored people within the racial hierarchy, these categories became far more fluid with emancipation.

Thus, a common thread in the escalation of uncertainty in the former slave societies of the Western Hemisphere was that the economic distinction of slave and free labor had served to anchor other social categories—black, white, and mulatto; feminine and masculine; lower and upper class—that became contested in the aftermath of emancipation. In the absence of slavery (or its appendages in programs of "gradual" emancipation), new institutional devices had to emerge to sustain historical patterns of racial, gender, and class inequality.

Conclusion

A core tenet of institutional analysis has long been that social institutions involve stable systems of rules, norms, and understandings that have an uncertainty-reducing effect. In the words of the Nobel Prize–winning economic historian Douglass North, "institutions reduce uncertainty by providing a structure to everyday life"; they determine "the opportunities in a society."[49] More recent incarnations of institutional theory have come to challenge this basic conception. Sociologists contend that institutions can be a source of instability as well as social order, as distinct rules and understandings come into conflict with one another, entail ambiguous interpretations, and favor the interests of the powerful over those of weaker social actors. The process of creating new institutional devices may have unintended consequences that yield ongoing sources of uncertainty. And, far from determining the opportunities in society, institutional change may eliminate old social categories and patterns of action without providing much guidance as to what new categories and patterns will come to replace them.[50]

The transition between slavery and capitalist institutions, perhaps the most profound social transformation in the history of the United States, as well as the Americas more generally, amply illustrates the advantages of the broadened conception of institutional change. Almost everywhere that slavery was eliminated in the New World, there were attempts to manage the uncertainty of abolition through programs of gradual, partial, and/or compensated emancipation. These institutional interventions generally acknowledged that uncertainty in wages, labor supply, competition among planters, and economic development would result from emancipation. But the interventions also sought to preserve the basic categories and social hierarchy of slave society, thereby ensuring stability (and durable inequality) in the economic possibilities that confronted the planter and freedman alike.[51]

Almost everywhere that these institutional interventions were implemented, they ultimately failed to minimize the uncertainty of emancipation or to prepare former slaves (and the white population) for freedom. The social organization of the household, agricultural production, commodity exchange, and race relations was fundamentally altered by the demise of slavery; in more subtle ways, so too were the class structure and urban life of former slave societies. The evolution of emancipation increasingly produced uncertainty around possibilities, not simply the probability of social outcomes.

As Arthur Stinchcombe reminds us, a key "aspect of freedom or liberty is that it enlarges the set of possibilities among which one can choose."[52] While this is a perceptive conceptualization, it does not imply that the escalation of uncertainty follows as a tautological consequence of freedom. Categorical uncertainty arises when the set of possibilities confronting human beings is ill defined or contested, not because it has been expanded. It reflects the precarious side of freedom, in which both (formerly) dominant and subordinate groups are unsure about their place in society following a period of profound institutional transformation. It may accompany the constriction of possibilities, as was the case in the forms of land tenure available to Southern blacks, as well as the expansion of possibilities.[53] Even in the twenty-first century, some of this durable uncertainty remains as we wrestle with the legacies of slavery and emancipation.

Appendix A. Data Sources and Sampling

The quantitative analyses in this book are based on a number of data sources covering individuals, organizations, and counties in the antebellum and postbellum South (see Table A.1). While some of the data sets are well known in cliometric or demographic circles, and have been carefully described elsewhere, others are new and have only recently been collected and coded. This appendix provides a brief overview of the data sets, as well as any special considerations or analytical corrections that have been applied in constructing the historical samples.

SLAVE PURCHASES, APPRAISALS, HIRES, AND WAGE LABOR

Chapter 2 draws on data comprising 75,099 transactions in the antebellum period, as well as 1,378 labor contracts in the postbellum era, to examine how the valuation of black labor was transformed between the 1830s and the years of emancipation. While many of the statistics reported in the chapter are based on the complete data, a key caveat in interpreting these findings is the issue of sampling bias. It is well known, for instance, that children and adolescents who were apprenticed to white employers in wage labor arrangements after the Civil War were typically either orphans or youth who were compelled to hire themselves out by destitute parents.[1] It is quite possible that the valuation of such child laborers is not comparable to that of young slaves in the antebellum period, owing to differences in skills and demographics. To guard against such sampling biases, I reexamined all of the results after matching black workers across labor markets on the basis of sociodemographic characteristics.

I first matched the samples geographically by limiting transactions to those conducted in a few Southern states that served as centers of the slave trade since the early American Republic, including Louisiana, Maryland, and Virginia. I constructed a core sample by beginning with 701 transactions between 1831 and 1863, with information on both slave appraisals and sales prices for the *same* individuals. Slave hires and wage laborers who were recruited in the same states were then linked to these records based on propensity score matching with a Mahalanobis metric.[2] The algorithm draws the hired worker or wage laborer who most closely matches a slave

Table A.1. Selected Sources of Data on Slavery and Reconstruction

Chapter	Data Set	Sources	Time Coverage	Unit of Analysis	Observations
2	Slave hires	Fogel and Engerman (2006a)	1831–65	Individual slaves	17,158
2	Slave sales and appraisals	Fogel and Engerman (2006b)	1831–65	Individual slaves	6,709 sales; 51,232 appraisals
2	Free labor contracts in D.C. and Virginia	Freedmen's Bureau (1865–70, 1865–72)	1865–67	Former slaves	1,378
3	Works Progress Administration interviews	Rawick (1972–79); Escott (1979); Ruef and Fletcher (2003)	1820s–1930s (retrospective)	Former slaves and free blacks	1,392
3	IPUMS linked sample of census records	Ruggles et al. (2010)	1860–80	Former slaves and free blacks	2,472
4	IPUMS 1 percent census samples (with black oversamples)	Ruggles et al. (2010)	1850–1900	Individuals	91,802[a]
5	Agricultural census	U.S. Bureau of the Census (1864a, 1872, 1883a)	1860–80	Counties	1,091
5	Southern farms	Ransom and Sutch (1999)	1880	Farms	11,202
6	Southern merchants, manufacturers, and traders	R. G. Dun Credit Reports; Ruef and Patterson (2009a)	1860–1900	Businesses	121,396[a]
7	Southern communities	R. G. Dun Credit Reports; Ruef and Patterson (2009b)	1870–80	Settlements	3,429[a]
7	Southern counties	Haines and ICPSR (2005)	1870–80	Counties	346[a]

[a] Some samples are limited to the five states in the Lower South (including Alabama, Georgia, Louisiana, Mississippi, and South Carolina).

observed in the purchase market based on gender, age, and occupational skill. The difference between workers is defined by the Mahalanobis distance d, where **u** and **v** are the values of the variables to be matched for a slave and hired/wage worker, respectively, and **C** is the sample covariance matrix for the matching variables from the full sample of laborers outside the slave purchase market:

$$d = (\mathbf{u} - \mathbf{v})^T \mathbf{C}^{-1} (\mathbf{u} - \mathbf{v}) \qquad (A.1)$$

Table A.2 shows the resulting reduction in standardized bias for age, gender, and occupational skill, computed as $100(1 - b_M / b_I)$, where b_I is the initial difference in sample means and b_M is the difference after matching.[3] The reduction in bias for all samples and covariates is substantial, ranging from 79 percent to 100 percent. After matching, t-statistics comparing the sample of wage workers and slave purchases suggest no statistically significant differences on these characteristics. For the sample of slave hires, differences in age composition persist, but covariate balance is improved considerably.

I computed weights for each observation to make the pool of hired slaves and wage laborers more representative of the population of black workers as a whole. I define $\hat{e}(x)$ to be a propensity score indicating the probability that a given individual will be hired out (antebellum period) or sign a wage contract (postbellum period), based on a logistic regression for each outcome that considers a combined sample of slave purchases and hires or slave purchases and wage contracts, respectively. Then the weight for hires and wage labor can be defined as $w = 1/\hat{e}(x)$. For the remaining sample of slave purchases and appraisals, the weight is calculated as $w = \hat{e}(x)/(1 - \hat{e}(x))$.[4]

Using samples that are matched to the data on slave purchases, Figure A.1 replicates the age-price profiles for black men and women following a propensity score analysis. One difference stands out compared to the results shown in Figure 2.4. Age-dependent price differences between the purchase market for slaves and the appraisal market largely disappear after the samples are matched. Insofar as the purchase market for slaves reflected the

Table A.2. Percentage Reduction in Standardized Bias from Logical and Propensity Score Matching

	Slave Appraisals (%)	Slave Hires (%)	Wage Labor (%)
Worker Attributes			
Age	100	79.3 ($t = 10.6$)	96.7 ($t = 0.50$)
Female	100	100.0 ($t = 0.00$)	100.0 ($t = 0.00$)
Skilled labor[a]	100	100.0 ($t = 0.00$)	100.0 ($t = 0.00$)

Note: All samples are matched to data on slave sales.

[a] All workers with occupational skills that do not involve field work or common labor are defined as skilled.

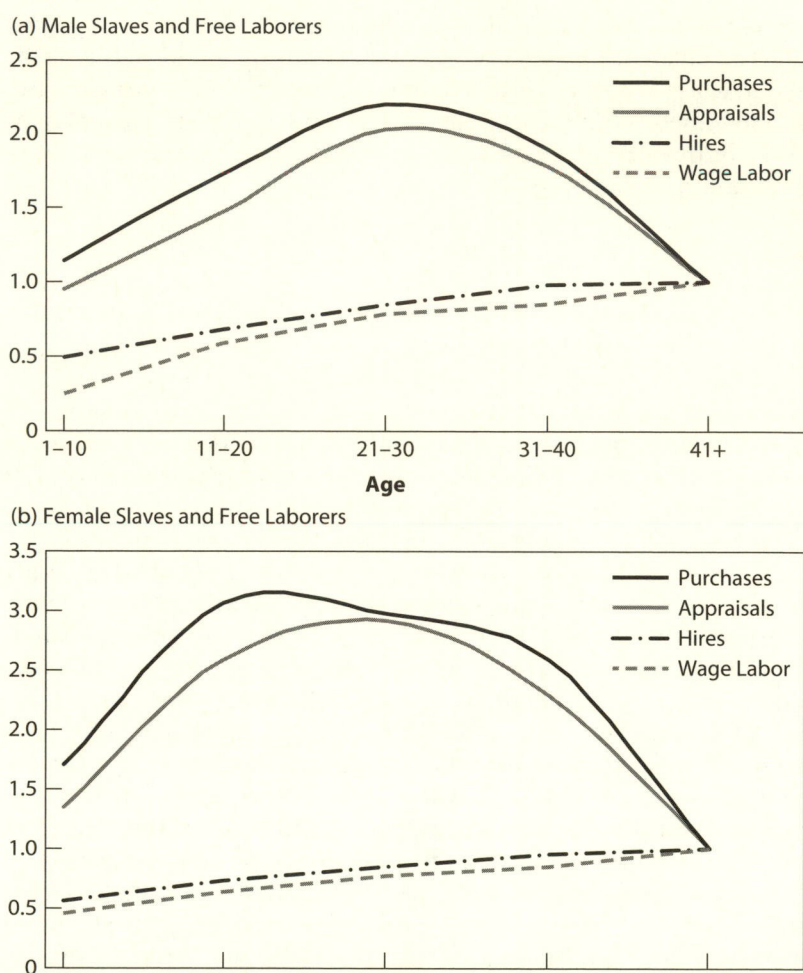

(a) Male Slaves and Free Laborers

(b) Female Slaves and Free Laborers

Figure A.1. Relative Price of Black Labor by Age Category, with Matched Samples:
(a) Male Slaves and Free Laborers, (b) Female Slaves and Free Laborers
Note: Prices are relative to reference category (= 1.0) for slaves or free laborers who
are older than forty years.

exploitation of young women and children, appraisers may have built the
value of such exploitation into their own assessments. The remaining variation across labor markets in the age-price profile centers around the distinction between short-term wage contracts (whether they involve slave or free
labor) and the perpetual ownership of labor.

Works Progress Administration Interviews

Using interviews conducted by the Works Progress Administration (WPA) in the 1930s, Chapter 3 examines the legacy of American slavery at the individual, intragenerational level. The data considered in the chapter include 1,590 interviews that elicited information from Southern blacks on their socioeconomic attainment during the postbellum period, as well as their status under slavery.[5] To be included in further analysis, respondents had to be born before or during the Civil War and reside in a slaveholding state (or territory) before emancipation. After removing cases that failed to meet these criteria, 1,471 remaining interviews were coded for identifying information, age, gender, family background, education, migration, and occupational attainment for each respondent.

For the education of interviewees, an imputation procedure was used to replace missing values and ensure that a maximum number of cases could be retained. Weights were assigned to cases with imputed education values in order to compensate for increased residual variance.[6] Cases with missing values on any of the other variables were removed by listwise deletion. This reduced the total number of cases to 1,392.

Although the aim of the WPA's Federal Writers' Project was to generate representative life histories of former slaves, limited systematic sampling was conducted. The archives contain narratives from roughly 2 percent of the ex-slaves still living in the 1930s, but feature considerable variation in the number of interviews collected from state to state. To account for geographic bias in the sample, I weighted all cases by state of origin to correspond to the slave and free black populations at the end of the antebellum era (as represented in the 1860 census). The sample sizes and case weights are shown by state in Table A.3.

Further issues of representativeness arise from the advanced age of respondents (a median of eighty-three in my subsample) and the possibility of varying mortality rates among respondents from different status backgrounds under slavery. Demographers have identified two primary correlates of mortality for slaves: slave occupation (e.g., domestic versus field hand) and plantation ecology (type of crop grown). Controlling for crop type, slaves engaged in domestic and skilled manual labor have been found to have mortality rates less than half those of field hands of the same age.[7] To account for this source of differential mortality, I applied a second set of weights based on the mix of slave occupations in the late antebellum South.[8]

The advanced age of respondents in the WPA archives also leads to questions concerning the accuracy of recall. WPA interviewers often undertook prior research to establish basic biographical details on respondents (such as age, family background, and the like). To improve reliability,

Table A.3. Distribution of WPA Sample across Former Slaveholding States and 1860 Census Weights

State	Cases	Case-to-Population Ratio	Case Weight
Ex-slave population			
Alabama	102	1:4,265	1.479
Arkansas	131	1:848	0.294
Florida	12	1:5,145	1.784
Georgia	159	1:2,907	1.008
Kentucky	42	1:5,369	1.861
Louisiana	73	1:4,544	1.576
Maryland	5	1:17,438	6.046
Mississippi	196	1:2,228	0.772
Missouri	45	1:2,554	0.886
North Carolina	93	1:3,560	1.234
Oklahoma (Indian Territory)	8	1:313	0.109
South Carolina	143	1:2,814	0.976
Tennessee	96	1:2,872	0.996
Texas	196	1:931	0.323
Virginia	69	1:7,114	2.467
Free black population			
Pooled for all states	30	1:7,699	2.577

Note: Figures are reported for sample of blacks with known social status within antebellum regime.

many interviewers were also instructed to visit respondents on at least two occasions, the second visit to "gather all the worthwhile recollections that the first talk has aroused." These multiple interviews primarily reveal problems of recall in complex chronological sequences (e.g., order of masters under the antebellum regime), rather than the more basic socioeconomic variables that are analyzed in this book. Moreover, interviews tended to be conducted around major life-cycle markers (emancipation, marriage, etc.), an approach that tends to improve the performance of long-term memory.[9]

INTEGRATED PUBLIC USE MICRODATA SERIES

To develop a more general portrait of Southern class structure and status attainment, this book employs representative samples of census data from the Integrated Public Use Microdata Series (IPUMS).[10] In Chapter 3, I use census records on African Americans from 1880 and consider whether they could be linked by name, birthplace, sex, race, and age to 1860 census records. African Americans who appeared in both the 1880 census and the 1860 census were identified as "free blacks" if they resided in a slaveholding state or territory before the Civil War. The remaining (unlinked) individuals were identified as former slaves if they were born in a slaveholding state or territory.[11] The resulting data set includes postbellum status outcomes on 2,472 blacks who lived in the antebellum South, including 229 free blacks and 2,243 former slaves.

Chapter 4 analyzes samples of whites and blacks that are not linked across censuses, but are organized as repeated cross-sections for every decade. These data include a 1 percent random sample of the free population in the Lower South, as well as a 2 percent oversample of blacks in 1860 and 1870. The initial data set encompasses 251,845 person records. Since the chapter defines class membership on an occupational basis, I restrict attention to individuals who were in the labor force and did not reside in group quarters (e.g., correctional facilities, military barracks, mental institutions, and poorhouses). The resulting sample includes 91,802 individuals in the Lower South between 1850 and 1900. To ensure comparability between the antebellum and postbellum eras, I also limit empirical analyses of human and financial capital to white adults, aged twenty and older. The smaller sample comprises 32,923 individuals between 1850 and 1900.

Agricultural Censuses

In order to examine the factors affecting the decline of the Southern plantation in the decades after the Civil War, Chapter 5 relies on county-level data from the U.S. Census Bureau Reports on Agriculture (1860–80), as well as a sample of eleven thousand farms from the 1880 manuscript census.[12] For purposes of analysis, I consider changes in the prevalence of plantation agriculture in all U.S. states having significant slave populations in 1860, including Alabama, Arkansas, Florida, Georgia, Kentucky, Louisiana, Maryland, Mississippi, Missouri, North Carolina, South Carolina, Tennessee, Texas, and Virginia. Slaveholding states with fewer than two thousand slaves in the 1860 census (Delaware, Kansas, and Nebraska) were not considered. This leads to a total of 1,091 counties that were available for the aggregate analysis and a smaller subset of 73 counties that could be analyzed on the basis of the manuscript census.[13]

The estimates in Figure 5.5 are based on raw organizational counts of plantation units, which offer some advantages over two alternative measures of plantation prevalence: (a) the ratio of plantations to all agricultural units in a county and (b) the degree of land concentration within the plantation system, rather than alternative forms of land tenure. Although useful for descriptive purposes (see Figure 5.2), the former measure is sensitive to simultaneity bias when the vector of predictor variables also contains components found in the ratio variable's denominator. The latter measure can only be estimated from county-level census records, since the largest farms are categorized in an open-ended interval (one thousand or more acres).[14]

CREDIT REPORTS ON SOUTHERN BUSINESSES

Chapters 6 and 7 employ data from the *Reference Book* of R. G. Dun and company, the most extensive listing of business classifications and credit ratings in the nineteenth century. To coincide with the timing of the U.S. census, I sampled firm data from five decennial cross-sections in the *Reference Book*, including 1860, 1870, 1880, 1889, and 1900.[15] The July 1860 edition of the *Reference Book* covered only 2,218 businesses in the Cotton South. The July 1870 edition identified 19,929 businesses in the region; the July 1880 edition contained 31,673 organizations (approximately 4 percent of all firms enumerated by Dun); 48,053 and 54,983 entries appeared in the 1889 and 1900 editions, respectively. For each case, information was coded on the business location, name(s) of proprietor(s), proprietor demographics, legal form of the business, capital assets, industrial classification, and credit rating. Listwise deletion removed cases that either were cross-listed duplicates or (in the postbellum period) had missing information on capital assets, leaving 121,396 cases for purposes of analysis.

Statistics based on these data are subject to many of the customary caveats regarding sampling methodology. For the time period analyzed here, there is no reliable universe of business firms that one can sample from. Consequently, the risk set for credit coverage pertains to those enterprises that Dun subscribers requested information on or that Dun agents were aware of. Many small or self-sufficient Southern businesses, especially in the domain of agriculture, are likely to be ignored by this sampling procedure.

Appendix B. Idiosyncrasy

In Chapter 7, the key variable assessing the degree of uncertainty surrounding a Southern county's pattern of postbellum development is the measure of idiosyncrasy. The measure evaluates the extent to which the profile of organizational forms in a county matches the pattern found in Southern postbellum counties on the whole. Because counties vary in their ability to sustain business activity, the measure is based not simply on matching industries across counties, but rather on the extent to which the appearance of businesses conforms to a nested pattern, conditioned on the diversity of organizational types in each county. I adapt an approach to nestedness that has been widely used in bioecology to analyze the hospitality and idiosyncrasy of habitats for diverse species.[1] Recent descriptive analyses in organizational sociology have suggested that this approach may also be useful in evaluating the typical order of appearance among organizational forms in human communities.[2]

For purposes of exposition, I will show how this approach can be applied to a small sample of counties from the South in 1870, involving ten counties from Alabama and the first ten organizational forms (alphabetically) in the list used by R. G. Dun and Company (excluding those forms that do not appear in any of those counties during that year). Figure B.1 illustrates the four steps used to derive a measure of county idiosyncrasy. We begin with a raw matrix indicating the presence or absence of each organizational form in the ten counties (Figure B.1a). Reading across the rows, for instance, we can see that Autauga County features at least one confectionary, cotton gin, drug store, dry goods store, and general store, but lacks a bank, blacksmith, butcher shop, carpentry, or clothier. Adopting the language of theoretical ecology, we refer to counties that feature a diverse set of forms as being *hospitable* to business activity and to organizational forms that thrive in a large number of counties as being *stable*. Conversely, counties featuring a small number of organizational forms are referred to as *inhospitable* and forms that exist in only a small subset of counties are called *tenuous*.[3]

The next step in the analysis permutes the rows and columns of the matrix (Figure B.1b), so that counties are ranked in order from hospitable to inhospitable and organizational forms are ranked from stable to tenuous.[4] If locales are *nested* within one another, such that the organizational forms in less hospitable counties always constitute a proper subset of the forms in more hospitable counties, then the resulting matrix should give rise to a

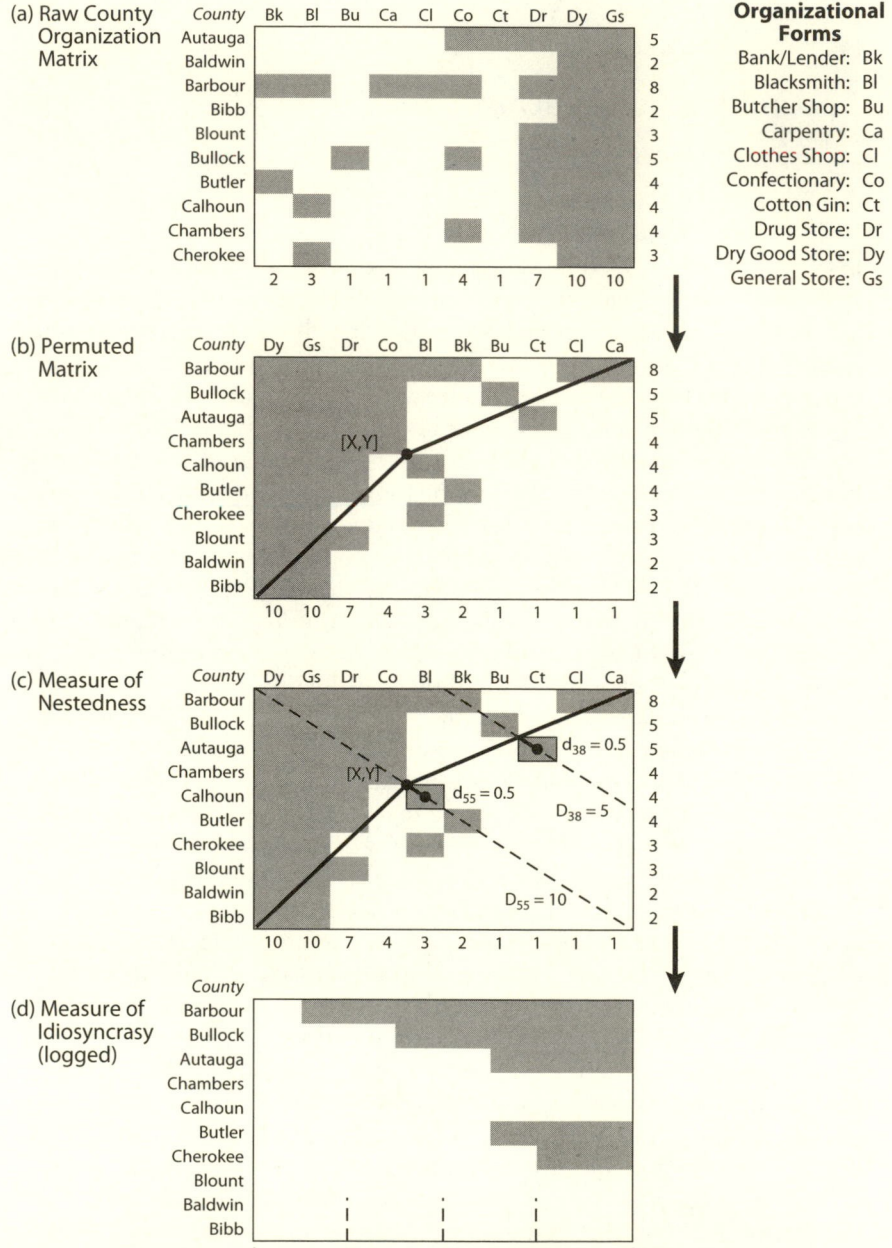

Figure B.1. Deriving a Measure of Idiosyncrasy from a County-Organization Matrix:
(a) Raw County-Organization Matrix, (b) Permuted Matrix, (c) Measure of Nestedness, (d) Measure of Idiosyncrasy (Logged)

predictable pattern, in which organizational presences are concentrated in the upper-left-hand corner of the permuted matrix and organizational absences are concentrated in the lower-right-hand corner.

Using the density of the presence-absence matrix, a perfect pattern of nestedness can easily be derived. We can identify a point [X,Y] along the matrix diagonal that divides the matrix into two areas, one consisting of only predicted presences and the other consisting of only predicted absences. If O is the number of organizational types, C is the number of counties, and Δ is the density of the matrix, we calculate X = $\Delta \times$ O and Y = $\Delta \times$ C. In the example, for instance, we have a county-organization matrix in which 40 percent of the cells are presences (Δ = 0.4). Thus, X = 0.4 $\times$ 10 = 4 and Y = 0.4 $\times$ 10 = 4. To divide the matrix, lines are drawn from the upper-right- and lower-left-hand corners to this point. Basic algebra verifies that the area above and to the left of these lines would contain all the presences in the matrix if they were concentrated in the most hospitable counties and stable organizational forms.

Several questions arise in analyzing the permuted matrix. First, to what extent do locales in a given region and historical period evidence a norm of nestedness? If strong norms of community structure prevail, the appearance of organizational forms will follow a predictable sequence. Locales that are inhospitable to organizing efforts will feature only the most stable organizational forms—such as dry goods and general stores, in our example. Locales that are exceptionally hospitable may feature even rare organizational forms (such as clothiers). To assess the strength of a norm of nestedness, I employ a measure based on deviations from the ideal-type pattern (Figure B.1c). Every empty cell above the dividing lines in the matrix represents an unexpected absence of an organizational type; every full cell below the dividing lines represents an unexpected presence. In theoretical ecology, these unexpected cells are identified as deviations (d_{ij}) from the dividing lines in the matrix along cross-cutting diagonals (whose length is denoted as D_{ij}).[5] Idiosyncrasy (I), the overall measure of deviation from nestedness in the matrix, is then calculated as,

$$I = \frac{100}{U_{max}} \frac{1}{C \times O} \left(\sum_{i=1}^{C} \sum_{j=1}^{O} \left(\frac{d_{ij}}{D_{ij}} \right)^2 \right) \qquad \text{(B.1)}$$

where C is the number of counties, O is the number of organizational forms, i and j index forms and counties (respectively), and U_{max} is a constant representing the maximum amount of deviation from nestedness that is possible for any given matrix. The measure I can range from 0, representing no deviation from nestedness, to 100, representing maximum deviation.

A cell from the example serves to illustrate how standardized deviations (d_{ij}/D_{ij}) are calculated to compose the metric of idiosyncrasy. Consider the

Table B.1. Organizational Forms Analyzed

Agent (NEC)
Agricultural implements/supply
Architect's office
Artist's studio
Auction house
Bakery
Bank/money lender
Bar/saloon
Barber shop
Billiard saloon
Blacksmith
Boarding house
Boatbuilder
Boilermaker
Bookbinder
Bookstore
Brewery
Brick/stone mason
Brickyard
Bridge builder
Broker, commercial
Broom factory
Builder/contractor
Building materials supply
Butcher
Cabinetmaker
Carpentry
Carpet store
Carriage-/wagonmaker
China/crockery/glass shop
Cigars/tobacconist
Cloth/linen store
Clothier (NEC)
Coal yard
Coffee house
Collection agency
College
Confectionary
Cooperage
Coppersmith
Cotton factor
Cotton gin/mill
Distillery (NEC)
Door/blind/sash maker
Drayage
Drug store
Dry goods store
Dyer
Engineer, civil
Express agency
Factor (NEC)
Factory (NEC)
Fancy goods store

Feed store
Ferry/tugboat/boat (NEC)
Fertilizer vendor
Fish/oyster monger
Foundry (NEC)
Furniture store
Gardener/nursery
Gas works
General store
Ginmaker
Grain store
Grist mill
Grocery
Gun-/locksmith
Hardware store
Harness maker
Hatter
Hide/leather store
Hotel
Huckstershop/peddler
Ice dealer
Insurance company
Ironworks
Jeweler
Justice of the peace
Lamp/kerosene store
Land/real estate agency
Law office
Limekiln/quarry
Liquor/wine store
Livery
Livestock dealer
Lumber yard/mill
Machine shop
Marble yard
Mechanic
Men's clothier
Merchant (NEC)
Milk/dairy delivery
Millinery/dressmaker
Millwright
Mine
Mineral spring
Music store
Music teacher/school
Newspaper/magazine
Newsstand
Oil mill
Paint/oil store
Painter
Paper mill
Paper store
Photography studio

Physician/dentist's office
Piano maker/tuner
Picture-frame maker
Plasterer
Plumber/gasfitter
Postmaster
Printer/publisher
Produce/provisions store
Railroad contractor/supplies
Railroad office
Restaurant
Rice mill
Saddlery
Sail maker
Saltworks
Saw/planing mill
School (NEC)
Seed vendor
Sewing machine vendor
Shingle mill
Ship chandler
Shipper/freighter
Shipwright
Shoemaker, boot/shoe store
Silver/goldsmith
Slater/roofer
Soap/candle factory
Soda (or other) bottler
Speculator
Stationary store
Steamboat
Stock brokerage
Stock raiser
Stone cutter
Stove vendor
Tailor
Tanyard
Tea shop
Telegraph company
Tinware shop
Toy store
Trunk maker
Turpentine distillery
Undertaker
Upholsterer
Warehouse
Watchmaker
Wharf
Wheelwright
Woodshop
Woodyard
Woolen mill

unexpected presence of a cotton gin factory in Autauga County. The deviation from the dividing line is small ($d_{38} = 0.5$), but the length of the cross-cutting diagonal is also fairly short ($D_{38} = 5$). The standardized deviation (d_{ij}/D_{ij}) informs us that this deviation represents 1/10 of the length of the cross-cutting diagonal.

When the occurrence of organizations within a set of locations gives rise to a pronounced pattern of nestedness, a second measurement issue emerges: how do we evaluate the idiosyncrasy of locales that do not conform to this pattern of community structure? Using the row totals that compose the measure of overall idiosyncrasy (I), a county-specific summation of deviations from nestedness ($I_C[i]$) is,

$$I_C[i] = \frac{100}{U_{max}} \frac{1}{O}\left(\sum_{j=1}^{O}\left(\frac{d_{ij}}{D_{ij}}\right)^2 \right) \qquad (B.2)$$

Figure B.1d illustrates the resulting measures of idiosyncrasy for the ten counties in the expository sample (in logged form). Autauga County is moderately idiosyncratic by this standard, since it lacks a bank and blacksmith shop, but does feature a rarer organizational form (the cotton gin factory). By contrast, Chambers County perfectly matches the expected pattern of organizational forms. As the figure suggests, measures of idiosyncrasy are sensitive to the inclusion of unique organizational forms, which appear in only a single locale in the matrix (note the relatively high scores for Barbour, Bullock, and Autauga). To guard against this problem, I include only those organizational forms in the analysis appearing at least *twice* in each wave of my data (see Table B.1 for list).

Notes

PREFACE

1. Savali (2013); Ramos (2013); Ellerson (2010).
2. Obama (2012). A prominent Lincoln scholar, Allen Guelzo, reported that he and others approached the White House about an event to recognize the sesquicentennial, but that "they blew us off ... somehow the idea of a celebration for the Emancipation Proclamation just got nixed" (Mackaman 2013).
3. CBS News (2011). I have weighted the sample of 848 respondents so that the statistics are representative of adults (age eighteen and over) living in the continental United States. The distinct views represented in the survey are not limited to the general public, but are commonly invoked in debates between interest groups, with some, such as the NAACP, associating the Civil War with the problem of slavery and others, such as libertarian and Southern heritage groups, closely linking it to economic disputes between an industrializing North and an agricultural South (Satris 2002: 74–75).
4. ABC News (1997). The sample includes 703 respondents, who are again weighted for representativeness. Craemer (2009) has shown that opinions on reparations for slavery are especially sensitive to how the issue is framed, considering *who* is to be compensated, by *whom*, and with *what* form of compensation. Between 1997 and 2002, national estimates of support for reparations ranged from an average of 11 percent to an average of 43 percent, partially as a function of question wording (ibid.: Table 1). In July of 2008, the U.S. House of Representatives issued a nonbinding resolution, apologizing to African Americans for slavery and Jim Crow laws, but leaving the thornier topic of financial reparations untouched (Daily Mail 2008).
5. Firestone (2000); CBS News (2000); Satris (2002). Partisan and race divisions around the flag issue parallel those found in debates around reparations. In the CBS News poll, the majority of blacks favored the removal of the Confederate flag (67 percent), compared with 42 percent of white Democrats and 35 percent of white Republicans. Among whites living in the South (both Democrat and Republican) support for removal of the flag dropped to 32 percent.
6. Whaples (1995: 142, 147–48). Percentages were calculated for the sample in the aggregate based on the subgroup statistics. Whaples identifies the aftermath of emancipation as one of the time periods with the most "substantial disagreement" among scholars, along with the causes of the Great Depression (ibid.: 139).
7. Torpey and Burkett (2010: 450, 454).

CHAPTER 1: INSTITUTIONAL TRANSFORMATION AND UNCERTAINTY

1. Twain and Warner (1873: chap. 18).
2. These estimates, obtained by David Hacker (2011) through an analysis of demographic differences between the 1860 and 1870 censuses, exceed older estimates that placed the male death toll from the Civil War at roughly 618,000. Because Hacker's method relies on a number of assumptions, it necessarily produces a broad margin of error, with a lower bound of 650,000 and an upper bound of 850,000 deaths.
3. Goldin and Lewis (1975).
4. Whaples (1995: 141); Goldfield (2012); Coclanis and Engerman (2013).
5. Blackmon (2008); Daniel (1972/1990); Jones (2010).
6. Fogel (1989: 64); see also Fogel and Engerman (1995); Kolchin (2003: 21–22). Stanley Engerman locates evidence for this economic flexibility in the antebellum South's "westward expansion, the introduction of canal and railroad improvements, and the diffusion of the cotton gin and its long-term impact on the mixture of southern crop production" (Coclanis and Engerman 2013: 81).
7. Hannan and Freeman (1984); Tilly (1998).
8. The Cotton South's institutional transformation has long been viewed with ambivalence. For members of the Dunning School, Radical Reconstruction was a political and economic failure, rooted in the incapacity of blacks who had never before experienced freedom. Starting in the 1950s, "revisionists" and "postrevisionists" began to debate the problems of the era through less racially tinged lenses, displacing the slander against freed slaves but preserving much of the Dunning School's emphasis on the shortcomings of carpetbagger government (Foner 2005).
9. Given the minimal troop presence in the South in the mid-1870s, the precise ending point of federal supervision is subject to dispute. By 1876, the military districts of the postwar period had been dismantled and only 3,230 army troops were stationed in the Southern states (Clendenen 1969: 242). The "withdrawal" of remaining troops arguably had little to do with the Hayes-Tilden compromise and was primarily catalyzed by Native American insurgencies in the West and railroad strikes in the Ohio River Valley.
10. As the political scientist Richard Valelly (2004: 2) has highlighted, "*No* major social group in Western history, other than African Americans, ever entered the electorate of an established democracy and then was extruded by nominally democratic means . . . forcing the group to start all over again."
11. Emigh (2005: 362).
12. Brown (2008); Ransom and Sutch (2001).
13. Beckert (1996: 804).
14. In referring to transitions from "precapitalist" institutions, I specifically exclude the rich literature on postsocialist transformations, which has often highlighted the role of uncertainty, particularly when written from the perspective of economic sociology (e.g., Guseva and Rona-Tas 2001; Bandelj 2008; Holm, Opper, and Nee 2013).
15. Easterbrook (1954: 348, 359–60). The lack of conceptual attention to uncertainty in studies of economic change has largely persisted. This gap extends more specifically to the transition between slavery and capitalism in the American South,

where few economists or historians have treated uncertainty as a central element in their explanations of postwar Southern development. One exception is Joseph Reid's (1976) work on sharecropping, which argues for the relative efficiency of this organizational form under conditions of uncertainty.

16. The problem of using retrospection to analyze historical events may lead to a number of fallacies, as David Hackett Fischer (1970) has outlined. Ignoring the uncertainty of historical subjects leads to a specific fallacy of motivation, in which a scholar acts as if "participants knew what was going on with great clarity and precision" as events unfolded (ibid.: 211).

17. Beckert (2002). See Knight (1921) for a classic discussion of the distinction between risk and uncertainty. Beckert (1996: 812–14) argues that postwar information economics has often ignored this distinction, seeking to reduce situations of uncertainty to ones of risk.

18. Beckert (1996: 827–30); Dequech (2003); Scott (2008: chap. 8).

19. DiMaggio and Powell (1983); Scott et al. (2000); Martin (2003); Fligstein and McAdam (2012).

20. These institutional changes are addressed in some detail in the next two chapters. For a more systematic overview of the elements involved in profound institutional change, with a different historical application, see Scott et al. (2000).

21. Fligstein and McAdam (2012: 20–21).

22. As Dirck notes, this has contributed to criticism—both past and present—"that the Emancipation Proclamation did not really free anyone, ignoring the slaves Lincoln could have freed in the loyal border areas while applying only to those slaves in the Confederacy he could not really reach" (2007: 101).

23. The quote from Garrison is cited in Dirck (2007: 102) and Mayer (1998). See Blair and Younger (2009) for a recent scholarly assessment of the reception of the Emancipation Proclamation.

24. Text of the Emancipation Proclamation.

25. Berlin et al. (1993: 28–29); Berlin, Reidy, and Rowland (1998).

26. Estimates suggest that roughly half a million former slaves and free blacks had been employed by the federal government by the spring of 1865. The context of employment varied from military service and logistical support to agricultural labor on plantations that had been occupied by federal authorities (Berlin et al. 1993: 76–77). Over time, as more and more ex-slaves proved their merit in free labor arrangements, Northern hysteria around black immigration began to subside. By the fall of 1863, for instance, Midwestern farmers welcomed an influx of one thousand former slaves who had been wasting away in a refugee camp in Arkansas (ibid.: 38).

27. Knight (1921: 205); Sarasvathy and Berglund (2010).

28. Knight (1921: 225, 259–60).

29. A notable feature of categorical uncertainty is that it becomes difficult to anticipate outcomes from preconditions or actions, even with historical hindsight (i.e., with knowledge of the future). Post hoc analysis can identify the range and frequency of outcomes that were observed in a historical situation. But it is far more challenging to "predict" the outcomes based on an individual's decision-making context, since the individual was unaware of the set of possible outcome categories when his or her decision was being made.

30. Aiken (1998: 28–33). Chapter 5 provides a more nuanced analysis of the different forms of "cropping" and alternative forms of agricultural tenure in the postbellum South.

31. Smith (1776); Stiglitz (1974); Reid (1976); Huffman and Just (2004). Newbery (1977) argues that risk regarding agricultural output is insufficient to justify sharecropping on economic grounds, but that it can be justified insofar as labor markets are risky (e.g., owing to variation in demand for agricultural labor).

32. Wells (1984: 20).

33. Aiken (1998: 23). See Emigh (1997) on the spread of sharecropping in fifteenth-century Tuscany.

34. Loring and Atkinson (1869: 130–48); Aiken (1998).

35. Royce (1993).

36. The idea of sharing risk as a potential benefit of sharecropping was explicitly rejected by historical observers in the South, precisely because the conditions that it insured against were unlikely to be repeated again (Loring and Atkinson 1869; Evans 1869; Royce 1993: 191–92).

37. Wells (1984); Royce (1993).

38. Under Special Field Order 15 in 1865. For a concise history, see Oubre (1978) on political opposition to Sherman's policy and to subsequent initiatives in favor of black landownership, such as the Southern Homestead Act of 1866.

39. At the end of the antebellum period, these states produced roughly four million bales of ginned cotton per year, or 75 percent of all cotton production in the United States (U.S. Bureau of the Census 1864a). My geographic definition of the Cotton South follows the state-level boundaries employed by Ransom and Sutch (2001).

40. On a per capita basis in 1849, the Cotton South had roughly one bank for every sixty-three thousand free residents and thirteen dollars in bank capital per resident. New England had one bank for every ten thousand residents and twenty-two dollars in bank capital per resident (per capita statistics based on 1840 census figures). A well-known issue in documenting statistics on antebellum banking is that unchartered bankers tend to be ignored (Polillo 2013).

41. All other banking institutions in Louisiana were bank branches, with one in Baton Rouge, one in Shreveport, and one in New Orleans itself. Homans (1860) did not identify branches as holding capital of their own.

42. Homans (1849, 1860); Ruef (2011: 218–19). In a telling comparison, the banks of the city of Boston had more capital in 1860 (nearly $37 million) than the entire Cotton South outside of New Orleans. The banks that did operate in the South were noteworthy, however, for their large amount of financial assets *per bank*, which reflected their function in servicing the factorage system and a few large corporations, with little attention to small business loans, real estate mortgages, or personal notes (Ransom and Sutch 2001: 107–8). Some historians have nevertheless debated the extent to which Southern banking was subordinated to the planter elite (see Polillo 2013: 97–101).

43. Atherton (1946).

44. Hidy (1939); Wyatt-Brown (1966); Olegario (2006). In a now classic account, Lewis Atherton offered a number of other reasons for the limited penetration of

formal credit rating in the antebellum South, including a tradition of "liberality with which some eastern houses [i.e., commission merchants] handled southern accounts" (1946: 550).

45. The estimate sums the capital assets of all businesses rated by Dun's Mercantile Agency (Robert Graham Dun and Company 1860–1900) and divides this measure by the total capital invested in agriculture and manufacturing, based on U.S. census records.

46. Kingston and Wright (2010) hypothesize that the absence of formal credit markets contributed to the institutionalization of dueling, a mechanism to defend honor that would have seemed archaic in more advanced economies. Duels often began with an accusation that had negative implications for the credit worthiness of the accused man. A man who retreated from the challenge tended to suffer a loss in reputation and credit rating, while a man who took on the challenge could restore his honor (ibid.: 1095–96).

47. Doyle (1990). The limited urbanization of the nineteenth-century South stands in stark contrast to more recent trends, in which Southern cities have experienced robust economic and demographic growth (Lloyd 2012).

48. Towers (2004: 19).

49. For a summary of the debates among economists and historians, see Fogel (2003), Kolchin (2003), and Smith (1998).

50. Tadman (1996: 112). See Chapter 2 on the terms of postbellum labor contracts.

51. Lebergott (1960: 455).

52. Estimates of the number of hires in Charleston can be computed because the city required a "badge" for slave hires and charged a tax once per year. The statistics presented here are taken from Greene, Hutchins, and Hutchins (2004), who calculate the number of badges issued every year as a function of total revenues divided by badge price (adjusting for heterogeneity in price by the occupation of slaves).

53. Dunaway (2003a: 38–39); Fogel and Engerman (1995: 56).

54. Lebergott (1960: 455); Genovese (1965). Among particular employers and industries, these structural constraints did not invariably yield an undersupply of workers. For instance, the burgeoning Southeastern textile industry, which began to take off in the 1830s, relied initially on a mix of slaves and poor whites to staff its mills. When plantation agriculture thrived after the 1837 to 1843 depression, the flow of slaves to the textile mills slowed to trickle, but mill owners could rely on an ample supply of unskilled white mill hands, consisting primarily of poor women and children (Terrill, Ewing, and White 1976).

55. U.S. Bureau of the Census (1854: Table XXII). The number of white laborers is calculated from IPUMS microdata (see Ruggles et al. 2010 and Chapter 4 in this book).

56. U.S. Comptroller of the Currency (1880); Ransom and Sutch (2001); Ruef (2011: 218–19). A "bank" could be a financial institution chartered by the state or federal government or an unchartered private entity (e.g., moneylenders who extend credit but lack the legal ability to create deposits). The latter organizational form was especially active in the years immediately after the Civil War.

57. The penetration of credit rating in the Southern economy leveled off for the remainder of the nineteenth century. It should be noted, however, that the

post-1870 decline of credit market integration in counties with urban centers, as shown in Figure 1.1, is largely an artifact of urban development. As settlements in rural counties attracted residents, they have been reclassified here as "urban" once they achieved a threshold of 2,500 inhabitants. The extent of market integration tended to lag behind demographic growth.

58. Evidence for the thesis of postbellum fragmentation in credit markets has typically been indirect, hinging on the lack of convergence of interest rates across geographic regions (e.g., Bodenhorn 1992).

59. Doyle (1990: 15). The impressive population growth of the "new" cities in the South's interior stood in stark contrast to some of the older, more established metropoles of the region. Charleston's demographic growth stagnated after the Civil War, with a mere 23 percent increase in population between 1860 and 1880. Charleston was embedded in the vestiges of the plantation economy, adopting a patrician business climate that was out of step with the emerging New South (ibid.: chaps. 6 and 7).

60. Kyriakoudes (2002).

61. Hahn et al. (2008); Etcheson (2009).

62. Du Bois (1935: 648).

63. Shlomowitz (1979). Of course, it is unclear whether contractual enforcement necessarily worked to the advantage of Southern blacks. Postrevisionist historians have argued that the contracts were an institutional device that supported an agenda of "forced employment" among freedmen and women (Harrison 2007: 207).

64. See Gaston (2002) on the "New South Creed," particularly its optimistic view of industrial development and racial harmony in the region.

65. Appendix A provides a general overview of the data sources analyzed in the book. Details on methodology are discussed in the notes to each chapter.

66. Fleck (2011: 311).

CHAPTER 2: CONSTRUCTING A FREE LABOR MARKET

1. Hereafter referred to as the "Freedmen's Bureau."

2. For the letter, see Document 75, "President of the Western Sanitary Commission to the Freedmen's Bureau Commissioner, and the Latter's Reply," pp. 358–61 in *Land and Labor, 1865*, an archival source edited by Steven Hahn and colleagues (2008). See Yeatman (1864) for his wartime assessment of the condition of Mississippi freedmen, as well as Span (2002: 200–201) and Foster (1982: 356–57, 360–61).

3. The use of leased slave labor was widespread in antebellum America, as Yeatman himself emphasized (the "hiring out of negroes was a common thing throughout the South"). Some historians have argued that the spread of leased labor was motivated by factors similar to those affecting the growth of the contingent work force today, including labor cost cutting and a desire for flexibility (Nash and Flesher 2005). From the perspective of nineteenth-century employers, hired slave labor also resolved many of the problems of absenteeism and control that arose with white workers.

4. Du Bois (1901) and Cimbala (1997) provide general overviews of the bureau's activities, while Harrison (2007) considers the historiography of the Freedmen's

Bureau. See Carpenter (1964/1999) and Thomson (2009) for biographical treatments of Oliver Otis Howard.

5. The Freedmen's Bureau was severely underresourced from its inception. When Howard was appointed commissioner in May 1865, the War Secretary gave him a house in Washington, D.C., for office space, a few clerks from the War Department, and a motley collection of documents regarding Southern blacks who had been freed during the war (Carpenter 1964/1999). By the end of that year, bureau personnel included only 85 men in the assistant commissioner's headquarters, 310 agents in district and local offices, and 77 medical officers and contract physicians (Hahn et al. 2008: 175). Upon hearing of the appointment, General Sherman himself wrote that the "Christian General" was taking on a Herculean task and that it was not in Howard's "power to fulfill one-tenth part of the expectations of those who framed the bureau for freedmen, refugees, and abandoned estates" (quote in Carpenter 1964/1999: 83).

6. Hahn et al. (2008: 360–61). There are a number of points of agreement in the correspondence as well. Like Yeatman, General Howard was pained by the low wages proposed by many bureau agents. Howard believed "a sort of morbid sympathy obtains from constant contact with those [slaveholders] who really feel that they have lost everything." As a result, agents did "not consider the past dues to the blacks, nor the ability of planters to secure land or crops in payment for labor." Shortly after writing his letter to Yeatman, Howard sent out a circular urging his agents to consider fair minimum wages that would vary according to local market conditions (Hahn et al. 2008: 361).

7. Hahn et al. (2008: 360).

8. For some bureau commissioners, the mere idea of wage setting raised the specter of paternalistic relationships between masters and slaves. Colonel Samuel Thomas, the assistant commissioner in Mississippi, argued that wage regulation would rob freedmen of the "opportunity of taking their first lessons in business, by thinking for them, instead of protecting them in their rights, and allowing them to do their own thinking" (Hahn et al. 2008: 317). Yeatman himself argued for a temporary federal intervention into wage setting, noting that "the sooner [freedmen] can be removed from all restraints, and . . . governed by the supply and demand for labor, the better—but for a while they need the tuteledge [*sic*] and protection of the government" (ibid.: 359).

9. Quote from Polanyi (1944: chap. 7). See also Marx (1867/1977: chap. 27) and Weber (1892). Even for the most linear treatments of history, a nuanced reading of classical scholarship reveals that the evolution from unfree to wage labor was seldom perceived as a straightforward development. For instance, Karl Marx's account of the British transition from feudalism to capitalism acknowledges a long intervening period in the late fourteenth and fifteenth centuries, when serfdom had practically disappeared but free peasant proprietors where able to maintain an independent livelihood (Katz 1993).

10. General critiques of the ahistorical view of wage labor arrangements can be found in Tilly and Tilly (1998), Stanley (1998), and Steinfeld (2001).

11. For a useful overview, see Mark Smith (1998). The development of Fogel and Engerman's account can be traced from *Time on the Cross* (1995, originally published in 1974) to Fogel's (1989) *Without Consent or Contract* and his (2003) retrospective

on the slavery debates. Genovese's view can be traced from his pathbreaking text on the *Political Economy of Slavery* (1965) to *Roll, Jordan, Roll* (1974) (see also Fox-Genovese and Genovese 2005).

12. On the division of unfree and free workers by contractual duration, see Steinfeld (2001: 13). On the regulation of hired slaves in antebellum Charleston, primarily via badge and licensing laws, see Greene, Hutchins, and Hutchins (2004).

13. For Weber's definition of free labor, see *Economy and Society* (1968: 127–28). The importance of regulation to free labor may seem curious to neoclassical economists, though Weber recognized that contracts may "be substantively regulated in various ways through a conventional or legal order governing the conditions of labor" (ibid.: 128).

14. Marx (1867/1977: 896).

15. The idea of human capital was initially developed in the 1950s and 1960s by economists such as Jacob Mincer (1958), Theodore Schultz (1961), and Gary Becker (1964). As Baron and Hannan (1994) argue, a common mistake is to simply equate human capital with years of education or training in a statistical regression model. The proper application of human capital theory requires that an attribute be "regarded as an investment for which there is a capital market and opportunity cost" (ibid.: 1124). Moreover, for there to be sustained rents from human capital investment, there must be barriers that prevent others from readily acquiring the same education or training.

16. Fogel and Engerman (1995: 233); Pritchett and Hayes (2011: 18).

17. Weber (1968: 155). For recent discussions of the ideology of the planter class, see Ruef and Harness (2009) and Fox-Genovese and Genovese (2005). Whether slave trading was indeed infrequent has been questioned by a number of scholars (e.g., Tadman 1996). Among planters, the temptation to sell was especially high when they owned teenagers and young adults, slaves who were in their prime working years. Nevertheless, the rate of turnover among purchased slaves was much lower than that of blacks hired on contract.

18. Fogel and Engerman appear to agree that this feature of skill acquisition under chattel slavery deviates markedly from the conditions of free labor markets. Under the typical logic of human capital investment, "the earlier an investment is made in occupational training, the more years there are to reap the returns on that investment" (1995: 150). Under slavery, however, the slaveholder would "treat entry into skilled occupations as a prize" (ibid.). This interpretation of occupations as incentive systems under slavery was subsequently questioned by other scholars (see David et al. 1976: 74–77).

19. This also implies that regions with surplus slaves and/or limited production of staple crops—such as Appalachia—witnessed a more pronounced equation between slavery and investment in human capital (Dunaway 2003a).

20. Collins (1979); Sørensen (2000); Weeden (2002).

21. Hanes (1996).

22. See Martin (2004) and Nash and Flesher (2005) on slave hiring in the antebellum South. As Zaborney (2012) has documented in a recent study of Virginia slave hires, the practice was widespread by the late antebellum period, with considerable variation depending on locale, slave characteristics, and the motivations of

employers and masters. The potential for ethnic competition with free white labor may have led some slaves to downplay their skills in the hire market, contributing to an attenuated effect of human capital (Bonacich 1975).

23. Early and influential treatments of statistical discrimination were offered by Phelps (1972) and Aigner and Cain (1977).

24. Fogel and Engerman (1995: chap. 3).

25. Weber (1968: 162–63). For an experimental analysis of statistical discrimination under conditions of risk, see Dickinson and Oaxaca (2009).

26. England (1984) offers a review and critique of neoclassical accounts of sex segregation in regulated markets for wage labor.

27. Sutch (1975); Dunaway (2003a). Fogel and Engerman (1995) dispute whether such statistical discrimination was built directly into the price mechanisms of the slave labor market. Indeed, the older perspective among cliometricians was "that slaveholders discouraged high fertility because female laborers were used in the fields to a greater extent than male workers" (as critiqued in Dunaway 2003a: 2).

28. Zelizer (1981: 1038).

29. Roughley (1823) (quoted in Fogel 1989: 54). On vacancy chains, more generally, see Harrison White (1970).

30. In 1860, twenty-one out of thirty-four states had adopted laws against interracial sex, though enforcement and penalties varied considerably (Robinson 2003).

31. See Collins (1904) and Tadman (1996: 142n14) on the Louisiana prohibition.

32. Schwartz (1970: 25–96) provides a legislative history of the Thirteenth Amendment to the U.S. Constitution.

33. Freedmen's Bureau (1865–70, 1865–72). Hahn et al. (2008: 291). In Washington and Alexandria, the average age of freedmen whose parents consented to long apprenticeship (greater than one year) was sixteen. These contracts, unsurprisingly, proved to be contentious among freedmen themselves. Joseph Hall, a black Maryland artisan, wrote to the D.C. bureau headquarters that he had seen "children bound out without the consent of their parents" and that some were "bound from the age of eight or ten years to the age [when they would be] twenty." These poor souls, he argued, "fared worse than they did when they were slaves" (Hahn et al. 2008: 566–67).

34. Freedmen's Bureau (1865–70: 108). Scholarly treatments that place the bureau's efforts in the comparative context of other efforts at labor market reform or social relief include Stanley (1998), Steinfeld (2001), and Goldberg (2006: chap. 2).

35. In total, the archive includes labor contracts with 1,378 individuals, covering such variables as the terms of service, attributes of freedmen (name, age, sex, occupation, family composition), names and locations of employers, and monthly wages (Appendix A).

36. Tadman (1996: Table 2.1) estimates that Virginia and Maryland were the only Southern states that were net exporters of slaves throughout the period from the 1790s until the 1850s. The coastal trade between the Chesapeake region and Louisiana was especially prominent, given the heavy labor demands of the sugar crop.

37. Wade (1964). The probate sample is taken from Fogel and Engerman (2006a); see Appendix A.

38. An in-depth treatment of Charleston's slave badge laws can be found in Greene, Hutchins, and Hutchins (2004). The most common occupational distinctions, according to slave badge designations, were those of mechanic, porter, house servant, huckster/fruit vendor, and fisherman/woman.

39. The exception to this generalization would seem to hold where a handful of municipalities attempted to set the wages of slave hires. Wade (1964: 42) acknowledges that such wage setting was likely to be arbitrary and "it is hard to know if the [wage] scales were enforced," particularly given their inflexibility to market conditions.

40. Murphy (2010: chap. 7). On the involvement and profit of Northern firms—including insurers—in the slave trade, see Farrow, Lang, and Frank (2005).

41. Coclanis (1982: 535); Dunaway (2003a: 36–37). Judicial sales offered locales for traders to meet and obtain important information regarding price trends (Tadman 1996). Fogel and Engerman's (2006b) probate records again provide data on the antebellum market for slaves (Appendix A).

42. Wahl cites the prototypical opinion of one South Carolina judge who suggested that "when men make contracts, and have fair opportunities of consulting their own prudence and judgment, there is no reason why they should not abide by them" (1996: 145; see also Wahl 2002).

43. Glen (1820–89) and Reid (1770–1910).

44. Quotations from planters appear in Breeden's (1980: 146, 195) sample of antebellum publications concerning slave management. Tadman (1996: 122, 143) provides a useful discussion of how concerns about reproduction influenced the pricing of slaves.

45. Breeden (1980: 26–27); Reid (1770–1910). For a slaveholder's views on religious instruction, see Breeden (1980: 226).

46. Earlier cases of slave emancipation in the Upper South had tended to occur on a piecemeal basis around federal military facilities, especially in tidewater Virginia and North Carolina (Berlin et al. 1993).

47. Berlin et al. (1993: 315–20). The understanding of child and female labor also displays a historical shift in the Freedmen's Bureau documents. Greene suggests that many freedmen will "have their wives, children, aged parents, dependent upon Government for shelter and rations" (ibid.: 316). In his eyes, this was hardly an unreasonable arrangement, as long as black children attended common school, women engaged in domestic trades, and freedmen of means (those earning more than twenty-five dollars per month) remitted a tax in support of the aged, indigent, infirm, and other dependents.

48. The question is especially salient since the preponderance of wage labor at Freedman's Village was limited, despite Elias Greene's aspirations. In September 1863, only 150 of the camp's 900 residents were able-bodied, employable men (Berlin et al. 1993: 255). Repeated efforts to move residents into private employment were met with mixed success.

49. See Cimbala (1997) on the activities of the Freedmen's Bureau in Georgia. Hahn et al. (2008: 551) and Kirk (1868).

50. Hahn et al. (2008: 334, 365); Cimbala (1997).

51. For example, see quotes from Howard's letter at the beginning of this chapter.

52. Hahn et al. (2008: 360–61); Farmer-Kaiser (2010).

53. To assess the valuation of labor across market interfaces, I estimate hedonic models of labor pricing. I control for variation in local market conditions (demand and supply) and inflation by using fixed effects for the county and year in which each transaction occurs. Standard errors are clustered by owner/employer to account for unobserved buyer-side characteristics that may affect a number of transactions. Substantively, the resulting regression model represents the (logged) price of labor (P) as a function of workers' ascribed characteristics (vector X_1), occupation (X_2), location (i), and year (t): $\ln P_{it} = \alpha_i + \beta_t + \delta'X_1 + \gamma'X_2 + \varepsilon$, where X_1 includes the age of each worker, the worker's sex and perceived health issues or disabilities (if any), and relevant interaction terms.

54. On slave occupations, see Fogel (1989: chap. 2), Moore and Williams (1942), and Ruef and Fletcher (2003). Rather than sorting occupations and trades into skill levels, the analysis presented here includes a fixed effect for every occupational label found in the probate data or labor contracts.

55. The findings presented here can also not rule out the possibility that *specific* occupations within the status hierarchy of slavery generated price premiums or penalties in the slave market. Based on Fogel and Engerman's (2006b) probate data, for instance, we find that common field laborers were appraised at levels that were two-thirds those of other slaves (net of demographic variables, such as age and gender). But the ability of occupational skills to explain price variation in the slave market on the whole is limited.

56. See Guo and Fraser (2010) and Appendix A on propensity score matching. The matched data exhibit several useful features in terms of sample composition: the workers evaluated in the slave appraisal market are identical to those evaluated in the purchase market; the workers evaluated in the wage labor market are statistically indistinguishable (by age, gender, or occupational skill) from those purchased or appraised; and the workers in the slave hire market, while still statistically distinguishable, are far more similar to those in the purchase market than they were in the original sample.

57. Eaton (1960: 678); Martin (2004).

58. The estimate of slave life expectancy is given by Fogel and Engerman (1995: 125). The postbellum statistics for occupation are based on the 1870 IPUMS 1.2 percent sample of all blacks in Georgia, Louisiana, Maryland, Mississippi, North Carolina, South Carolina, Tennessee, and Virginia (Ruggles et al. 2010). Given the relatively small number of wage labor contracts in the Freedmen's Bureau sample, it is not possible to reliably construct a corresponding distribution for the immediate postbellum period.

59. The plots in Figure 2.4 control for occupational skills. A methodological complication in estimating the age-price profiles is the relatively frequent problem of missing or imprecise data on the age of workers in the historical archives. Age data are missing entirely for over 25 percent of the cases in the sample of slave sales and appraisals, 69 percent of the cases in the Freedmen's Bureau sample of wage labor contracts, and 86 percent of the cases in the sample of slave hires. To retain a maximum number of cases for purposes of analysis, I employed multiple imputation for all analyses, drawing twenty imputations to construct each data set (Royston 2004). Listwise deletion of cases with missing age information does not produce findings that are substantively different from those obtained with multiple imputation.

60. Hahn et al. (2008: 336–41).
61. Letter to the Freedmen's Bureau Superintendent of the 2nd District of Virginia, December 30, 1865 (Hahn et al. 2008: 983–84). The same correspondence identifies other problematic labor conditions, such as black laborers who were held against their will and threatened if they sought employment elsewhere.
62. Freedmen's Bureau (1865–70).
63. Such compensation, based on fractions of the crop, represented an early phase of sharecropping, a development that will be reviewed in subsequent chapters. The terms of agricultural labor in the oral histories are taken from the Federal Writers' Project Slave Narratives and were coded by Paul Escott (1979). Chapter 3 and Appendix A offer a full discussion of these materials.
64. Freedmen's Bureau (1865–72). The weak provisions for medical care in labor contracting under the bureau reflect broader shortcomings of the federal health care effort at the time, which "did little to break the pattern of dependence [among Southern blacks] on whites" (Foster 1982).
65. E. W. Gantt, a former Confederate officer and general superintendent for the bureau in Arkansas, proclaimed that "when slavery ceased, the right to compel labor ceased. Whipping, or tieing up by the thumbs or any kind of bodily punishment to compel labor will not be tolerated" (Hahn et al. 2008: 307). Goldberg (2006: 40–41) notes, however, that early bureau policy tended to support disciplinary practices that reduced blacks to the status of slaves in the eyes of some contemporaries.
66. Specifically, the data include a 10 percent sample of payrolls and contracts in St. Martin and St. Mary's Parishes in Louisiana (Freedmen's Bureau 1863–72), as well as the complete payrolls of the McGavock plantation in Arkansas and the Anderson plantation in Mississippi.
67. See Rodrigue (1999) on the efforts of the Freedmen's Bureau to introduce wage labor in Louisiana and Hahn et al. (2008: 111) for the firsthand report on similar efforts in Mississippi.
68. The persistence of bondage in Arkansas was identified by Brigadier General J. W. Sprague in a report to General Howard, three months after the end of the war (Hahn et al. 2008: 26).
69. The contract for the McGavock plantation is reproduced in Hahn et al. (2008: 384–86).
70. Hahn et al. (2008: 386). It is not entirely clear what happened to McGavock's labor force after the complaint was filed, though one biographical treatment asserts that his "negroes were freed and scattered" at some point after the war (Goodspeed Publishing 1890). The same biography suggests that McGavock subsequently experimented with immigrants to work his cotton fields, including Irish women, German men, and Chinese laborers.
71. Correspondence of Chaplain James A. Hawley to Colonel Samuel Thomas, June 22, 1865 (Hahn et al. 2008: 110–27).
72. Labor Regulations by the General Superintendent of Freedmen in Alabama, Mississippi, and the Department of the Gulf, July 22, 1865 (Hahn et al. 2008: 333–35).
73. The most direct evidence for violations of Freedmen's Bureau policy comes from cases that were introduced in freedmen's courts, where the power of local

civil courts and magistrates was suspended owing to concerns of prejudice. In Alabama, for instance, three such courts were held in Mobile, Huntsville, and Selma in early 1866 (Bethel 1948: 53). Of the twenty-seven cases recorded there, most involved charges of nonpayment or assault and battery on the part of white employers; all but two were decided in favor of the workers.

74. Bell (1999: 140–42, 154).

75. Following Albert Hirschman, Fourcade and Healy (2007) identify a long legacy of claims among liberal economists that associate markets with such civilizing virtues as honesty, respect, cooperation, creativity, and freedom.

76. Smith (1776: 471).

77. Steinfeld (2001); Goldberg (2006).

78. Breeden (1980: 26–27).

79. On the uncertainty and ambiguity surrounding the policies of the bureau, see Goldberg (2006: chap. 2). On the tendency of organizations to decouple activities and goals in practice from institutionalized elements, see Meyer and Rowan (1977).

CHAPTER 3: STATUS ATTAINMENT AMONG EMANCIPATED SLAVES

1. Brown (1880: chap. 23).

2. See Du Bois (1935), Woodson (1918, 1922), Wesley (1927), Greene and Woodson (1930).

3. Influential treatments of the legacy of slavery and emancipation in the United States include Ransom and Sutch (2001), Foner (1988/2002), and Wright (1986/1996). Recent analyses of the intergenerational transmission of individual advantage or disadvantage for descendents of slaves include Sacerdote (2005) and Darity, Dietrich, and Guilkey (2001).

4. Scott (2008) provides a useful overview of research on the stability of social institutions.

5. Mills (1959).

6. Loury (2002); Tilly (1998). Charles Tilly emphasizes that mere attitudinal changes toward discrimination are typically insufficient to alter structured patterns of inequality (ibid.: 244).

7. Olson (1992).

8. Cohen (1991: 21). My 10 percent systematic sample of Freedmen Bureau contracts for St. Martin and St. Mary Parishes in Louisiana includes 150 cases; 42 involve share arrangements, with most contracts specifying either one-half or one-third shares. Interviews with former slaves conducted by the Federal Writers' Project suggest that these were the modal categories for share splits during Reconstruction in the South.

9. Greene and Woodson (1930: chap. 2); Foner (1988/2002).

10. The distinction was especially ambiguous in those states—Alabama, Florida, Georgia, Mississippi, North Carolina, and South Carolina—that enacted laws supporting peonage, in which ex-slaves where legally bound to serve a creditor until a debt was paid. Although such laws were unconstitutional from the standpoint of federal authorities, they remained a fact of life for many former slaves in the South (Cohen 1976; Daniel 1979; Mandle 1992).

11. Other examples of practices descendent from slavery institutions included the enforcement of Black Codes by police and the harassment of blacks by white patrols and vigilante groups that convened to regulate African American behavior. Of course, these were not identical practices under the antebellum and postbellum regimes. Slave patrols were instruments of the law before 1865, whereas night riders and other race terrorists operating after 1865 were criminals. But racist terrorist groups and vigilante groups drew inspiration from and employed tactics developed by slave patrols (see Hadden 2001).

12. Escott (1979: 164); Stinchcombe (1995); Tilly (1998: 90). In using the term "structural-functional," I do not intend to equate these perspectives on institutional reproduction with the familiar Davis-Moore (1945) theory of inequality. Rather, the accounts are structural-functional insofar as they assume that organizations adopting categorical inequalities from former institutional arrangements continue to be favored in new institutional contexts (Wright 2000).

13. These characteristics can be described more abstractly as control over work locale and control over work time. From a Marxist perspective, a defining element of precapitalist means of production is the absence of one (or both) of these elements among exploited classes. Slave hires typically lack control over work time, serfs lack control over work locale, while slaves who are not hired out lack both forms of control in the work process. Nominally free wage laborers, by contrast, exercise *some* control on both dimensions. See Wright (1997) for a general Marxist account of stratification.

14. Wright (1997).

15. Meyer (1994); Meyer and Jepperson (2000).

16. Stampp (1956); Genovese (1974). The degree of paternalism's degeneration is a topic of debate. Ochiltree (1998) questions the outright demise of paternalism but agrees with the prevailing conclusion in the literature that paternalism declined dramatically after 1865.

17. Litwack (1979: 449). Cohen (1991) argues that sharecropping was forced on planters by a freed working class that refused to participate in fieldwork reminding them of slavery. The sharecropping system was an improvement over slavery in that it gave workers substantially greater freedom over day-to-day work in the field and did not share (at least in theory) slavery's patterns of regulation through physical punishment.

18. My criterion for identifying states with substantial slaveholding activity involves the enumeration of at least two thousand slaves in the 1860 U.S. census. States meeting this criterion include Alabama, Arkansas, Florida, Georgia, Kentucky, Louisiana, Maryland, Mississippi, Missouri, North Carolina, South Carolina, Tennessee, Texas, and Virginia, as well as the Indian Territory (Oklahoma) and District of Columbia. For the larger sample of linked census records, I also add Delaware and Kansas to the analysis.

19. Wesley (1927); Moore and Williams (1942); Johnson (1986); Fogel (1989: chap. 2).

20. Miller (1979: 40).

21. Olson's estimates (1992: Table 8.14) place the number of black slave drivers per plantation in 1860 at roughly half the number in 1830, controlling for size of plantation, number of field hands, and type of crop produced.

22. Greene and Woodson (1930). Estimates of slave occupational composition, here and elsewhere in this chapter, are taken from Olson (1992), particularly Table 8.3.

23. Schwalm (1997); Johnson (1986).

24. U.S. Bureau of the Census (1864b).

25. Wesley (1927: 34–36).

26. Fogel (1989).

27. Williamson (1965: 301). There were other reactions, of course, including political advocacy and migration.

28. Spero and Harris (1931); Branch (2011).

29. Wiener (1979); Ferleger (1993); Alston and Ferrie (2005).

30. Du Bois (1935). The quotation and subsequent accounts from former slaves are taken from oral histories collected in Rawick (1972–79). George Albright's oral history is located in volume 6.1 (pp. 8–19).

31. Hartman (1997: chap. 5); Span (2002: 200–201). General Sherman quoted in Blassingame (1965: 152).

32. Du Bois (1935); Gutman (1987); Anderson (1988); Span (2009).

33. Rawick (1972–79: 1:267–74); Greene and Woodson (1930: 47).

34. The statistics are drawn from interviews conducted by the Works Progress Administration ($N = 1,392$). For the sake of representativeness, the sample is weighted by the occupational and geographic distribution of Southern blacks in 1860 (see Appendix A).

35. Washington (1901: 206–26); Du Bois (1903/1965: chaps. 3, 6).

36. The raw difference in literacy between children whose grandparents were born in slavery (many of whom remained in the South) and those who were not was larger, at roughly 16 percent (Sacerdote 2005: Table 2, Models 1 and 2). A notable shortcoming in studies that rely on census data is that they tend to infer the antebellum status of blacks (as free or slaves) exclusively based on birth year and place.

37. Woodson (1918). Migration immediately after emancipation can largely be attributed to attempts to reunify separated families, searches for economic opportunity, and desires to create distance from former owners (Davis 1993; Foner 1988/2002).

38. Cohen (1976, 1991).

39. Du Bois (1903/1965); see also Blau and Brown (2001). Quote from Rawick (1972–79: 9:1450–60).

40. U.S. Senate (1880: 7:281); Du Bois (1907); Douglass (1880).

41. The effects of migration on status attainment among blacks who had been free within the antebellum regime are more complex. These individuals had more extensive resources and support networks in their Southern communities than ex-slaves and may well have suffered status losses as a result of migration to the North or elsewhere (Woodson 1918: chap. 8).

42. Frederick Douglass wrote that emigration was likely to be considered "a mistake and a failure," as "it takes colored voters from a section of the country where they are sufficiently numerous to elect some of their number to places of honor and profit, and places them in a country where their proportion to other classes will be so small as not to be recognized as a political element, or entitled to be represented by one of themselves" (1880: 16).

43. See Appendix A for a discussion of this sample.

44. Estimates from linked 1860–80 census data (see Appendix A) and Collins (1997). The majority of demographic research on black out-migration from the South focuses on the Great Migration, which did not begin until the early twentieth century (e.g., Fligstein 1981; Tolnay 2003; Eichenlaub, Tolnay, and Alexander 2010). Historians studying black out-migration in the late nineteenth century have called attention to more specific movements, such as the Kansas Exodusters in 1879 and 1880 (Painter 1976/1992).

45. Litwack (1979).

46. Rawick (1972–79: 6.5:1939–42; 7.6:2455–56). Note that all of these presentations pertain to *social* identity—identity as perceived by strangers—rather than *personal* identity—as perceived by friends and intimates (Goffman 1963). Some ex-slaves may have shown equivocal attitudes toward freedom in public (especially when interacting with whites), while imbuing their new identity with positive valuation in private.

47. Cade (1935); Egypt, Masuoka, and Johnson (1945); Yetman (1984).

48. Erikson and Goldthorpe (1992). Even for postbellum status, the construction of prestige rankings is complicated by several factors. One typical approach to describing occupational desirability—the measurement of status or prestige (Blau and Duncan 1967; Wegener 1992)—requires information on education and income that is generally unavailable for the period considered here. While wages were recorded for industrial workers in turn-of-the-century census records, agricultural earnings can be computed only indirectly (e.g., Ng and Virts 1993; Irwin and O'Brien 2001). Educational experience is recorded in the 1900 census, but the corresponding "occupational" classifications in census data are industry-based. Moreover, education and income may be less robust determinants of occupational prestige during Reconstruction and the late postbellum period (Katz 1972) than in modern society. Despite these differences, correlations between nineteenth-century prestige rankings and twentieth-century SES scales tend to be high (Hauser 1982).

49. See Ganzeboom, De Graaf, and Treiman (1992).

50. Schultz (1998); Foner (1988/2002). Independent farmers still rank below skilled manual laborers along dimensions of income and advancement potential. In 1900, the average black-owned farm earned less than half the annual salary of a single carpenter (U.S. Bureau of the Census 1900). Nonagricultural workers also enjoyed chances for promotion to supervisory status.

51. U.S. Bureau of the Census (1890).

52. Expected counts are calculated assuming a model of statistical independence. Note that the comparable postbellum status rank for antebellum rank V (skilled domestics) is class IV, not V (which refers to independent farmers).

53. Since occupational prestige is measured on a ranked scale, multivariate methods for ordinal variables were applied. I estimated an ordered logit model based on the following specification, stated in terms of a continuous latent measure of prestige (Y^*): $Y^* = \beta_1 \times Age + \beta_2 \times Male + \beta_3 \times Free$. The observed counterparts to Y^* are the ranked prestige scores (Y) shown in Table 3.1, such that $Y = 1$ if $Y^* \leq \mu_1$, $Y = 2$ if $\mu_1 < Y^* \leq \mu_2, \ldots Y = 9$ if $Y^* > \mu_8$. The μ values are estimated threshold parameters

that distinguish ordered values, with the constraint that the first threshold parameter (μ_1) equal zero.

54. Horton and Horton (2001). This is not to say that slaves were unable to accumulate property during the antebellum period. Penningroth (2003) documents extensive extralegal property ownership among slaves, typically supported by social relationships with masters, kin, and other blacks. In the WPA interviews coded by Escott (1979), only 35 percent of the former slaves reporting on property ownership said that they had no money during slavery. Some 23 percent said they were able to possess small change, while 41 percent said they were able to accumulate larger amounts and savings. Common sources of funds included the sale of garden crops (from the small plots allocated to slaves), earnings from hiring out, and gifts and rewards from masters.

55. Analyses of antebellum census data (e.g., Wesley 1927) appear to contradict intuitions by some early historians that placed free blacks on par with, or even below, slaves in terms of occupational attainment. For instance, Greene and Woodson (1930: 4–5) contended that "it would appear that the Negroes as slaves had better opportunities to work at the trades than as free people of color. . . . As slaves they were frequently employed as blacksmiths, anchormakers, machinists, [etc.]. When free this was true to a less extent."

56. In the 1880 census of the Lower South (Alabama, Georgia, Louisiana, Mississippi, and South Carolina), only 1.5 percent of the black adult labor force were employed as artisans, independent professionals, or small business proprietors. Another 0.5 percent were employed as clerks or other white-collar employees. The changing distribution of occupational groups during the postbellum era is discussed more extensively in the next chapter.

57. To remove those individuals who only witnessed slavery as very young children and ensure comparability with the linked 1860–80 census sample, the WPA interviews analyzed here are limited to those of a respondent who was born in 1860 or before.

58. All estimates are derived from the same model discussed in note 53, with the addition of variables for antebellum occupational status, migration, and antebellum education. These indicators are available only from the WPA interviews.

59. As King (1995) documents, the children of slaves were also likely to have internalized submissive identities that were presented to others. Those without work duties were conditioned to avoid drawing attention to themselves by both whites and parents concerned with their safety. Some suffered the psychological trauma of seeing their parents beaten (or worse) or of being separated from family members (see also Patterson 1998: 39–41).

60. One potential concern with this interpretation of educational efficacy is that many WPA interviewees were relatively young during the antebellum regime. Given that the average respondent in the unweighted sample was approximately fourteen years old in 1865, it is reasonable to expect that a substantial proportion of the sample would not yet have reached school age. To explore this issue, I split the respondents into two subsamples, one comprising blacks who were ten years of age or younger in 1865 and one comprising those who were older than ten. The odds that the younger respondents who had received some schooling would

achieve a higher occupational status were 1.85 times those of young respondents who had received no schooling (significantly different from 1.0 at the $p < .05$ level). Among older respondents, this relationship was weaker—the odds of higher occupational status among those with antebellum schooling were only 1.15 times those who had no schooling (statistically insignificant).

61. The positive benefits of out-migration from the South in the late nineteenth century contrast with less propitious outcomes from the Great Migration of the twentieth century. Eichenlaub, Tolnay, and Alexander (2010) find that Southern-born black males who moved to the North did not have a significantly higher occupational status, employment rate, or relative income (compared to state medians) than those who remained in the South in 1940. The difference in outcomes is ironic since leaving the South altogether was an easier decision for the postbellum generation of blacks born in freedom, whose hopes of improving race relations in the South were destroyed during the Jim Crow period, than for the generation of freedmen and freedwomen (Litwack 1998).

62. Naidu (2010).

63. The ostensible ineffectiveness of Republican governments in advancing the cause of Southern blacks has been attributed to a number of factors, including corruption, party factionalism, and the delicacy of biracial coalitions. From the perspective of organizational theory, an even simpler explanation is Arthur Stinchcombe's (1965) oft-cited "liability of newness." In the years after the Civil War, Republican parties were established rapidly in the South, attempting to pass major legislation on public education, civil rights, labor law, and land reform in many of the former Confederate states (Valelly 2004). Given the organizing challenges faced by these new political parties, it is hardly surprising that all of them had been displaced by conservative Democratic parties within a decade.

64. The model used to derive these estimates builds on the specification discussed in note 53, with the addition of fixed effects for each respondent's state of residency in the postbellum South. The 1860–80 linked census data distinguish antebellum status only into slaves and free blacks. The WPA data also control for antebellum slave occupations, as shown in Figure 3.3.

65. Anderson (1988) provides a critical view of postbellum schooling in the South, suggesting that an educational system for the enlightenment of former slaves became co-opted by the agricultural and industrial interests of white elites. This view does not necessarily conflict with the finding, presented here, that participation in education proved propitious to the occupational attainment of individual blacks.

66. Horton and Horton (2001).

67. Cohen (1991); Williamson (1984); Litwack (1979); Gutman (1976).

68. For one theoretical overview, see Meyer and Scott (1983).

69. Some discussions of organized oppositional tactics among whites are outlined in Trelease (1971/1995), for the Reconstruction era, and Tolnay and Beck (1995), for the period after Radical Reconstruction.

70. Washington (2011); Woodward (1955/2002). The limited evidence available in the WPA archives suggests that one obvious explanation of advantage among free blacks—social or cultural capital handed down to those who had white ancestry—may not be especially viable. In particular, there is no significant

association in these data between freedom during the antebellum period and white parentage.

Chapter 4: Class Structure in the Old and New South

1. Twain and Warner (1873).
2. Ibid. (chap. 9).
3. Bendix (1956/2001); Blumin (1989); Doyle (1990); Price (1987); Tocqueville (1835–40/2003).
4. Marx and Engels (1848/1937); Urry (1973); Mills (1951: 5).
5. For a short overview of historical debates regarding these class formations in the American South, see the entries on "middle class" and "yeomanry" in Griffin and Hargis (2012).
6. Archer and Blau (1993). For other sociological critiques of dichotomous conceptions of class, see Hickox (1995) and Horton et al. (2000).
7. Mills (1951). Recent perspectives on neo-Marxist and occupational conceptions of class are reviewed by Wright (1997), Grusky and Sørensen (1998), and Weeden and Grusky (2005).
8. Blumin (1989); Davidoff and Hall (2003); Feldman (1999); and Woodward (1951).
9. Thompson (1963). The distinction between the subjective awareness of class position and its objective manifestation is especially central to Marxist analysis of class consciousness (see Fetscher 1991). Max Weber's (1946) conceptualization of class was limited to the material conditions—such as wealth, ownership of productive assets, and investment in education—that affected the economic life chances of a set of individuals.
10. Archer and Blau (1993). Other discussions of the diversity in the middling classes can be found in Bledstein and Johnson (2001).
11. For instance, observing economic development in southern Italy during the eighteenth century, Anthony Galt (1986: 421–22) remarks that "the distinction between the feudal era and the liberal order which follows it should not be seen as overly hard edged, since there existed an entrepreneurial middle class well before the abolition of feudalism."
12. Coclanis and Engerman (2013: 76–77).
13. Stinchcombe (1965: 146, 150–52).
14. Weber (1922). See also Polanyi (1944: chap. 5).
15. Wells (2004: 8, 14); Doyle (1990).
16. U.S. Bureau of the Census (1983); Doyle (1990: Figure 1.1).
17. Stinchcombe (1965: 150); Weber (1968).
18. The issue of artisanal literacy was raised more than a century ago by W. E. B. Du Bois (1902: 15), who noted that illiterate black artisans faced considerable obstacles in learning their trades during the antebellum era. The problem of illiteracy became more acute in the postbellum period, when, as Roger Ransom and Richard Sutch have written, "the skilled freedmen probably found illiteracy a major obstacle to pursuing artisan trades independently" (2001: 35), given the need to keep books and communicate with distant suppliers or customers.

19. On the historical role of newspapers and periodicals in middle-class culture, see Ryan (1981). On the role of numeracy and accounting skills, see Carruthers and Espeland (1991).
20. Wells (2004); Green (2007); Eelman (2004).
21. Ayers (1992).
22. Ruef and Patterson (2009a).
23. Carlton and Coclanis (2003: 101); Wells (2004).
24. Stinchcombe (1965); Thornton (1999: 26); Aldrich and Ruef (2006: 232–33).
25. Hannan and Freeman (1989: 127); Carroll, Delacroix, and Goodstein (1988).
26. Stinchcombe (1965: 147).
27. Weber (1968: 161–63).
28. Marx and Engels (1848/1937: 24–25). Subsequent treatments by Marx and his interlocutors have added nuance to the argument. Marx himself noted that his forecast did not imply that the middle class as a whole would disappear with capitalist development. For instance, in his *Theories of Surplus Value*, Marx discusses the *expansion* of the middle classes, presumably constituted largely by the growing ranks of office workers in bureaucratic enterprise (Urry 1973: 176–78).
29. Steinmetz and Wright (1989).
30. Ayers (1992: 21–22); Carlton and Coclanis (2003: chap. 6).
31. This issue leads some historians, such as Wells (2004), to exclude artisans entirely from the entrepreneurial middle class of the antebellum era. By contrast, this chapter includes master artisans, but not apprentices, given the capacity of the former group to establish independent, brick-and-mortar enterprise. Since the early American Republic, there was a growing social and economic divide between master craftsmen, on the one hand, and the journeymen and apprentices they employed, on the other (see, e.g., Wilentz 1984/2004).
32. Clapp (1854: 446).
33. See Appendix A.
34. Woodward (1951); Blumin (1989). On local variations in the rise of the postbellum middle class, see Doyle (1990).
35. The definition of the entrepreneurial class excludes factory operatives and apprentices in the trades, which are classified as common laborers. It also excludes individuals often employed in cottage industry (e.g., potters and basket makers), as well as the construction trades (carpenters, masons, etc.), since these occupations tended to be associated with self-employment but not proprietorship of brick-and-mortar enterprise.
36. Although the limited amount of nonfarm business proprietorship among farm owners may, at first glance, seem tautological, economic historians have noted the propensity of many planters to take on the entrepreneurial role of "landlord-merchants" after the Civil War (Ransom and Sutch 2001: 146–47).
37. On the difference between professions and quasi-professions, see Wilensky (1964). Using nineteenth-century census data, it is unfortunately not possible to draw more fine-grained distinctions, such as those cases where quasi-professionals are able to exercise greater autonomy as organizational founders (e.g., teachers who start their own schools), as opposed to working as employees.

38. Note that only the data on literacy are available for the full time span (1850—1900).

39. The probability (p) values at the bottom of the table indicate when a difference between a statistic and the mean for the entrepreneurial middle class is unlikely to have occurred by chance alone (owing to sampling error).

40. Although these statistics may be compared *within* each era, the averages in the body of the table are not strictly comparable *between* the antebellum and post-bellum eras. Census question wording for literacy changed between 1860 and 1870, with one question in 1860 identifying those who could not read *and* write and two separate questions in 1870 identifying those who could not read *and* those who could not write. This difference in question wording appears to lower the literacy rate artificially following the Civil War. Question wording for personal assets also changed, since the value of "other property" included slaves in the antebellum period.

41. During the antebellum period, these ratios were already high (about 67 for literacy and between 20 and 50 for material wealth), suggesting that the distinctions among the broad classes explained a good deal of the variation in human and financial capital. The sole exceptions, in this regard, were the entrepreneurial and bureaucratic factions of the middle class, which remained undifferentiated in terms of material wealth. Considering the data after the Civil War, on the other hand, the F-test ratio for literacy jumps to a value approaching 350 and the test statistic increases for material wealth as well (falling within the range of 30 to slightly over 50).

42. The census data for 1850 and 1860 consider only literacy rates for adult "children," age twenty or older. Consequently, these measures are not comparable to the postbellum measure of child literacy and are omitted from discussion here.

43. Woodward (1951: 218). Wesley (1927) uses city censuses to provide an overview of black business proprietorship in the nineteenth century.

44. Clearly, the status of such slave artisans cannot be equated with that of the entrepreneurial middle class at the time. Slave artisans did possess more autonomy and better living conditions than other slave laborers. Moreover, their technical skills offered a basis for independent employment following emancipation.

45. Green and Pryde (1997). These conclusions are based on an assessment of class prevalence in relative (i.e., percentage) terms. In raw numbers, the emerging black middle class of the 1870s and 1880s was far larger than the small number of free blacks engaged as artisans or business proprietors in the late antebellum period.

46. Table 4.3 (cf. Woodward 1951: 152 and Doyle 1990). As other scholars (e.g., Guest 2005) have documented, the expansion of clerical and sales positions in the late nineteenth century offered one of the best opportunities for upward mobility among young white men. Despite some growth of these white-collar occupations in the South, the region had the lowest rate of upward mobility (intra- and intergenerational) in the United States between 1880 and 1900 (ibid.: 148–49).

47. In the 1 percent IPUMS sample of the Lower South, for instance, I identified half a dozen individuals whose occupations were listed as a "dealer in slaves," "negro trader," "cotton broker," or "factor" in 1860. These individuals compose

little more than 0.1 percent of the sample of white male labor force participants as a whole.

48. Figure 4.2 reports the results from a logistic regression, with standard errors corrected for the geographic clustering of residuals due to unobserved heterogeneity at the county level.

49. Doyle (1990).

50. Du Bois (1903/1965); Ayers (1992).

51. Sylla (1969: 657–58); Marx (1867/1977: 777–78). Compounding these difficulties, debates about monetary standards (e.g., gold versus greenbacks) generated profound uncertainty about the nature of monetary exchange during the postbellum period (Carruthers and Babb 1996). In this environment, elements of the entrepreneurial class itself—and rural storekeepers, in particular—became key financial intermediaries, passing goods and credit from wholesalers to local farmers and proprietors through a consignment system (Ransom and Sutch 2001: 120–25), often at the cost of usurious interest rates.

52. Market integration is assessed as the proportion of capital in businesses (total pecuniary assets) within a county that are rated by the Dun Mercantile Agency (Robert Graham Dun and Company 1860–1900), relative to all capital investments identified by the U.S. census. For more information on nineteenth-century credit rating, see Ruef and Patterson (2009a) and Chapter 6.

53. Etcheson (2009: 237). Also see Chapter 3.

54. The measures are constructed based on the birth place and residential destination of census respondents. Persons born in the same state that they reside in are classified as "locals," while those originating from other parts of the Lower South serve as the reference category. The analysis also identifies persons originating from the Northeastern United States (i.e., "Yankees" from New England or the Mid-Atlantic states), from other parts of the United States, and from foreign countries.

55. A classic sociological treatment of the outsider as entrepreneur is provided by Simmel (1908/1950). Stinchcombe argues that the "level of organizational experience of a population is a main determinant of their capacity to form new organizations" (1965: 152), which suggests that one look to individuals from regions with a rich organizational life as a font of new enterprises within comparatively impoverished areas.

56. Tunnell (2006: 793–94).

57. Ferris and Greenberg (2006).

58. Harris (1890: 88).

59. Meyer and Rowan (1977); Scott (2008).

60. In 1887, a group of two hundred young Atlanta businessmen and professionals, including Henry Grady, formed the Gentlemen's Driving Club, a social association for the most notable "New Men" of the city (Doyle 1990). Less glamorous bases for social affiliation among the rising middle classes existed in business leagues, athletic clubs, hotel lobbies, and the Southern Methodist Church (Wells 2011). The American Missionary Association played a prominent role in catalyzing the idea of a black middle class in the South (Jewell 2007).

61. During the years before the Civil War, the American periodical literature barely registered the middling stratum as a noteworthy social construct, with only

sixty-two texts citing the term "middle class" in a large corpus of magazines and other journals published between 1840 and 1859. Between 1880 and 1899, the same corpus of periodicals invoked the term in over twenty thousand articles (based on the American Periodical Series, a digitized historical collection of magazines and journals published in the United States).

62. The ideology of the New South Creed was described most definitively by Gaston (2002). Examples of early twentieth-century scholars who promoted the tenets of the creed include John Spencer Bassett (1903) and Edwin Mims (1926).

63. Woodward (1951: 17, 20, 29). Despite the fact that C. Vann Woodward's book appeared over sixty years ago, its conclusions have been remarkably durable. In one retrospective in the early 1970s, Hackney (1972: 191) suggested that there was "little fundamental challenge to the outlines of [Woodward's] story" including the characterization of the postbellum South's "declining aristocracy [as] ineffectual and money hungry." Other retrospectives, written around the fiftieth anniversary of Woodward's book, critiqued the absence of women and blacks in his narrative (see, e.g., Gilmore and Fields in Boles and Johnson 2003), but were more hesitant to reconsider his thesis of decline in the white male planter elite.

64. Billings (1982: S57–61). See Genovese (1965) on the tension between planter control of unfree labor and industrialization.

65. Expanding on the beliefs of early Southern sociologists, such as George Fitzhugh and Henry Hughes, Chad Morgan (2005) has advanced the argument that planter-led, state-funded industrialization was already well established by the late antebellum period.

66. The data again involve a 1 percent random sample from the Integrated Public Use Microdata Series (Ruggles et al. 2010). The hypothesis that native-born Southerners are the same proportion of top wealth holders in 1870 as in 1860 can be rejected at the $p < .05$ level, but not at the $p < .01$ level of statistical significance (using a conventional two-tailed two-sample test).

67. The historian Lawrence Powell (1999) has provided the most systematic treatment of Northern emigrants who became part of the New South's planter elite during Reconstruction. He figures that five to seven thousand Northern entrepreneurs became involved in cotton cultivation in the Lower South after the Civil War, revising some of his earlier estimates (ibid.: xiii). Census data suggest that there was no substantive change in the prevalence of non-Southerners among the Lower South's planter aristocracy between 1860 and 1870. Before the Civil War, only 13 percent of the region's wealthiest planters (i.e., top 1 percent of the wealth distribution) were born outside the South; after the Civil War, this number remained virtually the same, at 12 percent of the wealthiest planters.

68. See Chapter 6 on the reorganization of Southern agriculture. Powell (1999: 54) suggests that competition from "hard-driving and calculating" Yankees may have shown the ex-slave owners the benefits of becoming a rentier class, though this claim cannot be substantiated on the basis of the relatively small number of Northern-born planters who came South.

69. Wiener (1978). Woodward (reprinted in Boles and Johnson 2003: 154–55) acknowledges some of the challenges posed by statistical data for his earlier claims of planter decline.

70. Franklin (1961: 221); Dunaway (2003b).
71. The Southern Agrarian poet and novelist Andrew Nelson Lytle, quoted in West (2008: 3).
72. West (2008: 11, 28–30).
73. Owing to the urbanization and industrialization of the South in the late nineteenth century, the persistence of the yeoman farmer was inevitably short-lived. From 1880 to 1900, the farm proprietors decline to 37 percent of the white adult labor force (Table 4.3).
74. West (2008: 109).
75. Ibid.; Hahn (1983/2006).
76. For a classic treatment of the antebellum yeoman farmer, see Owsley (1949).

CHAPTER 5: THE DEMISE OF THE PLANTATION

1. Quotation in Library of Congress (1941: 16.1:27–28). Planter quoted in Loring and Atkinson (1869: 4).
2. The survey had 158 named correspondents and an unknown number of additional anonymous respondents. Respondents were predominately cotton planters in the South, but the sample also included commercial brokers, real estate agents, judges, doctors, and the editors of *DeBow's Review*.
3. Loring and Atkinson (1869: 158). The statement is clearly more relevant in its symbolism than its facticity. An examination of the published correspondence from the report reveals only a single planter from Georgia who declared, with considerable hyperbole, that "there is not a single old slaveholder that is looking to a restoration of slavery" (ibid.: 81).
4. Ibid. (1869: 34–67, 98–99, 158).
5. Ibid. (1869: 17, 10, 5).
6. See Durkheim (1893/1997) and Macaulay (1963) for classic statements. The fragility of postbellum labor contracts was probably augmented by the transition from what Max Weber has called "status contracts," which circumscribed the entire existence of slaves in the antebellum South, to "purposive contracts," which attempted to achieve more specific economic outputs from free laborers (Weber 1968: 672–73; see also Swedberg 1999).
7. Loring and Atkinson (1869: 7).
8. Organizational scholars have undertaken extensive analyses of disbanding on the part of individual organizations (e.g., Carroll and Hannan 2000; Aldrich and Ruef 2006: chap. 10), as well as analyses of industry emergence (Ruef 2000; see also Stinchcombe 1965: 153–69). Studies of the extinction of entire forms of organizational activity have been far more limited.
9. The definition is similar to Edgar Thompson's classic conception that viewed the plantation as a "large landed estate . . . in which social relations between diverse racial or cultural groups are based upon authority, involving the subordination of resident laborers to a planter for the purpose of producing an agricultural staple which is sold in a world market" (1932/2010: 3). The *Oxford Dictionary* did not adopt a contemporary meaning of "plantation" until 1706. Previous usage had simply emphasized organizations involved in the "act of planting" or any

agricultural holding in a new or conquered territory (Thompson 1935: 318; Vlach 1993). Usage in this chapter does not identify slavery as an integral attribute of the plantation, although some coercive element is often required to sustain the labor intensiveness of the form (see, e.g., Paige 1997 on the political economy of coffee plantations).

10. Loring and Atkinson (1869: 129). On the antebellum prevalence of the plantation, see Elkins (1959: 47) and data from the U.S. Bureau of the Census (1883a).

11. Ransom and Sutch (2001: chap. 4); U.S. Bureau of the Census (1916); Rubin (1951). In an important critique, the geographer Charles Aiken (1998) has suggested that the thesis of plantation decline is largely mythological, driven by planter narratives of personal financial ruin, census figures that relabeled tenant units as farms, and the close cultural association between the American plantation system and slavery. While historical evidence supports Aiken's view that concentrated patterns of land ownership persisted after the Civil War (Chapter 4), it does not support stasis in the organizational form of Southern agriculture. As Aiken himself acknowledges (ibid.: 16–22), the rapid shift from nucleated to dispersed settlement patterns—and from gang system to familial labor—produced a New South "plantation" that was quite unlike its antebellum predecessors.

12. Litwack (1979); Wright (1978, 1986/1996).

13. The figure does not address trends in labor intensity, another defining feature of the plantation form. By the early twentieth century, Southern farms departed considerably from the labor intensity presumed by the plantation, with only 1.6 percent of all Southern farms reporting expenditures of over one thousand dollars for wage labor, compared to 3.3 percent for farms in all other regions of the United States (U.S. Bureau of the Census 1916: Table 23).

14. Aiken (1998: 3).

15. Florida planter Ethelred Philips, quoted in Litwack (1979: 337). Also see Wright (1986/1996) and Ransom and Sutch (2001).

16. Reid (1866/1965); Barrow (1881); Franklin (1961: 6). As this discussion highlights, the use of the term "wage plantation" does not mean that compensation was always monetary in character. Often, the "wages" took the form of crops, food rations, or housing, as revealed in labor contracts from the period. Contractual agreements aside, nonpayment of wages was a widespread concern for freedmen and women (Chapter 2).

17. Coulter (1947); Gates (1965).

18. U.S. Bureau of the Census (1864a, 1872); Ransom and Sutch (2001: 48). Owing to the inadequacies of the 1870 census, these figures should probably be regarded as lower bounds. Goldin and Lewis (1975) place a much larger value on the direct costs associated with the loss of physical capital in the South, though their calculation also includes declines in the value of land and other real estate.

19. Thompson (1935); U.S. Bureau of the Census (1883a); see also Figure 5.1. In advancing this hypothesis, Thompson echoed a long line of Malthusian arguments that were raised in the nineteenth century to predict the demise of slavery as a function of population growth (Coclanis and Engerman 2013: 82–83).

20. Smith (1987). Other scholars (e.g., Firebaugh 1979) have argued that plantation agriculture initially spurs urbanization in underdeveloped regions. This is

consistent with the model of dependent urbanization advanced by Smith and explains the relatively large size of urban centers such as Charleston in colonial America.

21. For a pioneering treatment of the impact of social movements among organizational members, see Zald and Berger (1978).

22. Granovetter and Soong (1988); Marwell and Oliver (1993); Chwe (1999). There are conceptual parallels between the abandonment of plantation agriculture among Southern blacks and other well-known threshold phenomena, such as worker strikes (see Granovetter 1978 for additional substantive examples).

23. Although the pattern of exits displayed in the figure is stylized, it is based on empirical estimates derived later in this chapter from interviews with former slaves.

24. Oberschall (1973); Granovetter (1978); Chwe (1999).

25. Barrow (1881); Reid (1866/1965). For a theoretical discussion of structural inertia, see Hannan and Freeman (1984).

26. Loring and Atkinson (1869: 22).

27. Ransom and Sutch (2001: 88); Du Bois (1901).

28. Loring and Atkinson (1869: 23).

29. See Chapter 3, Table 3.1. The calculation is based on adding the percentage of skilled (6.6 percent) and semiskilled manual workers (3.6 percent) in the antebellum period, divided by the size of the slave labor force as a percentage of the Southern black population (62.6 percent).

30. Snow, Zurcher, and Olson (1980); McAdam and Paulsen (1993).

31. Gutman (1976: 209); Escott (1979: chap. 2). In her analysis of the African American family in slavery, Dunaway (2003a: 78) suggests that as many as two-thirds of Appalachian slave children were separated from their fathers due to forced labor migration.

32. Gutman (1976). The theory implies that strong ties may be especially important in mobilizing those individuals with relatively high thresholds for abandoning an organizational form (i.e., late movers), in contrast to Chwe's (1999: 141–46) game-theoretic account, which suggests that the influence of strong ties is especially relevant for early mobilizers and that weaker ties, particularly those that transfer information, are of greater importance to holdouts.

33. Granovetter (1978: 1438–39).

34. Carroll and Hannan (2000: chap. 10).

35. Thompson (1935); Ransom and Sutch (2001: 74–75).

36. Fogel and Engerman (1995); Wright (1978: 85).

37. A diversity index of 1.0 indicates when crop acreage is completely heterogeneous in allocation, and an index of 0.0 indicates when all acreage is devoted to a single cash crop. Specifically, the diversity measure (D) is computed as,

$$D = -\sum_{i=1}^{n} \left(\frac{\log y_i}{\log n} \right) y_i$$

where n is the number of different crops and y_i is the proportion of crops listed within each crop category i.

38. Wright (1978: 47).
39. Ransom and Sutch (2001); Reid (1981); Raup (1973).
40. U.S. Bureau of the Census (1864a, 1872, 1883a). See Appendix A for additional information on the agricultural census data.
41. The data were originally collected by Ransom and Sutch (1999; 2001: Appendix G). Sampling weights allow generalization from these data to the entire South, subsuming all of the slaveholding states shown in Figure 5.2, with the exception of Kentucky, Maryland, and Missouri.
42. Although the information is available for only seventy-three counties, it is far more accurate than the 1880 Report on Agriculture, which combines cropland, pasture, and unimproved woodland in its enumeration of farm size distributions, introducing comparability problems with the 1860 and 1870 censuses.
43. A plantation is defined as an agricultural enterprise that is owner-operated (rather than rented or tenant farmed) and has five hundred or more acres of arable land. Some definitions of the postbellum plantation form use a more generous lower threshold (e.g., two hundred acres of cropland) in delineating the size of the organization but add the requirement that a substantial amount of production be handled by hired wage labor (Ransom and Sutch 2001: Table 4.3). Estimates of plantation prevalence by this standard are virtually identical to the definition employed here.
44. Litwack (1979: 351–53). Berthoff (1951: 328) notes that, until about 1907, Southern "planters, land speculators, railroads, industrialists, and the state governments strove … to tap the rushing stream of immigration to the United States." Consistent with the meager increase in the foreign-born population of the average county shown in Table 5.2, such efforts met with "little success" in the South (ibid.).
45. Missing census information from St. Bernard Parish in Louisiana led to the exclusion of this case. County-level increases or decreases in plantation density over time (dN_i/dt) are measured on an interval-level scale and are thus amenable to ordinary least squares estimation. Given potential heterogeneity in institutional influences on plantation density at the state level, I employed the following first-order difference specification with state-level effects,

$$dN_i/dt = \alpha_k + \boldsymbol{\beta'}\mathbf{dx}_i/dt + \gamma N_i + \varepsilon_i$$

where dN_i is the change in density of plantations in each county (i), α_k is the fixed effect for each Southern state (k), and $\mathbf{dx}_i$ corresponds to a vector of changes in county-level covariates over time (t). Consistent with model specifications in population ecology, the model assumes that the rate of change in plantation density is tied to antebellum density (N_i).
46. Gregor (1965) and Groth (1977) provide critiques of the frontier thesis.
47. See Reid (1981) on competition between different forms of agricultural tenure and Schumpeter (1942/1975) on creative destruction, more generally. There is little support for resource partitioning arguments, which suggest that plantations and smaller specialized farms thrived alongside one another in the late nineteenth century. From an evolutionary perspective, this resulted largely because small farmers increasingly abandoned subsistence farming in favor of

cash crop production (Wright 1978: 166), thus coming into direct competition with larger agricultural units.

48. This historical case of legitimacy spillovers between closely related organizational forms parallels colegitimation processes found in other organizational sectors (Ruef 2000).

49. Litwack (1979); Woodson (1918).

50. The analysis considers plantation prevalence in a representative set of seventy-three Southern counties between 1860 and 1880, serving as a safeguard against well-known shortcomings in the 1870 census (Ransom and Sutch 1999; 1975). Five counties from the original sample—including Grant (LA), Clay (MS), Lincoln (MS), Washington (MS), and Houston (TN)—were excluded from my analysis due to nonmatching census definitions or missing data between 1860 and 1880.

51. While a lack of annual data prevents us from exploring the issue more definitively, the rise in competition is entirely consistent with the density-dependent account offered by organizational ecology (Carroll and Hannan 2000) and extended to multiple organizational forms (Ruef 2000). In 1870, midsized farms represented fewer than one-quarter of agricultural units in the Cotton South and could be seen as complementary to the plantation form; by 1880, their numbers approached 40 percent of all agricultural units and they had to be recognized as a source of competition by larger producers.

52. Escott (1979: chap. 5); Alsberg (1937: 175). Weights were applied to the WPA data to deal with well-known sampling problems, particularly survivor bias among the elderly respondents (see Chapter 3). The weighting procedure generates a gender-stratified distribution of respondents across slave occupations that is representative for the late antebellum period.

53. Loring and Atkinson (1869: 18). Note that the estimates in the figure do not consider former slaves who came back to the plantation system as wage laborers after a period of absence. A small number of the slaves in the WPA sample (~1.5 percent) ended up returning to the same plantations that they had left earlier.

54. These statistics do not correspond strictly to the estimates plotted in Figure 5.6 due to missing values in the reasons given by former slaves.

55. Cf. Wright (1986/1996).

56. Event history techniques were used to analyze exit rates from the plantation system. I employed a semiparametric approach and estimated the following Cox (1972) model,

$$r(t) = h(t)\exp(\boldsymbol{\beta}'\mathbf{x})$$

where $r(t)$ is the plantation exit rate, $h(t)$ is an unspecified baseline rate (which controls for general temporal variation), $\mathbf{x}$ is a vector of covariates, and $\boldsymbol{\beta}'$ is the corresponding vector of coefficients. The vector $\mathbf{x}$ is positively related to individual variation in the propensities that ex-slaves have for abandoning the plantation system, with high rates corresponding to movers and low rates corresponding to stayers.

57. Given the average age of WPA respondents at the end the Civil War (~thirteen years old), a possible concern with this analysis is that many of the respondents

were too young to make their own decisions during emancipation. To verify the robustness of the results, I reestimated the exit rate models for a sample restricted to adolescents and adults. Results for the more limited sample are consistent with those reported here, although—as one might expect—status considerations explain more variance in the outcomes.

58. A measurement problem arises with respect to eliciting information on conditions on the plantation, since most WPA interviews were conducted by white interviewers in the 1930s (Blassingame 1975). This will lead to underestimates of adverse conditions, such as physical abuse. Because interest here focuses on contentious action, the reports provided by former slaves still prove useful. In effect, the mobilization of collective effort against plantation agriculture presumes that ex-slaves are willing to engage in some public denunciation of its practices.

59. To probe differences in network influences on "movers" and "stayers," I derived individual exit propensities (θ) for each respondent in the sample as $\theta = \exp(\boldsymbol{\beta}'\mathbf{x}) - 1$, using a Cox model and the estimates shown in Figure 5.7a. Higher values thus identify early movers, while lower values identify stayers.

60. Cf. Chwe (1999).

61. Wright (1978); Reid (1981). In some historical treatments, the rental farmers are referred to as "cash tenants," even though they might pay a landlord in either cash or agricultural commodities. Other treatments, including early twentieth-century censuses, differentiate between "standing rent tenants" and cash tenants. The crucial commonality to all of these arrangements was that the farmers paid a fixed amount, agreed upon in advance, to rent a landholding or farm acreage (Aiken 1998: 32–33).

62. Ransom and Sutch (2001: 86).

63. Zald and Berger (1978); Morrill, Zald, and Rao (2003).

64. Goffman (1961: 70–74).

65. Royce (1993).

66. Escott (1979: chap. 5); Wright (1978). As Patterson (1998: 48–49) has emphasized, the typical process of family formation among rural blacks in the postbellum period—involving early marriage, high fertility, and the widespread use of child labor—could be seen as either a consequence or cause of the sharecropping system. Rosenbloom (2002) provides one account explaining why familial networks tended not to connect black workers with northern labor markets in the late nineteenth century.

67. Hirschman (1970).

68. Litwack (1979).

69. Quoted in Wright (1986/1996: 236); see also Rubin (1951).

CHAPTER 6: CREDIT AND TRADE IN THE NEW SOUTH

1. Interview H-0098–2, Southern History Collection (#4007), Wilson Library, University of North Carolina at Chapel Hill.

2. John W. Snipes (1976/2006).

3. This argument has been put forward most provocatively by Roger Ransom and Richard Sutch (2001: chaps. 7 and 8). Despite its intuitive cogency, a survey of

scholars knowledgeable about the period found that nearly half of economists and a fifth of historians disagreed with the claim that "the monopoly power of the merchant … was used to exploit many farmers and to force them into excessive production of cotton"; around half of economists *and* historians disagreed with the corollary claim that "the crop mix chosen by most farmers in the post-bellum cotton South was economically inefficient" (Whaples 1995: 142). See Marler (2011) for a recent appraisal of the argument and Ransom and Sutch (1979) for an early response to critics.

4. Interview with Frank Durham (1979/2006). Guano is a nutrient-rich fertilizer made from the excrement of birds.

5. In economic sociology, the distinction of "upstream" and "downstream" is especially central to Harrison White's conception of markets. For White, "each market exhibits an orientation either upstream or downstream" (2004: 8) and the direction of this orientation is crucial to how we conceptualize uncertainty. For purposes of this chapter, the perspective of the market is oriented *toward* the country store or rural manufacturer as its object, so that suppliers are looking downstream, while farmers and consumers are looking upstream.

6. Ayers (1992: 93–94). One should not overstate the case, of course, that rural merchants provided a safety net for farmers in their communities. In an oral history, a former mill worker from North Carolina recounts how farming families, "got in such bad shape that they couldn't even get nothing to eat, hardly" even though "the merchants would carry them" for a while (Durham 1979/2006).

7. The census figures are likely to understate the role of drummers in the economy, since they tabulate only residents. Most drummers spent their time on the road, populating the hotels, eating houses, and railroad cars of the New South (Ayers 1992: 83–85).

8. Ibid. (84–86); John W. Hartman Center (2013).

9. Durham (1979/2006).

10. Ayers (1992: 83).

11. Hsu, Negro, and Koçak (2010) provide a useful overview of the current literature on organizational and product classification.

12. See Pred (1965) and Gamm and Putnam (1999) for analyses using these materials.

13. Madison (1974); Domosh (1990). See also Romanelli and Khessina (2005) on the regional identities produced by the spatial agglomeration of industry.

14. For informative accounts of early historical trends in commercial specialization, see Porter and Livesay (1971) and Doerflinger (1983).

15. Olegario (2006: 105).

16. Clark (1946: 31n13).

17. Author's analysis based on 2,218 entries in R. G. Dun's *Reference Book* for 1860. The average correlation in ratings across audiences was .84 for businesses that were classified unambiguously. The correlation fell to .77 for businesses that were not clearly classified by Dun. For a general discussion regarding the role of ambiguity and multiple audiences in business evaluation, see Pontikes (2012).

18. By 1860, these three cities included two-thirds of all businesses that were formally evaluated in R. G. Dun's *Reference Book* listings for the Cotton South.

19. Atherton (1946). In his influential book on the *Southern Country Store*, Lewis Atherton (1949) argued convincingly that the visibility of the cotton factor in the antebellum system of merchandising has been overstated by historians and that the mercantile activities of most small farmers dealt instead with storekeepers. If so, then the flow of transactions linking Northeastern wholesalers to the hinterland was often quite indirect, proceeding through factors and storekeepers before reaching "average" Southerners.

20. Although the change in ambiguous classification over time may appear small, it is statistically significant at the $p < .001$ level for each postbellum decade.

21. Images and quotations are taken from the collection of advertising ephemera at the John W. Hartman Center (2013) for Sales, Advertising, and Marketing History.

22. Again drawing on R. G. Dun's *Reference Book* (1860–1900) for the Cotton South, I find that the Pearson's *r* correlation between a firm's "pecuniary strength" (i.e., known assets) and the distinct categories of products/trades that the firm pursues is merely .03.

23. Sandage (2005: 10).

24. Earling (1890:55, italics added).

25. Sandage (2005: 142). To modern observers, this emphasis on focus may seem odd, particularly when we consider arguments touting the financial benefits of diversification. But it is also important not to equate diversification (or multibusiness enterprises) with the issue of categorical uncertainty in business classification. The former concept refers to a producer-side perspective, in which a firm hedges against risk by combining a number of (potentially unrelated) lines of business. The latter concept refers to an audience-side perspective, in which a firm is perceived to fall into multiple business categories and the extent of its commitment to any one is indeterminate (see also Hsu, Hannan, and Koçak 2009).

26. Madison (1974); Carruthers and Cohen (2006); Olegario (2006).

27. Foulke (1941). In New England, rudimentary credit reporting arose in the early nineteenth century through correspondents, who toured distant districts, collected debts, and made notes on business activities. In 1829, the London firm of Baring Brothers signed a contract with a prominent Boston merchant, Thomas Wren Ward, who was charged with the task of selecting correspondents in North America and organizing their credit reports in a "Private Remarks Book." Given Ward's extensive reliance on intimate connections, ranging from small merchants to presidents of the United States, critics regarded his approach as "antediluvian" by the 1850s (Hidy 1939: 87).

28. Foulke (1941); Carruthers and Cohen (2006).

29. Norris (1978). Previously, the absence of a reference book had been exploited by a Dun competitor, John Bradstreet, who in 1857 had begun issuing a bound volume that offered short-hand credit reports for a variety of enterprises. Bradstreet's initial volume contained reports on roughly seventeen thousand businesses in eight cities, none of them in the South (Foulke 1941: 298). Although Bradstreet's *Commercial Reports* had more limited coverage than Dun's book and focused on urban businesses, its availability had a devastating effect on the profits of the Mercantile Agency.

30. Foulke (1941: 313); Olegario (2006).

31. The full title of the 1860 edition is *The Mercantile Agency Reference Book (and Key), Containing Ratings on the Merchants, Manufacturers and Traders Generally, throughout the United States and Canada*. In this chapter, I refer to it, and subsequent editions, simply as the *Reference Book*.

32. For the sake of inclusiveness, the classification in the table broadens Dun's 1860 category of "boots and shoes" to all leather goods (including saddleries, harness makers, and tan yards). It narrows the heterogeneous category of "hardware, founders, metals, and house furnishings" to furniture, housewares, and hardware. And it replaces the very small category of "hats, caps, furs, and straw goods" with a far more common trade group tracking drug, dry goods, grocery, and general stores.

33. Credit reporters at Dun assigned firms to ten categories of "pecuniary strength," ranging from a class of small enterprises (referenced by the code K), with less than two thousand dollars in working capital, to the largest firms (referenced by A+), which possessed more than one million dollars in capital assets. These codes offered a crude assessment of the "worth" of an enterprise, based on information provided by credit applicants on real estate holdings, merchandise, personal property, and cash on hand (Olegario 2006).

34. Quotes in Norris (1978: 68–69). See also Vose (1916: 98).

35. Norris (1978: 83); Vose (1916).

36. Dun (Louisiana Credit Ledgers, 1882).

37. Ayers (1992: 83).

38. One simple quantitative indicator of this trend involves the inflation-adjusted net worth of the average business rated by R. G. Dun in the Cotton South. In 1860, the mean assets of a firm in the *Reference Book* can be estimated at around $28,624. Over the following decades, this mean drops to roughly $16,900 (1870), $15,500 (1880), and $16,000 (1900), in constant 1860 dollars (with calculations based on a GDP deflator).

39. Quoted in Norris (1978: 112).

40. Porter and Livesay (1971) provide a classic account of the industries that tended to witness forward integration by manufacturers in the nineteenth century (see also Williamson 1985: 108–17 for a transaction cost interpretation).

41. Norris (1978: 108, 157). Olegario (2006: 162) notes that Dun was one of the first major corporations in the United States to adopt the typewriter on a large scale.

42. Olegario (2006: 26–27, 48–49, 56); Wyatt-Brown (1966: 440). Earlier credit coverage had been provided by a correspondent named Sheldon P. Church, who may qualify as the first professional mercantile reporter in the United States. Starting in 1843, Church was hired by a group of New York businessmen to gather intelligence on Southern merchants, and he offered these assessments in an annual typeset series of "Church's Reports." Since Church had to undertake much of the reporting himself (aided by a network of contacts), the social organization of his operation underscores the limited institutionalization of credit reporting in the South before the middle of the nineteenth century (B. Cohen 2012: 137–43).

43. Sandage (2005: 184); Madison (1974); Olegario (2006).

44. Earling (1890: 301); Olegario (2006).

45. Scott (2008).
46. These efforts to manage uncertainty were not limited to Dun alone. According to Rowena Olegario (2006: 174–75), it was the closing decades of the nineteenth century that witnessed the birth of the "credit man" more generally, the professional who would complement the entrepreneur's reliance on "personal intuition, impressions and the variations of personal feelings" with a scientific approach that encouraged him "to transform uncertainty into calculated risk."
47. Norris (1978: 55).
48. Estimates are based on an ordered logit model predicting the ranking of each firm in the Dun credit rating system. The model controls for business assets, credit history, owner demography (gender and kinship), legal form of the business, local market conditions (number of other firms in a settlement and local population), year of evaluation, and distance of the business from the nearest branch office of the Mercantile Agency. Results are also robust to the inclusion of fixed effects for the most common industries in the postbellum South, including—in order of decreasing frequency—general stores, grocers, dry good stores, drug stores, saloons, farms, professionals' offices, saw mills, cobblers, millineries, commission merchants, blacksmiths, grist mills, confectionaries, and jewelers.
49. One question that arises in interpreting the "etcetera" designation is whether it might not simply reflect the need to abbreviate the classification of hybrids that were positioned in a large number of categories. There seems to be little support for this claim empirically, given that there is a negative correlation between the number of trade categories that were applied to Southern firms and the invocation of the residual category in Dun's reports ($r = -.019, p < .001$).
50. For the sake of consistency, the following analyses identify boundary violations for the 1870 and 1880 waves on a counterfactual basis—i.e., violations occur when combinations of trades are at odds with the second-order system of classification that was implemented in 1885.
51. A relevant concern in judging the causal impact of categorical uncertainty on credit is that there may be unmeasured proprietor characteristics that affect both the classification of a business and its credit rating. In particular, proprietors who suffered from low status or discrimination in a community (based on race, religious background, and the like) may also have tended to employ a strategy of trade diversification that allowed them to hedge their bets against the vagaries of any specific market niche. To help address this concern, I reorganized the data into groups of observations sharing a common proprietor and reestimated the model of credit ratings using a random effects specification for panel data. The key features of categorical uncertainty—hybridity, ambiguous classification, and boundary violation—continued to exhibit a strong negative correlation with credit rating.
52. Depending on model specification, the ratings premium for commission merchants and cotton factors—i.e., the estimated percentage receiving a fair (or better) credit rating above a grocer or general store with comparable assets— varies from as little as +1 percent to as much as +6 percent.
53. March and Simon (1958); Espeland and Stevens (2008).

54. Quoted in Norris (1978: 93). By "capital marking," Dun was referring to the Mercantile Agency's assessment of an enterprise's pecuniary strength.

55. The effect of business classification on variance in credit ratings can be modeled formally using a regression model with multiplicative heteroscedasticity (Harvey 1976). In this case, we specify the credit ratings as a function of the conditional mean based on assets, business classification, and other characteristics, as well as the variance of an error term, based on the hybridity and ambiguity of an enterprise's lines of trade.

56. Olegario (2006); B. Cohen (2012).

57. B. Cohen (2012: 333).

58. There is a marked contrast, for instance, in the tone of Dun's credit ledgers and the reports on Southern businesses issued by Sheldon Church in the 1840s. Church's "Black List" included proprietors who were accused, in mass-produced folios, of "knavery" and "depravity" (B. Cohen 2012: 142). Unsurprisingly, this lack of self-censorship also led to frequent legal challenges.

59. B. Cohen (2012); Patterson (2012). During the 1880s, an eighth credit category (4) was formally added to the *Reference Books* to denote financially unstable firms. In 1889, it was applied to 22 percent of the businesses identified by Dun in the Cotton South.

60. Patterson (2012: 60).

61. Patterson (2012: 60–64). See also Carruthers and Cohen (2001).

62. See Woodman's (1966: 1219; 2000) classic discussion of the decline of cotton factorage. Economic sociologists have theorized the conditions leading to failures in networks more generally. The factorage network, in particular, appears to be a victim of what Schrank and Whitford (2011) refer to as "contestation," in which some buyers and suppliers became more opportunistic in using railroad and communication systems to their advantage, at the same time that the standardization of credit information reduced ignorance among these network participants.

63. It is notable, in this respect, that the factorage system "did not disappear overnight," even "with buyers and suppliers on hand deep in the interior" of the Cotton South (Woodman 1966: 1230). According to Woodman, the remaining foothold of the cotton factors was the credit that they were able to offer to local sellers.

64. Nier (2009).

65. Using census microdata, Schweninger (1989) estimates that the total assets of 1,048 black business owners in the Lower South averaged around $7,000 in 1860. By 1870, the number of black business owners had tripled, to roughly 3,000, but the average assets for each proprietor had dropped to roughly $2,500. Meanwhile, the literacy rate among black business owners in the Lower South also declined from 82 to 54 percent, probably reflecting the influx of newly emancipated slaves.

Chapter 7: Paths to Development

1. Reprinted in Harris (1890: 90–91).

2. Wetherington (1994: 6); Malone (1986).

3. U.S. Bureau of the Census (1883b); Wetherington (1994); Malone (1986).

4. On the risk aversion of Southerners during the postbellum period, in particular, see Carlton and Coclanis (2003).

5. Hawley (1950) offers an early treatment of human ecology and the analysis of community structure. For an application to modern urban places, see Molotch, Freudenberg, and Paulsen (2000).

6. Dunlevy (1983); Ayers (1992).

7. Cf. Florida (2005); Molotch, Freudenberg, and Paulsen (2000).

8. Dotson (2008); Doyle (1990). Dotson notes that Roanoke was the fastest growing city in the South and the fourth fastest growing city in the United States during the 1880s. Birmingham's growth continued unabated into the early twentieth century, giving it the South's largest and tallest office buildings by 1920 (Brownell 1972). Despite the ravages of war, Atlanta's population nearly quadrupled between the beginning of the Civil War and 1880.

9. While studying boosterism in the collegiate Bluegrass town of Lexington, Kentucky, Morelock (2008) employs the term "civic folk mercantilism" to describe the latter perspective on competition between nineteenth-century cities.

10. For a useful overview in economic anthropology, see Plattner (1989); for a more critical perspective in economic sociology, see Irwin and Kasarda (1994).

11. Ayers (1992: 55–56).

12. Classic discussions of central place theory can be found in Christaller (1933/1966), Ullman (1941), and Mark and Schwirian (1967). A recent review and appraisal can be found in Mulligan, Partridge, and Carruthers (2012). Eberstein and Galle (1984) consider an application of the theory to the urban system of the American South.

13. In central place theory, the viability of the organizations that provide these goods and services depends further on other factors, including the range that consumers are willing to travel to obtain commodities and the homogeneity of consumers with respect to commodity preferences and purchasing ability. For discussions of the theory's limitations, see Shaffer, Deller, and Marcouiller (2004) and Krugman (1995).

14. Formally, cut-points on this distribution of settlements are employed to classify all settlements at different levels s within the central place hierarchy. Based on Christaller's theory, these cut-points are defined so that

$$\left(\frac{N_s}{m-1}\right) \approx \sum_{i=1}^{s-1} N_i$$

where N_s is the number of settlements in a given level of the central place hierarchy and $s = 1$ represents the class of the largest settlement (regional metropolis). Note that the formula employs the notation "approximately equal" ($\approx$) because ties in counts of business establishments may require that some classes of settlements be larger or smaller than this expectation.

15. Doyle (1990). The small scale of the Southern entrepôts relative to those in other parts of nineteenth-century America is worth noting. New Orleans only ranked fifteenth largest among U.S. cities around the turn of the century. Meanwhile, none of the other "cities" of the Cotton South had populations greater than fifty thousand before 1880 (Ransom and Sutch 2001: 301–5).

16. This procedure generated an average sample size of 133 settlements per focal region. Departures from central place predictions were evaluated as p levels based on a chi-square test,

$$\chi^2 = \sum_{i=1}^{k} \frac{(O_i - E_i)^2}{E_i}$$

where expectations (E_i) correspond to the distribution tabulated for each year in Table 7.1, observations (O_i) correspond to the settlement distribution in each sample, and $k = 4$.

17. Calculating the chi-square test statistic in note 16 for the 165 settlements in and around Autauga County, we have $\chi^2 = 0.082$ $(df = 3)$, which is statistically significant at the $p = .006$ level. In short, there appears to be less than a 1 percent chance that the array of settlements that may be accessed by county residents deviates significantly from the central place hierarchy of the Cotton South as a whole.

18. Prattville was founded on the Autauga Creek, a tributary of the Alabama River, less than fourteen miles away from Montgomery. The map shows a number of place names in central and northern Autauga county (e.g., Marbury, Vine Hill) that seem to have been recognized historically. But there is no evidence in credit reports that nonagricultural businesses were located there.

19. Goldfield (1997: 66n74). The debate regarding the urban evolution of the South figures in the question of whether the spatial and trade relationships of Southern cities converged with capitalist development to resemble that of other regions in the United States or remained rooted in their antebellum origins. Analysis of trade patterns among modern Southern cities has identified a low correlation with contemporary functional specialization and a high correlation with historical trade routes (Eberstein and Galle 1984).

20. Lösch (1944/1954).

21. Ransom and Sutch (2001). As a result of territorial merchant monopolies in Georgia, for instance, Ransom and Sutch estimate that interest rates charged to farmers during the 1880s hovered in the neighborhood of 60 percent per annum (ibid.: 130).

22. Ransom and Sutch (2001: 132–37, 140–42, 143).

23. While the state of railway lines was deplorable immediately after the war, virtually all lines had been restored by 1870 (Stover 1955). Railroad construction and expansion continued unabated, and by 1890 nine out of ten Southerners lived in a county that was serviced by a railroad (Ayers 1992: 9).

24. Kyriakoudes (2002).

25. For more extensive quantitative debates of the thesis of spatial monopolies among rural Southern merchants, see FitzRandolph (1981) and various contributors to a special issue in *Explorations in Economic History* (O'Brien and Shade 2001).

26. Examples of these case studies include Kyriakoudes (2002) on the Alabama black belt, Marler (2001, 2011) on central Louisiana, Aiken (1998) on the lower Georgia piedmont, and Wayne (1980/1990) on the Natchez district of the Mississippi Valley.

27. Kyriakoudes (2002); Wayne (1980/1990).

28. Lewis (1955); Smith (1975). Drawing on modern examples of developing countries, Escobar (2012) provides a counterpoint to the view that Lewis's dual-growth model is universal.

29. Evans (2001).

30. Evans (2001: esp. 124–25).

31. Ayers (1992: 20–21). See Table 7.3 in this chapter for a summary of county-level statistics in 1870 and 1880.

32. In extremis, these claims tend to be enshrined in assumptions that the population is evenly distributed, has equivalent consumption preferences and resources, and will minimize travel to the nearest settlement where a good or service is available.

33. Bauer (1956) offers an early critique of the dual-sector model of growth along these lines.

34. Harris (1890: 221).

35. Dotson (2008: 153); Newman (1996).

36. Hannan and Freeman (1989: 7). For perspectives emphasizing informal social organization and individual outcomes, see Park, Burgess, and McKenzie (1925) and a review by Sampson, Morenoff, and Gannon-Rowley (2002). For perspectives incorporating the role of formal organizations, see Hawley (1950) and Small and McDermott (2006).

37. Putnam (2000).

38. Wetherington (1994: 220).

39. As portrayed by Twain and Warner (1873), the far-fetched scheme for community development is made possible only due to the involvement of opportunistic local boosters and corrupt Washington politicians. After scandalous charges surrounding the "Industrial University Bill" emerge, not a single senator votes for the appropriation to the rural district.

40. Aldrich and Ruef (2006: chap. 11); Hanneman (2006).

41. Deviations from standards of community structure do not imply that idiosyncratic locales are less functional than prototypical locales with respect to any measure of individual well-being. Indeed, a comparison of county D in Figures 7.4a and 7.4b would suggest that the opposite may be true. While residents in the first case have an opportunity to consume alcoholic libations, those in the second may enjoy access to plays, operas, or music.

42. The data for Southern business enterprises come from Dun's *Mercantile Agency Reference Book* (1870, 1880), the most complete source of business information in the late nineteenth century. With the detailed descriptors employed by Dun's credit reporters, I coded businesses into 195 distinct organizational forms listed in the *Reference Book*. Organizational forms were dropped if (1) there were fewer than two instances of the form throughout the Deep South during either the 1870 or 1880 wave or (2) the form was purely agricultural (i.e., a farm or plantation). This left 158 organizational forms for purposes of analysis. Using the 1870 sample, I permuted the county-form matrix by the hospitality of counties and stability of forms (see Appendix B). This yielded the 342 × 158 cell matrix shown in Figure 7.5.

43. Clark (1944); Kyriakoudes (2002: 180).

44. To further test whether the pattern of nestedness is statistically significant, a Monte Carlo study of randomized replications was conducted. Specifically, one

hundred matrices were generated at random for both 1870 and 1880, where all matrices had the same density as the original data ($\Delta_{1870} = 0.10$; $\Delta_{1880} = 0.13$). I permuted each matrix by the frequency of organizational forms and calculated its overall idiosyncrasy on a 0 to 100 scale (Appendix B). The following table shows the results of this analysis:

Table. Monte Carlo Analysis of County Idiosyncrasy

	1870 Data	1870 Randomized[a]	1880 Data	1880 Randomized[a]
Idiosyncrasy	3.22	6.93	4.36	9.32
Density	0.10	0.10	0.13	0.13
Standard deviation	—	0.19	—	0.25
Z score	−19.61 ($p < .001$)		−19.67 ($p < .001$)	

[a] Based on 100 matrix replications.

    The idiosyncrasy of the actual and randomized county-organization matrices tends to be substantially greater than zero, the point where a perfectly predictable pattern of organizational development is observed. Still, the difference between the observed idiosyncrasy and mean of randomized matrix idiosyncrasies is also large for both periods. As a result, we can safely reject the null hypothesis that the presence of organizational forms in these locales is no different from what would be expected by chance. There appears to be a strong implicit norm governing the business structure of the postbellum communities in the Cotton South.

45. Solow (1956).
46. DiMaggio and Powell (1983).
47. Hannan (1988).
48. Carlton and Coclanis (2003: 104).
49. The foreign-born residents of the Cotton South were consistently less than 1 percent of the population in the 1870s and 1880s, suggesting that norms of community structure were unlikely to be affected by expectations introduced from other countries. Empirical support for the second scope condition can be found in note 44.
50. Molotch, Freudenberg, and Paulsen (2000: 791).
51. I specifically exclude the value of land when analyzing this outcome, since land is not subject to depreciation to the same extent as other forms of capital.
52. Formally, models for growth in county gross product (Y'), population (P'), and fixed capital investment (K') were specified as

$$Y' = \alpha P' + (1 - \alpha)K' + \beta_1 I_C + \gamma_1 X_1 + \dots \gamma_n X_n$$

$$P' = \theta(w) + \beta_2 I_C + \gamma_1 X_1 + \dots \gamma_n X_n$$

$$K' = s\left(\frac{Y}{K}\right) + \beta_3 I_C + \gamma_1 X_1 + \dots \gamma_n X_n$$

where I_c is the change in the idiosyncrasy of a county, w is the deviation of the local wage rate from the regional average at the beginning of the period, Y/K is the rate of return-on-capital (again, at the beginning of the period), and the vector X summarizes other variables that may affect economic or demographic growth (see Table 7.3). The parameter α estimates the share of output due to growth in the population (i.e., labor pool) and, conversely, $1 - \alpha$ estimates the share due to capital ($0 < \alpha < 1$). θ denotes the propensity of workers to be attracted to (and retained within) a locale based on the local wage rate, while s denotes the savings rate. Parameter β estimates the effect of county idiosyncrasy on growth in gross product, population, and capital investment.

53. Given the aggregated measurement of these outcomes, it is not possible to identify the micromechanisms that may underlie their association with local idiosyncrasy. In the case of demographic decline, for instance, migrants may not be attracted to counties that are idiosyncratic (leading to low in-migration), residents may be less inclined to stay in such counties (leading to high out-migration), and/or adults may be less likely to raise families (leading to lower fertility rates).

54. One critique that might be offered with respect to these findings is that the idiosyncrasy of counties may be negatively correlated with their economic scale, even when viewed cross-sectionally. Cross-sectional analyses suggest, however, that there is no empirical support for this claim. For the 1870 census, there is a moderate and *positive* correlation ($r = .11$, $p = .05$) between idiosyncrasy and county gross product in the Lower South; in the 1880 census, this correlation is weak and positive ($r = .05$, ns). These descriptive results dovetail with the sociological intuition that assigns a unique urban identity to larger centers of economic activity (Molotch, Freudenberg, and Paulsen 2000).

55. While these models suggest a correlation between changes in idiosyncrasy and economic and demographic growth, it must also be acknowledged that causal direction cannot be inferred decisively from these results. It is plausible, for instance, that entrepreneurs who move to a county will choose to create businesses that contribute to greater normative conformity in the composition of its business community (leading to an effect of population growth on organizational idiosyncrasy, rather than vice versa). Considering the relatively small number of entrepreneurs in the population of the postbellum South, though, it is unclear that this mechanism alone could account for the magnitude of the idiosyncrasy effect (see Chapter 4).

56. See Chapter 5 on the use of immigrant labor in Southern agriculture. Estimates of the effects of county demographic composition on local development may be found in Ruef and Patterson (2009b, Tables 3–5).

57. Schweninger (1989). For other examples of enclave economies in the postbellum South, see M. Cohen (2012) on Jewish ethnic networks and Doyle (1990) on the business districts created by German immigrants.

58. Ruef and Patterson (2009b: Table 4); Naidu (2010); also see Chapter 5.

59. Ransom and Sutch (2001); Ruef and Patterson (2009b). This decline appears to have been most severe in the heart of the Cotton South (Alabama and Georgia) and slightly less so in states that cultivated other cash crops, such as rice (e.g., Louisiana).

60. Portes (2006); Hoff and Stiglitz (2001).
61. Putnam (2000). For exceptions, see the articles by Molotch, Freudenberg, and Paulsen (2000) and Romanelli and Khessina (2005).
62. Carlton and Coclanis (2003: 104); Ayers (1992: 112); Foner (1988/2002). As discussed in Chapter 6, the economic link between the postbellum South and North existed in supply chains of goods and the mercantile credit that they relied on, rather than direct investment.
63. Among the counties of the postbellum South, a baseline model of growth in county gross product (see note 52) suggests that both labor supply and capital investment were highly correlated with economic output. Growth in the local population, however, had a far greater impact on economic output ($\alpha = .82$) than capital accumulation ($1 - \alpha = .18$).
64. See Figure 7.5 and DiMaggio and Powell (1983) on organizational fields, more generally.

CHAPTER 8: EMANCIPATION IN COMPARATIVE PERSPECTIVE

1. *New York Times* (1864).
2. *New York Times* (1864); *New York Times* (1863).
3. Cimbala (1997: xiv); Cimbala and Miller (1999).
4. As Bell (1999: 144) notes, Louisiana's hesitant transition to a free labor market became the legal template for restructuring the plantation system in much of the South.
5. Excerpt from the *Macon Telegraph* quoted in the *New York Times* (1865). The central irony of the commentator's view of emancipation—that former slaves would be "free" to work, while being highly constrained in their movements and other activities—was hardly limited to Southern conservatives. Indeed, Schmidt (1998) has suggested that this contradiction was inherent in the body of Northern labor laws that were deployed to construct the labor market of the postbellum South.
6. Tilly (1984).
7. In particular, see Stinchcombe's (1995) superb analysis of slavery and emancipation in the West Indies.
8. Fogel and Engerman (1995). The United States, more generally, exhibited a pattern where direct compensation to slaveholders was generally avoided. One notable exception was the District of Columbia, as discussed below.
9. For earlier overviews of paths to emancipation, see Goldin (1973), Fogel and Engerman (1995), and Stinchcombe (1995: part II).
10. Nash and Soderlund (1991). As a consequence of this policy, a child born to a thirty-year-old slave mother in 1809 may not have been released from bondage until 1837. The U.S. census indicates that there were still 403 slaves in Pennsylvania in 1830 and 64 in 1840.
11. Biddle and Dubin (2013). As Mary Farmer-Kaiser (2007: 429) documents, there was tremendous variation in the prevalence of child bondage by locale. In Lynchburg, Virginia, for instance, agents of the bureau were ordered to bind out *all* children when their parents received federal relief. Only a handful of the

bureau's contracts in Washington, D.C., and Northern Virginia involved child bondage (Chapter 2).

12. A more specific definition of partial emancipation requires that it occur without reference to a slave's age or birth cohort, or a future calendar year, thereby differentiating it from gradual emancipation.

13. Rodriguez (1999).

14. Blackmon (2008).

15. The description of the Moret Law as a "preparatory bill for the gradual abolition of slavery" signals its combination of partial and gradual elements of emancipation (Scott 1983: 452).

16. Goldin (1973: 71–72); Draper (2010); Rodriguez (1999).

17. The most notable effort to redistribute resources to former slaves in the United States was General Sherman's Special Field Order 15, which was revoked by President Andrew Johnson. While there have been a number of legal claims for reparations in the past few decades, no reparation program for slave descendants has been instituted in any other country (Posner and Vermeule 2003).

18. Clark-Lewis (2002). The value of the DC Emancipation Act as an act of war propaganda may have been lost because it received very limited media attention (Mitchell 1963/65).

19. Goldin (1973).

20. Scott (2008: 142); Douglas (1986).

21. Cimbala and Miller (1999: xxv); Cimbala (1997: 153).

22. See Meyer and Jepperson (2000) on the role of culture and institutional devices, more generally, in constructing individuals who are perceived as autonomous social actors.

23. For other comparative analyses of emancipation in the Americas and beyond, see Twaddle (1993), Kolchin (2003, 2012), and Drescher (1999). While there are important commonalities in the process of emancipation, as discussed in this chapter, it should also be acknowledged that the catalysts of abolitionist sentiment across societies are diverse and contested. One long-standing comparative-historical debate pits economic decline as the root cause of abolitionism (e.g., Williams 1944) against more subtle features of mass mobilization and political entrepreneurship (Drescher 1999).

24. Howard White (1970: 125).

25. Edwards (1997) provides a detailed analysis of the evolution of social roles in the Southern household as a consequence of institutional transformation after the Civil War.

26. Branch (2011); see also Chapters 3 and 5.

27. Woodman (1966: 1219; 2000); see also Chapters 4 and 6.

28. For one detailed case study, see Sheridan's (1993) discussion of the transition from chattel to wage slavery in Jamaica.

29. Note, however, that immediate emancipation was instituted in the Dutch Caribbean islands, including Aruba, Bonaire, Curacao, Saba, St. Eustatius, and St. Maarten (Emmer 1993: 87).

30. Emmer (1993).

31. Hu-Dehart (1993). Laborers from other ethnic groups were also well represented in colonial efforts to confront the cessation of the slave trade. Indentured

workers from East India were sent to British Guiana, Trinidad, Jamaica, the French colonies, and Suriname (ibid.: 68–69; Emmer 1993).

32. Hu-Dehart (1993: 72–73, 81).
33. In his discussion of semiservile labor in the British Caribbean, Stinchcombe (1995: 263–75) develops a typology of four forms of planter monopoly advantage under emancipation, including monopolies that attach (a) to persons (as in apprenticeship), (b) to consumption opportunities (e.g., via debt peonage in plantation shops), (c) to alternative production opportunities (e.g., by limiting peasant smallholding), and (d) to the exclusion of competition with other planters (e.g., through antienticement prohibitions).
34. Stinchcombe (1995).
35. Clarence-Smith (1993: 151–53).
36. See Chapters 3 and 5.
37. Chapters 4 and 6.
38. Branch (2011: 26–27); Sheridan (1993); Morrissey (1989). In the plantations of the American South, female slaves were well represented in unskilled field labor, though they were slightly outnumbered by male slaves by the late antebellum era (Olson 1992). Data from Jamaica in the early nineteenth century suggest that female slaves served as the *majority* of agricultural workers on many estates (Shepherd 1993: 45–46).
39. Quote in Sheridan (1993: 37).
40. Farmer-Kaiser (2010); Branch (2011: 34–35).
41. See Chapter 2 for a description of the sample of Freedmen's Bureau labor contracts.
42. Branch (2011: 19–21).
43. Valelly (2004: 80–81).
44. Tolnay and Beck (1995). As Valelly (2004: chap. 6) highlights, the reason that the post-Reconstruction era can be seen as one of profound uncertainty, rather than simply a reversal, for Southern blacks is that there were still ongoing federal initiatives to promote the cause of enfranchisement. A particularly strong piece of legislation, the Federal Elections Bill of 1890, received the support of the House, a Senate majority, and President Benjamin Harrison, but was nevertheless stymied by a filibuster among Southern Democrats.
45. Reitano (2010: 49); White (1991).
46. Washington (2011). Recent analyses of linked U.S. census data suggest that individual switching between mulatto and black racial categories was fairly common between 1870 and 1880, and patterned by changes in occupational status (Saperstein and Gullickson 2013). A possible inference is that racial boundaries were not yet fixed by the rule of hypodescent during the Reconstruction era, permitting a "tripartite" hierarchy of race (see also Bonilla-Silva 2004).
47. Lowenthal (1971). The distinction in race relations between the United States and the Caribbean was not limited to racial classification, but was also heavily influenced by historical demographics. Before emancipation, the meager numbers of free blacks in the American slave states—both Southern and Northern—did little to challenge the popular conflation of phenotypical black features with slavery. In the Caribbean, on the other hand, free colored people were far more common and assumed a far more prominent role in slave society (ibid.).

48. Lowenthal (1971: 372).
49. North (1990: 3,7).
50. Scott (2008); Fligstein and McAdam (2012); Portes (2010); Mahoney and Thelen (2009).
51. The emphasis on social stability was also promoted by British and American abolitionists, who generally "believed that a transitional period was necessary to educate slaves for freedom and to avoid the anticipated problems of social disorganization that emancipation might create" (Coclanis and Engerman 2013: 82).
52. Stinchcombe (1995: 321).
53. Royce (1993).

APPENDIX A.: DATA SOURCES AND SAMPLING

1. Farmer-Kaiser (2010).
2. Guo and Fraser (2010).
3. Rosenbaum and Rubin (1985).
4. Guo and Fraser (2010: 161).
5. See Escott (1979), Jacobs (1981), and Rawick (1972–79).
6. Little (1992: 1231).
7. Fogel (1989: 127–28).
8. The distribution of slave occupations is estimated using Olson's (1992) sample of plantation records. Unskilled agricultural workers tended to be undersampled in the WPA interviews, whereas domestics were oversampled (see also Escott 1979; Yetman 1984). The other characteristic impacting slave mortality—plantation ecology—is highly correlated with state of origin and is accommodated by the existing sample corrections for geographic bias.
9. Quote from Alsberg (1937). Also see Escott (1979).
10. Ruggles et al. (2010).
11. This empirical approach is based on the fact that only free blacks would have been enumerated in the 1860 census. One source of measurement error concerns the possibility that a small number of free blacks in 1860 may not have been linked to their 1880 records due to problems in matching names, age, birthplace, and/or gender. These matching problems would thus lead to cases where free blacks were misclassified as slaves. Based on the distribution of free blacks and slaves in 1860, however, the biases introduced by such linkage problems appear to be minor. By necessity, the procedure also excludes blacks who were born in slave colonies outside the United States.
12. U.S. Bureau of the Census (1864a, 1872, 1883a); Ransom and Sutch (1999).
13. Thirty-eight counties failed to provide agricultural census reports in 1860 or 1870 and were removed from the analysis.
14. The correlations between all three measures of plantation prevalence are high. For 1860, the raw count of plantations has a .76 correlation with the ratio metric comparing plantations to all farms and a .75 correlation with the estimated concentration of land under plantation tenure (treating the largest agricultural units as having 1,500 acres of cropland, on average).

15. Exploratory analyses suggest that Dun's coverage is more complete than that achieved by the Manufacturing Census and, moreover, includes a large number of sectors (retail, wholesale, hospitality, service, professional, etc.) that are not covered by the census at all. For 1889, coincidence with census data was not a consideration (owing to the destruction of the 1890 census), and sampling was timed for the sake of completeness of the archives in the Library of Congress.

Appendix B.: Idiosyncrasy

1. Atmar and Patterson (1993).
2. Hanneman (2006); Aldrich and Ruef (2006: chap. 11).
3. Atmar and Patterson (1993).
4. A basic version of this permutation process simply ranks counties and organizational forms based on their marginal row and column totals, respectively. As suggested by the example, however, this algorithm often does not yield a unique permuted matrix. Consequently, algorithms in theoretical ecology typically add a second step, in which a matrix permuted on the basis of marginal totals is permuted further in order to directly minimize deviations from a measure of nestedness.
5. Atmar and Patterson (1993).

References

ABC News. 1997. "ABC News 'Nightline' Slavery Poll." Computer file distributed by ICPSR. Radnor, PA: Chilton Research Services.

Aigner, Dennis and Glen Cain. 1977. "Statistical Theories of Discrimination in Labor Markets." *Industrial and Labor Relations Review* 30: 175–87.

Aiken, Charles. 1998. *The Cotton Plantation South since the Civil War*. Baltimore, MD: Johns Hopkins University Press.

Aldrich, Howard and Martin Ruef. 2006. *Organizations Evolving*. 2nd ed. London: Sage.

Allen, William and Andrew Burns. 1869/1880. *The Official Guide of the Railways and Steam Navigation Lines of the United States, Puerto Rico, Canada, Mexico and Cuba*. New York: National Railway.

Alsberg, Henry. 1937, July 30. "Memorandum to the State Directors of the Federal Writer's Project." Washington, DC: Works Progress Administration.

Alston, Lee and Joseph Ferrie. 2005. "Time on the Ladder: Career Mobility in Agriculture, 1890–1938." *Journal of Economic History* 65: 1058–81.

Anderson, James. 1988. *The Education of Blacks in the South, 1860–1935*. Chapel Hill: University of North Carolina Press.

Archer, Melanie and Judith Blau. 1993. "Class Formation in Nineteenth-Century America: The Case of the Middle Class." *Annual Review of Sociology* 19: 17–41.

Atherton, Lewis. 1946. "The Problem of Credit Rating in the Ante-Bellum South." *Journal of Southern History* 12: 534–56.

———. 1949. *The Southern Country Store, 1800–1860*. Baton Rouge: Louisiana State University Press.

Atmar, Wirt and Bruce D. Patterson. 1993. "The Measure of Order and Disorder in the Distribution of Species in Fragmented Habitat." *Oecologia* 96: 373–82.

Ayers, Edward. 1992. *The Promise of the New South: Life after Reconstruction*. Oxford: Oxford University Press.

Bandelj, Nina. 2008. *From Communists to Foreign Capitalists: The Social Foundations of Direct Investment in Postsocialist Europe*. Princeton, NJ: Princeton University Press.

Baron, James and Michael Hannan. 1994. "The Impact of Economics on Contemporary Sociology." *Journal of Economic Literature* 32: 1111–46.

Barrow, David. 1881. "A Georgia Plantation." *Scribner's Monthly* 21: 830–36.

Bassett, John Spencer. 1903. "The Industrial Decay of the Southern Planter." *South Atlantic Quarterly* 2: 112–13.

Bauer, P. T. 1956. "Lewis' *Theory of Economic Growth*." *American Economic Review* 46: 632–41.

Becker, Gary. 1964. *Human Capital: A Theoretical and Empirical Analysis, with Special Reference to Education*. Chicago: University of Chicago Press.

Beckert, Jens. 1996. "What Is Sociological about Economic Sociology? Uncertainty and the Embeddedness of Economic Action." *Theory and Society* 25: 803–40.

———. 2002. *Beyond the Market: The Social Foundations of Economic Efficiency*. Translated by Barbara Harshav. Princeton, NJ: Princeton University Press.

Bell, Caryn Cossé. 1999. "'Une Chimère': The Freedmen's Bureau in Creole New Orleans." Pp. 140–60 in P. Cimbala and R. Miller, eds., *The Freedmen's Bureau and Reconstruction*. New York: Fordham University Press.

Bendix, Reinhard. 1956/2001. *Work and Authority in Industry: Managerial Ideologies in the Course of Industrialization*. New Brunswick, NJ: Transaction.

Berlin, Ira, Steven Miller, Joseph Reidy, and Leslie Rowland, eds. 1993. *The Wartime Genesis of Free Labor: The Upper South*. New York: Cambridge University Press.

Berlin, Ira, Joseph Reidy, and Leslie Rowland, eds. 1998. *Freedom's Soldiers: The Black Military Experience in the Civil War*. New York: Cambridge University Press.

Berthoff, Rowland. 1951. "Southern Attitudes toward Immigration, 1865–1914." *Journal of Southern History* 17: 328–60.

Bethel, Elizabeth. 1948. "The Freedmen's Bureau in Alabama." *Journal of Southern History* 14: 49–92.

Biddle, Daniel and Murray Dubin. 2013. "'God Is Settleing the Account': African American Reaction to Lincoln's Emancipation Proclamation." *Pennsylvania Magazine of History and Biography* 137: 57–78.

Billings, Dwight. 1982. "Class Origins of the 'New South': Planter Persistence and Industry in North Carolina." *American Journal of Sociology* 88: S52–85.

Blackmon, Douglas. 2008. *Slavery by Another Name: The Re-Enslavement of Black Americans from the Civil War to World War II*. New York: Random House.

Blair, William and Karen F. Younger. 2009. *Lincoln's Proclamation: Emancipation Reconsidered*. Chapel Hill: University of North Carolina Press.

Blassingame, John. 1965. "The Union Army as an Educational Institution for Negroes, 1862–1863." *Journal of Negro Education* 34: 152–59.

———. 1975. "Using the Testimony of Ex-Slaves: Approaches and Problems." *Journal of Southern History* 41: 473–92.

Blau, Judith and Eric Brown. 2001. "Du Bois and Diasporic Identity: The *Veil* and the *Unveiling* Project." *Sociological Theory* 19: 219–33.

Blau, Peter M. and Otis D. Duncan. 1967. *The American Occupational Structure*. New York: John Wiley.

Bledstein, Burton and Robert Johnson, eds. 2001. *The Middling Sorts: Explorations in the History of the American Middle Class*. New York: Routledge.

Blumin, Stuart M. 1989. *The Emergence of the Middle Class: Social Experience in the American City, 1760–1900*. New York: Cambridge University Press.

Bodenhorn, Howard. 1992. "Capital Mobility and Financial Integration in Antebellum America." *Journal of Economic History* 52: 585–610.

Boles, John and Bethany Johnson, eds. 2003. *Origins of the New South, Fifty Years Later: The Continuing Influence of a Historical Classic*. Baton Rouge: Louisiana State University Press.

Bonacich, Edna. 1975. "Abolition, the Extension of Slavery, and the Position of Free Blacks: A Study of Split Labor Markets in the United States, 1830–1863." *American Journal of Sociology* 81: 601–28.

Bonilla-Silva, Eduardo. 2004. "From Bi-racial to Tri-racial: Towards a New System of Racial Stratification in the USA." *Ethnic and Racial Studies* 27: 931–50.

Branch, Enobong. 2011. *Opportunity Denied: Limiting Black Women to Devalued Work.* New Brunswick, NJ: Rutgers University Press.

Breeden, James. 1980. *Advice among Masters: The Ideal in Slave Management in the Old South.* Westport, CT: Greenwood.

Brown, Thomas, ed. 2008. *Reconstructions: New Perspectives on the Postbellum United States.* New York: Oxford University Press.

Brown, William Wells. 1880. *My Southern Home; or, The South and Its People.* Boston: A.G. Brown.

Brownell, Blaine. 1972. "Birmingham, Alabama: New South City in the 1920s." *Journal of Southern History* 38: 21–48.

Cade, John. 1935. "Out of the Mouths of Ex-Slaves." *Journal of Negro History* 20: 294–337.

Carlton, David and Peter Coclanis. 1989. "Capital Mobilization and Southern Industry, 1880–1905: The Case of the Carolina Piedmont." *Journal of Economic History* 49: 73–94.

———. 2003. *The South, the Nation, and the World: Perspectives on Southern Economic Development.* Charlottesville: University of Virginia Press.

Carpenter, John. 1964/1999. *Sword and Olive Branch: Oliver Otis Howard.* New York: Fordham University Press.

Carroll, Glenn, Jacques Delacroix, and Jerry Goodstein. 1988. "The Political Environment of Organizations: An Ecological View." Pp. 359–92 in B. Staw and L. Cummings, eds., *Research in Organizational Behavior.* Greenwich, CT: JAI.

Carroll, Glenn and Michael Hannan. 2000. *The Demography of Corporations and Industries.* Princeton, NJ: Princeton University Press.

Carruthers, Bruce and Sarah Babb. 1996. "The Color of Money and the Nature of Value: Greenbacks and Gold in Postbellum America." *American Journal of Sociology* 101: 1556–91.

Carruthers, Bruce and Barry Cohen. 2001. "Predicting Failure but Failing to Predict: A Sociology of Knowledge of Credit Rating in Post-Bellum America." Paper Presented at the American Sociological Association Meetings, Anaheim, CA.

———. 2006. "The Mechanization of Trust: Credit Rating in 19th-Century America." Paper presented at the American Sociological Association meetings, Montreal.

Carruthers, Bruce and Wendy Espeland. 1991. "Accounting for Rationality: Double-Entry Bookkeeping and the Rhetoric of Economic Rationality." *American Journal of Sociology* 97: 31–69.

CBS News. 2000, February. "CBS News Monthly Poll #1." Ann Arbor, MI: ICPSR (distributor).

———. 2011, April. "CBS News/60 Minutes/Vanity Fair National Poll" (#2). Ann Arbor, MI: ICPSR (distributor).

Christaller, Walter. 1933/1966. *Central Places in Southern Germany.* Englewood Cliffs, NJ: Prentice Hall.

Chwe, Michael. 1999. "Structure and Strategy in Collective Action." *American Journal of Sociology* 105: 128–56.

Cimbala, Paul. 1997. *Under the Guardianship of the Nation: The Freedmen's Bureau and the Reconstruction of Georgia, 1865–1870.* Atlanta: University of Georgia Press.

Cimbala, Paul and Randall Miller, eds. 1999. *The Freedmen's Bureau and Reconstruction: Reconsiderations*. New York: Fordham University Press.

Clapp, Milton. 1854. "The Prospects and Policy of the South, as They Appear to the Eyes of a Planter." *Southern Quarterly Review* 20: 431–57.

Clarence-Smith, William. 1993. "Struggles over Labour Conditions in the Plantations of São Tomé and Principe, 1875–1914." Pp. 149–67 in Twaddle, *Wages of Slavery*.

Clark, Thomas D. 1944. *Pills, Petticoats, and Plows: The Southern Country Store*. Indianapolis, IN: Bobbs-Merrill.

———. 1946. "The Furnishing and Supply System in Southern Agriculture since 1865." *Journal of Southern History* 12: 24–44.

Clark-Lewis, Elizabeth, ed. 2002. *First Freed: Washington, D.C. in the Emancipation Era*. Washington, DC: Howard University Press.

Clendenen, Clarence. 1969. "President Hayes' 'Withdrawal' of the Troops: An Enduring Myth." *South Carolina Historical Magazine* 70: 240–50.

Coclanis, Peter. 1982. "Rice Prices in the 1720s and the Evolution of the South Carolina Economy." *Journal of Southern History* 48: 531–44.

Coclanis, Peter and Stanley Engerman. 2013. "Would Slavery Have Survived without the Civil War? Economic Factors in the American South during the Antebellum and Postbellum Eras." *Southern Cultures* 19: 66–90.

Cohen, Barry. 2012. "Constructing an Uncertain Economy: Credit Reporting and Credit Rating in the Nineteenth Century United States." Unpublished Ph.D. dissertation, Department of Sociology, Northwestern University.

Cohen, Michael. 2012. "Cotton, Capital, and Ethnic Networks: Jewish Economic Growth in the Postbellum Gulf South." *American Jewish Archives Journal* 64: 112–36.

Cohen, William. 1976. "Negro Involuntary Servitude in the South, 1865–1940: A Preliminary Analysis." *Journal of Southern History* 42: 31–60.

———. 1991. *At Freedom's Edge: Black Mobility and the Southern White Quest for Racial Control, 1861–1915*. Baton Rouge: Louisiana State University.

Collins, Randall. 1979. *The Credential Society: An Historical Sociology of Education and Stratification*. New York: Academic Press.

Collins, William. 1997. "When the Tide Turned: Immigration and the Delay of the Great Black Migration." *Journal of Economic History* 57: 607–32.

Collins, Winfield. 1904. *The Domestic Slave Trade of the Southern States*. New York: Broadway Publishing.

Coulter, Merton. 1947. *The South during Reconstruction, 1865–1877*. Baton Rouge: Louisiana State University Press.

Cox, David. 1972. "Regression Models and Life Tables." *Journal of the Royal Statistical Society* 34: 187–220.

Craemer, Thomas. 2009. "Framing Reparations." *Policy Studies Journal* 37: 275–98.

Daily Mail. 2008, July 31. "U.S. House Apologises for History of Slavery." *Daily Mail*, 4.

Daniel, Pete. 1972/1990. *The Shadow of Slavery: Peonage in the South, 1901–1969*. Urbana: University of Illinois Press.

———. 1979. "The Metamorphosis of Slavery, 1865–1900." *Journal of American History* 66: 88–99.

Darity, William, Jason Dietrich, and David Guilkey. 2001. "Persistent Advantage or Disadvantage? Evidence in Support of the Intergenerational Drag Hypothesis." *American Journal of Economics and Sociology* 60: 435–70.

David, Paul, Herbert Gutman, Richard Sutch, Peter Temin, and Gavin Wright. 1976. *Reckoning with Slavery: A Critical Study in the Quantitative History of American Negro Slavery.* New York: Oxford University Press.

Davidoff, Leonore and Catherine Hall. 2003. *Family Fortunes: Men and Women of the English Middle Class, 1780–1850.* Rev. ed. London: Routledge.

Davis, Jack. 1993. "Changing Places: Slave Movement in the South." *Historian* 55: 657–76.

Davis, Kingsley and Wilbert Moore. 1945. "Some Principles of Stratification." *American Sociological Review* 10: 242–49.

Dequech, David. 2003. "Uncertainty and Economic Sociology: A Preliminary Discussion." *American Journal of Economics and Sociology* 62: 509–32.

Dickinson, David and Ronald Oaxaca. 2009. "Statistical Discrimination in Labor Markets: An Experimental Analysis." *Southern Economic Journal* 76: 16–31.

DiMaggio, Paul and Walter Powell. 1983. "The Iron Cage Revisited: Institutional Isomorphism and Collective Rationality in Organizational Fields." *American Sociological Review* 48: 147–60.

Dirck, Brian. 2007. "Abraham Lincoln, Emancipation, and the Supreme Court." Pp. 99–116 in B. Dirck, ed., *Lincoln Emancipated: The President and the Politics of Race.* DeKalb: Northern Illinois University Press.

Doerflinger, Thomas. 1983. "Commercial Specialization in Philadelphia's Merchant Community, 1750–1791." *Business History Review* 57: 20–49.

Domosh, Mona. 1990. "Shaping the Commercial City: Retail Districts in Nineteenth-Century New York and Boston." *Annals of the Association of American Geographers* 80: 268–84.

Dotson, Rand. 2008. "New South Boomtown: Roanoke, Virginia, 1882–1884." *Virginia Magazine of History and Biography* 116: 150–90.

Douglas, Mary. 1986. *How Institutions Think.* Syracuse, NY: Syracuse University Press.

Douglass, Frederick. 1880. "The Negro Exodus from the Gulf States." *Journal of Social Science* 11: 1–21.

Doyle, Don. 1990. *New Men, New Cities, New South: Atlanta, Nashville, Charleston, Mobile, 1860–1910.* Chapel Hill: University of North Carolina Press.

Draper, Nicholas. 2010. *The Price of Emancipation: Slave-Ownership, Compensation and British Society at the End of Slavery.* Cambridge: Cambridge University Press.

Drescher, Seymour. 1999. *From Slavery to Freedom: Comparative Studies in the Rise and Fall of Atlantic Slavery.* New York: NYU Press.

Du Bois, W. E. B. 1901. "The Freemen's Bureau." *Atlantic Monthly* 87: 354–65.

———. 1902. *The Negro Artisan: A Social Study.* Atlanta: Atlanta University Press.

———. 1903/1965. *The Souls of Black Folk.* New York: Penguin.

———. 1907. "Economic Co-operation among Negro Americans." In *Proceedings of the 12th Conference for the Study of Negro Problems.* Atlanta: Atlanta University Press.

———. 1935. *Black Reconstruction in America, 1860–1880.* New York: Russell and Russell.

Dunaway, Wilma. 2003a. *The African-American Family in Slavery and Emancipation*. New York: Cambridge University Press.

———. 2003b. *Slavery in the American Mountain South*. New York: Cambridge University Press.

Dunlevy, James. 1983. "Regional Preferences and Migrant Settlement: On the Avoidance of the South by Nineteenth Century Immigrants." *Research in Economic History* 8: 217–51.

Durham, Frank. 1979, September 10 and 17. Interview H-0067. Southern History Program Collection (#4007), Southern Historical Collection, Wilson Library, University of North Carolina at Chapel Hill (digitized in 2006).

Durkheim, Emile. 1893/1997. *The Division of Labor in Society*. New York: Free Press.

Earling, Peter. 1890. *Whom to Trust: A Practical Treatise on Mercantile Credits*. New York: Rand McNally.

Easterbrook, William Thomas. 1954. "Uncertainty and Economic Change." *Journal of Economic History* 14: 346–60.

Eaton, Clement. 1960. "Slave-Hiring in the Upper South: A Step toward Freedom." *Mississippi Valley Historical Review* 46: 663–78.

Eberstein, Isaac and Omer Galle. 1984. "The Metropolitan System in the South: Functional Differentiation and Trade Patterns." *Social Forces* 62: 926–40.

Edwards, Laura. 1997. *Gendered Strife and Confusion: The Political Culture of Reconstruction*. Champaign: University of Illinois Press.

Eelman, Bruce. 2004. "'An Educated and Intelligent People Cannot Be Enslaved': The Struggle for Common Schools in Antebellum Spartanburg, South Carolina." *History of Education Quarterly* 44: 249–69.

Egypt, Ophelia, J. Masuoka, and Charles Johnson. 1945. *Unwritten History of Slavery: Autobiographical Accounts of Negro Ex-Slaves*. Nashville: Fisk University Social Science Institute.

Eichenlaub, Suzanne, Stewart Tolnay, and J. Trent Alexander. 2010. "Moving Out but Not Up: Economic Outcomes in the Great Migration." *American Sociological Review* 75: 101–25.

Elkins, Stanley. 1959. *Slavery: A Problem in American Institutional and Intellectual Life*. Chicago: University of Chicago Press.

Ellerson, Lindsey. 2010, January 18. "On MLK Day, President Obama Posts Copy of Emancipation Proclamation in Oval Office." *ABC News*. http://abcnews.go.com/blogs/politics/ 2010/01/on-mlk-day-president-obama-posts-copy-of-emancipation -proclamation-in-oval-office/.

Emmer, Pieter. 1993. "Between Slavery and Freedom: The Period of Apprenticeship in Suriname (Dutch Guiana), 1863–1873." Pp. 87–113 in Twaddle, *Wages of Slavery*.

Emigh, Rebecca. 1997. "The Spread of Sharecropping in Tuscany: The Political Economy of Transaction Costs." *American Sociological Review* 62: 423–42.

———. 2005. "The Great Debates: Transitions to Capitalisms." Pp. 355–80 in J. Adams, E. Clemens, and A. Shola Orloff, eds., *Remaking Modernity: Politics, History, and Sociology*. Durham, NC: Duke University Press.

England, Paula. 1984. "Wage Appreciation and Depreciation: A Test of Neoclassical Economic Explanations of Occupational Sex Segregation." *Social Forces* 62: 726–49.

Erikson, Robert and John H. Goldthorpe. 1992. *The Constant Flux: A Study of Class Mobility in Industrial Societies*. New York: Oxford University Press.

Escobar, Arturo. 2012. *Encountering Development: The Making and Unmaking of the Third World*. Princeton, NJ: Princeton University Press.

Escott, Paul. 1979. *Slavery Remembered: A Record of Twentieth-Century Slave Narratives*. Chapel Hill: University of North Carolina Press.

Espeland, Wendy and Mitchell Stevens. 2008. "A Sociology of Quantification." *European Journal of Sociology* 49: 401–36.

Etcheson, Nicole. 2009. "Review: Reconstruction and the Making of a Free Labor South." *Reviews in American History* 37: 236–42.

Evans, Curtis. 2001. *The Conquest of Labor: Daniel Pratt and Southern Industrialization*. Baton Rouge: Louisiana State University Press.

Evans, W. H. 1869. "The Labor Question." *Southern Cultivator* 27: 54–55.

Farmer-Kaiser, Mary. 2007. "'With a Weight of Circumstances Like Millstones about Their Necks': Freedwomen, Federal Relief, and the Benevolent Guardianship of the Freedmen's Bureau." *Virginia Magazine of History and Biography* 115: 412–42.

———. 2010. *Freedwomen and the Freedmen's Bureau: Race, Gender, and Public Policy in the Age of Emancipation*. New York: Fordham University Press.

Farrow, Anne, Joel Lang, and Jenifer Frank. 2005. *Complicity: How the North Promoted, Prolonged, and Profited from Slavery*. New York: Ballantine.

Feldman, Lynne. 1999. *A Sense of Place: Birmingham's Black Middle-Class Community, 1890–1930*. Tuscaloosa: University of Alabama Press.

Ferleger, Louis. 1993. "Sharecropping Contracts and Mechanization in the Late Nineteenth Century South." *Agricultural History* 67: 31–46.

Ferris, Marcie and Mark Greenberg, eds. 2006. *Jewish Roots in Southern Soil: A New History*. Waltham, MA: Brandeis University Press.

Fetscher, Iring. 1991. "Class Consciousness." Pp. 89–91 in T. Bottomore, ed., *A Dictionary of Marxist Thought*, 2nd ed. Oxford: Blackwell.

Firebaugh, Glenn. 1979. "Structural Determinants of Urbanization in Asia and Latin America, 1950–1970." *American Sociological Review* 44: 199–215.

Firestone, David. 2000, May 11. "South Carolina Acts on Goals, but NAACP Isn't Happy." *New York Times*, A32.

Fischer, David Hackett. 1970. *Historians' Fallacies: Toward a Logic of Historical Thought*. New York: Harper and Row.

FitzRandolph, Peter. 1981. "The Rural Furnishing Merchant in the Postbellum United States: A Study in Spatial Economics." *Journal of Economic History* 41: 187–88.

Fleck, Robert. 2011. "The Political Economy of Progress: Lessons from the Causes and Consequences of the New Deal." Pp. 311–35 in P. Rhode, J. Rosenbloom, and D. Weiman, eds., *Economic Evolution and Revolution in Historical Time*. Stanford, CA: Stanford University Press.

Fligstein, Neil. 1981. *Going North: Migration of Blacks and Whites from the South, 1900–1950*. New York: Academic Press.

Fligstein, Neil and Doug McAdam. 2012. *A Theory of Fields*. New York: Oxford University Press.

Florida, Richard. 2005. *Cities and the Creative Class*. New York: Routledge.

Fogel, Robert. 1989. *Without Consent or Contract: The Rise and Fall of American Slavery*. New York: Norton.

———. 2003. *The Slavery Debates, 1952–1990: A Retrospective*. Baton Rouge: Louisiana State University Press.

Fogel, Robert and Stanley Engerman. 1995. *Time on the Cross: The Economics of American Negro Slavery*. Reissue. New York: Norton.

———. 2006a. *Slave Hires, 1775–1865*. Ann Arbor, MI: ICPSR.

———. 2006b. *Slave Sales and Appraisals, 1775–1865*. Ann Arbor, MI: ICPSR.

Foner, Eric. 1988/2002. *Reconstruction: America's Unfinished Revolution, 1863–1877*. New York: Harper Perennial.

———. 2005. *Forever Free: The Story of Emancipation and Reconstruction*. New York: Random House.

Foster, Gaines. 1982. "The Limitations of Federal Health Care for Freedmen, 1862–1868." *Journal of Southern History* 48: 349–72.

Foulke, Roy. 1941. *The Sinews of American Commerce*. New York: Dun and Bradstreet.

Fourcade, Marion and Kieran Healy. 2007. "Moral Views of Market Society." *Annual Review of Sociology* 33: 285–311.

Fox-Genovese, Elizabeth and Eugene Genovese. 2005. *The Mind of the Master Class: History and Faith in the Southern Slaveholders' Worldview*. New York: Cambridge University Press.

Franklin, John Hope. 1961. *Reconstruction: After the Civil War*. Chicago: University of Chicago Press.

Freedmen's Bureau. 1863–72. *Records of the Field Offices for the State of Louisiana*. Microfilm 1905, rolls 38 and 49. Washington, DC: National Archives.

———. 1865–70. *Records of the Field Offices for the District of Columbia*. Microfilm 1902, roll 18. Washington, DC: National Archives.

———. 1865–72. *Records of the Field Offices for the State of Virginia*. Microfilm 1913, roll 52. Washington, DC: National Archives.

Galt, Anthony. 1986. "Social Class in a Mid-Eighteenth-Century Apulian Town: Indications from the Catasto Onciario." *Ethnohistory* 33: 419–47.

Gamm, Gerald and Robert Putnam. 1999. "The Growth of Voluntary Associations in America, 1840–1940." *Journal of Interdisciplinary History* 29: 511–57.

Ganzeboom, Harry, Paul De Graaf, and Donald Treiman. 1992. "A Standard International Socio-economic Index of Occupational Status." *Social Science Research* 21: 1–56.

Gaston, Paul. 2002. *The New South Creed: A Study in Southern Mythmaking*. New ed. Montgomery, AL: NewSouth Books.

Gates, Paul. 1965. *Agriculture and the Civil War*. New York: Knopf.

Genovese, Eugene. 1965. *The Political Economy of Slavery: Studies in the Economy and Society of the Slave South*. New York: Pantheon.

———. 1974. *Roll, Jordan, Roll: The World the Slaves Made*. New York: Pantheon.

Glen, Tyre. 1820–89. *Letters and Papers*. Duke University, John Hope Franklin Collection.

Goffman, Erving. 1961. *Asylums: Essays on the Social Situation of Mental Patients and Other Inmates*. Garden City, NY: Doubleday Anchor.

———. 1963. *Stigma: Notes on the Management of Spoiled Identity*. Englewood Cliffs, NJ: Prentice Hall.

Goldberg, Chad Allen. 2006. *Citizens and Paupers: Relief, Rights, and Race, from the Freedmen's Bureau to Workfare.* Chicago: University of Chicago Press.

Goldfield, David. 1997. *Region, Race, and Cities: Interpreting the Urban South.* Baton Rouge: Louisiana State University Press.

———. 2012. *America Aflame: How the Civil War Created a Nation.* New York: Bloomsbury Press.

Goldin, Claudia. 1973. "The Economics of Emancipation." *Journal of Economic History* 33: 66–85.

Goldin, Claudia and Frank Lewis. 1975. "The Economic Cost of the American Civil War: Estimates and Implications." *Journal of Economic History* 35: 299–326.

Goodspeed Publishing. 1890. *Biographical and Historical Memoirs of Eastern Arkansas.* Chicago: Goodspeed Publishing.

Granovetter, Mark. 1978. "Threshold Models of Collective Behavior." *American Journal of Sociology* 78: 1420–43.

Granovetter, Mark and Roland Soong. 1988. "Threshold Models of Diversity: Chinese Restaurants, Residential Segregation, and the Spiral of Silence." *Sociological Methodology* 18: 69–104.

Green, Jennifer. 2007. "Networks of Military Educators: Middle Class Stability and Professionalization in the Late Antebellum South." *Journal of Southern History* 73: 39–74.

Green, Shelley and Paul Pryde. 1997. *Black Entrepreneurship in America.* New Brunswick, NJ: Transaction.

Greene, Harlan, Harry Hutchins, and Brian Hutchins. 2004. *Slave Badges and the Slave-Hire System in Charleston, South Carolina, 1783–1865.* Jefferson, NC: McFarland.

Greene, Lorenzo and Carter Woodson. 1930. *The Negro Wage Earner.* New York: AMS Press.

Gregor, Howard. 1965. "The Changing Plantation." *Annals of the Association of American Geographers* 55: 221–38.

Griffin, Larry and Peggy Hargis, eds. 2012. *Social Class.* Vol. 20 of *New Encyclopedia of Southern Culture.* Chapel Hill: University of North Carolina Press.

Groth, Philip. 1977. "Plantation Agriculture and the Urbanization of the South." *Rural Sociology* 42: 206–19.

Grusky, David and Jesper Sørensen. 1998. "Can Class Analysis Be Salvaged?" *American Journal of Sociology* 103: 1187–1234.

Guest, Avery. 2005. "Frontier and Urban-Industrial Explanations of U.S. Occupational Mobility in the Late 1800s." *Social Science Research* 34: 140–64.

Guo, Shenyang and Mark Fraser. 2010. *Propensity Score Analysis: Statistical Methods and Applications.* London: Sage.

Guseva, Alya and Akos Rona-Tas. 2001. "Uncertainty, Risk, and Trust: Russian and American Credit Card Markets Compared." *American Sociological Review* 66: 623–46.

Gutman, Herbert. 1976. *The Black Family in Slavery and Freedom 1750–1925.* New York: Random House.

———. 1987. "Schools for Freedom: The Post-emancipation Origins of Afro-American Education." Pp. 260–97 in *Power and Culture.* New York: Pantheon.

Hacker, J. David. 2011. "A Census-Based Count of the Civil War Dead." *Civil War History* 57: 307–48.

Hackney, Sheldon. 1972. "*Origins of the New South* in Retrospect." *Journal of Southern History* 38: 191–216.

Hadden, Sally. 2001. *Slave Patrols: Law and Violence in Virginia and the Carolinas.* Cambridge, MA: Harvard University Press.

Hahn, Steven. 1983/2006. *The Roots of Southern Populism: Yeoman Farmers and the Transformation of the Georgia Upcountry, 1850–1890.* Updated ed. New York: Oxford University Press.

Hahn, Steven, Steven Miller, Susan O'Donovan, John Rodrigue, and Leslie Rowland. 2008. *Land and Labor, 1865.* Series 3, vol. 1 of *Freedom: A Documentary History of Emancipation, 1861–1867.* Chapel Hill: University of North Carolina Press.

Haines, Michael and the Inter-University Consortium for Political and Social Research. 2005. *Historical, Demographic, Economic, and Social Data: The United States, 1790–2002.* Ann Arbor, MI: ICPSR.

Hanes, Christopher. 1996. "Turnover Cost and the Distribution of Slave Labor in Anglo-America." *Journal of Economic History* 56: 307–29.

Hannan, Michael. 1988. "Social Change, Organizational Diversity and Individual Careers." Pp. 161–74 in M. Riley, ed., *Social Structures and Human Lives.* Newbury, CA: Sage.

Hannan, Michael and John Freeman. 1984. "Structural Inertia and Organizational Change." *American Sociological Review* 49: 149–64.

———. 1989. *Organizational Ecology.* Cambridge, MA: Harvard University Press.

Hanneman, Robert. 2006. "Hierarchy in the Organizational and Community Ecology of the Western United States." Paper presented at the American Sociological Association meetings, Montreal.

Harris, Joel. 1890. *Life of Henry W. Grady, Including His Writings and Speeches.* New York: Cassell.

Harrison, Robert. 2007. "New Representations of a 'Misrepresented Bureau': Reflections on Recent Scholarship on the Freedmen's Bureau." *American Nineteenth Century History* 8: 205–29.

Hartman, Saidiya. 1997. *Scenes of Subjection: Terror, Slavery, and Self-Making in Nineteenth-Century America.* New York: Oxford University Press.

Harvey, A. C. 1976. "Estimating Regression Models with Multiplicative Heteroskedasticity." *Econometrica* 44: 461–65.

Hauser, Robert M. 1982. "Occupational Status in the Nineteenth and Twentieth Centuries." *Historical Methods* 15: 111–26.

Hawley, Amos. 1950. *Human Ecology: A Theory of Community Structure.* New York: Ronald Press.

Hickox, M. S. 1995. "The English Middle-Class Debate." *British Journal of Sociology* 46: 311–24.

Hidy, Ralph. 1939. "Credit Rating before Dun and Bradstreet." *Bulletin of the Business Historical Society* 13: 81–88.

Hirschman, Albert. 1970. *Exit, Voice, and Loyalty: Responses to Decline in Firms, Organizations and States.* Cambridge, MA: Harvard University Press.

Hoff, Karla and Joseph Stiglitz. 2001. "Modern Economic Theory and Development." Pp. 389–460 in G. Meier and J. Stiglitz, eds., *Frontiers of Development Economics.* New York: Oxford University Press.

Holm, Håkan, Sonja Opper, and Victor Nee. 2013. "Entrepreneurs under Uncertainty: An Economic Experiment." *Management Science* 59: 1671–87.

Homans, J. Smith, ed. 1849, September. "Increase of Bank Capital in the United States." *Bankers' Magazine and Statistical Register.*

———. 1860, June. "Banks of the United States." *Bankers' Magazine and Statistical Register.*

Horton, Hayward, Beverlyn Allen, Cedric Herring, and Melvin E. Thomas. 2000. "Lost in the Storm: The Sociology of the Black Working Class, 1850 to 1990." *American Sociological Review* 65: 128–37.

Horton, James Oliver and Lois E. Horton. 2001. *Hard Road to Freedom: The Story of African America.* New Brunswick, NJ: Rutgers University Press.

Hsu, Greta, Michael Hannan, and Őzgecan Koçak. 2009. "Multiple Category Membership in Markets: An Integrative Theory and Two Empirical Tests." *American Sociological Review* 74: 150–69.

Hsu, Greta, Giacomo Negro, and Őzgecan Koçak, eds. 2010. *Categories in Markets: Origins and Evolution.* Vol. 31 of *Research in the Sociology of Organizations.* Bingley, UK: Emerald.

Hu-Dehart, Evelyn. 1993. "Chinese Coolie Labour in Cuba in the Nineteenth Century: Free Labour or Neo-Slavery." Pp. 67–113 in Twaddle, *Wages of Slavery.*

Huffman, Wallace and Richard Just. 2004. "Implications of Agency Theory for Optimal Land Tenure Contracts." *Economic Development and Cultural Change* 52: 617–42.

Irwin, James and Anthony O'Brien. 2001. "Economic Progress in the Postbellum South? Implications from the Growth of Incomes of African-Americans in the Mississippi Delta, 1879–1913." *Explorations in Economic History* 38: 166–80.

Irwin, Michael and John Kasarda. 1994. "Trade, Transportation, and Spatial Distribution." Pp. 342–67 in N. Smelser and R. Swedberg, eds., *The Handbook of Economic Sociology.* Princeton, NJ: Princeton University Press.

Jacobs, Donald, ed. 1981. *Index to the American Slave.* Westport, CT: Greenwood.

Jewell, Joseph. 2007. *Race, Social Reform, and the Making of a Middle Class: The American Missionary Association and Black Atlanta, 1870–1900.* Lanham, MD: Rowman & Littlefield.

John W. Hartman Center. 2013. *Emergence of Advertising On-line Project: Advertising Ephemera Collection.* Database #A01060. http://library.duke.edu/digitalcollections /eaa.

Johnson, Michael. 1986. "Work, Culture and the Slave Community: Slave Occupations in the Cotton Belt in 1860." *Labor History* 27: 325–55.

Jones, Jacqueline. 2010. *Labor of Love, Labor of Sorrow: Black Women, Work, and the Family, from Slavery to the Present.* Rev. ed. New York: Basic Books.

Katz, Claudio. 1993. "Karl Marx on the Transition from Feudalism to Capitalism." *Theory and Society* 22: 363–89.

Katz, Michael B. 1972. "Occupational Classification in History." *Journal of Interdisciplinary History* 3: 63–88.

King, Wilma. 1995. *Stolen Childhood: Slave Youth in Nineteenth Century America.* Bloomington: Indiana University Press.

Kingston, Christopher and Robert Wright. 2010. "The Deadliest of Games: The Institution of Dueling." *Southern Economic Journal* 76: 1094–1106.

Kirk, Edward. 1868. *Educated Labor; or, Our Duty in Regard to the Americo-African Race: An Address Delivered before the American Missionary Association*. New York: Holt.

Knight, Frank. 1921. *Risk, Uncertainty and Profit*. Boston: Houghton Mifflin.

Kolchin, Peter. 2003. *A Sphinx on the American Land: The Nineteenth-Century South in Comparative Perspective*. Baton Rouge: Louisiana State University Press.

———. 2012. "Comparative Perspectives on Emancipation in the U.S. South: Reconstruction, Radicalism, and Russia." *Journal of the Civil War Era* 89: 203–32.

Krugman, Paul. 1995. *Development, Geography, and Economic Theory*. Cambridge, MA: MIT Press.

Kyriakoudes, Louis. 2002. "Lower-Order Urbanization and Territorial Monopoly in the Southern Furnishing Trade: Alabama, 1871–1890." *Social Science History* 26: 179–98.

Lebergott, Stanley. 1960. "Wage Trends, 1800–1900." Pp. 449–500 in *Trends in the American Economy in the Nineteenth Century*. Princeton, NJ: Princeton University Press.

Lewis, Arthur. 1955. *The Theory of Economic Growth*. London: Allen and Unwin.

Library of Congress. 1941. *Slave Narratives: A Folk History of Slavery in the United States from Interviews with Former Slaves*. Washington, DC: Works Progress Administration.

Little, Roderick. 1992. "Regression with Missing X's: A Review." *Journal of the American Statistical Association* 87: 1227–37.

Litwack, Leon. 1979. *Been in the Storm So Long: The Aftermath of Slavery*. New York: Knopf.

———. 1998. *Trouble in Mind: Black Southerners in the Age of Jim Crow*. New York: Knopf.

Lloyd, Richard. 2012. "Urbanization and the Southern United States." *Annual Review of Sociology* 38: 483–506.

Loring, F. W. and C. F. Atkinson. 1869. *Cotton Culture and the South Considered with Reference to Emigration*. Boston: A. Williams.

Lösch, August. 1944/1954. *The Economics of Location*. New Haven, CT: Yale University Press.

Loury, Glenn. 2002. *The Anatomy of Racial Inequality*. Boston, MA: Harvard University Press.

Lowenthal, David. 1971. "Post-emancipation Race Relations: Some Caribbean and American Perspectives." *Journal of Interamerican Studies and World Affairs* 13: 367–77.

Macaulay, Stewart. 1963. "Non-contractual Relations in Business: A Preliminary Study." *American Sociological Review* 28: 55–67.

Mackaman, Tom. 2013, April 3. "Understanding Lincoln: An Interview with Historian Allen Guelzo." *World Socialist Web Site*. https://www.wsws.org/en/articles/2013/04/03/guel-a03.html.

Madison, James. 1974. "The Evolution of Commercial Credit Reporting Agencies in Nineteenth-Century America." *Business History Review* 48: 164–86.

Mahoney, James and Kathleen Thelen. 2009. *Explaining Institutional Change: Ambiguity, Agency, and Power*. Cambridge: Cambridge University Press.

Malone, Ann Patton. 1986. "Piney Woods Farmers of South Georgia, 1850–1900: Jeffersonian Yeomen in an Age of Expanding Commercialism." *Agricultural History* 4: 51–84.

Mandle, Jay R. 1992. "Black Economic Entrapment after Emancipation in the United States." Pp. 69–84 in F. McGlynn and S. Drescher, eds., *The Meaning of Freedom:*

Economics, Politics, and Culture After Slavery. Pittsburgh, PA: University of Pittsburgh Press.

March, James and Herbert Simon. 1958. *Organizations.* New York: John Wiley.

Mark, Harold and Kent Schwirian. 1967. "Ecological Position, Urban Central Place Function, and Community Population Growth." *American Journal of Sociology* 73: 30–41.

Marler, Scott. 2001. "Merchants in the Transition to a New South: Central Louisiana, 1840–1880." *Louisiana History* 42: 165–92.

———. 2011. "Two Kinds of Freedom: Mercantile Development and Labor Systems in Louisiana Cotton and Sugar Parishes after the Civil War." *Agricultural History* 85: 225–51.

Martin, John Levi. 2003. "What Is Field Theory?" *American Journal of Sociology* 109: 1–49.

Martin, Jonathan. 2004. *Divided Mastery: Slave Hiring in the American South.* Cambridge, MA: Harvard University Press.

Marwell, Gerald and Pamela Oliver. 1993. *The Critical Mass in Collective Action.* Cambridge: Cambridge University Press.

Marx, Karl. 1867/1977. *Capital: A Critique of Political Economy.* Vol. 1. New York: Vintage.

Marx, Karl and Friedrich Engels. 1848/1937. *Manifesto of the Communist Party.* New York: International.

Mayer, Henry. 1998. *All on Fire: William Lloyd Garrison and the Abolition of Slavery.* New York: St. Martin's.

McAdam, Doug and Ronnelle Paulsen. 1993. "Specifying the Relationship between Social Ties and Activism." *American Journal of Sociology* 99: 640–67.

Meyer, John. 1994. "The Evolution of Modern Stratification Systems." Pp. 730–37 in D. Grusky, ed., *Social Stratification in Sociological Perspective.* Boulder, CO: Westview.

Meyer, John and Ronald Jepperson. 2000. "The 'Actors' of Modern Society: The Cultural Construction of Social Agency." *Sociological Theory* 18: 100–120.

Meyer, John and Brian Rowan. 1977. "Institutionalized Organizations: Formal Structure as Myth and Ceremony." *American Journal of Sociology* 83: 340–63.

Meyer, John and W. Richard Scott. 1983. "Centralization and the Legitimacy Problems of Local Government." Pp. 179–98 in J. Meyer and W. R. Scott, eds., *Organizational Environments: Ritual and Rationality.* Beverly Hills, CA: Sage.

Miller, Randall. 1979. "The Man in the Middle: The Black Slave Driver." *American Heritage* 30: 40–49.

Mills, C. Wright. 1951. *White Collar: The American Middle Classes.* New York: Oxford University Press.

———. 1959. *The Sociological Imagination.* New York: Oxford University Press.

Mims, Edwin. 1926. *The Advancing South: Stories of Progress and Reaction.* Garden City, NY: Doubleday.

Mincer, Jacob. 1958. "Investment in Human Capital and Personal Income Distribution." *Journal of Political Economy* 66: 281–302.

Mitchell, Mary. 1963/65. "'I Held George Washington's Horse': Compensated Emancipation in the District of Columbia." *Records of the Columbia Historical Society* 63/65: 221–29.

Molotch, Harvey, William Freudenberg, and Krista Paulsen. 2000. "History Repeats Itself, but How? City Character, Urban Tradition, and the Accomplishment of Place." *American Sociological Review* 65: 791–823.

Moore, Wilbert, and Robin Williams. 1942. "Stratification in the Ante-Bellum South." *American Sociological Review* 7: 343–51.

Morelock, Kolan. 2008. *Taking the Town: Collegiate and Community Culture in the Bluegrass, 1880–1917*. Lexington: University Press of Kentucky.

Morgan, Chad. 2005. *Planters' Progress: Modernizing Confederate Georgia*. Gainesville: University Press of Florida.

Morrill, Calvin, Mayer Zald, and Hayagreeva Rao. 2003. "Covert Political Conflict in Organizations: The View from Below." *Annual Review of Sociology* 29: 391–415.

Morrissey, Marietta. 1989. *Slave Women in the New World: Gender Stratification in the Caribbean*. Lawrence: University Press of Kansas.

Mulligan, Gordon, Mark Partridge, and John Carruthers. 2012. "Central Place Theory and Its Reemergence in Regional Science." *Annals of Regional Science* 48: 405–31.

Murphy, Sarah. 2010. *Investing in Life: Insurance in Antebellum America*. Baltimore, MD: Johns Hopkins University Press.

Naidu, Suresh. 2010. "Recruitment Restrictions and Labor Markets: Evidence from the Postbellum U.S. South." *Journal of Labor Economics* 28: 413–45.

Nash, Claire and Dale Flesher. 2005. "Employee Leasing. The Antebellum 1800s and the Twenty-First Century: A Historical Perspective on the Contingent Labour Force." *Accounting, Business, and Financial History* 15: 63–76.

Nash, Gary and Jean Soderlund. 1991. *Freedom by Degrees: Emancipation in Pennsylvania and Its Aftermath*. New York: Oxford University Press.

New York Times. 1863, September 20. "Emancipation in Maryland (Letter from Governor Bradford)." *New York Times*, 6.

———.1864, February 25. "No Gradual Emancipation." *New York Times*, 4.

———.1865, June 17. "Emancipation—Gradual or Immediate?" *New York Times*, 2.

Newbery, David. 1977. "Risk Sharing, Sharecropping and Uncertain Labor Markets." *Review of Economic Studies* 44: 585–94.

Newman, Harvey. 1996. "Atlanta's Hospitality Businesses in the New South Era, 1880–1900." *Georgia Historical Quarterly* 80: 53–76.

Ng, Kenneth and Nancy Virts. 1993. "The Black-White Income Gap in 1880." *Agricultural History* 67: 1–15.

Nier, Charles. 2009. "The Shadow of Credit: The Historical Origins of Racial Predatory Lending and Its Impact upon African American Wealth Accumulation." *University of Pennsylvania Journal of Law and Social Change* 11: 131–94.

Norris, James. 1978. *R.G. Dun & Co., 1841–1900: The Development of Credit-Reporting in the Nineteenth Century*. Westport, CT: Greenwood.

North, Douglass. 1990. *Institutions, Institutional Change and Economic Performance*. New York: Cambridge University Press.

Obama, Barack. 2012, December 31. "Presidential Proclamation—150th Anniversary of the Emancipation Proclamation." Washington, DC: White House, Office of the Press Secretary.

Oberschall, Anthony. 1973. *Social Conflict and Social Movements*. Englewood Cliffs, NJ: Prentice Hall.

O'Brien, Anthony and William Shade. 2001. *"One Kind of Freedom* Revisited." *Explorations in Economic History* 38: 1–5.

Ochiltree, Ian D. 1998. "'A Just and Self-Respecting System?' Black Independence, Sharecropping, and Paternalistic Relations in the American South and South Africa." *Agricultural History* 72: 352–80.

Olegario, Rowena. 2006. *A Culture of Credit: Embedding Trust and Transparency in American Business*. Cambridge, MA: Harvard University Press.

Olson, John. 1992. "The Occupational Structure of Southern Plantations during the Late Antebellum Era." Pp. 137–69 in R. Fogel and S. Engerman, eds., *Without Consent or Contract: The Rise and Fall of American Slavery*, Technical Papers, vol. 1. New York: Norton.

Oubre, Claude. 1978. *Forty Acres and a Mule: The Freedmen's Bureau and Black Land Ownership*. Baton Rouge: Louisiana State University Press.

Owsley, Frank. 1949. *Plain Folk of the Old South*. Baton Rouge: Louisiana State University Press.

Paige, Jeffrey. 1997. *Coffee and Power: Revolution and the Rise of Democracy in Central America*. Cambridge, MA: Harvard University Press.

Painter, Nell Irvin. 1976/1992. *Exodusters: Black Migration to Kansas after Reconstruction*. New York: Norton.

Park, Robert, Earnest Burgess, and Robert McKenzie. 1925. *The City*. Chicago: University of Chicago Press.

Patterson, Kelly. 2012. "Impression Management and Reputation Defense in 19th Century Credit Rating." Unpublished Ph.D. dissertation, Department of Sociology, Cornell University.

Patterson, Orlando. 1998. *Rituals of Blood: Consequences of Slavery in Two American Centuries*. New York: Basic Civitas.

Penningroth, Dylan. 2003. *The Claims of Kinfolk: African American Property and Community in the Nineteenth-Century South*. Chapel Hill: University of North Carolina Press.

Phelps, Edmund. 1972. "The Statistical Theory of Racism and Sexism." *American Economic Review* 62: 659–61.

Plattner, Stuart. 1989. "Markets and Marketplaces." Pp. 171–208 in Plattner, ed., *Economic Anthropology*. Stanford, CA: Stanford University Press.

Polanyi, Karl. 1944. *The Great Transformation: The Political and Economic Origins of Our Time*. Boston: Beacon.

Polillo, Simone. 2013. *Conservatives versus Wildcats: A Sociology of Financial Conflict*. Stanford, CA: Stanford University Press.

Pontikes, Elizabeth. 2012. "Two Sides of the Same Coin: How Ambiguous Classification Affects Multiple Audiences' Evaluations." *Administrative Science Quarterly* 57: 81–118.

Porter, Glenn and Harold Livesay. 1971. *Merchants and Manufacturers: Studies in the Changing Structure of Nineteenth-Century Marketing*. Baltimore, MD: Johns Hopkins University Press.

Portes, Alejandro. 2006. "Institutions and Development: A Conceptual Reanalysis." *Population and Development Review* 32: 233–62.

———. 2010. *Economic Sociology: A Systematic Inquiry*. Princeton, NJ: Princeton University Press.

Posner, Eric and Adrian Vermeule. 2003. "Reparations for Slavery and Other Historical Injustices." *Columbia Law Review* 103: 689–748.

Powell, Lawrence. 1999. *New Masters: Northern Planters during the Civil War and Reconstruction.* 2nd ed. New York: Fordham University Press.

Pred, Allan. 1965. "Manufacturing in the American Mercantile City: 1800–1840." *Annals of the Association of American Geographers* 56: 307–38.

Price, Roger. 1987. *A Social History of Nineteenth-Century France.* London: Hutchinson.

Pritchett, Jonathan and Jessica Hayes. 2011. "The Occupations of Slaves Sold in New Orleans: Missing Values, Cheap Talk, or Informative Advertising." Working paper 1113, Department of Economics, Tulane University, New Orleans, LA.

Putnam, Robert. 2000. *Bowling Alone: The Collapse and Revival of American Community.* New York: Simon & Schuster.

Ramos, Dorkys. 2013, January 2. "Obama Marks 150th Anniversary of the Emancipation Proclamation." *BET.* http://www.bet.com/news/national/2013/01/02/obama-marks-150th-anniversary-of-the-emancipation-proclamation.html.

Ransom, Roger and Richard Sutch. 1975. "The Impact of the Civil War and of Emancipation on Southern Agriculture." *Explorations in Economic History* 12: 1–28.

———. 1979. "Credit Merchandising in the Post-Emancipation South: Structure, Conduct, and Performance." *Explorations in Economic History* 16: 64–89.

———. 1999. *A Sample of Southern Farms, 1880.* Cambridge: Cambridge University Press.

———. 2001. *One Kind of Freedom: The Economic Consequences of Emancipation.* 2nd ed. Cambridge: Cambridge University Press.

Raup, Philip. 1973. "Corporate Farming in the United States." *Journal of Economic History* 33: 274–90.

Rawick, George, ed. 1972–79. *The American Slave: A Composite Autobiography.* Series 1–2, supplemental series 1–2. Westport, CT: Greenwood.

Reid, Joseph. 1976. "Sharecropping and Agricultural Uncertainty." *Economic Development and Cultural Change* 24: 549–76.

———. 1981. "White Land, Black Labor, and Agricultural Stagnation: The Causes and Effects of Sharecropping in the Postbellum South." Pp. 33–56 in G. Walton and J. Shepherd, eds., *Market Institutions and Economic Progress in the New South, 1865–1900.* New York: Academic Press.

Reid, Richard. 1770–1910. *Papers.* University of Virginia, Special Collections.

Reid, Whitelaw. 1866/1965. *After the War: A Tour of the Southern States, 1865–1866.* New York: Harper and Row.

Reitano, Joanne. 2010. *The Restless City: A Short History of New York from Colonial Times to the Present.* 2nd ed. New York: Routledge.

Robert Graham Dun and Company. 1860–1900. *The Mercantile Agency Reference Book (and Key), Containing Ratings on the Merchants, Manufacturers and Traders Generally, throughout the United States and Canada.* New York: Dun, Barlow & Company.

———. Various dates. Louisiana Credit Ledgers, R.G. Dun & Co. Collection, Baker Library, Harvard Business School.

Robinson, Charles. 2003. *Dangerous Liaisons: Sex and Love in the Segregated South.* Fayetteville: University of Arkansas Press.

Rodrigue, John. 1999. "The Freedmen's Bureau and Wage Labor in the Louisiana Sugar Region." Pp. 193–218 in P. Cimbala and R. Miller, eds., *The Freedmen's Bureau and Reconstruction*. New York: Fordham University Press.

Rodriguez, Junius. 1999. *Chronology of World Slavery*. Santa Barbara, CA: Greenwood.

Romanelli, Elaine and Olga Khessina. 2005. "Regional Industrial Identity: Cluster Configurations and Economic Development." *Organization Science* 16: 344–58.

Rosenbaum, Paul and Donald Rubin. 1985. "Constructing a Control Group using Multivariate Matched Sampling Methods that Incorporate the Propensity Score." *American Statistician* 39: 33–38.

Rosenbloom, Joshua. 2002. *Looking for Work, Searching for Workers: American Labor Markets during Industrialization*. New York: Cambridge University Press.

Roughley, Thomas. 1823. *The Jamaica Planter's Guide*. London: Longman, Hurst, Rees, Orme, and Brown.

Royce, Edward. 1993. *The Origins of Southern Sharecropping*. Philadelphia, PA: Temple University Press.

Royston, Patrick. 2004. "Multiple Imputation of Missing Values." *Stata Journal* 4: 227–41.

Rubin, Morton. 1951. *Plantation County*. New Haven, CT: Yale University Press.

Ruef, Martin. 2000. "The Emergence of Organizational Forms: A Community Ecology Approach." *American Journal of Sociology* 106: 658–714.

———. 2004. "The Demise of an Organizational Form: Emancipation and Plantation Agriculture in the American South, 1860–1880." *American Journal of Sociology* 109: 1365–1410.

———. 2011. "The Human and Financial Capital of the Southern Middle Class, 1850–1900." Pp. 202–24 in Wells and Green, *Southern Middle Class in the Long Nineteenth Century*.

———. 2012. "Constructing Labor Markets: The Valuation of Black Labor in the U.S. South, 1831 to 1867." *American Sociological Review* 77: 970–98.

Ruef, Martin and Ben Fletcher. 2003. "Legacies of American Slavery: Status Attainment among Southern Blacks after Emancipation." *Social Forces* 82: 445–80.

Ruef, Martin and Alona Harness. 2009. "Agrarian Origins of Management Ideology: The Roman and Antebellum Cases." *Organization Studies* 30: 589–607.

Ruef, Martin and Kelly Patterson. 2009a. "Credit and Classification: The Impact of Industry Boundaries in 19th Century America." *Administrative Science Quarterly* 54: 486–520.

———. 2009b. "Organizations and Local Development: Economic and Demographic Growth among Southern Counties during Reconstruction." *Social Forces* 87: 1743–76.

Ruef, Martin and David Reinecke. 2011. "Does Capitalism Produce an Entrepreneurial Class?" *Research in Organizational Behavior* 31: 225–52.

Ruggles, Steven, Trent Alexander, Katie Genadek, Ronald Goeken, Matthew Schroeder, and Matthew Sobek. 2010. *Integrated Public Use Microdata Series: Version 5.0*. Machine-readable database. Minneapolis: University of Minnesota.

Ryan, Mary. 1981. *Cradle of the Middle Class: The Family in Oneida County, New York, 1790–1865*. Cambridge: Cambridge University Press.

Sacerdote, Bruce. 2005. "Slavery and the Intergenerational Transmission of Human Capital." *Review of Economics and Statistics* 87: 217–34.

Sampson, Robert, Jeffrey Morenoff, and Thomas Gannon-Rowley. 2002. "Assessing 'Neighborhood Effects': Social Processes and New Directions in Research." *Annual Review of Sociology* 28: 443–78.

Sandage, Scott. 2005. *Born Losers: A History of Failure in America*. Cambridge, MA: Harvard University Press.

Saperstein, Aliya and Aaron Gullickson. 2013. "A 'Mulatto Escape Hatch' in the United States? Examining Evidence of Racial and Social Mobility during the Jim Crow Era." *Demography* 50: 1921–42.

Sarasvathy, Saras and Henrik Berglund. 2010. "On the Relevance of Decision-Making in Entrepreneurial Decision-Making." Pp. 163–82 in H. Landström and F. Lohrke, eds., *Historical Foundations of Entrepreneurship Research*. Northampton, MA: Edward Elgar.

Satris, Stephen. 2002. "The South Carolina State House and the Confederate Flag." *Teaching Ethics* 2: 71–76.

Savali, Kirsten. 2013, January 1. "President Obama Recognizes 150 Anniversary of Emancipation Proclamation. *NewsOne for Black America*. http://newsone.com /2118464/obama-150-emancipation-proclamation.

Schmidt, James. 1998. *Free to Work: Labor Law, Emancipation, and Reconstruction, 1815–1880*. Athens: University of Georgia Press.

Schrank, Andrew and Josh Whitford. 2011. "The Anatomy of Network Failure." *Sociological Theory* 29: 151–77.

Schultz, Mark. 1998. "The Dream Realized? African American Landownership in Central Georgia between Reconstruction and World War II." *Agricultural History* 72: 298–313.

Schultz, Theodore. 1961. "Investment in Human Capital." *American Economic Review* 51: 1–17.

Schumpeter, Joseph. 1942/1975. *Capitalism, Socialism and Democracy*. New York: Harper.

Schwalm, Leslie A. 1997. *A Hard Fight for We: Women's Transition from Slavery to Freedom in South Carolina*. Chicago: University of Illinois Press.

Schwartz, Bernard. 1970. *Statutory History of the United States—Civil Rights*. New York: Chelsea House.

Schweninger, Loren. 1989. "Black Owned Businesses in the South, 1790–1880." *Business History Review* 63: 22–60.

Scott, Rebecca. 1983. "Gradual Abolition and the Dynamics of Slave Emancipation in Cuba, 1868–1886." *Hispanic American Historical Review* 63: 449–77.

Scott, W. Richard. 2008. *Institutions and Organizations: Ideas and Interests*. 3rd ed. Thousand Oaks, CA: Sage.

Scott, W. Richard, Martin Ruef, Peter Mendel, and Carol Caronna. 2000. *Institutional Change and Healthcare Organizations: From Professional Dominance to Managed Care*. Chicago: University of Chicago Press.

Shaffer, Ron, Steve Deller, and Dave Marcouiller. 2004. *Community Economics: Linking Theory and Practice*. 2nd ed. Ames, IA: Blackwell.

Shepherd, Verene. 1993. "Alternative Husbandry: Slaves and Free Labourers on Livestock Farms in Jamaica in the Eighteenth and Nineteenth Centuries." Pp. 41–66 in Twaddle, *Wages of Slavery*.

Sheridan, Richard. 1993. "From Chattel to Wage Slavery in Jamaica, 1740–1860." Pp. 13–40 in Twaddle, *Wages of Slavery*.

Shlomowitz, Ralph. 1979. "The Transition from Slave to Freeman Labor Arrangements in Southern Agriculture, 1865–1870." *Journal of Economic History* 39: 333–36.

Simmel, Georg. 1908/1950. "The Stranger." Pp. 402–8 in K. Wolff, trans., *The Sociology of Georg Simmel*. New York: Free Press.

Small, Mario and Monica McDermott. 2006. "The Presence of Organizational Resources in Poor Urban Neighborhoods: An Analysis of Average and Contextual Effects." *Social Forces* 84: 1697–1724.

Smith, Adam. 1776. *An Inquiry into the Nature and Causes of the Wealth of Nations*. London: Strahan and T. Cadell.

Smith, David. 1987. "Dependent Urbanization in Colonial America: The Case of Charleston, South Carolina." *Social Forces* 66: 1–28.

Smith, Donald M. 1975. "Neoclassical Growth Models and Regional Growth in the U.S." *Journal of Regional Science* 15: 165–81.

Smith, Mark. 1998. *Debating Slavery: Economy and Society in the Antebellum American South*. Cambridge: Cambridge University Press.

Snipes, John W. 1976, November 20. Interview H-0098-2. Southern History Program Collection #4007, Southern Historical Collection, Wilson Library, University of North Carolina at Chapel Hill (digitized in 2006).

Snow, David, Louis Zurcher, and Sheldon Olson. 1980. "Social Networks and Social Movements: A Microstructural Approach to Differential Recruitment." *American Sociological Review* 45: 787–801.

Solow, Robert. 1956. "A Contribution to the Theory of Economic Growth." *Quarterly Journal of Economics* 71: 65–94.

Sørensen, Aage. 2000. "Toward a Sounder Basis for Class Analysis." *American Journal of Sociology* 105: 1523–58.

Span, Christopher. 2002. "'I Must Learn Now or Not at All': Social and Cultural Capital in the Educational Initiatives of Formerly Enslaved African Americans in Mississippi, 1862–1869." *Journal of African American History* 87: 196–205.

———. 2009. *From Cotton Field to Schoolhouse: African American Education in Mississippi, 1862–1875*. Chapel Hill: University of North Carolina Press.

Spero, Sterling and Abram Harris. 1931. *The Black Worker: The Negro and the Labor Movement*. New York: Columbia University Press.

Stampp, Kenneth. 1956. *The Peculiar Institution: Slavery in the Antebellum South*. New York: Knopf.

Stanley, Amy Dru. 1998. *From Bondage to Contract: Wage Labor, Marriage, and the Market in the Age of Slave Emancipation*. New York: Cambridge University Press.

Steinfeld, Robert. 2001. *Coercion, Contract, and Free Labor in the Nineteenth Century*. New York: Cambridge University Press.

Steinmetz, George and Erik Olin Wright. 1989. "The Fall and Rise of the Petty Bourgeoisie: Changing Patterns of Self-Employment in the Postwar United States." *American Journal of Sociology* 94: 973–1018.

Stiglitz, Joseph. 1974. "Incentives and Risk Sharing in Sharecropping." *Review of Economic Studies* 61: 219–56.

Stinchcombe, Arthur. 1965. "Social Structure and Organizations." Pp. 142–93 in James G. March, ed., *Handbook of Organizations*. Chicago: Rand McNally.

———. 1995. *Sugar Island Slavery in the Age of Enlightenment: The Political Economy of the Caribbean World*. Princeton, NJ: Princeton University Press.

Stover, John. 1955. *The Railroads of the South: 1865–1900*. Chapel Hill: University of North Carolina Press.

Sutch, Richard. 1975. "The Breeding of Slaves for Sale and the Westward Expansion of Slavery, 1850–1860." Pp. 173–210 in S. Engerman and E. Genovese, eds., *Race and Slavery in the Western Hemisphere: Quantitative Studies*. Princeton, NJ: Princeton University Press.

Swedberg, Richard, ed. 1999. *Max Weber: Essays in Economic Sociology*. Princeton, NJ: Princeton University Press.

Sylla, Richard. 1969. "Federal Policy, Banking Market Structure, and Capital Mobilization in the United States, 1863–1913." *Journal of Economic History* 29: 657–86.

Tadman, Michael. 1996. *Speculators and Slaves: Masters, Traders, and Slaves in the Old South*. Rev. ed. Madison: University of Wisconsin Press.

Terrill, Tom, Edmond Ewing, and Pamela White. 1976. "Eager Hands: Labor for Southern Textiles, 1850–1860." *Journal of Economic History* 36: 84–99.

Thompson, Edgar. 1932/2010. *The Plantation*. Columbia: University of South Carolina Press.

———. 1935. "Population Expansion and the Plantation System." *American Journal of Sociology* 41: 314–26.

Thompson, E. P. 1963. *The Making of the English Working Class*. New York: Pantheon.

Thomson, David. 2009. "Oliver Otis Howard: Reassessing the Legacy of the 'Christian General.'" *American Nineteenth Century History* 10: 273–98.

Thornton, Patricia. 1999. "The Sociology of Entrepreneurship." *Annual Review of Sociology* 19: 19–46.

Tilly, Charles. 1984. *Big Structures, Large Processes, Huge Comparisons*. New York: Russell Sage Foundation.

———. 1998. *Durable Inequality*. Berkeley: University of California Press.

Tilly, Chris and Charles Tilly. 1998. *Work under Capitalism*. Boulder, CO: Westview.

Tocqueville, Alexis de. 1835–40/2003. *Democracy in America*. New York: Penguin.

Tolnay, Stewart. 2003. "The African American 'Great Migration' and Beyond." *Annual Review of Sociology* 29: 209–32.

Tolnay, Stewart and E. M. Beck. 1995. *A Festival of Violence: An Analysis of Southern Lynchings, 1882–1930*. Urbana: University of Illinois Press.

Torpey, John and Maxine Burkett. 2010. "The Debate over African American Reparations." *Annual Review of Law and Social Science* 6: 449–67.

Towers, Frank. 2004. *The Urban South and the Coming of the Civil War*. Charlottesville: University of Virginia Press.

Trelease, Allen. 1971/1995. *White Terror: Ku Klux Klan Conspiracy and Southern Reconstruction*. Baton Rouge: Louisiana State University Press.

Tunnell, Ted. 2006. "Creating 'The Propaganda of History': Southern Editors and the Origins of 'Carpetbagger and Scalawag.'" *Journal of Southern History* 72: 789–822.

Twaddle, Michael, ed. 1993. *The Wages of Slavery: From Chattel Slavery to Wage Labour in Africa, the Caribbean and England*. London: Frank Cass.

Twain, Mark and Charles Warner. 1873. *The Gilded Age: A Tale of Today*. Hartford, CT: American.

Ullman, Edward. 1941. "A Theory of Location for Cities." *American Journal of Sociology* 46: 853–64.

Urry, John. 1973. "Toward a Structural Theory of the Middle Class." *Acta Sociologica* 16: 175–87.

U.S. Bureau of the Census. 1854. *Population of the United States in 1850, Compiled from the Original Returns of the Seventh Census.* Washington, DC: GPO.

———. 1864a. *Agriculture of the United States in 1860, Compiled from the Original Returns of the Eighth Census.* Washington, DC: GPO.

———. 1864b. *Population of the United States in 1860, Compiled from the Original Returns of the Eighth Census.* Washington, DC: GPO.

———. 1872. *The Statistics of Wealth and Industry of the United States, Compiled from the Original Returns of the Ninth Census (1870).* Washington, DC: GPO.

———. 1883a. *Report on the Production of Agriculture in the United States at the Tenth Census (1880).* Washington, DC: GPO.

———. 1883b. *The Statistics of the Population of the United States, Compiled from the Original Returns of the Tenth Census (June 1, 1880).* Washington: GPO.

———. 1890. *Special Report on the Statistics of Occupations in 1890.* Washington, DC: Department of Commerce.

———. 1900. *Twelfth Census of the United States.* Washington, DC: Department of Commerce.

———. 1916. *Plantation Farming in the United States.* Washington, DC: GPO.

———. 1983. *Census of the Population (1980), Characteristics of the Population (Volume 1).* Washington, DC: U.S. Bureau of the Census.

U.S. Comptroller of the Currency. 1880. *Annual Report of the Comptroller of the Currency.* Third session of the Forty-Sixth Congress. Washington, DC: GPO.

U.S. Senate. 1880. "Negro Exodus from the Southern States." Testimony before the Senate Select Committee, Washington, DC.

Valelly, Richard. 2004. *The Two Reconstructions: The Struggle for Black Enfranchisement.* Chicago: University of Chicago Press.

Vlach, John. 1993. *Back of the Big House: The Architecture of Plantation Slavery.* Chapel Hill: University of North Carolina Press.

Vose, Edward. 1916. *Seventy-Five Years of the Mercantile Agency: R.G. Dun & Co., 1841–1916.* New York: R.G. Dun & Co.

Wade, Richard. 1964. *Slavery in the Cities: The South 1820–1860.* New York: Oxford University Press.

Wahl, Jenny. 1996. "The Jurisprudence of American Slave Sales." *Journal of Economic History* 56: 143–69.

———. 2002. *The Bondsman's Burden: An Economic Analysis of the Common Law of Southern Slavery.* Cambridge: Cambridge University Press.

Washington, Booker T. 1901. *Up from Slavery: An Autobiography.* New York: A.L. Burt.

Washington, Scott. 2011. "Hypodescent: A History of the Crystallization of the One-Drop Rule in the United States, 1880–1940." Unpublished Ph.D. dissertation, Department of Sociology, Princeton University.

Wayne, Michael. 1980/1990. *The Reshaping of Plantation Society: The Natchez District, 1860–1880.* Urbana: University of Illinois Press.

Weber, Max. 1892. *Die Verhältnisse der Landarbeiter im Ostelbischen Deutschland.* Leipzig: Duncker and Humblot.

———. 1922. *The City (Non-Legitimate Domination)*. Reprinted in pp. 1212–1372 in Weber, *Economy and Society*.

———. 1946. "Class, Status, Party." Pp. 180–95 in H. Gerth and C. W. Mills, eds., *From Max Weber*. New York: Oxford University Press.

———. 1968. *Economy and Society: An Outline of Interpretive Sociology*. New York: Bedminster.

Weeden, Kim. 2002. "Why Do Some Occupations Pay More Than Others? Social Closure and Earnings Inequality in the United States." *American Journal of Sociology* 108: 55–101.

Weeden, Kim and David Grusky. 2005. "The Case for a New Class Map." *American Journal of Sociology* 111: 141–212.

Wegener, Bernd. 1992. "Concepts and Measurement of Prestige." *Annual Review of Sociology* 18: 253–80.

Wells, Jonathan. 2004. *The Origins of the Southern Middle Class, 1800–1861*. Chapel Hill: University of North Carolina Press.

———. 2011. "Reconstructing the Southern Middle Class: Professional and Commercial Southerners after the Civil War." Pp. 225–43 in Wells and Green, eds., *Southern Middle Class in the Long Nineteenth Century*.

Wells, Jonathan and Jennifer Green, eds. 2011. *The Southern Middle Class in the Long Nineteenth Century*. Baton Rouge: Louisiana State University Press.

Wells, Miriam. 1984. "The Resurgence of Sharecropping: Historical Anomaly or Political Strategy?" *American Journal of Sociology* 90: 1–29.

Wesley, Charles. 1927. *Negro Labor in the United States, 1850–1925: A Study in American Economic History*. New York: Vanguard Press.

West, Stephen. 2008. *From Yeoman to Redneck: In the South Carolina Upcountry, 1850–1915*. Charlottesville: University of Virginia Press.

Wetherington, Mark. 1994. *The New South Comes to Wiregrass Georgia, 1860–1910*. Knoxville: University of Tennessee Press.

Whaples, Robert. 1995. "Where Is There Consensus among American Economic Historians? The Results of a Survey on Forty Propositions." *Journal of Economic History* 55: 139–54.

White, Harrison. 1970. *Chains of Opportunity: System Models of Mobility in Organizations*. Cambridge, MA: Harvard University Press.

———. 2004. *Markets from Networks: Socioeconomic Models of Production*. Princeton, NJ: Princeton University Press.

White, Howard. 1970. *The Freedmen's Bureau in Louisiana*. Baton Rouge: Louisiana State University Press.

White, Shane. 1991. *Somewhat More Independent: The End of Slavery in New York City, 1770–1810*. Athens: University of Georgia Press.

Wiener, Jonathan M. 1978. *Social Origins of the New South: Alabama, 1860–1885*. Baton Rouge: Louisiana State University Press.

———. 1979. "Class Structure and Economic Development in the South, 1865–1955." *American Historical Review* 84: 970–92.

Wilensky, Harold. 1964. "The Professionalization of Everyone?" *American Journal of Sociology* 70: 137–58.

Wilentz, Sean. 1984/2004. *Chants Democratic: New York City and the Rise of the American Working Class, 1788–1850*. New York: Oxford University Press.

Williams, Eric. 1944. *Capitalism and Slavery*. Chapel Hill: University of North Carolina Press.

Williamson, Joel. 1965. *After Slavery: The Negro in South Carolina during Reconstruction, 1861–1877*. Chapel Hill: University of North Carolina Press.

———. 1984. *The Crucible of Race: Black-White Relations in the American South since Emancipation*. New York: Oxford University Press.

Williamson, Oliver. 1985. *The Economic Institutions of Capitalism*. New York: Free Press.

Woodman, Harold. 1966. "The Decline of Cotton Factorage after the Civil War." *American Historical Review* 71: 1219–36.

———. 2000. *King Cotton and His Retainers: Financing and Marketing the Cotton Crop of the South, 1800–1925*. Washington, DC: Beard.

Woodson, Carter. 1918. *A Century of Negro Migration*. Washington, DC: Association for the Study of Negro Life and History.

———. 1922. *The Negro in Our History*. Washington, DC: Associated Publishers.

Woodward, C. Vann. 1951. *Origins of the New South, 1877–1913*. Baton Rouge: Louisiana State University Press.

———. 1955/2002. *The Strange Career of Jim Crow*. New York: Oxford University Press.

Wright, Erik Olin. 1997. *Class Counts: Comparative Studies in Class Analysis*. Cambridge: Cambridge University Press.

———. 2000. "Metatheoretical Foundations of Charles Tilly's Durable Inequality." *Comparative Studies in Society and History* 42: 458–74.

Wright, Gavin. 1978. *The Political Economy of the Cotton South: Households, Markets, and Wealth in the Nineteenth Century*. New York: Norton.

———. 1986/1996. *Old South, New South: Revolutions in the Southern Economy since the Civil War*. Baton Rouge: Louisiana State University Press.

Wyatt-Brown, Bertram. 1966. "God and Dun & Bradstreet, 1841–1851." *Business History Review* 40: 432–50.

Yeatman, James. 1864. *A Report on the Condition of the Freedmen of Mississippi, Presented to the Western Sanitary Commission, December 17th, 1863*. St. Louis: The Commission.

Yetman, Norman. 1984. "Ex-Slave Interviews and the Historiography of Slavery." *American Quarterly* 36: 181–210.

Zaborney, John. 2012. *Slaves for Hire: Renting Enslaved Laborers in Antebellum Virginia*. Baton Rouge: Louisiana State University Press.

Zald, Mayer and Michael Berger. 1978. "Social Movements in Organizations: Coup d'Etat, Insurgency, and Mass Movements." *American Journal of Sociology* 83: 823–61.

Zelizer, Viviana. 1981. "The Price and Value of Children: The Case of Children's Insurance." *American Journal of Sociology* 86: 1036–56.

Index

Page numbers in *italics* refer to figures and tables.